INVISIBLE CONTRARIAN

Critical Studies in
the History of
Anthropology

SERIES EDITORS
Regna Darnell
Robert Oppenheim

Edited by Regna Darnell and Wendy Leeds-Hurwitz

INVISIBLE CONTRARIAN

Essays in Honor of Stephen O. Murray

University of Nebraska Press | Lincoln

© 2025 by the Board of Regents of the University of Nebraska

Acknowledgments for the use of copyrighted material appear on page 277, which constitutes an extension of the copyright page.

All rights reserved

The University of Nebraska Press is part of a land-grant institution with campuses and programs on the past, present, and future homelands of the Pawnee, Ponca, Otoe-Missouria, Omaha, Dakota, Lakota, Kaw, Cheyenne, and Arapaho Peoples, as well as those of the relocated Ho-Chunk, Sac and Fox, and Iowa Peoples.

Publication of this work was assisted by the Murray-Hong Family Trust, to honor and sustain the distinguished legacy of Stephen O. Murray in the History of Anthropology at the University of Nebraska Press.

Library of Congress Cataloging-in-Publication Data
Names: Darnell, Regna, editor. | Leeds-Hurwitz, Wendy, editor. | Murray, Stephen O., honouree.
Title: Invisible contrarian: essays in honor of Stephen O. Murray / edited by Regna Darnell and Wendy Leeds-Hurwitz.
Description: Lincoln: University of Nebraska Press, [2025] | Series: Critical studies in the history of anthropology | Includes bibliographical references and index.
Identifiers: LCCN 2024058225
ISBN 9781496243003 (hardback)
ISBN 9781496243218 (epub)
ISBN 9781496243225 (pdf)
Subjects: LCSH: Murray, Stephen O. | Sex—Anthropological aspects. | Anthropological linguistics. | LCGFT: Festschriften.
Classification: LCC GN484.3 .I69 2025 | DDC 306.7—dc23/eng/20250318
LC record available at https://lccn.loc.gov/2024058225

Designed and set in Arno Pro by K. Andresen

Cover watercolor: "Portrait of Stephen O. Murray" by Gary Bukovnik, 1991. Used with permission from artist and current owner, Stephen O. Murray and Keelung Hong Special Collections, Michigan State University Libraries; gift of Keelung Hong.

In memory of
Stephen O. Murray (1950–2019)

To Keelung Hong
For making this book
like so much else in Steve's life
possible

Contents

List of Illustrations...ix

Preface by Peter M. Nardi...xi

PART 1. INTRODUCTION

Introducing Stephen O. Murray as Invisible Contrarian...3
Wendy Leeds-Hurwitz and Regna Darnell

1. Stephen O. Murray in His Own Words: Extracts from His Journal...33
Prepared by Wendy Leeds-Hurwitz and Regna Darnell

PART 2. DISCIPLINARY HISTORY

2. The Breadth and Depth of Creativity in Stephen O. Murray's Research and Publications...53
Wendy Leeds-Hurwitz

3. Stephen O. Murray as Collaborator...81
Regna Darnell

4. Thinking through Area in the History of Anthropology...87
Robert Oppenheim

5. "AIDS and the Social Imaginary" Thirty Years Later: A Controversial Early Skirmish in the Decolonizing of Anthropology...115
Ralph Bolton

PART 3. HOMOSEXUALITIES

6. Stephen O. Murray's Legacy in the Comparative Study of Homosexualities...153
Barry D Adam

7. Stephen O. Murray's Contributions to Homosexuality Studies in Latin America ... 167
Milton Machuca-Gálvez

8. Stephen O. Murray and the Development of Queer African Studies ... 187
Marc Epprecht

PART 4. STEPHEN O. MURRAY GETS THE LAST WORD

9. John Gumperz in Context: 1977 and 1992 Interviews ... 199
Stephen O. Murray

10. Doing History of Anthropology ... 233
Stephen O. Murray

11. What Is a Conversation (in Anglo America)? ... 253
Stephen O. Murray

12. Introduction to *Male Sexual Subjectivities* ... 271
Stephen O. Murray

13. What Had Been ... 275
Stephen O. Murray

Source Acknowledgments ... 277

Appendix: Stephen O. Murray's Complete List of Publications ... 279
Compiled by Wendy Leeds-Hurwitz

Contributors ... 309

Index ... 311

Illustrations

PHOTOGRAPHS
    1. Stephen O. Murray...x
    2. SOLGA T-shirt...121

TABLES
    1. Murray's Books by Topic...4
    2. Conference Presentations and Attendance...15

Fig. 1. Stephen O. Murray, 1978, at the Norton Simon Museum in Pasadena, California. Photo by Peter M. Nardi.

Preface

Peter M. Nardi

A thinker, a traveler, an activist, a critic, an independent scholar, a contrarian. These are some of the thousand words that capture the personality and intelligence of Stephen O. Murray.

Widely published in an interdisciplinary range of scholarly and popular outlets, Steve often challenged the established ways of viewing sociology, anthropology, sociolinguistics, and the historical and cross-cultural social organization of homosexualities. His life work was to seek an understanding of sexual diversity by synthesizing and interrogating the cultures and social forces worldwide that shape human behavior and identity.

Although he could come across as shy and reticent in person, he never was at a loss for a critical opinion, often providing constructive points in his sharp and insightful writing. He posted reviews online and in academic journals on African cinema, Japanese culture, and Italian fiction, as well as scholarly anthropology and sociology books as he established his reputation as a "crusty curmudgeon." Steve was always willing to help others in reviewing manuscripts and providing feedback for early drafts, challenging them with contrary views to aid in their critical thinking and necessary revisions.

Always ready to fight injustice and discrimination, Steve was a founding member of the Sociologists' Gay Caucus (now LGBTQ Caucus) of the American Sociological Association in 1974 and involved in the formation of the American Anthropological Association's Anthropological Research Group on Homosexuality (renamed Society of Lesbian and Gay Anthropologists, then Association for Queer Anthropology). His activism with both organizations grew from his commitment, while still a graduate student, to bring about visibility for lesbian and gay scholars in professional associations. He regularly wrote about sexuality topics for these groups' newsletters and participated on academic panels that were sometimes seen as controversial events in the days when these associations marginalized gay and lesbian studies and ignored research on HIV/AIDS.

It was in those mid-1970s years that I first met Steve and participated in the founding of the Sociologists' Gay Caucus. Along with a handful of young scholars, we would gather at the annual sociology meetings, trying to get the organization to acknowledge our political issues and scholarly research. At times, these attempts for visibility would require protests, both written and in person, and I witnessed Steve's commitment to and ability to organize, critique, write, and protest.

Being the critic with contrarian views, he was asked to use his knowledge and skills to serve on the editorial boards of several important social science journals, including the *Journal of Homosexuality, Sexualities, Histories of Anthropology Annual*, and *Anthropology Today*. He wrote material for encyclopedias and for the online GLBTQ ENCYCLOPEDIA on HIV/AIDS, human sexuality, linguistics, and gay culture. He also was an editor for the Critical Studies in the History of Anthropology book series at the University of Nebraska Press. On top of all that, part of his book on African homosexualities, *Boy-Wives and Female Husbands*, coedited with Will Roscoe, was turned into a fifteen-minute performance piece in London by noted playwright Caryl Churchill.

Born on May 4, 1950, in St. Paul, Minnesota, Steve grew up in Blue Earth, Minnesota, graduating from the James Madison College of Michigan State University with a double major in social psychology and in justice, morality, and constitutional democracy. His 1975 MA degree from the University of Arizona and his PhD from the University of Toronto in 1979 were in sociology. At the University of California, Berkeley, he did postdoctoral work in anthropology.

With his life partner Keelung Hong, Steve was a regular international traveler, visiting historic sights and art museums, attending symphonies and operas, even birding, all the while keenly observing and taking notes for his extensive academic writings and critical reviews.

Anyone who ever visited Steve and Keelung's house in San Francisco, as I did over almost forty years, would benefit from an intellectual and culinary salon, when Keelung put together an amazing Chinese dinner for their guests. Conversations with both of them about movies, music, and travel as well as intellectual discussions about politics, literature, science, and scholarship would ensue. We would discuss each other's work and drafts. The community and culture sections of Steve's important 1996 book, *American Gay*, for example, gave me ideas and support for my own work on gay men's friendships, as well as our own experiences as friends. Steve provided his intellectual insights, encyclopedic memory and details, and—of course—his contrarian perspectives.

The contributions he made in so many areas live on and, as can be seen in the chapters of this book, have influenced so many others in their own personal and professional lives. His curmudgeonly views notwithstanding, Steve's ideas about everything from human sexuality to international films continue to stimulate others to push their knowledge and research to more sophisticated levels. Let this book be the creative guide for continuing his unique and diverse legacy.

INVISIBLE CONTRARIAN

PART 1 Introduction

Introducing Stephen O. Murray as Invisible Contrarian

Wendy Leeds-Hurwitz and Regna Darnell

This book memorializes and celebrates the prescient vision and interdisciplinary contributions of the late Stephen O. Murray (1950–2019), whose ways of practicing anthropology continue to provide a cogent example of an emergent, forward-looking approach that attends to multiple points of view in its broad range of work, which includes linguistics, regional ethnography, activism, migration studies, and the history of anthropology and the social sciences as a whole. In addition, it highlights Murray's methodological innovations, includes some of his own little-known work, and provides a complete list of his publications as an appendix. Anyone who has contributed as much over as long a period as Murray did deserves reexamination and sharing with contemporary and future audiences.

The book grew out of a panel at the American Anthropological Association convention in the fall of 2022. All of the contributors knew Murray well, most of us for decades. This book should be of interest to anyone who shares one or more of Murray's interests, whether in disciplinary history, sociolinguistics, regional ethnography, or homosexualities around the world. It serves as a good introduction for those who have not yet read his work; for those already familiar with him, it demonstrates the range of his accomplishments. Many potential readers will have run across one or a few of his publications, given the breadth of his interests, but it is highly unlikely that many will have explored just how much ground he covered. This book makes that obvious and hopes to spur further work in response.

Murray had two major projects: homosexualities (12 books mostly documenting the range of same-sex sexual relations around the world) and disciplinary history (5 books on the history of linguistic anthropology in North America). Yet he published another 7 books on additional topics: 4

can be described as regional ethnography or areal studies, and 3 are related to either fiction (his own, or critique of that by others) or film. For most of us, 7 books could easily represent a life's work, but for Murray, those books were only evidence of secondary interests. Other topics, such as his original contributions to sociolinguistic analysis, did not result in books but led to book chapters or journal articles. Across all topics he published dozens and dozens of book reviews of the work he read in preparing his own, as well as entries for various encyclopedias and dictionaries, either explaining key concepts or providing biographies of key people. Even the long list of his publications provided in the appendix does not encompass the thousands of reviews he posted online (of books, movies, music, and occasional events)—many of these are included in his journal, some are still available online, and some have been preserved in various collections (mostly his own), but others have now disappeared.

TABLE 1: MURRAY'S BOOKS BY TOPIC

HOMOSEXUALITIES	DISCIPLINARY HISTORY	AREAL STUDIES	FICTION/ FILM
Social Theory, Homosexual Realities	Group Formation in Social Science	Taiwanese Culture, Taiwanese Society	Collected Stories
Male Homosexuality in Central and South America	Theory Groups and the Study of Language in North America	Angkor Life	Reading 20th-Century Italian Fiction
Oceanic Homosexualities	American Sociolinguistics	Looking through Taiwan	An Introduction to African Cinema
Latin American Male Homosexualities	American Anthropology and Company	Reading Sicily	
American Gay	John Gumperz in Context		
Islamic Homosexualities			

Boy-Wives and Female Husbands

Homosexualities

Pacific Homosexualities

Heterogender Homosexuality in Honduras

21st-Century Representations of Muslim Homosexualities

Pieces for a History of Gay Studies

Murray's Life and Career

We begin by summarizing Murray's life and career, then return to his published work. He grew up in the town of Blue Earth, Minnesota; his father worked for Standard Oil, and his mother was a teacher, active in her church and the Republican party. He granted them much credit for his efforts, saying, "without my parents' encouragement, support, and high valuation of education, I would never have written this or any other book" (Murray 1983a, ix). For the BA, he completed a double major at Michigan State University in 1972, the first in social psychology and the second in justice, morality, and constitutional democracy (an interdisciplinary program intended mostly as preparation for law school). Not interested in law school and discovering that "there were no jobs for philosopher kings" (Murray, journal entry, February 19, 2007), he chose sociology for his MA at the University of Arizona, graduating in 1975. That degree was memorable in part for the response from one of his professors to his research proposal on gay men that "no one is interested in your lifestyle" (Murray 2021, xix); as a result, he "did not even think of doing gay research for my dissertation" (Murray 1996a, 277). He left the United States to earn his PhD at the University of Toronto in 1979, again in sociology. He served as teaching assistant and instructor while a graduate student at both Arizona and Toronto, his only formal teaching experiences. He settled in San Francisco in 1978 to write up the dissertation, becoming a postdoctoral fellow in anthropology at the University of California, Berkeley, under

John Gumperz from 1980 to 1982, courtesy of a National Institute of Mental Health fellowship. Awkwardly, Gumperz was absent the first year on a fellowship of his own at the Institute of Advanced Study at Princeton; however, in his absence, Murray got to know Gumperz's graduate students at the time, many of whom were international (for example, Niyi Akinnaso from Nigeria and Amparo Tusón from Spain, both of whom Murray later acknowledged for their support), and with many of whom he maintained lifelong connections. Along with other postdocs and graduate students, Murray (2010a) presented at the American Anthropological Association meeting in 1981, part of a double panel organized by peers Cheryl Ajirotutu and Douglas Campbell, with Frederick Erickson (in education) and Ronald Scollon (linguistics) as discussants. Many of those presentations, though not Murray's own, were published as chapters in Gumperz's 1982 collection *Language and Social Identity*.

Murray specifically mentions that as part of this peer group he was reading work by Gregory Bateson, Erving Goffman, and Alton Becker (in anthropology, sociology, and linguistics, respectively). He also read the work of French sociologist Pierre Bourdieu, whose concept of cultural capital "was a buzz word in this group" (Murray 2010a, 111). With Akinnaso, Murray audited a course offered by the Norwegian anthropologist Fredrik Barth in 1981 and attended lectures by French philosopher Michel Foucault, a visiting professor at Berkeley, in 1980 and 1983 (Murray 2010a, 2012b, 80–87). A subset of the group, "[Ruth] Borker, [Daniel] Maltz, ([Deborah] Tannen, already departed from Berkeley), and I[,] were also interested in genderlects and the relationships between sexuality and language patterns" (Murray 2010a, 110). Of the larger group of peers, he says: "We were immodestly confident that we were studying what was really going on in interaction, and that mismatched interpretive conventions used by speakers from differing backgrounds had important consequences, and, in particular, explained interactional breakdowns, failures of communication, and concomitant reinforcement of intergroup stereotyping in interethnic encounters, especially gatekeeping ones" (Murray 2010a, 110). Together these comments make clear that the postdoc significantly influenced his later research and publications across multiple topics and provided a cohesive group of others with common interests.

By 1981 Murray had met and married Keelung Hong, formally acknowledged in more than one book for his "unwavering and frequent support" (as in Murray 1998, 3) and decided to stay in the Bay Area. Given the lack of an academic offer once the postdoc ended, he took a non-academic job, working as a software analyst for PSP Information Group starting in 1982.[1] After being laid off in 1993, he never held another full-time position, though he occasionally identified himself as the research director at El Instituto Obregón (there were several other associates, it did have legal existence with the IRS, and when he published e-books, he named the institute as publisher; see chapter 7).[2] Because he did not obtain an academic position, he was an independent scholar across the majority of his career, which is why we have called him "invisible"—after 1982, he was not to be found at any university and had no graduate students of his own to support or carry on his projects. Murray attributed this lack primarily to his "lavender resumé," and mentioned that "selling myself is not one of my specialties" (Murray, journal entry, May 27, 2019; Murray et al. 2021, 257).[3] Having no full-time position did have a benefit in leaving him considerable time to write. In the end, he published far more than most academics manage, with his twenty-four books and hundreds of shorter publications.

Murray was HIV-positive by 1981 but did not progress to full-blown AIDS, calling himself "an AZT success story" (in conversation with Leeds-Hurwitz, and undoubtedly with others as well). This meant that he periodically was ill, sometimes quite ill, to the point of concern about whether he was dying; in consequence he pushed hard to publish as much as possible before that could occur. "Annual reports" sent around to numerous friends and colleagues at the end of every year always included details about his state of health as well as documenting both his travels and new publications. For example, his last one begins: "2018 has been a pretty good year for Keelung and a horrible one for Steve" (email to Leeds-Hurwitz and fifteen others, December 18, 2018); the horrible parts were all related to health issues.

Murray saw himself as a writer, first and foremost. One result was that he got used to spending much time alone and did not appreciate large groups, though he maintained many friendships for decades. He could be astonishingly blunt and caustic in print, but in person often did come off as the "quiet, polite Midwesterner," which he considered his primary self-presentation (Murray, journal entry, February 16, 1993). As Manuel

Fernández-Alemany ([2001] 2019) put it, "his sharp comments are often feared by authors of new publications. Yet for people who know him closely, Steve Murray is the most supportive and helpful reader of one's drafts one can find." Robert Oppenheim (email to Leeds-Hurwitz, November 10, 2023) suggests that "he knew how to be pointed in a way that had you laughing along with his insights about your work." Both of us (and many other contributors to this volume) were accustomed to exchanging drafts with Steve and severely miss his astute critiques.

Disciplinary History

Murray's first major achievements were in the area of disciplinary history. Three books were variations on a theme, and it is worth sorting this out because they comprise the heart of his contributions to that topic. Basically, he examined the ways in which theory groups function, building upon earlier work by Nicholas C. Mullins (1973; Griffith and Mullins 1972): the central insight is that ideas, even good ones, do not stand on their own but instead require groups of people to share them, promote them, and build upon them. The first version was his doctoral dissertation, "Social Science Networks" (1979c), revised for publication as *Group Formation in Social Science* (1983a). A second version was substantially revised, expanded, and updated, then published as an expensive hardcover, *Theory Groups and the Study of Language in North America* (1994c). Annoyed that it was now too expensive for many to purchase, he revised that into a shorter paperback, *American Sociolinguistics* (1998), with a tighter focus on the main argument. The longer version is the best for scholars doing disciplinary history who appreciate specific details and expansive coverage; the shorter version is more cogent, easier to work with, and appeals to a broader audience. Much later he collected essays he felt represented him well but that had not gotten as much attention as he thought they deserved in *American Anthropology and Company* (2013a; see chapter 2 herein). Basically, that book reprints many shorter publications relating to the history of linguistic anthropology (and also what he called "unanthropological linguistics," xvi) unrelated to the theory groups strand in his previous books.

The fact that Murray found multiple connections within his own intellectual genealogy to the well-known linguist Edward Sapir meant that even though his doctoral training was in sociology, he felt particularly well connected to linguistic anthropology specifically, and anthropology more generally—far more than just the experience provided by his postdoc would have suggested. At different times he highlighted the significance of Thomas Kuhn's (1962) contributions to his interest in the social history of science, as well as the role played by the University of Pennsylvania tradition. George Stocking, Dell Hymes, and Regna Darnell were all affiliated with Penn, and they all strongly influenced his publications in this area (Murray 2013a).

In his dissertation and the revised volumes that grew from it, Murray used American sociolinguistics, with a focus on the ethnography of communication, as the theory group forming his central case study. That he was both an insider (as someone with a clear academic genealogy in linguistics back to Sapir, but also as a postdoc with one of the founders of the ethnography of communication, Gumperz) and an outsider (not having a university position, and with degrees in sociology rather than either anthropology or linguistics) provided a useful combination of insight and distance. Murray began his dissertation with Griffith and Mullins's discussion of the central role played by "invisible colleges," testing it carefully against American sociolinguistics. In so doing, he prepared "the first detailed examination of the history of anthropological linguistics with a theoretical framework in the history of science" (Darnell 1983, i). He further examined the rhetoric of revolution in relation to previous ideas versus that of continuity with those ideas, and the role of group coherence, concluding that "the fate of ideas can be considered as depending on social processes rather than the intrinsic merit of ideas" (Murray 1994c, 490), something most people never even consider. And he demonstrated that group leadership becomes especially critical in an interdisciplinary group, given the many ways in which members remain tied to their disciplines of origin.

Over the various iterations of that work, he first tidied it up, then expanded it considerably, then compressed it down to more reasonable size again. But in each case, in every version of his work, he accomplished something few others had even attempted either before or since: a broad examination of who was doing what work, in what circumstances, with what peers, matched to a clear explanation of the difference between intellectual and organizational leadership, both of which turned out to be necessary to see an idea from initial consideration to eventual acceptance. He synthesized enormous amounts of material into a coherent story. Anyone who wishes to ensure their ideas are accepted either within a traditional discipline, or across an interdisciplinary collaboration, needs to understand what Murray had to teach us.

Asked whether he viewed his multiple research topics as separate or interrelated, Murray argued that they were interrelated, in large part because "the historical subject area in which I worked, anthropological linguistics, is also the area of some substantive (if uncollected) empirical work" (Murray et al. 2021, 252). Whatever the topic, his nature as a "contrarian" was often responsible for his interest, for "most of my research projects were stimulated by doubts about particular claims" (Murray 2013a, xvii), and this effort to sort out the facts motivated many (if not most) of his publications. However, it is important to mention that he was always willing to admit that he had been wrong, if clearly proved otherwise (see chapter 2).

When explicitly asked to name his intellectual influences, Murray emphasized Regna Darnell (originally the outside reader on his dissertation, later colleague, coeditor, and coauthor), Keith Basso (who introduced him to the ethnography of speaking at the University of Arizona), Robert Nisbet (also at Arizona, who introduced him to history of sociological theory and sent him on to Toronto), and John Gumperz (his postdoc supervisor at Berkeley; Murray et al. 2021). Many, many others who influenced him are mentioned throughout his publications, especially in the uncommonly extensive acknowledgments. He combined anthropology, sociology, and linguistics in ways that few others had comparable knowledge to manage (see Murray 2013a, 157–60). And fewer still have taken the time to sort out the history of how any of these have been studied, let alone all of them.

The minor book (only twenty-five pages) published in the set related to disciplinary history was *John Gumperz in Context* (2013c), consisting of two formal interviews Murray conducted in 1977 and 1992. It reveals much about how he conducted interviews, which formed a central component of his research, whether historical or ethnographic, and so it is reprinted in part 4 of this volume.

Murray also drafted two unpublished volumes relating to linguistic anthropology. The first, *"Interruptions" and Other Messy Things in Language*

Use, was designed to bring together all his analyses of sociolinguistic data, most of which had been previously published. "What Is a Conversation?" had not been, and it is also included in part 4. Interestingly, that volume would also have presented a revised version of "Deference, Domination and Solidarity in an Interactional Order," his unpublished MA thesis (Murray 1975). The second volume, *Essays on the History of Social Sciences*, was envisioned as a companion volume to *American Anthropology and Company*; it included a different set of mostly previously published papers that he felt had not received adequate attention. In emails to us both he called it his festschrift, despite the fact that one does not typically prepare one's own festschrift, but waits for one's students to do it—given that he had none, he took it upon himself to consider what he would want collected in such a volume.[4] In the draft introduction he argued that the selected essays "are typical of my skepticism for received wisdom" ("fest intro," Stephen O. Murray Papers, Michigan State University).

Homosexualities

Not the first, then, but the most numerous and arguably the most significant contributions Murray made were on the topic of homosexualities, covering a dozen volumes, or half of his books, as well as numerous shorter pieces. As he put it, "For a quarter of a century, I have been writing about gay identity and community, and about various roles around the world and across millennia that have involved same-sex sex" (unpublished foreword for Nicholas Charles Adams's *My Black Book*, Stephen O. Murray Papers). When he began this research, Murray applied much of what he had learned in sociology, describing himself as "a comparativist in the Max Weber and Émile Durkheim traditions" (Murray et al. 2021, 258). But his training in anthropology gets much of the credit for his interest in cross-cultural analysis and comparison. His ability to synthesize enormous amounts of data clearly, and his willingness to include historical and archival research, stood him well in his efforts to systematize what he learned and present it clearly to others.

The first of this set of books, *Social Theory, Homosexual Realities*, was published in 1984. At eighty-three pages, it is more a monograph than a full book, but it counts as a good first effort. As was his habit, he revised what he had written for inclusion in a later volume, in this case *American*

Gay (1996a). The last volume in this set was *Pieces for a History of Gay Studies* (2012b), published only as an e-book. In the introduction Murray applied what he had learned about disciplinary history to document the development of gay studies: where were the first courses taught, what program offered the first degree, who was the first faculty member to earn tenure in such a department, and so on. The chapters in that book focus mostly either on how anthropologists and sociologists responded to gay studies or document the history (and prehistory) of gay studies. As with other volumes produced in his last decade, most of the chapters had been previously published "in fugitive or otherwise difficult to find publications" (9); his effort to collect and republish them was intended to set them before a wider audience.

Nearly all the books published between these two were arranged geographically, and they all present same-sex sexual relations and role conception across various cultural regions. Essentially, the question Murray tried to answer through them was: "*what* social and historical factors explain both the occurrence of different same-sex patterns *and* the regularity within these patterns" (2021, xxxiv, original emphasis). The list includes *Male Homosexuality in Central and South America* (1987b), *Oceanic Homosexualities* (1992), *Latin American Male Homosexualities* (1995a), *American Gay* (1996a), *Islamic Homosexualities* (Murray and Roscoe 1997), *Boy-Wives and Female Husbands* (Murray and Roscoe 1998), *Pacific Homosexualities* (2002b), *Heterogender Homosexuality in Honduras* (Fernández-Alemany and Murray 2002), and *21st-Century Representations of Muslim Homosexualities* (2012e). Finally, *Homosexualities* (2000) was his grand synthesis, the place where he tried to tie together all the loose ends, the culmination of the entire project: "Yesterday I dispatched the proofs and index to *Homosexualities*. My life work is officially completed and I'm too exhausted to think about what I'll do with more borrowed time (a posthumous life)" (Murray, journal entry, January 8, 2000). This set of books is the focus of attention in part 3, where Barry D Adam provides a broad overview (emphasizing *Homosexualities* but including the patterns at work in the full set), while Milton Machuca-Gálvez emphasizes Murray's contributions to Latin American work, especially *Male Homosexuality in Central and South America* and *Latin American Male Homosexualities,* and Marc Epprecht focuses on Murray's contributions to queer African studies, highlighting *Boy-Wives and Female Husbands*.

A few comments follow to provide context for the books not discussed at length in part 3. *Heterogender Homosexuality in Honduras* began as Fernández-Alemany's dissertation; he was from Chile and earned a PhD in anthropology in the United States, then left for several years in the Himalayas, formally ceding responsibility to Murray for editing and revisions and insisting that Murray be listed as coauthor (Fernández-Alemany and Murray 2002, x). As such, that book provides better evidence of Murray's considerable support for others' research rather than his own. *Oceanic Homosexualities* is presented as being by Murray "with additional contributions by" eleven others, so it is best understood as the result of his attempts to collect relevant research on yet another geographic region, whether that by other scholars or resulting from his own archival efforts. (Other volumes in the subset on international homosexualities have a similar format, so that even when the cover lists him as "author," that should be understood to mean he was more of an editor who filled in any remaining gaps himself.) *American Gay*, however, was all his own: it incorporated not only a revision of *Social Theory, Homosexual Realities* but several conference papers and previous publications. It attracted substantial interest: as evidence, it was the subject of an "author meets critics" session at the Pacific Sociological Association meeting in San Diego (Murray 2002a, 245). It had taken an uncommonly long time to complete (especially for Murray, typically a quick writer): two decades (Murray 1996a, 275). *21st-Century Representations of Muslim Homosexualities*, an e-book published on the twentieth anniversary of the publication of *Islamic Homosexualities*, consists of book and film reviews, most of which he had previously published online, so collecting them into a single book was a way to preserve them.

There was one unpublished book related to this strand of research, occasionally described as his book on male desire, tentatively titled *Male Sexual Subjectivities*. The draft of the introduction lays out the mandate (as well as making clear the timing): "As I was concluding that long-running project of sorting out types of same-sex sexual relationships, I was also trying to encourage honest accounts of male-male sexual desire" ("desire intro," Stephen O. Murray Papers). The tentative table of contents includes mostly previous publications revised and reorganized. The draft introduction is included in part 4 for the overview it provides of his intent. Even uncollected articles could have substantial impact; for example, Epprecht (email to Leeds-Hurwitz and Darnell, October 27, 2023) notes, "I found his 'Five Reasons I Don't Take "Queer Theory" Seriously' very helpful and sent it around to African colleagues who seemed mesmerized."

Murray was given a number of awards or other forms of recognition acknowledging the significance of his work in one or another of this set of books. These included the Theory Development Award from the International Gay Academic Union in 1982, election to the Academy for the Empirical Study of Male Homosexualities in 1995, and the Polyvocality Award from that academy in 1996 ("UChi author questionnaire," Stephen O. Murray Papers).

Organizational Roles

Murray did not just study theory groups and what they needed to survive but put that knowledge to work helping to establish and then support multiple organizations. He was one of the founders of the Sociologists' Gay Caucus in 1974 and the Toronto Gay Academic Union in 1975. He said of himself at that time: "I was the one not doing research on homosexuality. I wanted to promote rather than do it, to read rather than write it" (Epprecht et al. 2018, 352). In later years he became editor of the *Sociologists' Gay Caucus Newsletter* (1977–79), a founding member of the Anthropological Research Group on Homosexuality in 1978 and editor of their newsletter as well (Murray 1991d), then editor and later book review editor of *Society of Lesbian and Gay Anthropologists Newsletter* (1989–92; Fuller 2009). And because he knew how important the memories of participants could be from his dissertation days, on several occasions he took time to document his experiences in helping to found gay and lesbian organizations (Murray 1994a, 2012b).

He started presenting at conferences as early as 1974 (see Murray 2012b) and did attend a lot, though certainly fewer, less consistently, and less often as a presenter, given his status as an independent scholar, than if he had been a faculty member with an expectation of routine participation. This makes sense because there was neither the reward of pay raises or promotions, nor financial support for expenses. And if the goal had been to travel, it made more sense to choose destinations where he and Hong could explore a new place together.[5] His publications mention a number of conferences he attended or presented at; the list (table 2) is impressive both for the range of organizations and disciplines—especially given that it is incomplete.[6]

TABLE 2: CONFERENCE PRESENTATIONS AND ATTENDANCE

YEAR	EVENT	LOCATION
1974	American Sociological Association	Montreal
1977	Georgetown University Round Table	Washington DC
1977	American Sociological Association	Chicago
1978	American Anthropological Association	Los Angeles
1978	Canadian Sociology and Anthropological Association	London, Ontario
1981	American Anthropological Association	Los Angeles
1981	Kroeber Anthropological Association	Berkeley
1984	Edward Sapir Centenary Conference	Ottawa
1986	Society for the Study of Social Problems	New York
1987	American Sociological Association	Chicago
1987	Homosexuality, Which Homosexuality?	Amsterdam
1988	American Sociological Association	Atlanta
1988	American Anthropological Association	Phoenix
1989	American Sociological Association	San Francisco
1989	American Anthropological Association	Washington DC
1989	North American Taiwanese Professors' Association	College Park MD
1992	American Anthropological Association	San Francisco
1993	American Sociological Association	Miami
1993	American Anthropological Association	Washington DC

1994	American Sociological Association	Los Angeles
1995	Emerging Lesbian and Gay Communities	Sydney, Australia
1995	Theorizing the Americanist Tradition	London, Ontario
1996	American Anthropological Association	San Francisco
1996	African Studies Association*	San Francisco
1997	American Anthropological Association	Washington DC
1997	Pacific Sociological Association	San Diego
1997	North American Taiwan Studies	Berkeley
1998	North American Taiwan Studies	Austin
1998	American Sociological Association	San Francisco
1998	CUNY Center for Lesbian and Gay Studies: Queer Middle Ages	New York
1998	U.S.-Chinese Tongzhi Conference	San Francisco
1999	American Sociological Association	Chicago
1999	Society for the Scientific Study of Sex	San Francisco
2001	American Anthropological Association	Washington DC
2001	Pacific Sociological Association	Anaheim CA
2002	American Anthropological Association	New Orleans
2004	Pacific Sociological Association	San Francisco
2006	American Sociological Association	Montreal
2008	American Anthropological Association	San Francisco
2012	American Anthropological Association	San Francisco

* Marc Epprecht (email to Leeds-Hurwitz and Darnell, October 27, 2023) notes that Murray was not participating in this conference; he showed up primarily to find recruits for *Boy-Wives and Female Husbands*.

Perhaps his most significant conference participation was one where he did not present a paper (see chapter 5). The response to the panel on AIDS at the American Anthropological Association in 1992 called upon him to fulfill multiple roles simultaneously: as a person who was HIV-positive, who had conducted research on gay populations, and who had helped establish gay organizations within anthropology. We will let Bolton tell that story and not repeat it here. Also, on some occasions, despite his lack of attendance at a conference, his work was discussed, as with the roundtable devoted to *Boy-Wives and Female Husbands* organized by Marc Epprecht for the 2018 Canadian Association of African Studies, which Murray could not attend as he was in the hospital at the time. At the African Studies Association meeting in 1996, participants were almost exclusively white, whereas by the time of the 2018 roundtable, participants included two African women and one Brazilian. In addition, "The audience (packed) had many Africans present from all over the continent and actively (constructively) contributing to the discussion—a big shift in part made possible (as the African presenters made clear) due to Steve's contributions" (Epprecht, email to Leeds-Hurwitz and Darnell, October 27, 2023).

Despite not holding an academic position, Murray served on editorial boards of multiple newsletters and journals (in addition to the five journals listed in Nardi's preface, also *Journal of the History of Sociology, Anthropology Today, Encyclopedia of Homosexuality,* and *Haworth Latin American/Hispanic Press*; "UChi author questionnaire") and coedited a major book series, Critical Studies in the History of Anthropology, at the University of Nebraska Press. In chapter 3 Regna Darnell reports on what he was like in their combined editorial activities across several decades; they jointly authored series editors' introductions to thirty-two books. In addition to editorial work, Murray (journal entry, August 9, 1999) served as an outside reviewer of proposals or manuscripts for multiple publishers sufficiently often that he once commented that "judging by my royalty checks, it's more lucrative and far less effort to review manuscripts than to write books, at least solo-authored ones." But writing was essential to who he was: "My self-presentation is as a writer. That is what I do most, and I have plenty of publications to bolster the claim. And it is more easily understood than the complexity of what I 'do for a living'" (Murray, journal entry, May 5, 1997). Later he expanded on just why he spent so much time writing: "I write to find out what I think. Different questions have led to different books" ("amazon interviews SM," Stephen O. Murray Papers).

Evidence that his research on disciplinary history and homosexualities meshed rather than being entirely separate can be found in the fact that he was awarded the Ruth Benedict Prize by the American Anthropological Association in 2000 for *Homosexualities*. In answer to a question about his job for a survey by Michigan State University, he said: "I don't know what my 'field' is. It seems no one else does either. Linguists and anthropologists think I'm a sociologist, sociologists think I'm an anthropologist (or possibly a linguist). Unlike Erving Goffman, whom everyone (sociology, anthropology, psychology, communications) wanted to claim, no one wants to claim me" (UChi author questionnaire). When the same survey asked: "What insight(s) can you offer to someone thinking about pursuing a career path like yours?" his answer was: "Don't! Being an 'independent scholar' is way too difficult." Later he glossed the phrase as "academic exiles (the euphemism is 'independent scholars')" (Murray 2021, xix).

Areal Studies

Although his books on homosexualities formed his major contribution, periodically Murray (journal entry, May 2, 1995) felt that considering other topics was appropriate: "A break from being a professional homosexual should be good." This particular entry describes a shift to preparing for a conference on disciplinary history, but there were other topics that occupied his time. We've categorized as areal studies two books written with Hong, *Taiwanese Culture, Taiwanese Society* (Murray and Hong 1994) and *Looking through Taiwan* (Hong and Murray 2005), one on Angkor Wat, *Angkor Life* (1996b), and an e-book on Italy, *Reading Sicily* (2012c). Obviously, the major topic here was Taiwan: the two books were supported by multiple shorter publications, many of which were then incorporated into one or the other book (see appendix for specific citations). Given that Robert Oppenheim's chapter 4 discusses this research strand in detail, we will only say here that the main point was to highlight the inappropriateness of the assumption by American anthropologists that it was reasonable to use Taiwan as a substitute for China in the years when the former was more accessible than the latter. This was an early topic of interest, for Murray (2013a, xxii) reports that "it was also while I was a Berkeley postdoc that Keelung Hong directed my attention at anthropological (mis) representations of Taiwan." While Hong served as the expert on Taiwan, Murray was the expert on American anthropology, and the one who helped bring these books and articles to the attention of American anthropologists. *Taiwanese Culture, Taiwanese Society* received the Ong Iotek Award from the Taiwan Foundation in 1995 ("UChi author questionnaire").

Murray (1996b) wrote *Angkor Life* because he could not easily find the guide he wanted when he finally visited Angkor Wat, a temple complex in Cambodia constructed in the twelfth century, and so he read everything he could locate upon returning to the United States, in the end deciding to prepare his own summary of "what we know or can reasonably infer about Khmer life during the late-Angkor era." As he explained in another context, "I write what I wanted to read but that no one had written" (Murray 2014, 141).

The introduction to *Reading Sicily* states that Murray (2012c, 7) looked to literature "to try to understand something of 'native views' (culture)" and "I look at 'high culture' to gain some access to 'culture' in the anthropological sense, fully aware that documenting what interests a sociologist or an anthropologist was not the aim of the writers of fiction examined." Supporting the categorization of the book as areal studies are some of the pieces he chose to include, and his discussion of similarities between his readings of literature and his own fieldwork in Mexico and Guatemala, but this volume could also have been placed in the fiction and film category. This was another e-book, and so another opportunity for Murray to present his work without the delays of traditional publishers.

Fiction and Film

The final category is labeled "fiction and film" because it includes one book with fiction he wrote, one about fiction by others, specifically from and about Italy, and one describing films from Africa. The e-book *Collected Stories* (2012a) includes a dozen stories, of which he says only one was based on his own life: "How Can We Be 40, Let Alone at a 40th Class Reunion?" Interestingly, he arranged the stories in chronological order by the age of the narrators, all of whom are looking back at their lives, something he himself was certainly doing at the time. The dozen poems are described as a complete collection of those he wrote. As with other of his books, some of these selections had previously been published, mostly online, so his goal was to gather them together and preserve them. And it was a good thing he did: all the publications and websites listed as the original sources have by now folded.

As with other books included in this category, *Reading 20th-Century Italian Fiction* (2012d), another e-book, falls clearly in the "minor works" category: minor both in terms of importance to Murray and in terms of the influence it has had on others. This book makes the shift to just reviewing literature rather than trying to fit the pieces together with ethnographic reports, and so it seems best to categorize it with other fiction and film discussions. As with *Reading Sicily*, most reviews included had been published previously online. His modest goal was "to introduce some readers to some Italian novels and novelists whose work has made it into print in English" (6).

Similarly, the e-book *An Introduction to African Cinema* (2013b) is based on his online reviews of films then readily available in the United States, and so forms a subset of what had been produced by then, intended for a specific audience. Given that, the breadth is impressive, with seventy-five movies included. But again, this book never found a large audience.

Briefer Publications

Although the focus to this point has been on books, since they form his most substantial and generally best-known contributions, Murray published an impressive number of journal articles and book chapters on sociolinguistics, most often on gay speech, based on his fieldwork in the United States, Canada, Mexico, Guatemala, and Taiwan (Covelli and Murray 1980; Murray 1979a, 1979b, 1980, 1983b, 1985, 1987a, 1991a, 1991b, 1991c, 1994b, 1995b, 1995c, 1996c, 2010b; Murray and Covelli 1988; Murray and Arboleda G. 1987). Interestingly, he started this research while still a graduate student. He describes the research eventually published in "The Art of Gay Insulting" as having occurred during 1975, and "by 1977 I was presenting reports at sociology meetings of my own research on gay male speech" (Murray 2012b, 72). Clearly the Toronto context proved far more welcoming to this strand of his research than Arizona had been. In addition to original research, he synthesized and summarized, rediscovered or provoked fieldwork by others for short descriptions in many of the books on homosexualities. A few chapters in his books highlighted original research, such as "Ethnic and Temporal Differences in Coming Out and in Moving to San Francisco" (in Murray 1996a), using interviews he conducted. Most relevant here is that he found a way to combine his background in linguistics, sociology, and anthropology with his interest in gay studies, giving us data-driven analyses most often based on either interviews or participant observation. This and others were designated for inclusion in *"Interruptions" and Other Messy Things in Language Use*, assuming it had been accepted for publication. And, of course, there were many shorter publications in both disciplinary history and homosexualities never incorporated into a book.

Plan of This Book

We begin and end by letting Murray speak for himself. Part 1 presents "Introducing Stephen O. Murray in His Own Words" with extracts from the journal he kept from 1969 to 2019. It seems appropriate to give someone who wrote so much about himself as well as others the opportunity to introduce himself to readers. The original journal includes literally tens of thousands of pages consisting mostly of reviews—of films, books, concerts, and more (most often published online on Epinions, Netflix, Amazon, Tangent Group, other platforms, or his own website, Japanese Culture Reflections). Many of the selections chosen for inclusion here were written as the lead or conclusion to a review in which he related his primary topic to his own life experience. The first entry provided, his self-introduction on Epinions, has been moved out of chronological order to supply basic autobiographical details at the beginning. All entries have been lightly edited, and most comments about specific individuals omitted.

Chapters in part 2 emphasize Murray's contributions to disciplinary history. In "The Breadth and Depth of Creativity in Stephen O. Murray's Research and Publications" Wendy Leeds-Hurwitz examines Murray's breadth—that is, the way in which his publications spanned disciplines—and also his depth—that is, his use of multiple methods of investigation. In terms of breadth, he gave special emphasis to anthropology's disciplinary borderlands: sociology, linguistics, psychology, and history. He was particularly interested in how social research occurs, devoting much time to the development and influence of theory groups, including the connections between individual scholars over time, as well as how ideas come to be adopted and expanded upon. He provides an exemplar of how contemporary scholars can follow his lead in being open to crossing disciplinary boundaries when studying disciplinary history. This chapter highlights how he spoke for himself in his late collection *American Anthro-*

pology and Company. In terms of depth, Murray was not just interested in what should be studied (the topic) but also how (the method), and this chapter documents the ways in which he moved between qualitative and quantitative approaches, frequently combining methods others considered quite distinct. A final section analyzes his writing style, for he considered good writing essential to good research.

In "Stephen O. Murray as Collaborator," Regna Darnell reports on their joint editorial activities over several decades. Murray and Darnell coedited the series Critical Studies in the History of Anthropology at the University of Nebraska Press from 2001 to 2019, which required frequent contact to decide what to include in the series; they also edited the books and wrote series editors' introductions together. Darnell explains how Murray worked as a collaborator in these multiple roles: he could be both incredibly detail oriented (especially when it came to remembering who had said what) and, at the same time, incredibly sloppy (with citations especially).

In "Thinking through Area in the History of Anthropology," Robert Oppenheim examines one of two books Murray coauthored with Keelung Hong, *Looking through Taiwan*, along with its intellectual antecedents. That book offers a strong critique of Cold War American anthropology, which used Taiwan as a proxy for engaging in the ethnography of "traditional China" at a moment when the People's Republic of China itself was mostly closed to outside researchers. Hong and Murray declaimed the complicity of this anthropology with a Kuomintang-associated intellectual erasure of indigeneity and Taiwanese identity on this basis. Rather than rehearsing, extending, or evaluating the ongoing salience of a critique written in a very different era, this chapter addresses the broader implications of the book's central metaphor of transparency and displacement for the practice of the history of anthropology. The metaphor of "looking through" underscores the need to analyze the ways in which area or place figure in history of anthropology research, thereby offering a methodological contribution that directs our attention to the variety of expressions of area in anthropologies past and present.

In "'AIDS and the Social Imaginary' Thirty Years Later: A Controversial Early Skirmish in the Decolonizing of Anthropology," Ralph Bolton details a panel at the annual meeting of the American Anthropological Association in 1992. Participants were prominent figures in the field from elite graduate institutions, while representatives of people living with AIDS, members of the LGBTQ anthropological community, researchers from the well-established AIDS and Anthropology Research Group, and younger, less visible scholars who had already devoted years to the study of HIV/AIDS were excluded from the panel. The organizers circumvented the annual meeting rules to turn down paper proposals by AIDS researchers because of lack of slots on the program, exacerbating the tensions caused by such exclusions. Murray had a key symbolic role in this encounter, as someone living with HIV/AIDS and a specialist on homosexualities. This chapter provides a contextualized account of this event as an early skirmish in the process of decolonizing anthropology, one in which a disdained and discriminated-against minority refused to cede control of the narrative to the power elite within the discipline.

Part 3 turns to Murray's publications on homosexualities, where he applied what he had learned in sociology, anthropology, and linguistics. "Stephen O. Murray's Legacy in the Comparative Study of Homosexualities," by Barry D Adam, provides an excellent overview. From his magnum opus, *Homosexualities*, to his areal surveys of same-sex behavior, Murry's work is grounded in a comparative, structural tradition of identifying major patterns from an encyclopedic array of data. Like Lévi-Strauss's *Elementary Structures of Kinship*, which sought to plot the full range of family structures available to human imagination and practice, his work aimed to make sense of a vast but fragmentary set of observations on same-sex sexual bonding. As LGBTQ and queer studies have subsequently become preoccupied with poststructuralist approaches, it is germane to consider Murray's legacy to spur a much-needed renewal of interest in the systematic analysis of sexualities.

In contrast to Adam's overview, "Stephen O. Murray's Contributions to Homosexuality Studies in Latin America" by Milton Machuca-Gálvez examines one strand of that research, in one geographic region. Ethnographic perspectives on male homosexuality in Latin America have grown exponentially since the publication of Murray's *Male Homosexuality in Central and South America* in 1987. Murray subsequently revisited his ideas as a comprehensive theoretical introduction to the topic in *Latin American Male Homosexualities*, as a reflection on his work as a gay anthropologist in Guatemala in "Male Homosexuality in Guatemala," and, finally, as a global synthesis in *Homosexualities*. No examination has been made of Murray's contributions to the field in terms of cultural continuity and change, including attitudes, values, and laws regarding male homosexuality in the region, despite his three-decade span of work on male homosexuality in Latin America. A comprehensive review of Murray's position on male homosexuality studies in Latin America, this chapter begins with his disciplinary position and traces how it evolved over time. Machuca-Gálvez suggests ways to explore the key concepts and positions Murray held about homosexuality in Latin America, specifically in his ethnographic work in Mesoamerica, and their relevance for contemporary social scientists.

Similarly, in "Stephen O. Murray and the Development of Queer African Studies," Marc Epprecht focuses on one strand of the research. As Epprecht put it when originally proposing the chapter, "Murray was definitely not an Africanist; nor was he a cheerleader for queer theory, but with coeditor Will Roscoe, and to a lesser extent with Epprecht, he helped to lay the foundations for what has become a vibrant field of study." This chapter considers the lasting, albeit often unacknowledged, traces of Murray's approaches to the study of (and political activism for) homosexualities in Africa.

Unpublished or Underappreciated Works

It seemed appropriate to include at least a few pieces by Steve himself in this volume, which leads to the question of which ones. For part 4, we chose pieces both for their significance and representativeness, and for their failure to receive prior attention, sometimes because they were never published. These chapters illustrate his method in history of anthropology, sociolinguistics, and some varieties of sociology and span multiple topics he wrote about across multiple disciplines and over decades of his research.

Elsewhere in this volume, Leeds-Hurwitz describes one method Murray used to good effect: to interview "elders" who participated in the time periods he was examining in his historical research. *John Gumperz in Context: 1977 and 1992 Interviews* was published as an e-book in 2013 but never received as much attention as deserved. The gap between these two interviews is critical. In 1977 Murray was interviewing someone he did not know, although he was connected to him through his dissertation adviser.

From 1980 to 1982 Gumperz was the supervisor for Murray's postdoctoral fellowship at the University of California, Berkeley, so by the second interview in 1992, they knew one another reasonably well. The circumstances and timing of the two interviews shed light on what he did when he interviewed elders—to wit, on his method. Among other comments, Gumperz specifically says, "Reviews don't matter very much" (Murray 2013c, 23). It's impressive that Murray didn't argue the point given how many thousands of reviews he devoted the time to write, and so this chapter demonstrates his assumptions about what should happen during interviews. In terms of process, Murray transcribed the audiotapes. A few notes on the editing of this chapter: Murray included lifespans for scholars mentioned, but since that does not fit the format used in the other chapters, we have omitted these. We have repaired obvious typos and done very limited editing, revising the format of the references he included and, for publications mentioned during the interviews, providing citations in endnotes where they do not intrude.

Murray prepared "Doing History of Anthropology" for an anthropology department colloquium at the University of California, Davis, in 1991, marked it for inclusion in the unpublished book *Essays on the History of Social Sciences*, and revised it as the conclusion to *American Anthropology and Company*, both books that collect his research on disciplinary history. We find the content extremely relevant for contemporary and future readers and want to bring it more attention than yet received, even in published form, because in this piece Murray clearly and concisely explains what he considers important in disciplinary history and what lessons he wants to pass on. We began with the published version, added references and notes, and edited lightly.

"What Is a Conversation?" began life as a working paper during his time at the University of California, Berkeley (1981), and foreshadowed a much later description of the milieu at Berkeley when he was there (2010a). It was substantially revised several times in later years (for example, a journal entry for June 17, 1987, indicates that he worked on it during a trip to Austria) but never published. The version here, dated 1993, was intended for inclusion in the unpublished *"Interruptions" and Other Messy Things in Language Use*. Its content illustrates what Murray thought about conversation analysis, explaining that he hated it because he took for granted Gumperz's assumption that one must understand interaction in context. Thus, he objected strenuously to the lack of context that those following conversation analysis guidelines took for granted and objected when conversation analysis scholars expand the meaning of the term "conversation" to include all speech, arguing that this is both misguided and wrong.

Fourth, we have included the draft introduction to the unpublished book *Male Sexual Subjectivities*, written in 2014. Like the other books prepared near the end of his life, this one would have been composed mostly of revised and expanded versions of previously published articles or chapters. Inclusion of this draft is merited because it describes quite clearly research Murray thought had not yet been done but desperately needed doing. Among other asides, it incorporates a quote that explains much about his willingness to spend so much time reading fiction: "Poems, plays, and fiction speak from the inside" (Smith 1991, 25).

Finally in this section we have a single brief poem, "What Had Been," taken from his *Collected Stories*. We know it was published in 2012 but do not know when it was written. Murray (2012a, 6) mentions, "The poems are included in chronological order of composition, I think." It was used as the final poem for that book, and we think it makes a nice final statement here. One possible interpretation would be that it describes the exhilaration of getting an idea down on paper and the need to celebrate that accomplishment. Readers are welcome to develop other interpretations.

Appendix

Every festschrift summarizing a scholar's contributions must include a list of publications, and so the final section in this book provides that. Murray kept a list, but unfortunately it turned out to be both incomplete and inaccurate; this one is as complete and accurate as possible.[7] The final list reveals that Murray contributed a surprising number of short entries to *The Encyclopedia of Homosexuality*; *Encyclopedia of Lesbian, Gay, Bisexual and Transgender History in America*; *Global Encyclopedia of Lesbian, Gay, Bisexual, and Transgender and Queer (LGBTQ) History*; *The Encyclopedia of Language and Linguistics*; *Dictionary of Anthropology*; *International Dictionary of Anthropologists*; *Biographical Dictionary of Social and Cultural Anthropology*; and *The Oxford Encyclopedia of Women in World*

History. These include essays on individuals as well as locations, cultures, and more general topics. The significance of these short pieces is that, first, such contributions take a remarkable amount of time to produce in exchange for limited reward, and second, they serve as a final testament to his reputation as a scholar: someone whose work is unknown to the editors is unlikely to be asked to produce such entries. His approximately one hundred published book reviews and review essays for a wide range of publications, both academic and popular, are equally significant for the same reason.

Notes

1. Details about Murray's life come from a copy of his résumé (and most are mentioned in various publications or his journal as well). The résumé and journal are now available in the Stephen O. Murray Papers, Stephen O. Murray and Keelung Hong Special Collections, Michigan State University (https://findingaids.lib.msu.edu/repositories/4/resources/6615). As a warning to anyone wishing to consult it, the résumé is a very abbreviated and incomplete document, but presumably accurate as far as it goes.
2. The longer version of the story is that he and several others filed suit for wrongful termination, the case was settled out of court, and he invested the settlement wisely. The story is told across several documents; see "JMC Alumni," and "amazon interviews SM," Stephen O. Murray Papers.
3. He said variations of the same thing in person and in email, for example: "Those of us foolish enough to write about homosexualities in the late-1970s certainly did not get jobs (even someone like me whose dissertation topic was not 'lavender')" (email to Michael Banton, June 11, 1997, taken from a document titled "Banton re AT 97," Stephen O. Murray Papers).
4. He asked Leeds-Hurwitz to write a preface when he was still hoping it could be completed and published in spring 2019; that draft was incorporated into Murray et al. (2021).
5. They did do an enormous amount of travel over the years. The list is far too long to include here, but a few countries that Murray felt deserved their own separate files in his journal were Austria, Ecuador, France, Peru, and Turkey. The one for "Peru trip, 1985" begins with a nice summary of his view of travel: "Journeys begin and end at home. Indeed, so much self is carted about, many wonder what point there is in traveling at all only to end, after incredible exertions, back with one's familiar self. Travel is not automatically broadening; the alien is glimpsed rather than lived

from within, and the taste that remains of the 'tristes tropiques,' as Lévi-Strauss says, is one of ashes." The journal is available in the Stephen O. Murray Papers.

6. Interestingly, given his attention to documentation in other areas, Murray does not seem to have maintained a list of his own conference presentations, and none are included in his résumé. The presentations here typically were mentioned in his publications, naming where material had first been presented; conferences he merely attended were often noted in journal entries. We have combined these two lists given that multiple entries were difficult to confirm.

7. Librarians at New Mexico State University, Texas A&M University, University of Pennsylvania, University of Vermont, University of Wisconsin–Madison, University of California, Berkeley, University of Southern California, and Michigan State University were especially helpful in tracking down details of some fairly obscure publications, as their special collections permitted.

References

Covelli, Lucille H., and Stephen O. Murray. 1980. "Accomplishing Topic Change." *Anthropological Linguistics* 22 (9): 382–90.

Darnell, Regna. 1983. "Preface." In *Group Formation in Social Science* by Stephen O. Murray, i–viii. Edmonton AB: Linguistic Research.

Epprecht, Marc, Stephen O. Murray, Kuukuwa Andam, Francisco Miguel, Aminata Cécile Mbaye, and Rudolf P. Gaudio. 2018. "*Boy Wives, Female Husbands* Twenty Years On: Reflections on Scholarly Activism and the Struggle for Sexual Orientation and Gender Identity/Expression Rights in Africa." *Canadian Journal of African Studies / Revue canadienne des études africaines* 52 (3): 349–64.

Fernández-Alemany, Manuel. (2001) 2019. "On Homosexualities: An Interview of Stephen O. Murray." Tangent Group. https://www.tangentgroup.org/on-homosexualities/.

Fernández-Alemany, Manuel, and Stephen O. Murray. 2002. *Heterogender Homosexuality in Honduras*. Lincoln: iUniverse.

Fuller, Amy Elisabeth. 2009. "Murray, Stephen O. 1950–." In *Contemporary Authors*, vol. 279, edited by Amy Elisabeth Fuller, 302–5. Farmington Hills: Gale eBooks.

Griffith, Belver C., and Nicholas C. Mullins. 1972. "Coherent Social Groups in Scientific Change: 'Invisible Colleges' May Be Consistent Throughout Science." *Science* 177 (4053): 959–64.

Gumperz, John, ed. 1982. *Language and Social Identity*. New York: Cambridge University Press.

Hong, Keelung, and Stephen O. Murray. 2005. *Looking through Taiwan: American Anthropologists' Collusion with Ethnic Domination*. Lincoln: University of Nebraska Press.

Mullins, Nicholas C. 1973. *Theories and Theory Groups in American Sociology.* New York: Harper and Row.

Murray, Stephen O. 1975. "Deference, Domination and Solidarity in an Interactional Order." Unpublished MA thesis, University of Arizona.

———. 1979a. "The Art of Gay Insulting." *Anthropological Linguistics* 21 (5): 211–23.

———. 1979b. "The Institutional Elaboration of a Quasi-ethnic Community." *International Review of Modern Sociology* 9 (2): 165–77.

———. 1979c. "Social Science Networks." Unpublished PhD dissertation, University of Toronto.

———. 1980. "Lexical and Institutional Elaboration: The 'Species Homosexual' in Guatemala." *Anthropological Linguistics* 22 (4): 177–85.

———. 1981. "What Is a Conversation?" *Working Papers of the Language Behavior Research Laboratory,* No. 52. Berkeley: University of California, Berkeley.

———. 1983a. *Group Formation in Social Science.* Edmonton AB: Linguistic Research.

———. 1983b. "Ritual and Personal Insults in Stigmatized Subcultures: Gay, Black, Jew." *Maledicta* 7: 189–211.

———. 1984. *Social Theory, Homosexual Realities.* New York: Gay Academic Union.

———. 1985. "Toward a Model of Members' Methods of Recognizing Interruptions." *Language in Society* 14 (1): 31–40.

———. 1987a. "Dangers of Lexical Inference II: Some Aymara Terms." In *Male Homosexuality in Central and South America,* edited by Stephen O. Murray, 165–67. New York: Gay Academic Union.

———, ed. 1987b. *Male Homosexuality in Central and South America.* New York: Gay Academic Union.

———. 1991a. "Ethnic Differences in Interpretive Conventions and the Reproduction of Inequality in Everyday Life." *Symbolic Interaction* 14: 187–204.

———. 1991b. "'Homosexual Occupations' in Mesoamerica?" *Journal of Homosexuality* 21 (4): 57–66.

———. 1991c. "Knowledge, Beliefs and Attitudes about AIDS in Los Angeles." *Society of Lesbian and Gay Anthropologists Newsletter* 13 (3): 54–55.

———. 1991d. "Letter to the Editor." *Archives of Sexual Behavior* 20 (6): 587–88.

———. 1992. *Oceanic Homosexualities.* New York: Garland.

———. 1994a. "A Memoir of the Founding of the Caucus." *Sociologists' Lesbian and Gay Caucus Newsletter* 79: 1–2.

———. 1994b. "Sex and the Economy of Speaking Turns." *Journal of Pragmatics* 21 (2): 215–24.

———. 1994c. *Theory Groups and the Study of Language in North America: A Social History.* Amsterdam: John Benjamins.

———. 1995a. *Latin American Male Homosexualities.* Albuquerque: University of New Mexico Press.

———. 1995b. "Modern Male Homosexuality in México and Peru." In *Latin American Male Homosexualities*, 145–49. Albuquerque: University of New Mexico Press.

———. 1995c. "Stigma Transformation and Relexification in the International Diffusion of *Gay*." In *Beyond the Lavender Lexicon: Authenticity, Imagination and Appropriation in Lesbian and Gay Languages*, edited by William L. Leap, 297–315. New York: Gordon & Breach.

———. 1996a. *American Gay*. Chicago: University of Chicago Press.

———. 1996b. *Angkor Life: Pre-Cambodian Life 800 Years Ago in the Society That Created the Stupendous Monuments of Angkor Wat and Angkor Thom*. Bangkok: Bua Luang Books.

———. 1996c. "Male Homosexuality in Guatemala: Possible Insights and Certain Confusions from Sleeping with the Natives." In *Out in the Field: Reflections of Lesbian and Gay Anthropologists*, edited by Ellen Lewin and William L. Leap, 236–60. Urbana: University of Illinois Press.

———. 1998. *American Sociolinguistics: Theorists and Theory Groups*. Amsterdam: John Benjamins.

———. 2000. *Homosexualities*. Chicago: University of Chicago Press.

———. 2002a. "Five Reasons I Don't Take 'Queer Theory' Seriously." In *Sexualities: Critical Concepts in Sociology*, vol. 4: *Sexualities and Their Futures*, edited by Ken Plummer, 245–48. London: Routledge.

———. 2002b. *Pacific Homosexualities*. Lincoln: iUniverse.

———. 2010a. "Interactional Sociolinguistics at Berkeley." In *The Social History of Language and Social Interaction Research: People, Places, Ideas*, edited by Wendy Leeds-Hurwitz, 97–126. Cresskill NJ: Hampton Press.

———. 2010b. "Mexico." In *The Politics of Sexuality in Latin America: A Reader on Lesbian, Gay, Bisexual, and Transgender Rights*, edited by Javier Corrales and Mario Pecheny, 60–65. Pittsburgh: University of Pittsburgh Press.

———. 2012a. *Collected Stories*. San Francisco: El Instituto Obregón.

———. 2012b. *Pieces for a History of Gay Studies*. San Francisco: El Instituto Obregón.

———. 2012c. *Reading Sicily (in English)*. San Francisco: El Instituto Obregón.

———. 2012d. *Reading 20th-Century Italian Fiction*. San Francisco: El Instituto Obregón.

———. 2012e. *21st-Century Representations of Muslim Homosexualities*. San Francisco: El Instituto Obregón.

———. 2013a. *American Anthropology and Company: Historical Explorations*. Lincoln: University of Nebraska Press.

———. 2013b. *An Introduction to African Cinema*. San Francisco: El Instituto Obregón.

———. 2013c. *John Gumperz in Context: 1977 and 1992 Interviews*. San Francisco: El Instituto Obregón.

———. 2014. "Appendix: 1997 and 2002 Interviews of the Author by Stephen Murray." In *Flipping* by Ricardo Ramos, 141–60. Floating Lotus.

———. 2021. "The Genesis of *Boy-Wives and Female Husbands.*" In *Boy-Wives and Female Husbands: Studies in African Homosexualities*, 2nd ed., edited by Stephen O. Murray and Will Roscoe, xix–xxiv. New York: St. Martin's.

Murray, Stephen O., and Manuel Arboleda G. 1987. "Stigma Transformation and Relexification: 'Gay' in Latin America." In *Male Homosexuality in Central and South America* by Stephen O. Murray, 130–38. New York: Gay Academic Union.

Murray, Stephen O., and Lucille H. Covelli. 1988. "Women and Men Speaking at the Same Time." *Journal of Pragmatics* 12 (1): 103–11.

Murray, Stephen O., and Keelung Hong. 1994. *Taiwanese Culture, Taiwanese Society: A Critical Review of Social Science Research Done on Taiwan*. Lanham, MD: University Press of America.

Murray, Stephen O., Wendy Leeds-Hurwitz, Regna Darnell, Nathan Dawthorne, and Robert Oppenheim. 2021. "An Interview with Stephen O. Murray on Stephen O. Murray as Historian of Anthropology (and More)." In *Centering the Margins of Anthropology's History*, edited by Regna Darnell and Frederick W. Gleach, 243–68. Lincoln: University of Nebraska Press.

Murray, Stephen O., and Will Roscoe, eds. 1997. *Islamic Homosexualities: Culture, History, and Literature*. New York: New York University Press.

———. 1998. *Boy-Wives and Female Husbands: Studies in African Homosexualities*. New York: St. Martin's.

Smith, Bruce. 1991. *Desire in Shakespeare's England: A Cultural Poetics*. Chicago: University of Chicago Press.

1 Stephen O. Murray in His Own Words

EXTRACTS FROM HIS JOURNAL

Prepared by Wendy Leeds-Hurwitz and Regna Darnell

February 19, 2007: Where I'm Coming From

Forebears
My father's mother's forebears, the Wadsworths, arrived in Massachusetts by 1640. My father's grandfather emigrated from Ayrshire, Scotland, in the 1870s and worked on the Illinois Central Railroad. My mother's grandparents were Danish Baptists whose fathers were named Peter and they took the family name "Peterson" when they immigrated, at about the same time as my Scottish great-grandparents, and took up farming in Freeborn County, Minnesota.

The only family story that resonates with me is of a great-grandmother who wore a feather in her hat to church one day. This led to much clacking of disapproving tongues. My great-grandmother looked over her (no doubt dowdy!) detractors and said, "I'm sure the Lord won't mind."

Parents
My paternal grandparents moved (along with livestock) by train to Pilot Grove in Minnesota in 1913, when my father was one. Other than military service during the Second World War, and wintering in Arizona for a number of years, he has lived his whole life in Minnesota's Faribault County. He worked for Standard Oil (of Indiana, which became Amoco, and then BP).

My mother's mother died a hideously prolonged and painful death of cancer. Her father then wanted his two daughters to stay with him and take care of him, although they wanted to go to college. They did, with no support from him, to put it mildly, and completed the two years necessary (in those days) to get teaching certificates. Even after my grandfather got a daughter-in-law whose duties included catering to his demands, he continued to resent being "abandoned" by his daughters.

My mother began teaching in a one-room country schoolhouse and taught 4th grade except for two years working in a post office in San Diego while my father was stationed there during WWII. The school superintendent there liked my mother and rehired her when she returned even though married women usually were not hired (the "rule" was "relaxed" to the extent of employing married women without children).

My mother, in particular, valued education very highly and was determined to make sure that her children were encouraged rather than blocked. There was never the slightest doubt that I was going to college and would be the first in the family to graduate from college.

Before I came on the scene, my mother was also the county Republican chair. She had been a friend of the then-future "boy-wonder" Minnesota governor Harold Stassen in church camp and was more of the internationalist (Wendell Wilkie) than the isolationist (Ohio Senator [Robert A.] Taft) wing of the GOP before it was taken over by Southern bigots. One of her raps against Democrats remained that Democratic presidents had taken the U.S. into war (Wilson, Roosevelt, Truman, Johnson were born during the Taft administration and she didn't remember McKinley, let alone Lincoln).

The local Baptist church, of which my maternal grandmother was a pillar, opposed dancing, makeup, and card-playing. My mother loved her bridge parties, would not go out without putting her face on [i.e., makeup] and sometimes went to a "supper club" with dancing; so I was raised and confirmed in the Evangelical United Brethren Church, which did not have edicts on such lifestyle issues.

I didn't realize how German the EUB church was until decades later I thought of the names of the families among its membership. I didn't think to ask if there had been covert fights between my mother and my father's mother about her refusal to join the local Baptist church, covert because my mother and my father's mother never fought with each other. Her rejection of the narrow-mindedness of the church seemed natural to me ("the Lord won't mind" redux).

My father nearly died while he was in the Navy during World War II, stationed in the Great Lakes Training Center on Lake Michigan, when his appendix burst. He enlisted when he was 40 and spent most of the war in San Diego. After the war, I assume to be close to their parents, they moved, and this subjected me to Minnesota winters. I only had to trek seven blocks to school through blizzards, unlike the three miles my mother made much of (until I saw an old photo and learned that she had a horse to ride to school). My father started school in a one-room country schoolhouse less than a mile from the farm on which he grew up as the third son with no prospects of inheriting it.

Both my maternal grandfather and my paternal grandfathers retired "into town" where they had wood-burning stoves for cooking and cisterns with hand-operated pumps for water. My paternal grandmother burned corncobs, my maternal grandfather wood. Both were given electric stoves by their children but continued to use the wood-burning ones.

Nothing bothered my mother more than unloved children; she was appalled at the idea of any woman being forced to bear a child she did not want. In response to the embrace by the local and national Republican Party of seeking to recriminalize abortion, this lifelong Republican whose first presidential election vote had been for Herbert Hoover in 1932 voted for Clinton in 1992.

and me

At the ripe old age of 14, I had made three speeches supporting Barry Goldwater for president. I loathed both Lyndon Johnson and Hubert Humphrey and my opposition to the U.S. military involvement in Vietnam came partly from distrust of LBJ and partly from familial distaste for and distrust of foreign military campaigns.

I actually remember the radio reports of the Gulf of Tonkin "incident" which I listened to while on a rowboat in some northern Minnesota lake where I was also reading Gore Vidal's novel about Julian the Apostate. Because I had little trust for Lyndon Johnson, I was skeptical about his rationale for the entry of U.S. fighting forces (given that there had been military "observers" before) to try to prop up the Republic of Vietnam whose Catholic dictator the U.S. had been complicit in assassinating during the Kennedy administration.

During my senior year in high school, I joined the grassroots "children's crusade" to topple Johnson. Back in 1960, I had been very impressed by the speech that our then junior (to Humphrey) senator Eugene McCarthy had made by nominating Adlai Stevenson. I experienced no cognitive dissonance working against Johnson in the Republican Party.

I was intermittently active during college in my opposition to Nixon's continuance of the Vietnam debacle, although I was acutely aware of and recurrently wrote about the need to persuade those who recoiled from long-haired (etc.) opponents of the war. I still keenly feel that the failure to appeal to what Nixon claimed was a "silent majority" is the major failure of our "Question Authority" generation and that too many of my agemates were dismissive of those sent to fight while the Dick Cheneys, Dan Quayles, and George W. Bushes who "supported" the war ensured that they would not have to fight it, along with the Bill Clintons who opposed the war but also ensured that they would not have to fight it. I was born on a good day: my lottery number was 270 and the draft never came close to it.

I could not vote in the 1968 presidential election but I was of the "There's no real difference" persuasion and had a visceral repugnance for Humphrey. With the "Southern Strategy" designed for Nixon by Kevin Phillips, there turned out to be a big difference and the U.S. has been dominated by reactionary Southerners ever since.

In many ways, I think that I remain a conservative in the Goldwater/libertarian mode: anti-statist, very skeptical of social engineering ("nation-building"), and acutely aware that there are always unanticipated consequences. This was true well before I took any sociology courses.

I took a double major in social psychology and "Justice, Morality, and Constitutional Democracy" (try to fit that into a box for "major"!) in James Madison College, an "experimental living-learning unit" within the vast multiversity of Michigan State University.[1] . . .

Because I was so argumentative from grade school on, everyone assumed that I would become a lawyer; JMCD was a major primarily for future lawyers, there were no jobs for philosopher kings. My advisor was one of the later (Claremont) students of Leo Strauss and my other mentor had been a student of Sheldon Wolin; the first introduced me to the writings of

Tocqueville, the second to Freud's metapsychology, as well as Plato, Aristotle, Augustine, Machiavelli, Hobbes, Locke, Marx, and Weber. I thought we were studying classical political theory but when I got to graduate school in sociology, I discovered that classical political theory and classical social theory were largely the same. According to Robert Nisbet (the leading historian of French conservative social theory), I did as well on the pretest he gave his social theory class as he would have scored himself. . . .

Although I didn't plan to go so far forward into my own influences, anyone who made it through the first two parts of these entries probably noticed that I came from a family that did not accept rules its members thought unjustified before becoming a part of the "Question Authority" generation.

May 14, 1988
Paper is piling up around me and I don't have the energy to sort it or the will to throw it out, although it's not like me to have unanswered letters. I think that I am becoming more introverted.

February 9, 1993
I recognize my crankiness in delaying dealing with Konrad's endless provocations.[2] I'll have to start over if I burn that bridge which will take time and that is my scarcest commodity. On the other hand, I don't want to spend the rest of my life, or any more of my life, on the formalities that substitute for grappling with substance in his editorial practices. I am ready to give him an ultimatum to give me a contract or else. It's not a bluff, but if he calls it, I may be forced to deal with the demands of other publishers to reduce the bibliography or have to fight for footnotes. I don't understand why endnotes continue to exist in the 1990s!

February 16, 1993
Others have remarked on the disparity between my "hard chic" writer's persona and the quiet, polite Midwesterner encountered in person.

March 13, 1993
As journal rejections mount, I worry about possible neurological bases for the decline of my ability to develop an argument. We know that HIV can cross the blood/brain barrier. I don't know that it has in me, but whether or not it is in my brain, my mind is like a popcorn popper with no lid, in

which some kernels are warming up and waiting to pop, flying off individually in many directions when they do; they certainly don't get strung together, or even piled up into a bowl. I can at least produce sentences, even if one bears little relationship to its neighbors!

March 25, 1993
I sent off the manuscript to Amsterdam.[3] What a relief! This is how an elephant must feel after giving birth or how a rhinoceros would feel after giving birth to an elephant! I feel as if I have been working on this book continually since 1976 and hope that its interest will outlast me. I think there is a lot of information in it that is not available elsewhere and that it offers some unique interpretations. Having recently read it from one end to the other (for the first time ever) and then skimmed it again for the (infernal) name index, I realize that it flows at different speeds. For example, the syntax is rarely simple; I have transformed some (not enough) sentences into active voice, even at the cost of being the agent of some of them.[4] There are some sentences I like. I frequently don't like how I have allocated information across sections. I think that I could or should have been a bit more narrative and a bit less comparative; but linearity is not my way; fortunately, it is also quite unfashionable at present. My life expectancy is too short to try to reorganize and rewrite it all.

May 11, 1993
The day I was laid off from my first and maybe only fulltime job.

May 14, 1993
[What follows is part of an exercise in training for the "What do you want to do?" question during interviews.]

POST-DOC

What did you like in your jobs?
- Autonomy (practically total!)
- Solving analytical problems, focus on analyzing data
- Having influence (at least at San Francisco, if not from PSP)[5]
- Some of the people I work with, both peers and customers
- Truly collegial project meetings
- Access to resources like computation, printing, photocopying and some storage

- Never having to make work or to appear busy
- Flexible hours and no requirement to work in my Berkeley office

What did you not like in your jobs?
- I rarely had the satisfaction of helping people solve what they perceived as problems, although I didn't recognize the ego satisfactions this brings at the time.
- Lack of integration due to liminal status and living in San Francisco
- Being in Berkeley (I didn't particularly mind getting there)

TEACHING

What did you like in your jobs?
- Autonomy (pretty considerable)
- Mentoring (meeting with students and helping them understand something)
- Serious discussions about interesting phenomena
- Respect (from students and faculty)
- Never having to make work or to appear busy
- Flexible hours and minimal requirement of office hours

What did you not like in your jobs?
- Lecturing
- Certainty of having to leave and sell myself elsewhere
- Lack of resources (neither of these would apply to a real [i.e., tenured] professorship)

WRITING

What did you like in your jobs?
- Autonomy (generally considerable to total)
- Feedback, especially occasional serious discussions about interesting phenomena
- Recognition (when I get it): seeing someone else use my ideas and knowing that someone else has gotten something s/he finds interesting or useful from what I have written.
- Collaboration (when I get it!)
- Seeing what I think (which sometimes surprises me. I don't know something and then write it; opinions, and even knowledge, emerge through writing for me)
- Seeing my name in print
- Freedom to live and work where I want

What did you not like in your jobs?
- Dotting i's to ensure communication of my ideas
- Lack of feedback and influence (writing is a solitary activity, even in collaboration with others)
- Marketing myself
- Low or non-existent compensation (and concomitant lack of resources)
- Willful misinterpretation bothers me less than the silent obliteration of being ignored

What do you conclude from these lists?
- Respondent likes autonomy and respect and solving problems, does not like to be locked up in an office, especially with capricious and paternalistic bosses. Distaste for (nervous lack of confidence in) public speaking, especially having to sell self or product to hostile audience.
- The surprise is that I like working with people more than with data; collaborating is more gratifying than the solitary splendor of problem-solving. I already knew that I like to work on a range of unconnected problems at the same time rather than grind one to completion before starting the next one. In my employment, as in my real work, once I know what the solution to a problem is, I lose interest in it. I suppose that is why I have trouble communicating the solution and making sure that it is applied (or even that it really works, I suppose!). I suppose this parallels a greater relish for criticizing and identifying what should be problematic than for explicating what is good, true, beautiful. I am quite deferential to those I see as having accomplished something, but most of those I see who regard themselves or their courtiers as emperors have threadbare or no clothes!
- The lengthening list of dissatisfactions in the jobs as opposed to valued activities shows how increasingly unhealthy was the position I occupied to stay insured. I've never been in a position with any real job security (tenure, union, or civil service seniority).
- I'm not very focused on *skills*. Is originality a skill (or a curse!)?
- Editing (evaluating, clarifying, and improving the expression of others' arguments)
- Writing (not just academic)
- Synthesizing ideas to solve diverse sorts of problems
- Analyzing data (sketchy qualitative data, as well as large quantitative data sets)

- Collaborating on identifying (potential as well as present) problems, solutions, and establishing procedures to avoid problems' occurrence or recurrence

What, then, do I want from this historical survey?
- autonomy
- challenges (not impossible ones! but not the same ones over and over either)
- flexibility of where and when to do the work
- bright, sane, convivial coworkers
- (and incompatibly?) security

*Is there any way to avoid **both** working for others or repeatedly marketing myself?*

July 5, 1993
My first unpaid national holiday since Labor Day of 1982, but I nonetheless recognize how fortunate I am compared to most of the people who have lived on this earth. I have the leisure and the cultivation to enjoy central masterworks of Western (and other) civilizations, viz., to reread *The Tempest* and listen to Brahms' first symphony. Rather than wondering where there will be a next meal, we feast on duck, and I can choose grapes, cherries, blueberries, or raspberries. No one knows how long I'll be able to enjoy these luxuries but I feel that I have known more of the world than most people have or do, and that despite being unemployed and HIV+, I have genuinely lived. Half the AIDS obituaries are still of men younger than I am. I want to see and enjoy and live much more but I am happy to have seen and enjoyed and lived as much as I have.

October 25, 1993
Is my lifework done? I don't seem to have much drive to undertake anything new and seem to be writing retrospectively like someone nearing the end of a career.

November 11, 1993
I need to live (which for me means mostly reading and writing) now. I am here and intact now. Visualizing my death and beyond wastes time and that is what I have all too little of.

January 6, 1994
Was I contrary before puberty? Was I born oppositional? I was certainly argumentative in high school and often sustained my point of view which is why everyone, including myself, assumed I would become a lawyer. By the time of my first ongoing battle with a teacher in 7th grade, I had already reached puberty. I can remember what strikes me as only a childish flare-up in sixth grade. Almost a decade later, I readily believed Marcuse in *Eros and Civilization* that there is an intrinsic connection between homosexuality and social criticism or opposition. This was an important legitimation for me at the time. I still think I was oppositional before I was gay, though I have come to realize that many people find (closeted) homosexuality and hyper-conformity a comfortable fit. Now I wonder when my own intransigence started.

April 20, 1994
Between approaching the anniversary of being laid-off and reading AIDS fiction, I guess I have reason to be somewhat depressed. I feel that I should be using my time better....

For me, adolescence was a time of nearly total alienation, isolation from others. Like now, I read a lot. Then I read about sex; at least in the last week... I have been reading about deterioration and death. Anticipation in both cases? ... I feel guilt that I don't have more to show from a year of not having to go to work.

October 17, 1994
Whether I'm hot, gay studies are hot, or Will's proposals are very enticing (or some or all these), there's interest in both the books we're proposing (African and Islamic). My energy has revived some, feeding off incipient recognition.

December 31, 1994
I sent off two book manuscripts this week (Angkor and N. America) and a paper.[6] I should dig out from the accumulated paper that surrounds me, none of which unfortunately relates to any of the three dispatched manuscripts. Perhaps my latest anti-retroviral... is working.... I've had more energy and better concentration of late, albeit I have to lie down sometimes.

May 2, 1995
Other than during our trip to San Diego, I feel that I have read nothing unrelated to homosexuality other than the Sunday paper, *Newsweek*, and the *New Yorker* for months. A break from being a professional homosexual should be good.

May 4, 1995
Unlike . . . many others, I have attained a 45th year. I feel very lucky to feel fairly good, to be productive and, most of all, to be loved and secure.

May 20, 1995
My recent writing, instead of beginning by attacking others, lays out conventional ignorance or mistakes that I shared. This seems to be received less well by referees than is attacking existing literature. I want to engage readers in how I corrected my own views, not just those of others but also the strict separation of the process of discovery from the "logic" of justification that is resolutely maintained, even in anthropology.

August 27, 1995
Yesterday I called his hospital room but got no answer.[7] Without guests, I planned to be more persistent in calling today but it's too late. Now I am wracked with guilt that I didn't get there. . . . I wish I could believe there was a heaven in which he would be rewarded, but if there is an omnipotent god who permits such things as AIDS to happen and him to die alone, he is unimaginably evil. I prefer to believe none exists. Since I have chosen my work over being there for sick and dying friends, I'd better make it good.

November 11, 1995
I wish everyone would write more about the basis for selecting examples. No one, least of all myself, has ever provided a very good rationale explaining why we choose the examples we do or for establishing that they are typical.

December 20, 1995
I don't fail to appreciate how lucky I am to be almost healthy fourteen or more years after infection, to have insurance and some income, Keelung's support (which extended to taking me along to Hawai'i). The combination of these blessings has given me at least two and a half years of being able

to do what I regard as my real work.... I am also aware that some people's jobs are more central to their selves than mine was.... I sometimes feel too isolated and miss the sociability around work, but I have other things to do that are more important in my view. Writers typically overvalue writing: I realize that writing is not well rewarded in American society and that its mystique is limited, though it is not limited only to writers.

March 4, 1996
A downside of my seemingly extending life expectancy is having to make my teeth last longer. I may even have to start making longer-range plans rather than waking up, checking if I still feel fine, and then figuring out what to work on.

July 9, 1996
My first-ever personal appearance in a bookstore went fairly well.[8] My worst fear was that no one would turn up, but there were about 35, ten standing. And there were some questions.... Keelung... remarked that the audience listened very intently. I don't think any had read the book.

April 18, 1997
I was dreading both being attacked and that the panel on *American Gay* would draw no audience.[9] I was exhilarated to have my work taken seriously and subjected to careful reading. It received thoughtful praise and thoughtful criticism.

May 5, 1997
My self-presentation is as a writer. That is what I do most and I have plenty of publications to bolster the claim. It is more easily understood than the complexity of what I "do for a living."

August 1, 1999
I have been self-driven primarily to complete my lifework before HIV cut me down. Having done so, I feel that I am drifting.... Since I always work on multiple things rather than one project at a time, I know that starting one doesn't close off another and I should get moving.

August 9, 1999
Judging by my royalty checks, it's more lucrative and far less effort to review manuscripts than to write books, at least solo-authored ones.

January 8, 2000
Yesterday I dispatched the proofs and index to *Homosexualities*. My life work is officially completed and I'm too exhausted to think about what I'll do with more borrowed time (a posthumous life). I'll produce reviews and chapters and a talk that I've promised and do some AAA centennial work. And work on less academic projects (books even!).

May 4, 2000
It's astounding that I have made it to age 50, since I didn't expect to make it to age 40 or to finish *Homosexualities*.

April 9, 2001
I was not craving ice cream and welcomed a chance for solitude.[10] I am used to being alone most of the time and group life wears on me, particularly with inadequate sleep.

September 11, 2002
I enjoy books in which people describe their experiences living in a culture/environment different from the one in which they grew up. I consume a lot of books about experiences of immigrants to Anglophone societies and enjoy books about Anglophone emigrants' long-term experiences more [than] "travel writing."

December 30, 2002
Being contrary by temperament . . .

June 20, 2005
For me, the main pleasures of reading someone else's diary are (1) reading what the person says about me and (2) reading what someone I know writes for himself or herself and did not intend to share (that is, stealing glances).

August 28, 2006
My experience as an editor of a book series that has been very heavy on biographies is that biographers tend either to over-identify with the biographical

subject and engage in special pleading for him or her or become so irritated at the person they are writing about that they write "pathographies."

October 18, 2006
I think helping someone to finish it who cannot help himself is different from aiding or condoning suicide. I believe that suicide is a right (did I pick that up from [Albert] Camus as a college freshman?) but I have worked very hard at staying alive.

April 13, 2008
It would not take great intuition for anyone to guess that I have spent a lot of time in libraries or that this began at an early age. . . . I want to salute both the librarian at my hometown public library when I began checking out books (I'd guess when I was in second grade), Miss Gooseberry (I kid you not!), and school librarian Judith Hanks. Both encouraged me in multiple ways and provided a guidance so subtle that I did not notice it at the time.

In passing through libraries at the four universities I attended, I sometimes went intending to cruise, but was invariably distracted by (absorbed into) the books. (I get bored fast and my tolerance for boredom has not increased with age!)

Libraries have also been important sources of music for me.

May 4, 2008
I am bemused by having survived so long. . . . At the age of 46, there was little likelihood of living to 50, though by the age of 48 it seemed a strong possibility because of the protease "revolution." Now it seems that barring an accident of some sort, I will reach 60 and even 62 (to start collecting Social Security).

January 31, 2009
Luc[y] Sante writes in reviewing Susan Sontag's youthful journal (NYT), "You might say there are two kinds of writers: those who keep a journal in the hope that its contents might someday be published, and those who do not keep a journal for fear that its contents might someday be published. In other words, no journal-keeping by a writer who harbors any sort of ambition is going to be entirely innocent. The complicated, somewhat voyeuristic thrill the reader might derive from seemingly prying open the

author's desk drawer is therefore, to a certain extent, a fiction in which both parties are complicit." I think my journal has become like hers in mostly pasting in reviews. As [Sante] says of some of hers, perhaps "sometimes the intellectual items sound more naked and the private items more hedged."

August 8, 2009
Before the ASA [American Sociological Association] thematic session on sexual communities, I was resenting not being invited to be on it, not because I wanted to talk or had any new research or new thoughts on "community," but aren't I the prophet of "gay community"? Placated by being the only author quoted in Gayle Rubin's presentation. . . . It occurred to me that I should have organized a session.

April 2, 2012
I was asked about my just-up Kindle book.[11] My reply: I was frustrated that it's taking four years from submission to publication of my book *Anthropology and Company: Border Perspectives* by a university press, even in a series I co-edit. The gay studies part was originally the third part of that book, but the book was too long.

I did not want to wait for the inane referee comments and my usual battle with copyeditors (in my experience failed writers who want to take out their frustrations on authors).

The instant gratification was too instant because I realized that I had missed some references that I added in the last chapter and had to resubmit the file (though this only cost about twelve hours of availability!) . . .

I am addicted to footnotes, which Kindle doesn't support, so I had to insert them directly into the text. Scientific citation style also seemed an obstacle for readers, so I generally put the titles of books I discuss in the text. This is, of course, more a problem for history of discourses than for ethnography or memoirs.

But the book is available at a low price ($3.39); with 70% royalties, royalties per copy are as great or greater than most of my books published by academic publishers. . . .

I like the covers of some of my earlier books published by university presses, was very unhappy with the one from the imprint of the second-biggest publishing conglomerate in the world. Not everyone wants to design/do their own covers, but I do, so this was another plus for me.

December 4, 2014

What DO I want beyond a more stable digestive system and no more dental work? I'm feeling old and professionally underappreciated (though I never had a position as a "professional"). Under cited and unappreciated, not un- or under loved. I try not to take for granted what I have, but it's the other stuff that gnaws, alas.

March 5, 2015

Perhaps because it is easier to write about something with which I have faults to find, I sometimes can't find anything to say about works I greatly admire.

April 20, 2015: Parachute ID

What am I?
- writer
- analytical/critical
- interested in differences (observing & interpreting)
- gay
- editor (and other ways of bringing out the best work in insecure others)
- oppositional/individualistic (too prone to isolation)
- shy (too prone to isolation)
- researcher
- cultured (in the high, not anthropological sense of "culture")
- interested in understanding HIV+
- resentful (increasingly, at lack of recognition, funding, position)
- insecure

What am I not or not very good as?
- speaker
- orthodox
- team player (for large entities: I think I am good at collaborating with limited numbers)
- meticulous (a programmer or proofreader)

- expecting longevity
- gracious/generous

May 4, 2015
I should try to come up with some attainable goals for my "golden years."[12]

November 19, 2016
I periodically feel guilty about how little I am accomplishing and the high price in medicine and medical practitioners needed to keep me functioning.

December 28, 2016
I believe that a reviewer should assess how well an author did what s/he tried to do, not opine about what he or she should have done instead.

January 6, 2016
There's much more to do to organize my archive. Once the desktop surfaces are cleared, I should go in and pitch various folders of stuff I have not and will now never write about.

May 4, 2018
Back in Long Hospital, initially with a temperature of 103. . . . I'm discouraged about surviving the treatment. How can my system get ready for another round of chemo like this? And is the high cost (in my discomfort, never mind hospital charges) worth the possible gain in longevity? What do I want to do that I haven't done? I've said that there is nowhere left on my "bucket list." I've loved and been loved. I've done what I can of research/writing. Living longer is not going to increase the impact or in/visibility of my work.

September 9, 2018
I am tired of being weak, tired of not being able to sit comfortably, tired of neuropathies. I feel as if I have sand between my toes without being on Fire Island. . . . I have fought too hard to live to contemplate suicide.

May 27, 2019
With a partly "lavender resumé," I could not even get a job interview, let alone a tenure-track job.

[The following has no date, but is the final entry in the last journal of 2019]
I have been too flummoxed with information about recent health status information to write anything while deciding whether to die today or not.

Notes

1. He took no undergraduate courses in sociology or anthropology.
2. Konrad is Konrad Koerner; the publication is *Theory Groups and the Study of Language in North America*.
3. *Theory Groups and the Study of Language in North America*.
4. In fact, in editing these journal entries, transforming sentences into active voice is one of the changes we have made.
5. PSP is the company that had just laid him off.
6. The two books were *Angkor Life* and *American Gay*.
7. A friend had died during the night, and Steve had not gone to see him for a few days due to having had visitors.
8. He does not say which book, but the bookstore was A Different Light, a gay/lesbian bookstore in San Francisco, so probably *American Gay*.
9. He was at the Pacific Sociological Association convention.
10. He was on a birdwatching trip to Costa Rica.
11. The book being discussed is *Pieces for a History of Gay Studies*.
12. This was his sixty-fifth birthday.

PART 2 Disciplinary History

2 The Breadth and Depth of Creativity in Stephen O. Murray's Research and Publications

Wendy Leeds-Hurwitz

Disciplines are social constructions, although we often forget that they are made rather than found (Leeds-Hurwitz 2012).[1] Students today are frequently trained in single disciplines and discouraged from crossing their boundaries to investigate others. Understanding that disciplines are socially constructed means that the boundaries between them are also made things, and thus flexible, changing over time. Stephen O. Murray had formal training in several disciplines and was comfortable doing history of not only anthropology but also linguistics and sociology, occasionally bringing in psychology as well.[2] My focus here will be on the essays he collected in *American Anthropology and Company* (2013a) as, in many ways, this was the culmination of his historical writing.[3] He introduces the volume by explaining, "Collecting some of my writings about research on the history of American anthropology and its social science neighbors (history, linguistics, psychology, and at greatest length, sociology) provides the opportunity to reflect on how they came about and to see some relationships between a range of research projects aiming to answer questions about some things that happened and some that did not but seemingly could have along the relatively unfortified borders of twentieth-century American anthropologies" (Murray 2013a, xv).

Murray was uncommon not just due to the breadth of his research (that is, across disciplines) but also due to the depth (that is, his use of not one single method, but multiple methods, a strategy which permitted him to delve deeply into those topics of greatest interest).[4]

Breadth

Murray's background in sociology was the most obvious, given that he had a PhD in that discipline (from the University of Toronto). If additional support for the idea that he used his qualifications in sociology is required, it is worth mentioning that multiple publications appeared in sociology journals (such as Murray 1979b, 1987a, 1991a; Murray and Poolman 1982; Murray, Rankin, and Magill 1981). In terms of anthropology and linguistics, he said, "my path into or toward sociocultural anthropology was through linguistic anthropology" (Murray 2013a, xix).[5] Occasionally he referred to himself as being "a linguistic anthropologist (which I sometimes think I am)" (Murray 2013a, xvi) and said, "I consider myself a practitioner of linguistic anthropology, rather than an 'alien' analyst" (Murray 1996a, 355). He could legitimately make this claim due to the training provided through his postdoctoral fellowship with John Gumperz at the University of California, Berkeley (see Murray 2013b).[6] On occasion he specifically claimed to have "gone native": "Having taken postgraduate courses in anthropology for four years at three universities, I 'went native' to some extent, joined the American Anthropological Association, presented research and served as a discussant at sessions of its annual meetings (on subjects other than the history of anthropology), and have published research that is not history of the fields in anthropological and linguistic anthropology journals" (Murray 2013a, 316n3).

He also was occasionally accused by others of having "gone native," sometimes by joining the linguists rather than the anthropologists: "Sociologists... have wondered if I went native and became more interested in the history of linguistics than in sociological generalization" (Murray 1998a, 2).[7] He published multiple analyses of language used in interaction with major journals (including Covelli and Murray 1980; Murray 1979a, 1980b, 1985; Murray and Covelli 1988; Payne and Murray 1983), which should certainly make clear that he was able to function as a linguistic anthropologist. On occasion, he specifically documented his lineage from Sapir: "Each of my successive anthropological linguistic mentors provide a link to Sapir: Keith Basso through Clyde Kluckhohn, William Samarin through Mary Haas and Murray Emeneau, John Gumperz through Kenneth Pike" (Murray 2013a, 316n5). He also explicitly pointed out the connections between his research and Sapir's: "A number of us feel that we are working in programs of research sketched by Sapir" (Murray 1991c, 317).

His work in disciplinary history was published in multiple journals with "history" in the name (such as Murray 1980a, 1980c, 1981a, 1982, 1991b; Payne and Murray 1983). By his own report, "As a historian, I approached the anthropology-sociology border from anthropology, having approached sociocultural anthropology from linguistic anthropology and linguistic anthropology from the Durkheimian/Lévi-Strauss tradition" (Murray 2013a, xiv).[8] Unlike these other disciplines, psychology (and it is worth noting that one of his undergraduate majors was psychology) was not considered on its own but became relevant only when he looked at such topics as "culture and personality" (as in Murray 1986b) or when briefly consulted for additional documentation (as when citing a book review from *Transcultural Psychiatric Research*, in Murray 2013a, 140).[9]

Interestingly, he occasionally drew a sharp distinction not only between being a disciplinary historian and being a practitioner of that discipline but between being a historian of institutions and a historian of ideas. For example, he said in one review, "Regna Darnell, who is a historian of early American anthropology as well as an ethnolinguist, clearly regards Sapir as a legitimating ancestor of contemporary work. In this book, the historian predominates over the practitioner of ethnolinguistics, and, within that category, it is the historian of institutions and of the "invisible college" of the American social science elite in the 1920s and 1930s more than the historian of ideas who is in evidence" (Murray 1991c, 317).[10]

A note of caution is important here: I realize the citations to this point may make it look like most of Murray's work in disciplinary history and sociolinguistics was conducted and written before most of his work on homosexuality, but that is not in fact the case. For example, it's useful to realize that he was one of the founders of the Sociologists' Gay Caucus in 1974 and one of the editors of their newsletter by 1979 (Murray 2021). In fact, he worked on multiple topics simultaneously, even if some projects have later publication dates. As he explained at one point, the year he published something could not be relied upon to illuminate the year it was written:

> Year of publication ill reflects composition. Parts of AMERICAN GAY [published as Murray 1996a] date back to 1976; parts of ISLAMIC HOMOSEXUALITIES [published as Murray and Roscoe 1997] to 1981. Only ANGKOR LIFE [published as Murray 1996b], which is quite short (reflecting how little is known) stems from recent work (1994). That is, I have a considerable backlog (including an African book [Murray and Roscoe 1998], parts of which also date back to 1980–1, two collections of essays and a sort-of-book reaching back to work done during the 70s).[11] (email to Leeds-Hurwitz, June 27, 1996)

This means that he was actually doing something far more difficult than moving from one topic to another over time as his interests changed: he consistently balanced multiple, substantially different topics simultaneously throughout his career.

One of the reasons Murray (2013a, 157; see also 194) combined sociology and anthropology was due to the "initially porous boundary between sociology and anthropology." That boundary has become more rigid over time, since "social science disciplines were less ossified into distinct entities during the 1920s" (173) than they are today. He documented this through a detailed examination of publications by leading anthropologists in sociology journals (175), of student enrollment across disciplinary boundaries (190–91), and of citations to anthropology versus sociology faculty members in sociology dissertations (192). He clearly demonstrated that, at least at the University of Chicago in the 1920s and 1930s, the boundary was porous indeed. Then Murray went on to examine the extent to which publications by anthropologists were reviewed in major sociology journals between 1921 and 1951 (198), demonstrating the same early fluid boundary existed far beyond Chicago. At times he used the phrase "human science" to refer to the combination of anthropology and sociology (and potentially psychology as well), which has not yet coalesced but still may one day (210).[12] When explicitly asked about the interrelationship between the disciplines he studied, he answered, "my historical work seems to me to be work on the boundaries of disciplines as they have been organized in Anglo North America, particularly the ones dividing anthropology from sociology and anthropology from psychology" (Murray et al. 2021, 252).

Although Murray had originally started publishing in the history of sociology, particularly within the *Journal of the History of Sociology*, that journal "collapsed in 1987, not for lack of material being submitted but for lack of financial support" (Murray 2013a, 159), and he began publishing in other journals. Whatever the discipline, when doing historical work, he always followed historicist rather than presentist assumptions (Stocking 1965). Briefly, *historicism* means examining what previous scholars did in context, while *presentism* means looking to see how the early work led to the modern work. As he explained: "I think that understanding past thinkers as they understood themselves is ultimately impossible but nonetheless is a worthy aspiration, which is to say I consider my work 'historicist.' . . . I do not think that trying to figure out what people in the past thought they were doing disallows criticism of how they did—and failed to do— what they wanted to do" (Murray 2013a, xxiv).

Elsewhere, he expanded on this: "I also believe that the job of historians is to try to establish what happened and to explain why it happened" (Murray 1996d, 12). In fact, he argued strongly against presentist history:

> "presentist," which is to say that in writing about the past their primary purpose is making sense of the present, legitimating present preoccupations with some sort of tradition and development, and lauding those who made contributions that are either accepted in the present or believed to have led to present understandings of whatever phenomena are of concern to science, or would be if only others would value the proposed progenitor as the author does. . . . These do not aim to make sense of scientists in their own world with their own assumptions but as prefiguring "what we know now." (Murray 2013a, 282)

Despite the difficulty of historicist research, he offers advice for this impossible task, bringing the goals of presentism and historicism together: "The goal of scientific history, even of that concerned with implications for present work, must be to explicate why scientists did what they did, rather than to denigrate them for not pursuing contemporary problematics with contemporary methods" (Murray 1983a, 360n2).[13]

In addition, Murray distinguished between "insider" and "outsider" historians (those trained and working within the discipline and those not), and "internalist" (concerned with "internal dynamics of the institutionalized disciplines"; Murray 1996c, 355) versus "externalist" (considering the influence of events and people from outside the discipline). He was particularly annoyed when linguist Charles Hockett, serving as reviewer of one of his disciplinary history books (Murray 1994c), considered him an outsider and expected more attention paid to external factors, whereas Murray (1996c, 355) considered himself to be an insider, focusing on internal events; he complained that Hockett thus "consigns me to outer darkness." In the process, Murray (1996c, 355–56) clarifies that his dissertation, defended in 1979 (published as 1983b), was "an internalist history by an outsider," whereas the book Hockett reviewed was "an internalist history by an insider of sorts—one with four years of post-graduate coursework in linguistic anthropology and two decades of participation (including publication) in the tradition that was my original interest and that remains the central case study of my 1994 book. Having been supervised by linguists who were students of Sapir's students, I can claim legitimate descent as a 'third-generation Sapirian.'"

He was particularly annoyed when Hockett classified him as a sociologist (the reason Hockett considered Murray an outsider), given that he had by then "published more in anthropological linguistic journals than in sociology journals" (Murray 1996c, 356).

Periodically, Murray would compare what scholars in one discipline were writing with what those in others prepared. For example, in a review essay he summarized what was being written on a single topic (AIDS) by historians, anthropologists, and sociologists: "It seems from these two books that historians are freer to criticize the biomedical paradigm of AIDS transmission than anthropologists, who are, in turn, less subservient to the orthodoxy than sociologists, even though we should be the ones best able to see what is wrong with the conceptualizations, data collection, and statistical analyses on which the orthodoxy rests" (Murray 1994a, 752).

In an ideal world, more scholars would know enough of how different disciplines approached a topic to provide this sort of framing more often. In such a world, it would be difficult to maintain that disciplinary boundaries have greater importance than subject matter or that scholars in different disciplines never have anything to contribute to one another's research.

Given the breadth of Murray's research, an obvious question to ask would be how he chose which projects to pursue. Most researchers choose topics they encounter that have not yet been studied, and he was no different. For example, in a chapter describing the study of anthropology at the University of California, Berkeley, in the 1950s, he says, "I have chosen to focus on the 1950s in part because the early decades of Berkeley anthropology have been well described in print and Berkeley of the 1960s has been much written about. Berkeley anthropology of the 1950s has not" (Murray 2013a, 115). Another time, he pointed out that others "have ignored opportunities to compare the gathering of information about alien ('barbarian') cultures by earlier, non-'Western' writers, notably Arab, Chinese, and Indian explorers and traders," saying this is what led to his own research on Zhou Daguan's thirteenth-century writing (Murray 1994d, 15).

However, this accounts for only a small number of Murray's publications. Clearly, he often started research projects because he was unhappy with something someone else published. He explicitly said at one point, "Most of my research projects were stimulated by doubts about particular claims," and he often was attempting "to correct misapprehension" (Murray 2013a, xvii, xxiv). Whenever someone else made a claim he found questionable, he would take the time to investigate (Murray 1999a being but one particularly good example of this). Obviously, if he discovered that they were right, there was no need to publish on the topic, so nearly all his publications began when he discovered a problem in someone's argument, or disagreed with what they said, and took time to gather evidence to document the facts of the case. He summed this up by saying, "Being contrarian, I set out in search of data that would not fit the typology" (Fernández-Alemany [2001] 2019). He was speaking here of a specific project, though the generalization would account for many others as well. This approach occasionally had the result of making him seem at least a little cranky.[14] His suggestion that Alfred Kroeber was "one of American anthropology's most critical evaluators" (Murray 2013a, 59) applies equally well to Murray himself. His warnings against "simpleminded 'just-so' stories" (xvii, see also 273) are important reminders to all of us to question what we read, whether or not we end up carving out time to prepare and publish a response.[15]

In addition, Murray paid at least some attention to publications in disciplines beyond the central ones under discussion here. For example, in making a comment about research topics he thought should seem obvious but were not explored by anthropologists, he pointed to research within political science (Murray 2013a, 132), a discipline not otherwise frequently mentioned but which it obviously made sense to him to take the time to check in this case. Similarly, when commenting that the Linguistic Society of America had no written code of professional ethics, he contrasted that with the American Medical Association's having established one in 1847 (Murray 2001c, 1934). Most scholars ignore publications in disciplines outside their own, so it is a further comment on Murray's breadth of concerns that he did not. To state the point more generally, Murray (2013a, 274) would pursue a topic "that should be—but has not been—of interest."

Depth

I have described Murray's willingness to cross disciplinary boundaries as breadth; now I will move on to his willingness to cross methodological boundaries, referring to that as depth. Murray (2013a, 273) was interested in both "what should be studied and how." The "what" refers to the specific topic; many of these have been mentioned as examples in the first part of this paper. The "how" he explained as "shared practices—methods rather than methodologies" (273). He made the distinction between these two explicit: "what was done (my method) rather than . . . how research should in the author's opinion be done (a methodology)" (Murray 1994c, 491). He used a wide range of approaches in doing history, moving readily between what others often separate as quantitative and qualitative. Whatever the approach, he was especially good at reading carefully and looking at details, and at pulling together ideas that others might ignore.[16] One of his earliest book reviews argues that the authors provide an "exhaustively researched but succinctly presented case study" (Murray 1978, 35), and another critiqued work whose "scholarship is shoddy" (Murray 1981b, 744), demonstrating that he was clear from his first publications about what he valued. He expected others to adhere to this high standard and could be harsh when they did not.[17] At its best, his work has been called "encyclopedic"; in fact, the entire quote says "'Encyclopedic' is too dull a term for this engrossing work" (Dickemann 2001, 269).

It may be useful to explicitly sort through the different methods Murray used across publications. To gather information for his dissertation, he began with a questionnaire, sent to specific authors in areas he was interested in examining (Murray 1998a, 261). Although he was not one to choose either quantitative or qualitative methods for a particular research topic, in expanding his dissertation research he also conducted interviews with central figures. He specifically acknowledged the willingness of these interviewees to answer his questions about the past: "Many scholars patiently and generously answered questions that at times must have seemed tedious and/or perverse" (1983b, xi).

He spent an enormous amount of time conducting interviews of everyone relevant to his dissertation and later historical projects and, once, in describing interviews with George Foster, referred to these as "elicitation of memories from elders" (Murray 2013a, 80). That stands as a particularly apt description of Murray's own interviews of senior scholars. Reciprocally, he was always willing to fact check even statements by respected elders, since "in my experience interviewing our elders, chronology is not remembered well, and what seems to them to fit together often has been put together in recollection. Actual historical connections are rarely so neat" (Murray 2013a, 276). This is part of why he combined qualitative methods such as interviewing with quantitative methods such as counting. To him, this was a necessary way to put all the pieces together in the search for a coherent whole.

In addition, it is worth mentioning that on several occasions he published interviews in order to make them accessible to a wider audience. The first was an interview not by him, but by Earle Edward Eubank of Marcel Mauss (Murray and Mauss 1989), which he found in the Eubank Papers at the University of Chicago Library. What is most relevant to a discussion of historical research is his comment about the interview: "How much is paraphrase and how much transcription cannot be determined, since the original notes are not extant. As with archived fieldnotes, we cannot ask the follow-up questions that Eubank failed to ask, and must interpret the material that has been preserved" (163). He contributed what he could by making the interview public. The second example was one he conducted of Mary Haas as part of his dissertation research in 1978 (Murray 1997b). This was published as an epilogue for "Mary R. Haas: A Memorial Issue." Murray lets us know what he appreciated about the interaction: "I am struck by her ability and her willingness to answer what I was asking—in a number of instances, before I articulated a clear question" (695). He tells us what else he now wishes he had asked: "If I could return to that afternoon... I would ask much more about the specifics of how she did the analysis she did, especially during the 1930s" (696). The third example was a pair of interviews of John Gumperz, from 1977 and then in 1992. He interviewed Gumperz first at the 1977 Georgetown University Round Table, then obtained a National Institute of Mental Health postdoctoral fellowship to work with him at Berkeley in 1980–82. While at Berkeley, he says he "had been endeavoring to 'go native' and was more participant than observer while there'" (Murray 2013b, 2) but did include analysis of that context in two publications (Murray 1998a, 2010). He explicitly presents these interviews as part of the "raw data" from his dissertation, which should now be made available to others (Murray 2013b, 3). Given the focus on theory groups, it makes sense that mostly Murray asked Gumperz questions about his research topics as well as his network of teachers and colleagues and how this changed over time.

Let us now return to the listing of methods. His interviews did not stand alone but required considerable preparation. "In addition to—and in preparation for—interviewing, I looked at books, journals, and archived correspondence" (Murray 1998a, 264).[18] Archival research was particularly important to him given that it was something "relatively unfunded researchers can do by themselves" (Murray 2003, 137), which explains part of the attraction; I suspect the rest was joy at learning things other did not know or had long forgotten. He was especially good about taking time to track down obscure publications and reviews, as well as unpublished manuscripts (often located in the same archives as unpublished correspondence). He excelled in locating significant but long-forgotten quotes from these archival materials.[19] And he occasionally made it clear that he highly valued synthesis of such content, as when praising Darnell's work because "it synthesizes an enormous amount of manuscript material" (Murray 1991c, 321).[20]

In fact, he did not just read what people had written before meeting them; he began his analysis then. "Thorough examination of research literature shows who published where, acknowledging and citing whom, which one should know before seeking information directly from informants.... Patterns of acknowledgment and citation provide unobtrusive measures of connection, although only acknowledgments evidence social connection" (Murray 1998a, 264).[21] Just as there was work to be done in preparation for interviews, there was yet more work to be done after the interviews occurred: he typically supplemented these with letters, either asking follow-up questions, or sent to those he was unable to interview face-to-face (261). Also, he "made considerable use of reviews and obituaries" (Murray 1994c, 498).[22]

Once he had a draft, he circulated that for comments on his conclusions. These he did not always accept, since "I do not think that 'the natives' are invariably right, even about what they have done or why," but at least he always recorded them, in case on occasion "readers will agree with 'the natives' rather than with the alien observer" (Murray 1998a, 262). Correspondence from archives he found especially useful, for "more than in their publications, the 'natives' of those researching the history of social science speak for themselves in their correspondence" (Murray 1994c, 499). Whether through their archived letters or letters to him directly, he often let others speak for themselves, using extensive quotes, because he was "committed to multivocality in 'inscribing' history as much as in writing ethnography" (499).

Given his attention to detail, it infuriated him when others ignored data that did not support their argument, as when he said he had found "another example of Freeman's reckless disregard of data contrary to his theses" (Murray 2013a, 44).[23] It was an equal problem when predecessors were not acknowledged, something he viewed as "the antithesis of scholarship" (47). He was similarly unhappy with lack of documentation altogether, as when writing of a book by Bourdieu: "he totally avoids any systematic historical analysis or any longitudinal data," and "nor does he provide any evidence for the claim" (Murray 2002a, 389, 390).

Presumably because he attended so carefully to acknowledgments by others, Murray was meticulous in writing his own. Those for *American Anthropology and Company* take up five pages (Murray 2013a, 289–93) and are organized by chapter, typically including such details as what archival collections were consulted, which interviews were relevant, whose comments were useful (even distinguishing between more casual conversations and formal written responses to drafts), and presentation or publication of any previous versions. Because it provides just the sort of setting in context of his own work that he typically provided for that of others, it seems worth quoting in detail just one of these sets of notes for one chapter:

> An earlier version of "The Postmaturity of Sociolinguistics" appeared in *History of Sociology* 6(2) (1986): 75–108, a variant of my Sapir centenary conference paper presented in Ottawa in 1984, published as Murray (1986a). The original impetus for this investigation was discussion with William Samarin about the tardy and marginal institutionalization of the study of language within sociology. In addition to the published literature, this research drew on the Kroeber and Lowie collections preserved in the Bancroft Library of the University of California at Berkeley, on the Sapir papers at the National Museum of Man in Ottawa, and on the Ogburn, Park, Redfield, Wirth, and anthropology department archives in the Regenstein Library of the University of Chicago. It also greatly benefited from patient answers to the author's numerous queries by Herbert Blumer, Martin Bulmer, Bingham Dai, Regna Darnell, Fred Eggan, Murray Emeneau, Robert Faris, William Fenton, Paul Friedrich, Mary Haas, Philip Hauser, Everett Hughes, Theodora Kroeber, Weston LaBarre, Barbara Laslett, David Mandelbaum, Kenneth Pike, Stanley S. Newman, Edward Shils, Anthony F. C. Wallace, and Ellen Black Winston. The text was clarified and otherwise improved by comments from Regna Darnell, Fred Eggan, Wendy Leeds-Hurwitz, Yakov Malkiel, James Nyce, and Michael Silverstein and by close editorial scrutiny from the father of the sociology of science, Robert K. Merton. (Murray 2013a, 292)

This is one of the more detailed lists, but most of his publications provide comparable explanations, presumably to anticipate the needs of later disciplinary historians by providing what he would have wanted to know about someone else's work (and which others rarely provided to his satisfaction). In addition, such a listing demonstrates that he was a stickler for details, tracking down all potentially relevant documentation to include in an analysis. In some other examples, he even documented the readings that influenced him most (as in Murray 1991b, 1n1).

One of the reasons to spend time looking at acknowledgments is to document someone's "invisible college" (a term popularized by Crane

1972). This is a metaphor based on a standard college or university context, where a disciplinary historian might expect departmental colleagues to collaborate on research, or at least talk about it, and thus influence one another in visible ways. But, in addition, each scholar has what Crane also calls "social circles" (138), that is, groups of people who are not obviously connected to them, at least not in ways so visible to outsiders, but who also influence their ideas. An invisible college might be made up of those who once were students together. After leaving to take positions in various cities or countries, it may not be obvious to readers that there is a connection between them. To find his invisible college, one might look not just at Murray's acknowledgments but at the publications of others for acknowledgments of his influence. This can be seen clearly in an article by Jay Bernstein (2002, 559), whose acknowledgments include this line: "Finally, I thank Stephen O. Murray, a valued member of my invisible college, for suggesting that I submit this article to the *American Anthropologist*." Murray and Bernstein both were housed in the anthropology department at the University of California, Berkeley, in overlapping years in the 1980s (Bernstein earned an MA and PhD there). Theresa Montini (2000, S129) commented that "Stephen O. Murray read and commented on successive drafts of this article more times than either of us could keep track of. His persistent and patient nursing of this project is duly noted and much appreciated." Again, she was part of Murray's invisible college, with an MSW from Berkeley and a PhD from the University of California–San Francisco. To Murray (2019, 261), "citations are a kind of behavior, a behavior of scholars and scientists," and as such, they should be studied the way anthropologists study other types of human behavior.

One of the methods Murray used in a number of studies is ethnography, the classic method for anthropology, requiring participant observation in naturally occurring occasions as the central technique. At one point, he wrote, "The author has been engaged in participant observation of North American anthropology since 1974. Results of that include *Theory Groups and the Study of Language in North America: A Social History* (Amsterdam, 1994[a]) and *Taiwanese culture, Taiwanese society* (Lanham MD, 1994, with Keelung Hong)" (Murray 1997a, 2). Among his publications using at least some elements of ethnography are "Accomplishing Topic Change" with Covelli, "Deference, Domination and Solidarity in an Interactional Order," "The Art of Gay Insulting," "Lexical and Institutional Elaboration," "Ritual and Personal Insults," "Toward a Model of Members' Methods of Recognizing Interruptions," "Power and Solidarity in 'Interruption,'" and "Ethnic Differences in Interpretive Conventions." However, he did not think all of this work was ethnographic; in fact,

> It could be said that I also began fieldwork on homosexuality both north (Canada) and south (Mexico and Guatemala) of the United States during those years, although I didn't see my explorations as ethnography (as I explained in my chapter in *Out in the Field*). I did some formal lexical elicitation ("white-room ethnography") in Guatemala City and in San Francisco, wrote about a speech genre ("ritual insults") with mostly Canadian data and examined the supposedly "technical" social science criteria of "community," finding that the Toronto gay community of the late-1970s fit them better than Toronto ethnic communities. (Fernández-Alemany [2001] 2019)

Rather, he saw these as examples of anthropological linguistics, as made clear in his answer to whether he saw the different strands of his work as separate or interrelated: "I'd say interrelated, not least in that the historical subject area in which I worked, anthropological linguistics, is also the area of some substantive (if uncollected) empirical work" (Murray et al. 2021, 252). Murray was sufficiently interested in this area that he even at one time put together a potential collection of relevant publications, to be titled *"Interruptions" and Other Messy Things in Language Use* (email to *Pragmatics and Beyond*, July 30, 1996). It was to include his unpublished master's thesis, "Deference, Domination and Solidarity in an Interactional Order"; "Toward a Model of Members' Methods of Recognizing Interruptions"; "Power and Solidarity in 'Interruption'"; "Ethnic Differences in Interpretive Conventions"; Review of *You Just Don't Understand!*; "Sex and the Economy of Speaking Turns"; and "Accomplishing Topic Change" with Covelli, among other selections.

On a few occasions, his use of quantitative techniques moved far beyond merely counting citations, as when he wrote about dependent variables (see Murray 1998a, 265) or stepwise regression (Murray 2013a, 143). On many other occasions, he simply counted things, whether members of the Linguistic Society of America as an obvious way to document the growth of linguists in the 1950s (Murray 1994c, 241), or sales of Leonard Bloomfield's (1933) *Language* as a way to document that the book actually sold more copies in the 1960s than the 1930s (Murray 2001c, 1933), despite popular assumptions to the contrary.

One of the methods Murray refused to use, and argued against, was something quite common in past anthropology, typically named "the ethnographic present." Specifically, he considered this to be the "change-obscuring ethnographic present" (Murray 2013a, 34) and pointed out that "it seems hard for anthropologists to give up the unfortunate practice of writing in an 'ethnographic present'" (Murray 2000, 748). Beyond his own brief early attempts, he mostly was not thrilled by "white room ethnography" (that is, taking the native informant out of context for the convenience of the researcher, rather than observing a functioning culture; see Murray 2013a, 279 and 312; Murray 1992a, 680).[24] On the one occasion when he considered the very earliest precursors of linguistics, he was equally unimpressed by the predecessor tradition of "armchair theorists" (Murray 2001a, 1914).

Murray felt it essential to critique sloppy or incomplete work, as when one of his reviews said the topic "requires more rigorous collection of other kinds of data than are available in this book" (Murray 1992a, 681), or even that "the last section includes data from a pathetically incompetent questionnaire" (Murray 1999c, 306). And he was particularly adamant that "historians should look at what scientists (including linguists) do, not what they say they do" (Murray 1992b, 64). However, he occasionally voiced strong support for methods rarely used, as when pointing out that "Winkin (1988), Daubenmier (2008), and Migliore et al. (2009) provide exemplars of what I would like to see explored more often in field sites: eliciting memories from the 'natives' and their views on how their culture was represented by the alien observer" (Murray 2013a, 280). It is worth noting that in a book about Taiwan, where Keelung Hong grew up, the first chapter is titled "Experiences of Being a 'Native' Observing Anthropologists" (Hong and Murray 2005). Related to this, Murray (2013a, 302n25) argued that "in my view, the stories anthropologists tell about themselves in various locales threaten to drown out the stories that other people tell them." He deemed such behavior unforgivable.

Qualitative and quantitative methods are often separated, but, both for Murray and many others, it is frequently their combination that makes the most sense. This is presumably why Murray moved between methods, not just in his historical research, but also when he practiced what he otherwise described. For example, this could mean starting with open-ended interviews (qualitative) leading to better design of a questionnaire (quantitative; Murray and Poolman 1984). In either case, the key was to systematically gather data, rather than simply providing opinions and impressions.[25]

Writing

In addition to examining the breadth and depth of Murray's research, it is worth spending a little time looking at his writing, for, although his syntax could often be complex, he was a strong writer who could use metaphors gracefully.[26] A few examples will make this clear. A chapter on anthropology at Berkeley concludes: "The department now, like the American Anthropological Association more than a hundred years old, continues and a later owl than I can evaluate whether the luster has been or will be recovered" (Murray 2013a, 121). In a review of Konrad Koerner, he wrote, "In my view he is hunting for unicorns, finding only sheep and goats who claim to be the mythic creature, or, at least, to be related to it" (Murray 1992b, 64). And in describing the "halo effect" (that when a trusted source says something, the researcher may not bother to locate confirming evidence), he suggests there is a parallel "reverse halo (horns?) effect" leading researchers to distrust information from a usually unreliable source (Murray 1998a, 264).[27] Often he provides an exceedingly memorable analysis, as when he described Bloomfield as "identifying himself with Galileo rather than with an established church" (Murray 1994c, 163). Other times he simply relies on a lucid analysis.[28]

Murray's opinions are often uncommonly bluntly stated, as when he concludes that "claims of virtue or of novelty provoke close scrutiny, so let those who make them beware" (Murray 1991e, 399), or "'cannot' is a word that wise sociologists should eschew. As prophecy, this diatribe was singularly inept" (Murray 2004a, 131). When he thought a source was seriously flawed, he did not hesitate to explain all the problems, as in this review: "Khaled el-Rouayheb's book reads like the revised PhD thesis (Cambridge University) that it is, with the de rigueur opening in which everything that has previously been written on the subject is dismissed, a straw-man is put forward to be torn apart, and a great deal of pedantic detail follows in the main body.... He makes no attempt to look for any development or other kinds of change within the two centuries of his time frame.... What is missing from the book is evidence about what people did" (Murray 2006, 11–12).[29] He makes quite explicit that what he valued (in addition to good and complete research respecting documented facts as well as historical and geographic differences) are ideas: "Although I have questioned both the novelty and soundness of some of them, there are ideas in Hoad's book" (Murray 2009, 171).

Murray was always willing to recognize the distinction between quality of work and the degree to which he counted someone as a friend or trusted scholar, so he often critiqued poor work even by friends and praised good work even by those whose ideas he otherwise strongly critiqued—often in the same publication. For example, of the same book, he said at one point that what was written "is so inadequate that it would have been better to have written nothing on the topic" but concluded overall that it is "exceptionally fair-minded for a historical memoir" (Murray 1991d, 653, 654). He saw no contradiction here, for his focus was on evaluating the work and neither the person nor his personal connection to the author. He made this explicit in 2019: "When I think something is wrong, I say so. It doesn't matter who said what I think is wrong, even if that person is myself.... I think that both my friends and my enemies know I am going to say what I think and let the chips fall where they may. My friends already know I am going to say that a claim is unwarranted or wrong if I think it is. I guess some enemies have been puzzled when I accept that they got something right" (Fernández-Alemany [2001] 2019). Clearly, for Murray, it made perfect sense that the same person would be capable of good work at one point and sloppy work at another. Appropriately, he was quite willing to change his opinion given documentation that contradicted his earlier conclusions, even if he had already published them. He could be gracious when shown to be wrong—all you had to do was provide conclusive evidence.[30]

Conclusion

Ultimately, Murray (2013a, 281) argued for the history of anthropology as a form of anthropology: "I think that we can no more recover the past than we can enter into the full native sense of cultures other than those in which we were raised. Again, searching across time is similar to reaching across space or across social/cultural distances within a place to so-called subcultures. Nonetheless, I think that these ultimately impossible goals are ones we should reach for and try to approximate."

He supported this argument of doing history of anthropology as akin to doing anthropology by saying, "The danger for history as for anthropology is, I think, inordinate haste in applying etic labels—this is a 'shaman,' that is a 'structuralist'" (Murray 2013a, 286). Both history and anthropology were, for him, about "making sense of the ways of others," and he felt strongly this was the "raison d'être of social science" (287).

One of Murray's strengths was in locating obscure or forgotten documentation in archives, combining that with interviews and his own correspondence with those still alive, and adding uncommon data analysis (such as citation and acknowledgment analysis) to weave together a coherent story, one that often was new to readers and which often contradicted common assumptions.[31]

For Murray (1996c, 358), "the essence of science is in openness to correction," and he made a substantial distinction between "truth-seeking" and "truth-proclaiming." Thus his efforts to catch errors, or fill in gaps in our knowledge of what had happened in the past, were all part of the effort to ensure he was doing good science. His willingness to use such a wide variety of methods, and to cross disciplinary boundaries, and to write in a way that would catch attention, were all part of his effort to do good research.

Notes

1. A previous version of this chapter was presented at the American Anthropological Association's convention, November 9–13, 2022, Seattle.
2. At one point he mentioned his "more than a third of a century of observing anthropologists, sociologists, and linguists" (Murray 2013a, 264).
3. I'm not ignoring Murray's longer works on disciplinary history but have already written extensively about them elsewhere (Leeds-Hurwitz 1987, 1996, 2002, 2021;

Murray et al. 2021). However, I will draw on dozens of his publications for brief comments.
4. He was also uncommon in never holding an academic position. Every so often he would mention the issue, as here: "In my view the 'outlaws' are those of us subsisting in exile from academia or consigned to multiple simultaneous part-time positions without any security or benefits, not to tenured faculty able to pose as chicly transgressive" (Murray 1998b, 566).
5. Earlier, he had written that "my path to sociolinguistics was so indirect as to defy plausibility: I discovered the American/Americanist tradition exploring *Tristes Tropiques*, and linguistics through the still less likely vehicle of the *political* writings of Rousseau, Merleau-Ponty and Chomsky" (Murray 1983b, ix–x, emphasis in original).
6. As he explained, "My participation with too minimal observation as a postdoctoral fellow in Berkeley's Language Behavior Research Laboratory (1980–82) provided me more intense, but narrow insider perspectives" (Murray 1998a, 263).
7. He wrote of "the natives whom I studied (i.e., linguists)" in the longer draft of a response published only in shortened form (Murray 1986a, 1).
8. However, he also admitted "when push comes to shove I am a sociologist more than a historian" (Murray 1994c, 492).
9. In describing his education, he described himself as "an undergrad with a second major in psychology (the first was in 'Justice, Morality, and Constitutional Democracy')" (email to Leeds-Hurwitz, December 18, 2018).
10. The original source is Taylor (1972).
11. The "sort-of book" was most likely the collection of essays on sociolinguistic topics described elsewhere.
12. "Human science" on analogy to the French phrase *sciences humaines*.
13. This publication is included in Murray (2013a), but the footnotes were inadvertently omitted, so I am citing the original publication.
14. Witness the introduction by the interviewer to a discussion of one of Murray's books: "Controversial and proudly free of political correctness, his sharp comments are often feared by authors of new publications. Yet for people who know him closely, Steve Murray is the most supportive and helpful reader of one's drafts one can find." Later in the same interview, Fernández-Alemany ([2001] 2019) asks: "Have you ever been criticized for being too confrontational and bold?" and Murray replies, "Not to my face, though, perhaps some people think this. My own self-conception is that I am an inordinately polite and very nonconfrontational rural Midwesterner."
15. See also his comment that "we can only hope that someone pays attention to the research priority suggested but ignored in practice by Arthur Wolf" (Murray

2013a, 129). Or his devastating critique that "social scientists have too often supported—in their words, in their presence, and in their deeds—the paternalistic claims of rulers suppressing the very cultures the anthropologists want to study" (153). Or his clear irritation with authors who "make spectacularly unfounded claims to originality for themselves and demonstrate considerable unfamiliarity with [relevant] empirical studies" (Murray 2009, 168).

16. This is not my opinion alone; his work has often been held up as a model. For example, Koerner (2002, 256) at one point says of two other scholars covering some of the same topics that their book "does not compare at all in thoroughness with Murray's work." Or, as Epstein (1997, 1484) says: "I think it safe to say that absolutely no one has mastered the social-scientific literature on sexuality and homosexuality any better than Murray has; indeed, this book is worth owning simply for the extensive bibliography and the abundance of detailed, often fascinating, footnotes."

17. In response to an article by Laura Martin, he points out that "As is not the case for most research reported in the journal, the views of the natives represented by Martin can be readily checked in their original context, unmediated by the anthropologist reporter" (Murray 1987b, 443). That commentary concludes: "If as readily available a record as well-known publications by Boas, Whorf, and Brown can be so distorted in the *American Anthropologist*, one must wonder about the validity of reports resting entirely on ethnographers' accounts of what more or less exotic peoples said and mean!" (444). It is ironic that Martin was in fact attempting to argue for more careful statements herself, specifically against the inappropriate reduction of the complexity of reality: "As scholarship in linguistic anthropology, this treatment is wholly inadequate" (Murray 1986, 419).

18. A detailed list of what archives he consulted is provided in Murray (1994c, 498–99). Since that volume of the three major iterations of his dissertation research (1983b, 1994c, 1998a) was based on the largest collection of materials, this list can stand for all three books.

19. As an example, he points out that Robert Redfield complained, "I miss the guidance of general ideas," only to get the reply from John Embree that "as a benighted empiricist, I am against having a theme song drown out the words" (Embree to Redfield, June 4, 1940, as cited in Murray 2013a, 73).

20. He was equally willing to state clearly what he did not like in the books he reviewed, as here: "What I find disturbing are his [the author's] lack of discussion about choosing which texts to analyze, his assumption that absence of evidence is evidence of absence, his confusion of coining a word with the origin of a phenomenon or a concept, and the hyper-idealist premises underlying his whole endeavor" (Murray 1995, 264).

21. For example, he did an analysis of citations by others of Mead's books, to learn whether Freeman's claims were correct; he found they were not (Murray 2013a, 46).
22. Given how useful he found these, it should not be surprising that he published an uncommon number of biographies, often for well-known anthropologists, such as Ruth Benedict (Murray 2001b) or Robert Redfield (Murray 2002b). He knew others could benefit from what he had taken time to learn and was willing to take a little more time to share the results.
23. See also detailed refutation of a comment by Robert Murphy, since "looking at the immediately postwar volumes of the official journal of the American Anthropological Association does not substantiate this, as table 1 shows" (Murray 2013a, 96–97), with even more evidence provided by documentation of regional expertise and dissertation field sites on 97–98.
24. In other comments about methods, he said: "My frustrations with unrepresentative sampling, postmodernist jargon, reliance on anecdotage, and a lack of interest in trying to assess effects of explanatory variables (such as class and country of birth) are triggered by most contemporary ethnographies and make me wonder if ethnography can sort out (let alone explain!) the diversities within a population dispersed across a metropolis and extensively linked to a distant homeland" (Murray 2004b, 953).
25. I am paraphrasing here from a review he wrote, where he critiqued an author by saying, "He does not seem to have systematically gathered data... but provides his impressions and value judgments" (Murray 1999b, 575).
26. Johnson refers to Murray's (2001, 490–91) "heavy-handed academic voice," which can be "dense and at times difficult to read." However, the same reviewer highlighted Murray's grasp of "theory, cultural and historical range, use of examples and presentation of multiple perspectives."
27. See also the extended set of metaphors relating to Chomsky and transformational generative grammar as "a delta with many channels (and even more swamps)" (Murray 1994c, 493).
28. For example, a chapter written with Keelung Hong on how American anthropologists conducting research in Taiwan have made conclusions about China, puts one of the conclusions particularly cogently: "The massiveness of these archives has been taken as prima facie proof of the validity of the records, as if, because there is so much, it must be accurate" (Murray 2013a, 126).
29. Occasionally, such bluntness in his reviews led to reciprocal bluntness by others, so that in a review of one of his books (Murray 1984), the reviewer complains of "an overabundance of caustic barbs directed at writers with opposing views" (Corzine 1986, 119).

30. An example is this comment: "By securing employment records from the Department of State Leeds-Hurwitz (1990n20) showed that the linguists were not all purged when the first Eisenhower administration began—a piece of folklore Murray (1989, 158 uncritically perpetuated)" (Murray 1991b, 23n34; end parenthesis in the wrong place in the original).
31. This was occasionally recognized in reviews, as when one of his books is described thus: "Ranging from 18th-century publications to material from the late 1990s, the approximately 25-page bibliography and accompanying preface, introduction, and four section overviews are as comprehensive a set of summaries of literature as any I have seen on a subject about which so little has been previously compiled. The editors have done a stellar job in pulling together a wide range of resources and information" (Nardi 2000, 847).

References

Bernstein, Jay H. 2002. "First Recipients of Anthropological Doctorates in the United States, 1891–1930." *American Anthropologist* 104 (2): 551–64.

Bloomfield, Leonard. 1933. *Language*. New York: Holt, Rinehart & Winston.

Corzine, Jay. 1986. Review of *Social Theory, Homosexual Realities* by Stephen O. Murray. *Contemporary Sociology* 15 (1): 118–19.

Covelli, Lucille H., and Stephen O. Murray. 1980. "Accomplishing Topic Change." *Anthropological Linguistics* 22 (9): 382–90.

Crane, Diana. 1972. *Invisible Colleges: Diffusion of Knowledge in Scientific Communities*. Chicago: University of Chicago Press.

Dickemann, Jeffrey M. 2001. "Global Homo: Review of *Homosexualities* by Stephen O. Murray." *Journal of Sex Research* 38 (3): 266–69.

Epstein, Steven. 1997. "Review of *American Gay* by Stephen O. Murray." *American Journal of Sociology* 102 (5): 1483–85.

Fernández-Alemany, Manuel. (2001) 2019. "On Homosexualities: An Interview of Stephen O. Murray." Tangent Group. https://www.tangentgroup.org/on-homosexualities/.

Hong, Keelung, and Stephen O. Murray. 2005. *Looking through Taiwan: American Anthropologists' Collusion with Ethnic Domination*. Lincoln: University of Nebraska Press.

Johnson, Corey W. 2001. Review of *Homosexualities* by Stephen O. Murray. *Gender and Society* 15 (3): 490–91.

Koerner, E. F. K. 2002. *Toward a History of American Linguistics*. London: Routledge.

Leeds-Hurwitz, Wendy. 1987. Review of Stephen O. Murray, *Group Formation in Social Science*. *Language* 63 (3): 668–71.

———. 1996. Review of Stephen O. Murray, *Theory Groups in the Study of Language in North America*. *Communication Theory* 6 (1): 104–7.

———. 2002. Review of Stephen O. Murray, *American Sociolinguistics: Theories and Theory Groups*. *Journal of the History of the Behavioral Sciences* 38 (2): 195–96.

———. 2012. "These Fictions We Call Disciplines." *Electronic Journal of Communication/La Revue Electronique de Communication* 22 (3–4). https://www.cios.org/ejcpublic/022/3/022341.html.

———. 2021. "The Role of Theory Groups in the Lives of Ideas." *History of Media Studies* 1. https://doi.org/10.32376/d895a0ea.0b35e36e.

Martin, Laura. 1986. "'Eskimo Words for Snow': A Case Study in the Genesis and Decay of an Anthropological Example." *American Anthropologist* 88 (2): 418–23.

Montini, Theresa. 2000. "Compulsory Closets and the Social Context of Disclosure." *Sociological Perspectives* 43 (4), Supplement: A Tribute to Anselm Strauss: S121–S132.

Murray, Stephen O. 1975. "Deference, Domination and Solidarity in an Interactional Order." Unpublished master's thesis, University of Arizona.

———. 1978. Review of *Africville: The Life and Death of a Canadian Black Community* by Donald H. Clairmont and Dennis W. Magill. *Contemporary Sociology* 7 (1): 34–35.

———. 1979a. "The Art of Gay Insulting." *Anthropological Linguistics* 21 (5): 211–23.

———. 1979b. "Institutional Elaboration of a Quasi-Ethnic Community." *International Review of Modern Sociology* 9 (2): 165–77.

———. 1980a. "Gatekeepers and the 'Chomskian Revolution.'" *Journal of the History of the Behavioral Sciences* 16: 73–88.

———. 1980b. "Lexical and Institutional Elaboration: The 'Species Homosexual' in Guatemala." *Anthropological Linguistics* 22 (4): 177–85.

———. 1980c. "Resistance to Sociology at Berkeley." *Journal of the History of Sociology* 2 (2): 61–84.

———. 1981a. "The Canadian 'Winter' of Edward Sapir." *Historiographia Linguistica* 8 (1): 63–68.

———. 1981b. Review of *Language and Control* by Roger Fowler, Gunther Kress and Tony Trew; *Language as Ideology* by Gunther Kress and Robert Hodge. *American Journal of Sociology* 87 (3): 743–45.

———. 1982. "Role Distance 'South of the Slot.'" *Journal of the History of Sociology* 4 (2): 90–95.

———. 1983a. "The Creation of Linguistic Structure." *American Anthropologist* 85 (2): 356–62.

———. 1983b. *Group Formation in Social Science*. Edmonton, Canada: Linguistic Research.

———. 1983c. "Ritual and Personal Insults in Stigmatized Subcultures: Gay, Black, Jew." *Maledicta* 7: 189–211.

———. 1984. *Social Theory, Homosexual Realities*. New York: Gay Academic Union.

———. 1985. "Toward a Model of Members' Methods of Recognizing Interruptions." *Language in Society* 14 (1): 31–40.

———. 1986a. "Comment on Newmeyer." Unpublished manuscript. [Shortened version was published in 1986, in *Language* 62 (4): 966–67.]

———. 1986b. "Edward Sapir in the 'Chicago School of Sociology.'" In *New Perspectives on Language, Culture and Personality: Proceedings of the Sapir Centenary Conference*, edited by William Cowan, Michael K. Foster and E. F. K. Koerner, 241–92. Amsterdam: John Benjamins.

———. 1987a. "Power and Solidarity in 'Interruption.'" *Symbolic Interaction* 10 (1): 101–10.

———. 1987b. "Snowing Canonical Texts." *American Anthropologist* 89 (2): 443–44.

———. 1991a. "Ethnic Differences in Interpretive Conventions and the Reproduction of Inequality in Everyday Life." *Symbolic Interaction* 14 (2): 187–204.

———. 1991b. "The First Quarter Century of the Linguistic Society of America, 1924–1949." *Historiographia Linguistica* 18 (1): 1–48.

———. 1991c. Review of *Edward Sapir: Linguist, Anthropologist, Humanist* by Regna Darnell. *Language in Society* 20 (2), 317–22.

———. 1991d. Review of *A Life for Language: A Biographical Memoir of Leonard Bloomfield* by Robert A. Hall Jr. *Language* 67 (3): 653–54.

———. 1991e. Review of *More Man Than You'll Ever Be! Gay Folklore and Acculturation in Middle America* by Joseph P. Goodwin. *Journal of American Folklore* 104 (413): 397–99.

———. 1992a. Review of *Bodies, Pleasures, and Passions: Sexual Culture in Contemporary Brazil* by Richard G. Parker. *Journal of the History of Sexuality* 2 (4): 679–82.

———. 1992b. Review of *Practicing Linguistic Historiography*, E. F. Konrad Koerner, ed.; and *First Person Singular II*, E. F. Konrad Koerner, ed. *Journal of the History of the Behavioral Sciences* 28 (1): 63–68.

———. 1992c. Review of *You Just Don't Understand! Women and Men in Conversation* by Deborah Tannen. *Journal of Pragmatics* 18 (5): 507–14.

———. 1994a. Review of *The Time of AIDS: Social Analysis, Theory, and Method* by Gilbert Herdt and Shirley Lindenbaum; *AIDS: The Making of a Chronic Disease*, Elizabeth Fee and Daniel M. Fox, eds. *Contemporary Sociology* 23 (5): 751–53.

———. 1994b. "Sex and the Economy of Speaking Turns." *Journal of Pragmatics*, 21 no. 2: 215–24.

———. 1994c. *Theory Groups and the Study of Language in North America: A Social History*. Amsterdam: John Benjamins.

———. 1994d. "A Thirteenth Century Imperial Ethnography." *Anthropology Today* 10 (5): 15–18.

———. 1995. "Discourse Creationism: Review of *The Invention of Heterosexuality* by Jonathan Ned Katz." *Journal of Sex Research* 32 (3): 263–65.

———. 1996a. *American Gay*. Chicago: University of Chicago Press.

———. 1996b. *Angkor Life*. Bangkok: Bua Luang.

———. 1996c. "Historical Truths and Partisan Misrepresentations." *Anthropological Linguistics* 38 (2): 355–60.

———. 1996d. *Toward a Sociology of Linguistic Knowledge: A Memoir*. Unpublished manuscript.

———. 1997a. "Explaining Away Same-Sex Sexualities When They Obtrude on Anthropologists' Notice at All." *Anthropology Today* 13 (3): 2–5.

———. 1997b. "A 1978 Interview with Mary Haas." *Anthropological Linguistics* 39 (4): 695–722.

———. 1998a. *American Sociolinguistics: Theorists and Theory Groups*. Amsterdam: John Benjamins.

———. 1998b. Review of *Academic Outlaws: Queer Theory and Cultural Studies in the Academy* by William G. Tierney. *American Anthropologist* 100 (2): 565–66.

———. 1999a. "How *The Logical Structure of Linguistic Theory* Did Not Appear during the 1950s or 60s." In *The Emergence of the Modern Language Sciences: Studies on the Transition from Historical-Comparative to Structural Linguistics in Honour of E. F. Konrad Koerner*, vol. 1, edited by Sheila Embleton, John E. Joseph, and Hans-Josef Niederhe, 261–64. Amsterdam: John Benjamins.

———. 1999b. Review of *Machos, Maricones, and Gays: Cuba and Homosexuality* by Ian Lumsden. *Archives of Sexual Behavior* 28 (6): 575–77.

———. 1999c. Review of *Queerly Phrased: Language, Gender, and Sexuality* by Anna Livia and Kira Hall. *Language in Society* 28 (2): 304–8.

———. 2000. Review of *Beyond Carnival: Male Homosexuality in Twentieth-Century Brazil* by James N. Green; *Beneath the Equator: Cultures of Desire, Male Homosexuality, and Emerging Gay Communities in Brazil* by Richard Parker. *Journal of the Royal Anthropological Institute* 6 (4): 747–48.

———. 2001a. "Attempts at the Professionalization of American Linguistics: The Role of the Linguistic Society of America." In *History of the Language Sciences*, vol. 2, edited by Sylvain Auroux, E. F. K. Koerner, Hans-Josef Niederehe, and Kees Versteegh, 1932–1935. Berlin: Walter de Gruyter.

———. 2001b. "Benedict, Ruth F." In *Who's Who in Gay and Lesbian History: From Antiquity to World War II*, edited by Robert Aldrich and Garry Wotherspoon, 48. London: Routledge.

———. 2001c. "The Ethnolinguistic Tradition in 19th-Century America: From the Earliest Beginnings to Boas." In *History of the Language Sciences*, vol. 2, edited by Sylvain Auroux, E. F. K. Koerner, Hans-Josef Niederehe, and Kees Versteegh, 1909–23. Berlin Germany: Walter de Gruyter.

———. 2002a. Review of *Masculine Domination* by Pierre Bourdieu. *Journal of the Royal Anthropological Society* 8 (2): 389–90.

———. 2002b. "Robert Redfield." In *Celebrating a Century of the American Anthropological Association*, edited by Regna Darnell and Fred W. Gleach, 105–8. Lincoln: University of Nebraska Press.

———. 2003. "Sociology." In *Encyclopedia of Lesbian, Gay, Bisexual and Transgender History in America*, vol. 3, edited by Marc Stein, 134–38. New York: Charles Scribner's Sons.

———. 2004a. "Humphreys vs. Sagarin in the Sociological Study of Gay Movements." *International Journal of Sociology and Social Policy* 24 (3/4/5): 128–45.

———. 2004b. Review of *Global Divas: Filipino Gay Men in the Diaspora* by Martin F. Manalansan. *Journal of the Royal Anthropological Institute* 10 (4): 952–53.

———. 2006. Review of *Before Homosexuality in the Arab-Islamic World, 1500–1800* by Khaled el-Rouayheb. *Committee on Lesbian and Gay History Newsletter* 20 (2): 11–12.

———. 2009. Review essay: Southern African Homosexualities and Denials. *African Intimacies: Race, Homosexuality, and Globalization* by Neville Hoad; *Imperialism within the Margins: Queer Representations and the Politics of Culture in Southern Africa* by William J. Sperlin; and *Unspoken Facts: A History of African Homosexualities* by Gays and Lesbians of Zimbabwe. *Canadian Journal of African Studies / Revue canadienne des études africaines* 43 (1): 167–72.

———. 2010. "Interactional Sociolinguistics at Berkeley." In *The Social History of Language and Social Interaction Research: People, Places, Ideas*, edited by Wendy Leeds-Hurwitz, 97–126. Cresskill NJ: Hampton Press.

———. 2013a. *American Anthropology and Company: Historical Explorations*. Lincoln: University of Nebraska Press.

———. 2013b. *John Gumperz in Context: 1977 and 1992 Interviews*. San Francisco: El Instituto Obregón.

———. 2019. *Stephen O. Murray and the History of Human Sciences*. Unpublished manuscript.

———. 2021. "The Genesis of *Boy-Wives and Female Husbands*." In *Boy-Wives and Female Husbands: Studies in African Homosexualities*, 2nd ed., edited by Stephen O. Murray and Will Roscoe, xix–xxiv. Albany: State University of New York Press.

Murray, Stephen O., and Lucille H. Covelli. 1988. "Women and Men Speaking at the Same Time." *Journal of Pragmatics* 12 (1): 103–11.

Murray, Stephen O., and Keelung Hong. 1994. *Taiwanese Culture, Taiwanese Society: A Critical Review of Social Science Research Done on Taiwan.* Lanham MD: University Press of America.

Murray, Stephen O., Wendy Leeds-Hurwitz, Regna Darnell, Nathan Dawthorne, and Robert Oppenheim. 2021. "An Interview with Stephen O. Murray on Stephen O. Murray as Historian of Anthropology (and More)." In *Centering the Margins of Anthropology's History,* edited by Regna Darnell and Frederick W. Gleach, 243–68. Lincoln: University of Nebraska Press.

Murray, Stephen O., and Marcel Mauss. 1989. "A 1934 Interview with Marcel Mauss." *American Ethnologist* 16 (1): 163–68.

Murray, Stephen O., and Robert C. Poolman, Jr. 1982. "Strong Ties and Scientific Information." *Social Networks* 4 (3): 225–32.

———. 1984. "Socially Structuring Prototype Semantics." *Forum Linguisticum* 8 (1): 95–102.

Murray, Stephen O., Joseph H. Rankin, and Dennis W. Magill. 1981. "Strong Ties and Job Information." *Sociology of Work and Occupations* 8 (1): 119–36.

Murray, Stephen O., and Will Roscoe. 1997. *Islamic Homosexualities: Culture, History, and Literature.* New York: New York University Press.

———. 1998. *Boy-Wives and Female Husbands: Studies in African Homosexualities.* New York: St. Martin's.

Nardi, Peter M. 2000. "Review of *Boy-Wives and Female Husbands* by Stephen O. Murray and Will Roscoe." *American Journal of Sociology* 106 (3): 846–48.

Payne, Kenneth W., and Stephen O. Murray. 1983. "Historical Inferences from Ethnohistorical Data: Boasian Views." *Journal of the History of the Behavioral Sciences* 19 (4): 335–40.

Stocking, George W., Jr. 1965. "On the Limits of 'Presentism' and 'Historicism' in the Historiography of the Behavioral Sciences." *Journal of the History of the Behavioral Sciences* 1 (3): 211–18.

3 Stephen O. Murray as Collaborator

Regna Darnell

I collaborated with Steve in various editorial capacities at the University of Nebraska Press from when I invited him to join various editorial boards in the early 1980s until his death over a quarter of a century later. He became my coeditor in the Critical Studies in the History of Anthropology series in its planning stages and was seminal to choosing the series title, with "critical" as its key term. I was in contact with Steve in multiple capacities from the time of his dissertation research so perhaps knew him longer than anyone else in his professional life who is still living.

I first met Steve in person at the joint meetings of the American Anthropological Association and the Canadian Anthropology Society in Toronto in 1972. This initiated conversations about a range of interdisciplinary interests, such as linguistics, language, and culture, interests I shared and that reflected my training. Thereafter, I responded to him as a colleague sharing common interests. Conferences were important to him; in 1998 he was "bummed out" by transportation delays that made it impossible for me to get to a conference he had attended mainly so we could meet (email, December 7, 1998). We entered into periodic correspondence that was more important than occasional meetings at conferences because we did not attend the same conferences. This was the beginning of an uncommon relationship of collaboration that persisted until his death.

As part of his dissertation research around 1977–78 Steve emailed me among many others with a questionnaire on the history of anthropology. I responded but realized that no one in Canada would be likely to respond unless they knew who he was. So I emailed Canadian colleagues with interests in history of anthropology expressing my support for him and his project and urging them to respond; many did so.

Once his dissertation was complete, I served as its external examiner in 1979. Since all of the regular members who knew his work were on leave, I found myself in the bizarre position of being an anthropologist explaining a sociology dissertation to the sociology committee members. Steve was virtually catatonic after a redeye flight from the West Coast, leaving me as his spokesperson. His relief at passing the defense was palpable, and we adjourned to a nearby restaurant for a celebratory toast. Without this context, it would be startling to learn that I had reviewed a sociology dissertation for a student when I was not on his committee.

Steve and I coedited thirty-two books for the Critical Studies in the History of Anthropology series; for the last one we added Robert M. Oppenheim as the third editor with the intent of maintaining Steve as a courtesy during his lifetime (see series list in the back matter). Steve died while I was still arranging this with the press, so the effort proved to be moot. I chose Steve as coeditor for his expertise in sociology and his use of quantitative approaches, both areas where I was weak. I continued to list myself as senior editor of the three series in history of anthropology I edit for the University of Nebraska Press: Critical Studies in the History of Anthropology; Histories of Anthropology Annual, which I coedit with Frederic W. Gleach; and the Franz Boas Papers, which I edit alone. I felt that my own interdisciplinary identity would unify the three series and encourage readers with a range of backgrounds to access University of Nebraska Press publications, thus contributing to the sustainability of the series and the press. At an interactional level, however, I treat my coeditors as equal partners in making decisions. Steve chose Oppenheim as his successor to cover a range of topics important to him (South Asia, Latin America); I accepted his right to choose his successor, though I then knew Rob as editor of one volume in the series (Oppenheim 2016), and we worked closely together only after he joined the editorial team. On the contrast of our editorial personae, Steve wrote: "I live by the sword, more than you do," and added the observation that he liked to work in collaboration (email, April 29, 1997). Steve continued to be listed as the second editor during his lifetime (Kubica 2020).

Although Steve and I did not always agree, the working agreement in our collaboration was to recommend publication if one or the other of us felt strongly. I provide some examples of this collaboration below. Steve was not always a contrarian, only when his ire was roused by shoddy scholarship or willful blindness to the evidence of facts. This is characteristic of the way both of us operated and drew on each others' networks in our collaboration. The editor most knowledgeable about or committed to a particular project drafted the letter to the press board recommending publication. The balance in kinds of submitted manuscripts ensured a reasonable division of labor over the long haul.

To give some examples of our decisions and the reasons underlying them, Steve liked R. Lee Lyman's 2016 volume *Theodore E. White and the Development of Zooarchaeology in North America* because it was a topic in anthropology rarely mentioned by anthropologists, and he thought that including it might attract an audience otherwise oblivious to our series. I accepted his reasoning.

I liked Robert Jarvenpa's *Declared Defective: Native Americans, Eugenics, and the Myth of Nam Hollow* (2018) because it fit with the list we were beginning to develop in critical race studies (Brownell 2008; Weiss-Wendt and Yeomans 2013; and later McMahon 2019). Steve was "uninterested" in the subject but approved it as a "single-authored and critical text" (email, July 18, 2016). He accepted my reasons for wanting to include it in the series because this is the way our editorial collaboration worked.

Steve pushed hard for *Looking through Taiwan* (2005), which he coauthored with his life partner Keelung Hong. He was eager to elaborate the decades-long collaboration underlying everything that he wrote and to disseminate both his work and his method as widely as possible. Their collaboration extended far beyond the scope of these publications, but his approach to collaboration was the same in all cases. He was passionate about the project because he had a stake in it (which I suspect was the cause of hesitation by the press editor). I found him equally passionate and tenacious with every project he argued for. He provided documentation for his decisions about what to include in his collected essays (Murray 2013). The press hesitation contrasted sharply to that for my own collected essays in the series (Darnell 2001). Steve commented on the manuscript with his usual meticulous style.

We both liked *Irregular Connections: A History of Anthropology and Sexuality* (Lyons and Lyons 2004) but for different reasons. Mine were personal friendship and respect for a partnership of balanced strengths like the one I had developed with Steve and other collaborators at Nebraska. I don't know why Steve liked it. He commented, "We have yet to do an edited book, but Gary assured me at the outset that as long as they were in a minority, we could do some" (email, June 4, 2004). Steve did not consider biographies critical, as required by the series title we chose together, and found the preponderance of biographies in our list (twelve of thirty-two titles) annoying. For example, at one point, when reviewing yet another proposal for a biography, he said "Just what we need—another biography championing the author's favorite underacclaimed anthropologist" (email, July 1, 2017). He accepted my reasoning that biographies constituted a critical commentary on the genre when read en masse (Barnhart 2005; Cole 2003; Gershenhorn 2004; Gordon 2018; Kan 2009; Kubica 2020; Leeds-Hurwitz 2004; Lyman 2016; Peace 2004; Seymour 2015; Young 2005; Zumwalt 2019). This is characteristic of our modus operandi.

Steve treated the collections in the series (Blustain and Wheeler 2018; Brownell 2008; McMahon 2019; Weiss-Wendt and Yeomans 2013) on their merits, no differently than other submissions. By contrast, he actively liked the more general histories, like Joyce's 2001 *The Shaping of American Ethnography*, of which he said: "we should communicate to the two Nebraska editors that we don't just think it should be published but should be published in our series" (email, March 20, 1999).

Steve was incredibly detail oriented when it came to remembering which scholar said what when but could be incredibly sloppy when it came to citations (witness the numerous missing references provided as an addendum after the publication of *Group Formation in Social Science* in 1983). He could be gracious about edits to his own writing: "if you misunderstand the sentence, it definitely needs revision, and I've substituted 'Nevertheless' (one of my favorite words, along with 'alas')" (email, May 13, 2003; under discussion was the series editors' introduction for Leeds-Hurwitz 2004). He was a great reader of drafts because he was interested and knew enough about the topics I wrote on that he could give me serious and relevant feedback. I got serious responses. Several of his critiques for our comments to the authors on revising their draft manuscripts before final submission reflected his enthusiasm or lack thereof; the series editors' introductions always reflect both of our assessments. His commentaries were designed "not to convince but to start a conversation" (email, November 28, 1997).

Steve's actions as series editor tell us much about his drive for success under the pressure of living with HIV/AIDS. He was driven to do as much work as he could and to disseminate it as broadly as possible because he accepted that his lifespan was limited and realized that he would not be able to share his work in person. The reprieve of retrovirus therapy extended his circumscribed future, but his lifespan was still finite, a question most of us do not consider on a day-to-day basis. His drive remained unchanged, and he was still working with a laptop on his bed the morning of his death by MAID (medical assistance in dying). In response to a critique he considered frivolous and mistaken, he wrote: "I'm unlikely to become more taciturn on my deathbed" (email, August 17, 2019). I believe that Steve thrived on the affirmation of his role both through our editorial collaboration and the platform it provided for his research and its dissemination. My own editorial practice continues to reflect the methods and values I acquired from my collaboration with him. I still hear his voice in my ear as I do my own work. I have collaborated with many others in the intervening years but never matched the intense learning experience of collaborating with Steve.

References

Barnhart, Terry A. 2005. *Ephraim George Squier and the Development of American Anthropology*. Lincoln: University of Nebraska Press.

Blustain, Malinda Stafford, and Ryan J. Wheeler, eds. 2018. *Glory, Trouble, and the Renaissance at the Robert S. Peabody Museum of Archaeology*. Lincoln: University of Nebraska Press.

Brownell, Susan, ed. 2008. *The 1904 Anthropology Days and Olympic Games: Sport, Race, and American Imperialism*. Lincoln: University of Nebraska Press.

Cole, Sally. 2003. *Ruth Landes: A Life in Anthropology*. Lincoln: University of Nebraska Press.

Darnell, Regna. 2001. *Invisible Genealogies: A History of Americanist Anthropology*. Lincoln: University of Nebraska Press.

Gershenhorn, Jerry. 2004. *Melville J. Herskovits and the Racial Politics of Knowledge*. Lincoln: University of Nebraska Press.

Gordon, Robert J. 2018. *The Enigma of Max Gluckman: The Ethnographic Life of a 'Luckyman' in Africa*. Lincoln: University of Nebraska Press.

Hong, Keelung, and Stephen O. Murray. 2005. *Looking through Taiwan: American Anthropologists' Collusion with Ethnic Domination*. Lincoln: University of Nebraska Press.

Jarvenpa, Robert. 2018. *Declared Defective: Native Americans, Eugenics and the Myth of Nam Hollow*. Lincoln: University of Nebraska Press.

Joyce, Barry Alan. 2001. *The Shaping of American Ethnography: The Wilkes Exploring Expedition, 1838–1842*. Lincoln: University of Nebraska Press.

Kan, Sergei. 2009. *Lev Shternberg: Anthropologist, Russian Socialist, Jewish Activist*. Lincoln: University of Nebraska Press.

Kubica, Grażyna. 2020. *Maria Czaplicka: Gender, Shamanism, Race*. Translated by Ben Koshalka. Lincoln: University of Nebraska Press.

Leeds-Hurwitz, Wendy. 2004. *Rolling in Ditches with Shamans: Jaime de Angulo and the Professionalization of American Anthropology*. Lincoln: University of Nebraska Press.

Lyman, R. Lee. 2016. *Theodore E. White and the Development of Zooarchaeology in North America*. Lincoln: University of Nebraska Press.

Lyons, Andrew P., and Harriet D. Lyons. 2004. *Irregular Connections: A History of Anthropology and Sexuality*. Lincoln: University of Nebraska Press.

McMahon, Richard, ed. 2019. *National Races: Transnational Power Struggles in the Sciences and Politics of Human Diversity, 1840–1945*. Lincoln: University of Nebraska Press.

Murray, Stephen O. 2013. *American Anthropology and Company: Historical Explorations*. Lincoln: University of Nebraska Press.

Oppenheim, Robert. 2016. *An Asian Frontier: American Anthropology and Korea, 1882–1945*. Lincoln: University of Nebraska Press.

Peace, William J. 2004. *Leslie A. White: Evolution and Revolution in Anthropology*. Lincoln: University of Nebraska Press.

Seymour, Susan C. 2015. *Cora Du Bois: Anthropologist, Diplomat, Agent*. Lincoln: University of Nebraska Press.

Weiss-Wendt, Anton, and Rory Yeomans, eds. 2013. *Racial Science in Hitler's New Europe, 1938–1945*. Lincoln: University of Nebraska Press.

Young, Virginia Heyer. 2005. *Ruth Benedict: Beyond Relativity, Beyond Pattern*. Lincoln: University of Nebraska Press.

Zumwalt, Rosemary Lévy. 2019. *Franz Boas: The Emergence of the Anthropologist*. Lincoln: University of Nebraska Press.

4 Thinking through Area in the History of Anthropology

Robert Oppenheim

In a series of publications culminating in their 2005 book *Looking through Taiwan*, Keelung Hong and Stephen O. Murray offered a trenchant and politically pointed critique of the American anthropology of Taiwan from the 1940s into the 1990s.[1] During much of this period, the People's Republic of China (PRC) was closed to most outside anthropological researchers, with the result that some American researchers turned to Taiwan as an available site to study Chinese society and culture. Frequently, this practice of research by proxy was animated by the implicit or explicit notion that Taiwan was somehow "the place where Chinese culture was best preserved"—an idea that Hong and Murray (2005, 58) noted was unknown before it became convenient in the 1950s, took for granted the proposition that the modernizing and mobilizing Japanese colonial state of 1895–1945 had ruled with an exceptionally light hand, and would have been ludicrous to late Qing officials and intellectuals. In a sense, Hong and Murray contended that there was, with some signal exceptions, really no American anthropology of Taiwan at all in this era, because Taiwan was treated by many anthropologists doing research there as a transparency, a window onto China, a site *looked through*, in the metaphor of the title, in order to see something and someplace else. Hong and Murray accused anthropologists who operated in this vein of ignoring divergent Taiwanese cultural practices, of rendering terms in Mandarin (or "Beijinghua," which highlights the implications of the choice) rather than the Hokkien/Holo or Hakka spoken as a first language by most of their informants, and of avoiding the topics of Taiwanese identity and nationalism. And when the PRC reopened to American anthropological research, the authors noted, many anthropologists were all too happy to move on. Furthermore, Hong and Murray argued that these acts of intellectual make-believe made American anthropology complicit in the political project of the Kuomintang (KMT)–led authoritarian regime that had been dominant in Taiwan for almost forty years, grounding its claim to be the legitimate government of all China in a notion of a Chinese cultural unity that included the island. Up to the present, to chronicle Taiwanese sociocultural differences, let alone the divergent aspirations of some portion of Taiwan's population, is at least inconvenient for "one China" fictions demanded by the PRC that circulate on both sides of the Taiwan Strait and considerably beyond.

I begin this paper with an outline of Hong and Murray's critique because it is the central conceptual basis of *Looking through Taiwan*. In the first section, I examine earlier forms of their argument through a series of previous publications that were in dialog, sometimes tense, with anthropologists working in Taiwan. Whether with an eye to past or present anthropological work conducted in Taiwan, however, I intend neither to endorse Hong and Murray's criticisms nor to refute them nor to extend them. I take this position primarily because I am not qualified to assess their critique on its merits. My background is not in the anthropology of Taiwan, nor of China in any sense. I read none of the associated languages. Rather, my training has been in the anthropology of Korea, or more precisely, the Koreas. There do exist some similar patterns in modern Taiwanese and Korean history that have sometimes led Taiwan and South Korea to be compared and considered together: both were developmental states, both have confronted hostile adversaries in contests over legitimacy and national representation since the 1940s, and both had rightist authoritarian regimes that relied domestically on states of emergency and, until the 1980s, claimed the sole prerogative to imagine national futures. There are notable differences as well: Korean division after 1945 was, in fact, the partition of a political domain that had existed in close to the same form for the better part of a millennium before the twentieth century. While there are certainly critiques that one might make of the Cold War anthropology of Korea, they are not the same critiques, and I find reasonable none that approach the scale or fundamentality of Murray and Hong's excoriation of the practice of Taiwan anthropology.[2] Consequently, I would not argue that Hong and Murray's more scathing points about the constitution of the project of studying Taiwan necessarily transfer to the historical critique of the anthropology of other relatively comparable places.

As a result, my ultimate goal is to suggest the value of a broader and admittedly less critical-political reading of *Looking through Taiwan*, a reading that can, I think, coexist with the critical intervention of the book without being dependent upon it. This reading reflects the relatively narrow pathway along which I came to know Murray's work (in this case, his jointly authored work) and, eventually, although I dare to say not as well as many, Murray himself—not as an anthropologist of homosexualities and especially of gay male lives,[3] nor as a multifaceted historian of the social sciences whose conceptualization of theory groups stands among his signal achievements, but as a historian of anthropology sometimes dissatisfied with biography as the default mode into which much history of anthropology writing falls and consequently interested in alternative ways of organizing history of anthropology projects, for example around the internal and external relations that studies of area engender. In this vein, I turn to Hong and Murray's central metaphor of "looking through." Through this metaphor, they raise the issue of one area being a transparency to another in a way that foregrounds and highlights the value of making the variable relationship between area as a locus of study and area or theory as object of knowledge a more explicit item of attention in history of anthropology research. Read in this light, while *Looking through Taiwan* offers a critique, it also charters a productive agenda for the history of anthropology. I consider these readings in succession, first tracing Hong and Murray's objections regarding the American anthropology of Taiwan as well as reviews of and responses to their criticisms from the late 1980s through their culminating publication on the topic, then sampling more recent publications that suggest other possibilities of their central idea.

Taiwan Unseen

The first appearance of Murray and Hong's critique in anthropological publications followed a review in *American Anthropologist* by David K. Jordan of Robert Weller's 1987 *Unities and Diversities in Chinese Religion*. Weller's (1987, 2) book, based on research conducted in and around the Taiwanese town of Sanxia, was framed around "debates about unity or diversity ... of religion in complex societies." Jordan's (1987) review was largely positive, declaring the discussion of the text "full of provocative insights both about the diversity of beliefs and about their relationships and underpinnings." However, having noted Weller's "recurring theme" of "a running conflict between, on the one hand, folk interpretations too diverse to form an adequate basis for opposition and, on the other hand, a government assumed to be interested only in its own power," Jordan went on to express his "misgivings about considering religion so specifically and constantly from a political perspective." One element of these objections was Weller's alleged tendency to "attribute motivation without demonstrating it" when writing of Taiwanese government officials' attitudes toward popular religion. Jordan's own "experience interviewing Taiwanese government personnel suggest[ed] much less rigid and self-interested motives" than Weller appeared to take for granted (1987, 995). Jordan also complained that Weller's preference for transcribing terms using Hokkien rather than Mandarin pronunciations necessitated frequent recourse to the list of Chinese-character terms in the back of the book.

In a commentary in *American Anthropologist* the following year, Murray and Hong (1988) took issue with Jordan's review and in the process opened up several other lines of argument that would become central to their longer publications critiquing the American anthropology of Taiwan. They began by addressing the fact that Jordan had found Weller's Hokkien transcriptions at all "remarkable." They wrote, "It is hard to imagine an anthropologist today writing about a cultural phenomenon anywhere in the world except Taiwan listing the 'native terms' not in the language the natives use to talk about it, but rather substituting 'the official language' (e.g., presenting Zapotec terms in Spanish)." Murray and Hong (1988, 976) themselves considered it noteworthy that Jordan had thought "that the way to find out why a dictatorial regime attempts to suppress native festivals, language, and religion is to ask its functionaries." From these specific objections to Jordan's review, Murray and Hong expanded their argument to lay out some of the fundamentals of their eventual larger critique. Invoking Talal Asad's examination of the imbrication of past anthropologies within colonial endeavors, they hoped "anthropologists would be more careful in providing ideological service to current colonial regimes" but lamented in contrast that "two generations of Sinologists, especially anthropologists wishing to do community studies, have shared the Go Min Dong's"—Kuomintang, pointedly in Hong's regional dialect of Hokkien—"interest in considering Taiwan to be China" (Murray and Hong 1988, 976; Asad 1975). "Taiwan is not traditionally a part of China," they continued, "let alone the most traditional part"; the obvious alternative was "to study *Taiwanese* culture" in a more transparent fashion (Murray and Hong 1988, 977). Weller's book deserved praise for its documentation of government suppression of folk religion. "What Go Min Dong personnel say is less important than what their regime and preceding ones have done," Murray and Hong (1988, 977) concluded. "It behooves anthropologists not to be complicit with such ethnocide."

Jordan's (1988) invited response to Murray and Hong's criticism was brief. He reiterated that he felt it "preferable to try to establish that people do in fact have the motivations and intent one attributes to them even if they are government policymakers." With respect to the question of transcriptions, he explained that "most readers familiar with Chinese religion would have to consult Weller's character table more frequently than would have been the case had he used Mandarin for expressions where Mandarin transcriptions are already conventional, and hence familiar." To Murray and Hong's final line about complicity with ethnocide, Jordan (1988, 978) responded, "I do not follow their logic, but I am sorry to have made them unhappy."

A sharper response to Murray and Hong by Stevan Harrell (1989) appeared in *American Anthropologist* the next year, to which they in turn responded as well. Harrell's title, and the bulk of his comment, addressed what he considered Murray and Hong's "errors," including the claim that Taiwan had not traditionally been a part of China (Harrell chronicled a history of migration from the mainland extending back to early Qing in contrast to the relative recency of Chinese sovereignty) and the nature of Nationalist (KMT) rule (Harrell [1989, 1026] acknowledged that it was "ethnocidal and dictatorial" in some periods but emphasized that it was "complex and paradoxical" over its full extent and had, for instance, encompassed "rises in living standards, public health, and literacy" during the 1950s). Turning to the more complicated "issue of the relationship between language, culture, ethnicity, and political legitimacy," Harrell restated the question as "how 'Chinese' is Taiwan," and what political difference does that make? Linguistically, Harrell noted, both Hokkien and Hakka are

Chinese languages that use the same written forms as Mandarin. Culturally, while he allowed that Taiwan had been relatively isolated from the southern Chinese mainland from 1895 to 1987, Harrell stated that Taiwanese isolation "never has been absolute" and was diminishing again at time of writing; folk religion in particular, the key topic for both Weller and Jordan, had "diverged much less" than other cultural domains. "Taiwan," concluded Harrell (1989, 1027), "is not *representative* of China ... but its religion is very much the same as that of Fujian" (emphasis in original). Murray and Hong's larger "error," Harrell opined, had been to grant such issues objective significance in relation to political legitimacy in the same manner as Beijing and KMT nationalists had done, albeit with opposite valence: "Murray and Hong, who favor independence for Taiwan, assume that their position can only be supported if Taiwan is not Chinese. They thus swallow their Nationalist opponents' line that ethnicity is something objective, and that national borders are the same as ethnic-group boundaries. There is a good case to be made for an independent Taiwan, but on the basis of political realities of the past 40 years, not imagined ethnic differences" (1027).

Only after these broader arguments did Harrell turn to Murray and Hong's critical response to Jordan's review.[4] Harrell (1989, 1027) denied that Jordan's decision to render terms in Mandarin rather than Hokkien pronunciations held any significance for the broader scholarly community beyond convenience: "it certainly does not indicate complicity with government efforts to suppress the rituals." He also supported Jordan's efforts to ask government officials about their "motives," taking exception to Murray and Hong's assumption "that these officials' motives must lie in the suppression of an ethnic group," declaring it "no better methodology than the one they criticize." Harrell surmised that most such officials had been "propagandized" into beliefs that they now sincerely held: "it takes an anthropologist to see a social function where most educated people see superstition and waste" (1028).

Hong and Murray's (1989, 1028) reply began by noting the complexity of Ming- and Qing-era migration to Taiwan and underscoring the concomitant complexity of resulting identifications, in contrast to the simplifying "Go-min-dang (GMD) myth (repeated by Harrell)" that associated such migrants primarily with Ming loyalism and thus residual "Chinese" identity. They doubled down on Harrell's own claim of the complex aspects of Nationalist rule: should Harrell want "to distribute plaudits to authoritarian rulers," they noted acerbically, consistency would require him to extend the favor to Japanese colonial government and the regime of U.S. support for Taiwan as well (1028). With respect to language, Hong and Murray pointed out the existence of scripts for Hakka, Hokkien, and Taiwan's Austronesian languages but continued to base their more fundamental critique on the substitution of Mandarin or "Beijinghua" for Hokkien or Hakka native terms when anthropologists' transcription of such terms as spoken is "taken for granted for publication of fieldwork done everywhere else but Taiwan" (1029). They wrote, "It does not seem to require excessive analytical insight to see that when a linguistic minority makes its language the official language and forces it on a majority population, and foreign observers represent what they observe in the language of the rulers rather than in the language used by those whom they observe, they are helping legitimate both the language policy and the domination of the majority by the minority" (1029).

With respect to the question of the motives of government officials, Hong and Murray (1989, 1029) reiterated that they had mainly sought to induce "skepticism" toward such officials' self-justifications. In any case, they claimed, whether in discussing government functionaries or the positioning of anthropologists, motivation or conscious intention was less the issue than "*unconscious* complicity" with an ethnocidal state agenda (emphasis in original).

By the time of the follow-up exchange with Harrell, however, Murray and Hong were already envisioning their critique of the anthropology of Taiwan in wider terms. During the summer of 1988, Murray made a speech, "The Invisibility of the Taiwanese," to a Taiwanese American summer camp, the text of which was later published in a Taiwanese American journal. Framing his talk around Thomas Jefferson's statement that "eternal vigilance is the price of liberty" and thereby highlighting the problem of the conflation of Taiwan with China in both academic and popular publications, Murray (1988, 3–4) called for a broad social project of "the correction of misrepresentation of Taiwan as the KMT or as China wherever they appear." "To mobilize support for Taiwanese self-determination," he argued, "it is first necessary to establish that there are Taiwanese, that interests are not the same as KMT policies, and that there are important historical and cultural differences between Taiwan and mainland China and that the interests of the Taiwanese majority are neither represented nor advanced by the mainlander oligarchy" (4).

Murray announced the contribution to this project that he and Hong planned to undertake, the terms of which clearly exceeded their critique of the critique of Weller. "Having recently criticized one KMT running dog anthropologist," Murray (1988, 6) declared, "we are beginning a review of all the work American social scientist[s] have done on Taiwan, seeing how widespread studying Taiwan and writing about China is, and also how common translating Taiwanese terms into Beijinghua is."[5]

Murray and Hong's efforts culminated in a substantial 1991 article, appearing in *Dialectical Anthropology*, that in turn formed a core chapter in each of their two books on the topic. "American Anthropologists Looking through Taiwanese Culture" (Murray and Hong 1991) introduced the visual and spatial metaphor of "looking through" for the first time. It was initially explained in an introductory section, attributed to Hong alone, that described his experiences of the slaughter of Taiwanese by Chiang Kai-shek's forces and the suppression of Holo (Hokkien) language and culture in Nationalist-run schools in the following years.[6] Despite his hopes for the potential of anthropology as a discipline, he had found little solace in American village ethnographies that preferred to render terms in Mandarin (or, again, "Beijinghua") rather than Hokkien or other local languages. This disappointment underwrote the article's core critical insight:

> I soon realized that American anthropologists and mainland Chinese in Taiwan were not interested in Taiwanese culture. They seemed to be looking at us, but were really looking through us to try to see traditional Chinese culture without seeing us, our culture, or our historical experiences. Being invisible or transparent constituted only a slight promotion in the value of our culture, because this work legitimizes robbing us of our language and subordinating our culture to the so-called great tradition of Chinese civilization, just as we are economically and politically subordinated to the ethnic minority dictatorship that still rules Taiwan under the fiction of being the government of China. (Murray and Hong 1991, 273)

The bulk of the article examined both current and past American anthropological writings on Taiwan, beginning with those of Arthur Wolf, whom Murray and Hong (1991) deemed most central to the field. They called Wolf to task for substituting "Chinese" for "Taiwanese" throughout his work but most notably in his titles, which overwrote the occasional acknowledgment that data from Taiwan "may not be representative," as well as for singularizing concepts such as "Chinese society," "the Chinese family," and, especially, "Chinese religion" (Murray and Hong 1991, 274, 275). The former act rendered Taiwan "unthinkable," whereas the latter tended to make Taiwanese internal diversity unseeable (in contrast to which Murray and Hong cited anthropologists' emphasis on "multiple religious realities" in Thailand; 275). From here, the article turned to brief considerations of the anthropological representation of folk religion and of class and ethnicity, with Murray and Hong highlighting the "salient emic distinction" of the "Taiwanese/mainlander dichotomy... inconvenient though it may be ... to anthropologists" (278). Murray and Hong then examined and often excoriated older anthropological works with the aim of providing an analysis of "historical sources of Taiwanese invisibility" (280). As they drew toward their conclusion, however, they cited two topical examples as exceptions to the overall pattern of rendering Taiwan invisible, namely the study of ethnomedicine, where unlike the case of religion "the pragmatic diversity in medical behavior ... and the intracultural variation in the salience and content of medical beliefs" had been featured in anthropological scholarship, and the study of female factory laborers in the context of Taiwanese capitalist industrialization (287, 288).

Slightly expanded, revised, and retitled as "Looking Forward to Taiwan to See 'Traditional' China," the *Dialectical Anthropology* article formed the narrative core of Murray and Hong's (1994) book *Taiwanese Culture, Taiwanese Society*. The bulk of the book, meanwhile, was devoted to a critical annotated bibliography of anthropological and selected other social scientific publications on Taiwan, a project close to the raw result of their review of the literature (Murray and Hong 1994, 77–213), while a preface by Hong reflected the spirit of the introductory section of the *Dialectical Anthropology* paper. A significant new element, however, was a separate introduction by Murray, in which he stated of the book as a whole that "although the English phrasing of the critique is mine, most of the ideas ... are [Hong's]"; it also noted that Murray had been for the first time able to visit Taiwan himself, accompanying Hong, after Hong's blacklisting ended in 1992 (8). Murray's introduction did the work of locating their critique with respect to the history of anthropology, with its historical respect for and usage of "native terms" (7), even as he tied it to contemporary general anthropological debates, specifically the then-prevalent topic of nationalism. In rejoinder to the criticism of those such as Harrell and in anticipation of a similar argument from Joseph Bosco discussed later, Murray explicitly denied reliance on an objectivist or essentialist notion of culture. "We do not endeavor," he wrote, "to substitute a more-constrained-in-space-and-time essence of 'Taiwanese culture' for the essence 'Chinese culture' stretching across millennia and a huge space" (10). While he and Hong favored the self-determination of Taiwan (and Tibet), their position "need not depend on the existence of a distinct culture (or language or history or religion).... There is no fixed and value-free standard of the amount of cultural difference that justifies a state" (11). In making this argument, Murray and Hong agreed in principle with some of their own critics, but Murray insisted that enunciating Taiwanese difference held a second, complicating and productively discomfiting role in the face of actually-existing patterns of anthropological discourse: "Asserting that the existence of a separate Taiwanese reality tends to correlate to other politics than the conceptual ethnic-cleansing of positing a single Chinese essence" (11). "Either claim," he continued, "has political repercussions"; a footnote highlighted the asymmetry of a situation in which "some [anthropologists] consider using 'Taiwanese' as 'political' and 'Chinese' as neutral" (11, 11n10). In short, Murray suggested that it was not he and Hong who had invited the bêtes noires of nationalism and "politics" to the party; they were rather already fully ensconced in the practice of seeing China through Taiwan.

Taiwanese Culture, Taiwanese Society was somewhat sparsely reviewed. Writing in *The China Quarterly*, Joseph Bosco (1995) had perhaps the most critical response. After outlining Murray and Hong's arguments, he took issue with the scathing tone of the book, which he thought impeded its argumentation. "The essay's rhetorical excesses and sarcasm make it easy to dismiss even the valid points of its argument, especially the issue of China being higher prestige than Taiwan and the focus of sinological anthropology on understanding traditional China rather than the present" (Bosco 1995, 873). Bosco went on to defend a particular focus of Murray and Hong's criticism, Arthur Wolf, as having been more attuned to "local variation" (of marriage forms) than they had given him credit for (873). He expressed reservations with *Taiwanese Culture*'s romanization and its annotated bibliography. Most fundamentally, echoing Harrell's earlier criticism while skipping over Murray's responsive text, Bosco alleged that Murray and Hong simply substituted one nationalist reading for another: "The book is another example of how scholars cannot avoid being dragged into nationalist debates about cultural authenticity. The question of Taiwan's political independence is separate from—and does not hinge on—Taiwan's cultural distinctiveness. In their denial of Taiwan's Chinese-ness, Murray and Hong merely mirror Kuomintang nationalist discourse. . . . Rather than transcending nationalist discourse, they are embroiled in it" (874).[7]

In contrast, Astrid Winterhalder (1996, 623), reviewing the book for *Anthropos* with an extensive German-language summary, pronounced it a useful introduction to the subject of Taiwan in American social science. Meanwhile, in *China Information*, Peter Jeffrey Herz (1996, 159) praised the book overall for raising "important questions." He also noted some "drawbacks": Murray and Hong, he claimed, had overstated the importance of foreign scholars' reliance on Mandarin while underappreciating the historical role of the language within Taiwan and were "mistaken in identifying the pre-Koxinga population of Taiwan as 'Polynesian'" (158). His major contention, however, was that Murray and Hong did not sufficiently develop the larger significance of their argument, which had potential relevance beyond Taiwan itself. "The authors rightly raise the question of how legitimate it is to generalize a lost 'traditional China' from Taiwanese data. But in doing so, they may have unwittingly raised the question of whether social science research has wrongly homogenized the whole Sinitic world. Intra-Han diversity remains a stubborn fact in most of south-eastern China and South-east Asia, despite the efforts of Chinese nationalists of all stripes to overcome it" (158).

Hong and Murray's argument reached its final form more than a decade later in their second book on the topic, *Looking through Taiwan* (Hong and Murray 2005), published as part of the same University of Nebraska Press Critical Studies in the History of Anthropology series in which the present volume appears. The eponymous chapter, in a form largely congruent with the 1991 original, formed the core of the middle section of the work, "American Social Scientists' Complicity with Domination." This central part documented the violence and repression of early KMT rule in Taiwan, beginning with the 228 Incident of 1947 (so called for its occurrence on February 28) and the White Terror that followed, as well as the inadequate response of American social science to these events. The key analysis of the American gaze focused on the "pseudo-objectivity" of a 1991 Hoover Institution study of the 228 Incident (Hong and Murray 2005, 27, referencing Lai, Myers, and Wei 1991). An introductory section of *Looking through Taiwan* included a chapter in Hong's voice, as a "'native' observing anthropology," that also reiterated some of the argumentative clarifications of his and Murray's previous book. It underscored that the distinctiveness of Taiwanese culture and the case for Taiwanese self-determination did not logically or ethically depend on each other while emphasizing the asymmetry and irony of anthropologists noting "politics" only in the assertion that Taiwan is *not* Chinese, and not the opposite proposition (Hong and Murray 2005, 7–9).[8] A second chapter tied American community studies of Taiwan into a genealogy of anthropological practice that began with salvage ethnography of Native American groups and the extension of its assumptions across the Pacific to the U.S. overseas colony in the Philippines; the chapter discussed Japanese colonial research on Taiwanese Indigenous populations and culminated in a postwar rise of community-based research (13–15). The third chapter of the first section provided a short history of Taiwan's government. A final major section of the book, then, considered the anthropology of Taiwan in the 1990s. Its chapters on the question of the erasure of Taiwanese women's names and on anthropological considerations of Taiwanese spirit possession engaged in close critique of more recent assertions by American anthropologists. The final chapter documented a turn in the overall situation through which "most of the American anthropologists who did fieldwork on Taiwan when China was closed to them moved on to their real interest when the post-Mao communist regime allowed foreigners greater access to China" (109). Even so, Hong and Murray argued, many continued to occlude the Taiwanese basis of their new comparative insights in a variety of ways.

Across the gamut of reviews of *Looking through Taiwan*, even the most critical deemed the book in touch with something significant. Joseph Bosco (2007, 196), returning to evaluate Hong and Murray's second joint volume, remained mostly negative, contending that while "the book discusses important issues and has some interesting ideas and arguments... it often takes these points to an extreme and illogical conclusion." He described their "degree of animosity toward anthropology" as "puzzling" and their "polemical, combative and tendentious tone" as counterproductive: "The authors are frustrated and irritated at not being taken seriously by anthropologists, but this book will not do much to make most anthropologists pay more attention" (198). Their protestations notwithstanding, Bosco continued to argue that Hong and Murray had failed to escape the trap of nationalist essentialism, noting as an example their "nationalist rhetoric that biologizes Taiwaneseness" (197). "Not all Taiwan independence supporters, even those who emphasize the ethnic differences between Mainlanders and Taiwanese, deny being Chinese," Bosco wrote. "The authors claim that they do not rest their claim for Taiwan's independence on Taiwan's cultural distinctiveness (p. 9), yet the book is primarily an attempt to prove that distinctiveness. Any research that attempts to place Taiwan in a larger context of Chinese culture is attacked as politically motivated" (197).

Bosco also highlighted positive effects of the history of American anthropological research on Taiwan and Taiwanese religion specifically, notwithstanding the KMT umbrella under which it had taken place, including the building of American public sympathy for the island and the countering of local elite dismissals of popular religious practice as superstition (197). While it bought no appreciation for *Looking through Taiwan*, Bosco linked the work to a larger anthropological problem that it unwittingly indexed. He claimed that, during the period Hong and Murray scrutinized, "a major question of the anthropology of Chinese societies was that of unity and diversity within Chinese culture, or how to understand 'Chinese culture' on the basis of any particular local study. Research in Hong Kong or Hunan can sometimes be helpful in understanding wider Chinese patterns," just, he implied, as research in Taiwan might be (196).

Another two-sided review by Sylvia Li-chun Lin (2006, 134) was somewhat less grudging overall. She found Hong and Murray's criticism of the Hoover Institution analysis of the 228 Incident out of place, simply on the grounds that the Hoover authors were not anthropologists. Lin invited readers to parse the question of when "complicity," perhaps a passive acceptance of the affordances of research under KMT government auspices, "slides into collusion" with such a regime (133). She hesitated at Hong and Murray's "politicized" quickness to read anthropological complicity as "deliberate conspiracy," preferring to situate anthropologists themselves as "products of particular political, cultural, and academic systems" (135). Moreover, she pointed to the twenty-first-century complexity of identity on Taiwan, noting that "many in Taiwan still consider themselves Chinese (or at least Chinese first and Taiwanese second)," and thus "one cannot completely write off anthropological works that claim to be about Chinese culture, if some people in Taiwan still consider their culture Chinese, not Taiwanese." Yet this statement came hand-in-hand with an acknowledgment of the previous and (though she did not say this explicitly) formative pre-1987 situation that had given rise to the first iteration of Hong and Murray's critique, in which such complexity had been strongly suppressed. "Under martial law," she wrote, "many Taiwanese were reluctant to express their identification with Taiwan, for fear of political persecution. It was only after 1987 that Taiwanese were not afraid to stand up and proclaim 'We are Taiwanese'" (136). Overall, Lin's review balanced her assessment of the "flaws" of *Looking through Taiwan* with an appreciation of its "merits," listing its authors' "several good cases against anthropological studies of Taiwan" (135).

In the French Southeast Asia journal *Moussons*, Chantel Zheng (2006) struck a similar tone, describing *Looking through Taiwan* as a "vitriolic indictment" that did not always appear "objective" but at the same time praising it as "courageous" and its criticisms of anthropology as "fair play."[9] It was left for another review, and perhaps not incidentally another European scholar, to warn (American) anthropology most strongly against too glib a dismissal of Hong and Murray's appraisal. Although Paul-François Tremlett (2006, 497) characterized *Looking through Taiwan* as a "self-consciously angry book," that did not mean that it could or should be set aside: "No doubt some critics will point to Hong and Murray's frequent appeals to polemic and hyperbole. Those critics would do well to acquaint themselves with Nietzsche's observation that dispassionate or objective modes of writing are special instances of polemic that consciously seek to mask their own partisan nature." Tremlett considered the volume "compulsory reading" and hoped that "contemporary anthropological scholarship on Taiwan (and elsewhere) takes on board this critique and that anthropologists think twice before becoming partners with states for which the prosecution of violence and terror against their own populations is routine" (497, 499).

The iterations of Hong and Murray's critique of the American anthropology of Taiwan (or of "China" via Taiwan) and the reception of this critique by anthropologists over the course of more than fifteen years resist easy summary, but several points merit highlighting. Murray and Hong did not hide their anger, and many commentators accused them of being too personal, tendentious, or unbalanced in their presentation, or of committing errors of fact or interpretation. Tremlett had the best eventual response to this all-too-easy path to dismissal. It is not, he suggested, the job of critique to be measured or objective or even "fair" when it swims against the tide of accepted practice. It is the job of critique to spur reflexivity, when necessary through its own extremity; Hong and Murray's critique did that. Hong and Murray wore their opposition to the KMT and pro-Taiwanese independence sentiments on their sleeves, and especially during the 1980s–1990s heyday of the critique of nationalism within both anthropology and historical studies, it was easy to accuse them of being enmeshed in nationalism's logics. By the time of *Looking through Taiwan*'s publication in 2005, moreover, their argument could seem obviated by Taiwan's democratization and the new freedom of its residents to negotiate complex, non-exclusive identifications openly. Yet it was also only roughly then when reviewers such as Lin followed Murray and Hong's contention of a decade earlier that Chinese nationalism in Taiwan and Taiwanese nationalism in Taiwan might not be regarded as equivalent cases of a generic problem within a pre-1987 situation in which the former was mandatory and the latter bordered on unspeakable—an owl of Minerva taken wing only after the dusk of authoritarianism had fallen.

There was also a final strand in the reception of Murray and Hong's argument that straddled its more negative and positive respondents, conjoining, for instance, Bosco's consideration of unity and diversity in Chinese culture with Herz's insistence on the fact of intra-Han variability. This strand took their work as a springboard to further consideration of the spatial and ontological characters of Chinese and Taiwanese being.

Space, Ontology, and the Rise of Taiwan Studies

More recent scholarly reassessments of Hong and Murray's critique have been conditioned by the changed situation of Taiwan studies in the Euro-American academy—indeed, it might be said, the rise of Taiwan studies as such. Simultaneously, intellectual trends within anthropology as a discipline have complexified the space, place, and reference of ethnographic research. One consequence has been a complexification of the relationship of area as locus of study vis-à-vis area as object of knowledge, or where research is done versus where and what research is done about, away from the taken-for-grantedness of the community studies model to which Murray and Hong referred.

With respect to the first of these dynamics, there has been a considerable overall change in tone. The last section of *Looking through Taiwan* had registered something of a dark night of the soul for the anthropology of Taiwan, insofar as American scholars had reacted to the new openness of the PRC by shifting from studying Taiwan as a proxy for China to not bothering to study the island at all. Taiwan scholars, not necessarily anthropologists, who have more recently recalled this period around the turn of the millennium have described it in similarly forlorn terms. Taiwan was "a marginal topic on the edge of Chinese Studies"; Taiwan studies itself was a "desert" (Fell and Hsiao 2019, 1, quoting "desert" from Fell 2008, 5). Niki J. P. Alsford (2020, 14) quotes at length from an unpublished talk given by Murray Rubinstein (2013, 2) in which Rubinstein described the period from 1979 to 1999 as one in which "'Taiwan as China' [was] put to death." Rubinstein would title a separate talk given just a few years before "Is Taiwan Studies Dead?" and Alsford himself (2020, 15, 16) recalls being asked "why Taiwan?" on several occasions early in his career, a question that carried, among other implications, the hint that painstakingly acquired language skills (whether Mandarin, Hokkien, or Hakka) might be put to better use across the straits. He also quotes Shu-Mei Shih, who contended in 2003 that Taiwan had been "written out of mainstream Western discourse" and was indeed "illegible" because "knowing Taiwan does not carry 'value,' either symbolic or material, as the significance required for value production is either missing or not recognized" (Alsford 2020, 16, quoting Shih 2003, 144). Melissa J. Brown (2019, 123) recalls assimilating the critical perspective of Murray and Hong's *Taiwanese Culture, Taiwanese Society* while also facing pressure from the potential publisher of her first book, the University of California Press, to have "China" or "Chinese" in its title for the sake of marketing. Her solution to this dilemma was to reframe the demand as a question and to have the book published as *Is Taiwan Chinese?*[10]

More recently, however, there has been a shift away from this pessimistic, somewhat literally funereal outlook for the field toward a broad optimism. Rubinstein emerged from his consideration of the possible demise of Taiwan studies heartened and "re-energize[d]" (Alsford 2020, 16). Dafydd Fell and Hsin-Huang Michael Hsiao (2019, 1) proclaim the present to be a "golden age of international Taiwan Studies," pointing to a variety of institutional developments including conferences, dedicated journals, a book series, expanded course offerings, and the development of Taiwan-focused degree programs at several universities (notably including my own).[11] At the most basic intellectual level, the study of Taiwan for Taiwan's sake, or possibly through some comparative lens but in any case not as an unacknowledged stand-in for an unavailable China, has been validated and invigorated. Within this positively transformed environment, one tendency has been to anteriorize or historicize Hong and Murray's critique of the practice of American anthropology and to regard it, however transformative or successful or "fair" in its moment, as having concluded its business with the field. There are some exceptions. Megan Steffen (2020, 3), for instance, builds upon Hong and Murray in arguing against a still-extant tendency for "anthropologists writing in English about the PRC [to] lump past studies of Hong Kong and Taiwan into the anthropology of China." Steffen takes the position "that anthropologists working in the PRC today should stop treating past work done in Hong Kong and Taiwan as historical predecessors and instead think of them as comparative studies" and that they should call the PRC "the PRC" (2, 4). Most provocatively, she asks, in a bid for specificity, "why use the term

'China' in anthropology at all," given its confounding surfeit of potential referents (1)?

Steffen's argument links the overall tonal shift in Taiwan studies with a second development within American anthropology as a whole. Partially in parallel with the turn toward optimism in Taiwan studies and sometimes in connection, a variety of efforts to foreground categories of space, place, area, location, and similar spatial concerns have emerged within anthropology since roughly 1990. These have appeared in conjunction with more methodologically oriented efforts to denaturalize community or village studies, which had often entailed the assumption that small-scale research automatically speaks to a larger, commonly national cultural whole; trends toward such topics as diaspora, globalization, and transnationalism as well as toward explicitly "multi-sited" ethnographic practice are the most glaring manifestations of these phenomena.[12] Against this backdrop, Murray and Hong's critique of seeing China through a Taiwan thus rendered transparent becomes a special, politically obnoxious case of a more general issue that is in itself politically ambivalent. The spatial and ontological indexicality of anthropological research has now become a heightened focus of theoretical attention. In light of this focus, Hong and Murray's argument and their central metaphor of "looking through" become not merely corrective but enabling of projects, critical and otherwise, that ask what one sees by looking in a variety of new ways. Paul-François Tremlett (2009, 4), the same Nietzschean defender of *Looking through Taiwan*, for example, cites Hong and Murray as precursors of his own state-of-the-field reflection that embraces these new developments, writing that "re-articulations within the island of Taiwan concomitant with wider, globalizing or re-territorializing processes and pressures—in terms of political identity, the organization of the economy and polity, relations to the past, and hopes and anxieties about the future (to name only three)—suggest the need to re-visit (the representation of) Taiwan, and the fissures and instabilities at play in those representations."

Writing in the inaugural issue of a new journal dedicated to Taiwan, Scott Simon (2018) reviews the "ontologies" of Taiwan studies as they relate to Indigenous studies. He cites *Taiwanese Culture, Taiwanese Society* in recounting the emergence of a confident Taiwan studies from its past encompassment by Chinese studies, in the process recalling a past of the field that Murray and Hong might recognize. "In the 1990s," Simon (2018, 13) writes, "when I started arguing at anthropology conferences that we need to study Taiwan as a society in its own right rather than as an avatar of Chinese culture, senior colleagues warned me against being 'so political.' They were reluctant to admit the political implications of their own statements, such as: 'You must admit that Taiwan is culturally Chinese.'" Simon proceeds to take Murray and Hong as a launching pad for a new possibility, offering Taiwan as a potential "paradigmatic case" in a new, more global formulation of Indigenous studies that might center questions of Taiwanese indigeneity and Indigenous nationalisms (13). After reviewing several ways in which Taiwanese Indigenous studies might be articulated—for instance, with the broader concerns of Austronesian studies or with the local indigenization (*bentuhua*) movement that emerged in the 1980s—Simon arrives at his point that these are fundamentally, even ontologically, different things. "Indeed," he writes, "this is why we have to reflect upon Chinese studies, Taiwan studies, Austronesian studies, and Indigenous studies, and so forth, as not just different topics of research, but as different genres of writing that are based in fundamentally different ontological projects" (17–18). Beyond the stifling situation to which Hong and Murray originally responded and the specific critical intent of their writings, Simon regards them as having opened a box of multiplicity, licensing a variety of ways of thinking through and mapping research that might be physically conducted in Taiwan.

Other appropriations take the "looking through" metaphor as a basis for inspiring productive questions for research in the history of anthropology. My own work on late nineteenth- and early twentieth-century American anthropology and the study of Korea drew on this concept as the inspiration for a concept I called *figuration*. With it, I intended to flag "the multiplicity of ways in which Korea was looked upon and [here referring to Hong and Murray] 'looked through' by American anthropologies of the time," emphasizing the variable relationship between area as a locus of study and its linked object of knowledge that *Looking through Taiwan* helped open up (Oppenheim 2016, 4). For a readership that I imagined to include post-Boasian anthropologists but also area studies readers who tend to take for granted the idea that the point of studying Korea has always been to know Korea, I felt the need to outline dynamics of theoretical universalism and comparativism in American anthropology's past that made this not always the case. The result was to highlight the point that Korea, in various anthropological ventures of the era, could stand "for evolutionary pasts, racial anchorages or contact zones, the regrettable but unavoidable collateral damage of secondary imperialisms, and the problem of the national being of small nations" (4). I was not necessarily critical of this fact, at least not in the same way that Hong and Murray were critical of the way that seeing Taiwan as a proxy for China rendered Taiwan itself invisible, but in part that was simply because the anthropology of Korea before 1945 did not have the same stakes for the present at the moment in which I was writing.

Hong and Murray's "looking through" metaphor can also be brought into conversation with other ways of understanding the sociology of knowledge entailed in the Western anthropological project of studying China during its era of inaccessibility. Chris Vasantkumar (2013), for instance, considers Taiwan as not a proxy per se but the broader study during this epoch of "residual China," a term he derives from Maurice Freedman.[13] Versus the visual perspectivism of Hong and Murray's "looking through" metaphor, Vasantkumar employs an alternative theoretical language of social topology, with an end goal, consideration of which is beyond the scope of this chapter, of contributing to the development of topological methods. Vasantkumar does not cite Hong and Murray and is not fully critical of the turn to "residual China," mostly following Freedman's sense that the "closure" of China forced conceptual innovation upon China studies that stood it in good stead while the rest of anthropology was later to come to the realization that it needed to start thinking about ways cultures exist in diasporas and other transnational circuits rather than solely within place-based stabilities. As Vasantkumar (2013, 918–19) puts it, "the end of China anthropology on the familiar terrain of Euclidean space was followed by the rise of China(s) in more-than-Euclidean topologies with anthropologies to match." Despite the differences between Vasantkumar's and Hong and Murray's projects, especially in this era of a newly confident Taiwan studies, I would argue that there is room for both their points to coexist and be in conversation because they are fundamentally reciprocal. If Vasantkumar is about what the topology of "residual China" connected and interiorized and figured in, it seems to me that the more critical half of

Hong and Murray's argument is about what was not figured, not connected, or disconnected in the very same process: some version of "Taiwan itself." In terms that Vasantkumar would recognize, the formation of topologies also enacts "othered out-theres," "absences as Otherness," the potentially relevant rendered invisible, outside, or spectral (Law 2004, 84). A given topology might also be considered through the prism of its absencings.

Conclusion

It is probably safe to say that Murray is better known within American anthropology as a comparative scholar of homosexualities as well as a critic of anthropological business as usual surrounding the AIDS epidemic and the representation (in the "speaking for" sense of the word) of HIV-positive persons than for the critiques of Taiwan anthropology that he and Hong coauthored. This is not surprising in itself; area literatures are area literatures, and few within them read beyond their own. As a matter of biography and intellectual history, however, the experiences that gave rise to each intervention were connected for Murray. In the wake of what Deb Amory anointed the "panel from Hell," the 1992 American Anthropological Association annual meeting panel "AIDS and the Social Imaginary," which drew strong protest notably from members of the Society of Lesbian and Gay Anthropologists for its marginalization of the "native" voices of those already deeply enmeshed in AIDS-related research and activism (see Bolton, a fellow participant objector, in this volume), Murray published and reflected upon his oral comments at the event. "Being rendered invisible here—looked through or looked beyond," he said, "I understand better what my Taiwanese friends feel about privileged outsiders coming in and profiting from their oppression, speaking in the language of the oppressor, and seizing their suffering as means to advance their already-inflated reputations."[14] The allusion and the intertextual link were to Hong's initial comments on "being invisible or transparent" in their *Dialectical Anthropology* article of the year before (Murray and Hong 1991, 273).

With respect to Taiwan, as with AIDS, Murray (and Hong) were willing to take critique to scathing and personal levels to make their point. Whether or not this violated some unwritten rule of scholarly decorum (on which issue one might consult Tremlett's response), a more interesting question for the present is whether one might declare victory on their behalf. Euro-American Taiwan studies has been reinvigorated on newly self-confident terms, against the grain of universities the world over simultaneously following the money to the PRC,[15] and some commentators on this development see Hong and Murray as among its heralds. Even in this new era, some such as Steffen regard Murray and Hong's critique of the too-easy conflation of Taiwan and "China" as retaining its salience. It could also be argued that Hong and Murray's central problematics of the politics of representation and the complicity of anthropological practice and silence have taken on new importance with emergent forms of repression in Xinjiang (cf. Fiskesjö 2020) and Hong Kong, the perennial problem of Tibet, and indeed from new shadows over Taiwan's future. There are others, though, who beyond Hong and Murray's obvious critical intent take, or might well take, their "looking through" metaphor as enabling of new prescriptive, conceptual, and historical projects in anthropology. This has been my own bias in reading their work, which suggests to me that a foregrounding of the need for finer-grained attention to the question of what one sees when one looks at areas should be taken as among the significant legacies of Murray's career.

Notes

1. Antecedent works are discussed later in this chapter. Hong and Murray switched authorial priority in various publications. When discussing a specific work, I refer to them in the order in which they are listed in that work; when discussing them more generally, I have tried for a rough alternation of who is listed first.
2. Some potential criticisms of Korea anthropology basically dovetail with a broader questioning of the assumptions of much of American anthropology, or indeed the interdisciplinary American academy, in this period. Cold War anthropology of Korea can be accused of being sometimes too complacent with the assumptions of modernization theory, for instance. There were "China effects" in the anthropology of Korea as well. Ethnographies of South Korea written in the 1970s and 1980s bear the marks of an unsubtle pressure to include a "comparative chapter" juxtaposing Korean, Japanese, or Chinese (or Taiwanese) phenomena—this at a time before the Korean wave and flashy South Korean economic success, when studies of Korea were not assumed to be sufficiently interesting to a broad readership to stand on their own. Yet the net result of this pressure was definitively not the elision of local particularity and diversity that Hong and Murray allege

for the Taiwanese case (see, for instance, Janelli and Janelli 1982, 177–95, and Kendall 1985, 170–78).

Meanwhile, anthropology of North Korea, closed to outside scholars as the PRC was, was basically not done at all between the 1950s and 1990s. But the low prestige of Korean studies overall meant that such studies were not really missed; if there was perhaps a broad assumption that North Korean patterns might be grasped at the intersection of South Korean culture and society with patterns of socialist development knowable from the USSR and PRC, then that assumption was rarely actualized in the sorts of "study by proxy" that Hong and Murray document. More recent efforts to conduct the anthropology of North Korea have not danced around the issues of doing "anthropology at a distance," but rather have made them explicit objects of theoretical attention (for instance, Ryang 2021, 8–11).

3. This is to employ categories that Murray himself preferred (see Murray et al. 2021, 261–62).

4. Harrell also took issue with Murray and Hong's passing criticism of Emily Martin Ahern and Hill Gates in the course of their address to Jordan.

5. Murray also suggested an earlier iteration of his and Hong's concern with the (non-) representation of Taiwan in American scholarship, noting that in 1982 they had "criticized the *Harvard Encyclopedia of American Ethnic Groups* for including separate entities for very small groups under Russian domination within the Soviet Union and not distinguishing Taiwanese and Tibetans from 'Chinese'" (7). This is true: Kalmyks, Tatars, and "Germans from Russia" have full entries in the Harvard book (Thernstrom 1980) while Taiwanese and Tibetans lack even cross-references (Taiwan comes up in the entry for Chinese, while a cursory examination [there is no index] reveals no mention at all of Tibetans). But the volume also has an overall lumping tendency, such that, for instance, a few years after 1975, the entries for Vietnamese, Cambodians, and "Laotians" all cross-reference to a vast entry for "Indochinese," while Hmong receive no mention. As, perhaps, an impossible undertaking that thoroughly explores its own impossibility, when it comes to the Harvard volume it is difficult to distinguish the signal of political decisions about representation from the noise of its overall idiosyncrasy and randomness.

6. Most likely this referred to the February 28 (or 228) Incident (or Massacre) of 1947, though there were other events.

7. Deliberately or not, by failing to acknowledge Murray's address to this very question of nationalism Bosco's review stifled a potential opportunity for scholarly conversation.

8. Here I might note, guiltily, that I failed to appreciate Hong and Murray's analysis of the asymmetry of anthropological perspectives on subsumptive and

anti-subsumptive nationalisms before writing my own (Oppenheim 2010, 2016, 223–58).
9. I.e., "de bonne guerre"; my translations.
10. Brown notes that she later came in for criticism in *Looking through Taiwan*, despite the fact that her basically negative answer to her own question concurred with Hong and Murray's position.
11. On which development see also Fell and Chang (2019).
12. There is, of course, a vast literature here. Some important early works include Appadurai (1990), Gupta and Ferguson (1992), and Marcus (1995). My own early ethnographic and theoretical writing bore some allegiance to this trend (Oppenheim 2007, 2008).
13. It is worth noting in passing that Murray and Hong (1994, 114) were critical of Freedman in an early iteration of their critique.
14. Murray, "Colonizing AIDS Discourse," commentary in Amory (1993), 23–24.
15. On the global promotion of Confucius Institutes as one aspect of this trend, see Paradise (2009).

References

Alsford, Niki J. P. 2020. "Finding the Threads in Taiwan History and Historiography." *European Journal of East Asian Studies* 19 (1): 13–47.

Amory, Deb, ed. 1993. "The 1992 AAA Panel from Hell—'AIDS and the Social Imaginary.'" *SOLGAN* 15 (1): 20–32.

Appadurai, Arjun. 1990. "Disjuncture and Difference in the Global Cultural Economy." *Public Culture* 2 (2): 1–24.

Asad, Talal. 1975. *Anthropology and the Colonial Encounter*. London: Ithaca Press.

Bosco, Joseph. 1995. Review of *Taiwanese Culture, Taiwanese Society: A Critical Review of Social Science Research Done on Taiwan*, by Stephen O. Murray and Keelung Hong. *China Quarterly* 143 (September): 873–74.

———. 2007. Review of *Looking through Taiwan: American Anthropologists' Collusion with Ethnic Domination*, by Keelung Hong and Stephen O. Murray. *China Journal* 57 (January): 195–98.

Brown, Melissa J. 2019. "Tigers on the Mountain: Assessing *Is Taiwan Chinese?* in 2018." In *Taiwan Studies Revisited*, edited by Dafydd Fell and Hsin-Huang Michael Hsiao, 112–40. New York: Routledge.

Fell, Dafydd. 2008. "The Role of SOAS in the Development of European Taiwan Studies." In *Proceedings for Taiwan Studies in Global Perspectives*, 1–15. Santa Barbara: Center for Taiwan Studies, University of California at Santa Barbara.

Fell, Dafydd, and Sung-sheng Yvonne Chang. 2019. "Developing Taiwan Studies Teaching Programmes in Europe and the U.S.: The Experience of SOAS University of London and the University of Texas at Austin." *China Quarterly* 240 (December): 1108–34.

Fell, Dafydd, and Hsin-Huang Michael Hsiao. 2019. "Taiwan Studies Revisited." In *Taiwan Studies Revisited*, eds. Dafydd Fell and Hsin-Huang Michael Hsiao, 1–12. New York: Routledge.

Fiskesjö, Magnus. 2020. "Cultural Genocide is the New Genocide." *Pen/Opp*, May 5. https://www.penopp.org/articles/cultural-genocide-new-genocide.

Gupta, Akhil and James Ferguson. 1992. "Beyond 'Culture': Space, Identity, and the Politics of Difference." *Cultural Anthropology* 7 (1): 6–23.

Harrell, Stevan. 1989. "Politics and Scholarship on Taiwan: Some Errors of Murray and Hong." *American Anthropologist* 91 (4): 1026–28.

Herz, Peter Jeffrey. 1996. Review of *Taiwanese Culture, Taiwanese Society: A Critical Review of Social Science Research Done on Taiwan*, by Stephen O. Murray and Keelung Hong. *China Information* 11 (1): 157–59.

Hong, Keelung, and Stephen O. Murray. 1989. "Complicity with Domination." *American Anthropologist* 91 (4): 1028–1030.

———. 2005. *Looking through Taiwan: American Anthropologists' Collusion with Ethnic Domination*. Lincoln: University of Nebraska Press.

Janelli, Roger L., and Dawnhee Yim Janelli. 1982. *Ancestor Worship and Korean Society*. Stanford: Stanford University Press.

Jordan, David K. 1987. Review of *Unities and Diversities in Chinese Religion*, by Robert P. Weller. *American Anthropologist* 89 (4): 995.

———. 1988. "Response to Murray and Hong." *American Anthropologist* 90 (4): 978.

Kendall, Laurel. 1985. *Shamans, Housewives, and Other Restless Spirits: Women in Korean Ritual Life*. Honolulu: University of Hawai'i Press.

Lai Tse-Han, Ramon H. Myers, and Wei Wou. 1991. *A Tragic Beginning: The Taiwan Uprising of February 28, 1947*. Stanford: Stanford University Press.

Law, John. 2004. *After Method: Mess in Social Science Research*. New York: Routledge.

Lin, Sylvia Li-chun. 2006. Review of *Looking through Taiwan: American Anthropologists' Collusion with Ethnic Domination*, by Keelung Hong and Stephen O. Murray. *China Review International* 13 (1): 133–37.

Marcus, George. 1995. "Ethnography in/of the World System: The Emergence of Multi-Sited Ethnography." *Annual Review of Anthropology* 24 (October): 95–117.

Murray, Stephen O. 1988. "The Invisibility of the Taiwanese." *Taiwan Culture* 18:3–8.

Murray, Stephen O., and Keelung Hong. 1988. "Taiwan, China, and the 'Objectivity' of Dictatorial Elites." *American Anthropologist* 90 (4): 976–78.

———. 1991. "American Anthropologists Looking through Taiwanese Culture." *Dialectical Anthropology* 16 (3/4): 273–99.

———. 1994. *Taiwanese Culture, Taiwanese Society*. Lanham MD: University Press of America.

Murray, Stephen O., Wendy Leeds-Hurwitz, Regna Darnell, Nathan Dawthorne, and Robert Oppenheim. 2021. "An Interview with Stephen O. Murray on Stephen O. Murray as Historian of Anthropology (and More)." In *Centering the Margins of Anthropology's History*, edited by Regna Darnell and Frederic W. Gleach, 243–68. Lincoln: University of Nebraska Press.

Oppenheim, Robert. 2007. "Actor-Network Theory and Anthropology after Science, Technology, and Society." *Anthropological Theory* 7 (4): 471–93.

———. 2008. *Kyŏngju Things: Assembling Place*. Ann Arbor: University of Michigan Press.

———. 2010. "Revisiting Hrdlička and Boas: Asymmetries of Race and Anti-Imperialism in Interwar Anthropology." *American Anthropologist* 112 (1): 92–103.

———. 2016. *An Asian Frontier: American Anthropology and Korea, 1882–1945*. Lincoln: University of Nebraska Press.

Paradise, James F. 2009. "China and International Harmony: The Role of Confucius Institutes in Bolstering Beijing's Soft Power." *Asian Survey* 49 (4): 647–69.

Rubinstein, Murray. 2013. "Studying 'Taiwan Studies': The Evolution and the Transformations of a Multi-Disciplinary Sub-field, 1600 CE to 2013 CE." Accessed March 5, 2023. https://aacs.ccny.cuny.edu/2013conference/Papers/Rubenstein%20murray_1.pdf.

Ryang, Sonia. 2021. *Language and Truth in North Korea*. Honolulu: University of Hawai'i Press.

Shih, Shu-Mei. 2003. "Globalisation and the (In)significance of Taiwan." *Postcolonial Studies* 6 (2): 143–53.

Simon, Scott. 2018. "Ontologies of Taiwan Studies, Indigenous Studies, and Anthropology." *International Journal of Taiwan Studies* 1 (1): 11–35.

Steffen, Megan. 2020. "Refusing to Inherit 'China': The Troubled Histories and Continuities of an Anthropological Object." *Transnational Asia: An Online Interdisciplinary Journal* 4, no. 1 (March). https://doi.org/10.25615/9bgt-hz22.

Thernstrom, Stephan, ed. 1980. *Harvard Encyclopedia of American Ethnic Groups*. Cambridge: Belknap Press of Harvard University Press.

Tremlett, Paul-François. 2006. Review of *Looking through Taiwan: American Anthropologists' Collusion with Ethnic Domination*, by Keelung Hong and Stephen O. Murray. *Bulletin of the School of Oriental and African Studies* 69 (3): 497–99.

———. 2009. "Introduction: Re-writing Culture on Taiwan." In *Re-writing Culture in Taiwan*, edited by Fang-long Shih, Stuart Thompson, and Paul-François Tremlett, 1–14. New York: Routledge.

Vasantkumar, Chris. 2013. "The Scale of Scatter: Rethinking Social Topologies via the Anthropology of 'Residual' China." *Environment and Planning D: Society and Space* 31 (5): 918–34.

Weller, Robert P. 1987. *Unities and Diversities in Chinese Religion*. Seattle: University of Washington Press.

Winterhalder, Astrid. 1996. Review of *Taiwanese Culture, Taiwanese Society: A Critical Review of Social Science Research Done on Taiwan*, by Stephen O. Murray and Keelung Hong. *Anthropos* 91 (4/6): 620–23.

Zheng, Chantal. 2006. Review of *Looking through Taiwan: American Anthropologists' Collusion with Ethnic Domination*, by Keelung Hong and Stephen O. Murray. *Moussons* 9–10. https://doi.org/10.4000/moussons.1957.

5 "AIDS and the Social Imaginary" Thirty Years Later

A CONTROVERSIAL EARLY SKIRMISH IN THE DECOLONIZING OF ANTHROPOLOGY

Ralph Bolton

A session at the annual meeting of the American Anthropological Association (AAA) incites controversy and confrontation every few years. The year 2022 marked the thirtieth anniversary of one such unsettling event, the incendiary panel entitled "AIDS and the Social Imaginary" organized by Nancy Scheper-Hughes and Paul Rabinow for the 1992 meeting in San Francisco. This controversial session took place in an atmosphere of intense emotions and resistance and attracted a standing-room-only audience with attendees sitting on the floor as well as standing along all the walls of the large conference room; others tried to listen from the hallway beyond the open doors. Many who had planned to attend could not get in because of the crowded conditions of the room. An estimated three hundred people squeezed into the auditorium, attracted by the big names of the official panelists, by the topic of AIDS, and by advance reports that the event would prove to be contentious.

Although younger generations of scholars may not know about this event, its importance at that time is beyond doubt; it unsettled the landscape of professional anthropology and was a significant forerunner to contemporary efforts to unsettle the landscapes of power within anthropology. The event garnered press coverage locally in the *Bay Area Reporter* (Conkin 1992), a widely circulated LGBTQ publication, and nationally among academics in the *Chronicle of Higher Education* (Coughlin 1992). Scheper-Hughes (2021b) has displayed ongoing preoccupation with the event more recently. Her memoir after Rabinow's death devoted five of its six pages to the session and AIDS and included little else (Scheper-Hughes 2021b). Although Rabinow is well-known for many of his works, as per the notice of his death on the University of California, Berkeley website (Anwar 2021) and his Wikipedia page, research or publications on AIDS are not salient among them.

I decided to document this event for three reasons: Steve was a key participant in the social imaginary event in 1992; he had a strong interest in the history of anthropology; and he was among the pioneers who fought for gay rights within the anthropological and sociological contexts. I thought it important to have a correct historical record, given misinformation as well as fading memories, and not to allow elitist, revisionist accounts to go unanswered and uncorrected.

Numerous anthropologists wrote to Steve after the event to express their support and to comment on the session, using such terms as "appalling" to describe what they had witnessed on the part of the panelists. They often stressed the significance of the session as being of singular importance in the history of twentieth-century anthropology and as "moving." One correspondent asserted that there had not been such a powerful critique of the "colonial politics" of anthropology since the days of the Vietnam War and that the event opened the first public discussion of how the discipline, inadvertently or not, acts to wound its own members. Without permission of the authors, copyright laws prevent me from including these letters here, despite their relevance. One distinguished anthropologist refused permission to quote her, even "anonymously." Such censorship of materials related to the session renders a comprehensive account of the event problematic, and the cowardice of self-censorship is reprehensible. Such regrettable gaps indicate how far we must go to reach a point at which our anthropological analyses handle issues responsibly and honestly.[1]

This session was seared into the memory of many in the LGBTQ and HIV/AIDS communities and was deeply painful to them. One activist attendee, a graduate student at a Bay Area university at the time, wrote to me as I was preparing this chapter: "I'm almost 60, and these events from 30 years ago still haunt me" (personal communication, November 11, 2022). Another person involved stated: "It's not an episode I enjoy thinking about. . . . I realize now that the pain it triggers is connected to the fact that it was a moment of being reminded how powerless you were as a queer. Which is a moment of shame" (personal communication, May 12, 2021).

Session on "AIDS and the Social Imaginary"

The program of the ninety-first annual meeting of the American Anthropological Association, San Francisco, December 2–6, 1992 (American Anthropological Association 1992), lists this session:

3-050 AIDS AND THE SOCIAL IMAGINARY YOSEMITE B

12:00	Chairs: PAUL RABINOW (California–Berkeley) and NANCY SCHEPER-HUGHES (California–Berkeley)
1:30	PAUL RABINOW (California–Berkeley)
	NANCY SCHEPER-HUGHES (California–Berkeley)
	JEAN COMAROFF (Chicago)
	RENATO ROSALDO (Stanford)
	EMILY MARTIN (Johns Hopkins)
	MICHAEL TAUSSIG (New York)
	ARTHUR KLEINMAN
	JOHN O'NEIL

The "List of Panel Participants" included in the program does not correspond to the list of scholars who actually spoke. Media and individual accounts indicate that presentations were made by Scheper-Hughes, Rabinow, Taussig, Rosaldo, and Comaroff. Kleinman, Martin, and O'Neil did not show up.[2] To clarify the absence of these three scholars, I wrote to each of them to inquire about their apparent absence. Emily Martin replied that after looking for relevant materials, she found nothing and remembers nothing about the session. She does not list it on her curriculum vitae. Arthur Kleinman reported no memory of this event or knowledge of the controversy and had no idea if he had participated or agreed to participate. I googled the name John O'Neil and found someone by that name who replied to my query. He responded that, after checking his files, "I wracked my brain" and found nothing. Although no affiliation was given for him on the program, he received his degree at the University of California, Berkeley and knew Scheper-Hughes but had not yet worked on AIDS at the time of the session; he did so many years later. He thought it might be some other John O'Neil. This led to a John O'Neill, a sociologist, also in Canada, who had recently passed away. O'Neill published "AIDS as a Globalizing Panic" in *Theory, Culture & Society* in 1990, an article mentioned in the syllabus for a course on AIDS co-taught by Rabinow and Scheper-Hughes (1992). Most likely, then, O'Neill was the one listed in the program.

The session was billed as a panel discussion and provided no paper titles, nor did any papers go through the normal vetting process for AAA conferences. From the outset the session was designed to present papers by distinguished and powerful anthropologists working at elite universities. Scheper-Hughes and Rabinow explained their purposes for organizing this session in a letter to the participants; they acknowledged that they were not experts on AIDS and had done little or no research on the topic but thought they could call attention to the epidemic and underscore its importance by lending their good names to the cause, despite the remarkable hubris this implied. It is possible to argue that they intended the session to be a provocation from the outset. Some correspondence suggests that the organizers conveyed to the AAA staff that they expected a disturbance, and there was discussion about extra hotel security to monitor the situation.[3]

When the preliminary program for the 1992 annual meeting became available, knowledge of the panel's scheduling became public. An immediate, vigorous reaction was reflected in a flurry of communications between the organizers, the leadership of the Society of Lesbian and Gay Anthropologists (SOLGA), the program committee of the AAA, and the leadership and staff of AAA.

The Resistance: SOLGA and AARG

Members of two organizations that hold sessions during annual meetings of the AAA expressed their consternation: the Society of Lesbian and Gay Anthropologists, later renamed the Association of Queer Anthropologists, and the AIDS and Anthropology Research Group (AARG), a subunit of the Society for Medical Anthropology. Members of these two organizations spearheaded the reaction to the panel. The immediate aim of the resistance was to expand the panel to include someone who could speak on behalf of communities most affected by AIDS. The senior cochair of SOLGA, Jeffrey Dickemann principally, the panel organizers, and the leadership of AAA entered into negotiations. The panel organizers refused to consider this request, and we are not privy to the reasons for the rejection. With three listed panelists not participating, adding one more speaker designated by SOLGA or AARG for the discussion would have been simple. At the time of these negotiations, however, the organizers may still have expected the participation of seven of the eight people listed in the program. They sent a memo to the anticipated participants urging them to keep their presentations to ten minutes each, for a total of seventy of the ninety minutes allotted to the session. The actual session did not include a discussion because presentation of the prepared papers filled the time available.

The panel organizers proposed a "compromise" in which someone from SOLGA would be the first recognized speaker after the papers were presented. Dickemann advocated for a designated first commentator after the panelists read their papers. The panel eventually agreed to this plan, although at one point, Scheper-Hughes communicated with Dickemann telling him to hold off notifying me as Scheper-Hughes was still negotiating this with Rabinow. My selection for this position made sense since I was the incoming senior cochair of SOLGA that year, I had a history of working on AIDS that began in 1983–84, I was active in the leadership of AARG and served as its chair in 1991, I was a member of the AAA AIDS and Anthropology Task Force, and I was an openly gay anthropologist. At the same time, I was not part of the negotiations and did not offer to be this designated person. Once appointed, I was told that I would have one minute to respond.

When the panelists finished delivering their papers, I was invited to the podium to respond. I wanted to put a face on the topic, a real human being, not an imaginary one. We needed someone who lived in this community that had suffered so much, who was living with HIV, and was surrounded by the epidemic every day from the onset of the epidemic, someone who had excellent credentials as a specialist on homosexualities around the world, and who had fought for the rights of LGBTQ people within the American Anthropological Association and the American Sociological Association beginning in the 1970s. Thus I invited Stephen Murray to deliver the first remarks as someone who could represent the community of persons living with AIDS. Stephen was not eager to do it but acquiesced. Regna Darnell reports: "I sat next to him, and he was shaking, nervous but determined" (personal communication, September 14, 2020).

I spoke briefly after Stephen concluded his remarks. The thrust of my remarks was: "Where have you [i.e., the panelists] been? Why were you not speaking out ten years ago when it really mattered, and your high-profile status as elite members of the profession could have made a difference? Why were you silent then?" Although time had run out, audience members insisted on speaking. Little time was left for them to talk since the papers had taken up almost the entire allotted time. The session ended when it was necessary to clear the room for the next session. Scheper-Hughes fled out the back door of the auditorium, reportedly in a state of emotional distress (tears), on her way to her next paper session, which was about to begin (Michael Clatts, personal communication, independently confirming what I witnessed, April 30, 2020).

Objections to the Session

Much of the drama that unfolded that day could have been avoided, in my opinion, if the organizers had permitted the addition of one speaker to represent one or more of the communities most severely affected by AIDS, both locally and within the profession, the "natives." The organizers' intransigence was perceived as arrogant, insulting and condescending, an infliction of further alienation and discrimination, an expression of elite hubris, power, and control. SOLGA and AARG members fought back: leaflets denouncing the panel and panelists were distributed as people entered the room before the session. Many members of both organizations wore T-shirts with the slogan "These natives can speak for themselves." The time for speaking truth to power had arrived. Those who managed to speak during the closing minutes of the session did not hold back in denouncing the panel.

Reasons for the antipathy toward this panel include, first, the lack of diversity on it. The panel consisted of white, presumably heterosexual anthropologists from elite institutions, none of whom was at that point seriously engaged in research on AIDS or an activist on the AIDS front or involved in gay rights concerns. Specifically, there was no openly gay

> *These Natives can speak for themselves*
>
> SOLGA

Fig. 2. SOLGA T-shirt. Photo by Ralph Bolton.

member of the panel. By this time in the pandemic many gay anthropologists had been engaged with the AIDS crisis for years. Gilbert Herdt (Chicago) comes to mind as someone who would have been an appropriate choice. He was well-known in the profession and teaching at an elite institution. He has no memory of having been invited to be on the panel (personal communication, October 29, 2022). No one for whom AIDS was a major research interest was on the panel. Paul Farmer (Harvard University and Partners in Health) would have been a logical person to represent serious AIDS researchers; as a specialist on Haiti, he was drawn early to the topic to defend Haitians against blame for the epidemic leveled against them (Farmer 1992). Herdt and Farmer do not appear anywhere in the 1992 program, so their participation would not have violated conference rules on multiple presentations. Herdt recalls that he was in the audience and thinks Farmer was present also (personal communication, October 30, 2022).

Rosaldo, the son of an Anglo mother and a Mexican father, identifies as Chicano and could be considered to represent a person of color on the panel. He seems to have recognized the problematic nature of the panel's composition. In the *American Anthropologist* in 1994, he published a piece about cultural studies that recognized the need for inclusiveness, with an obvious allusion to the "AIDS and the Social Imaginary" debacle. He wrote: "Changing search procedures to get appropriate qualified people in the room should apply to conference panels, academic committees, reading groups, classroom teaching, authors assigned in courses, and authors cited in talks, published articles, and books. Of course, men should speak about women and vice versa, but would an all-male panel speak about women? Should an all-white edited collection address issues of race or multiculturalism? How often should all-straight, all-white panels talk about AIDS? There are differences between speaking as an X, discussing with an X, and talking about an X" (Rosaldo 1994, 528). In short, the panel consisted of individuals who were least impacted by the pandemic. If a panel on racism had no person of color on it, it would be condemned. If a panel on women's issues had no women on it, it would be condemned. If a panel on antisemitism included no Jews, it would be condemned. And if it took negotiations to try to gain representation with just one individual, there would be outrage.

The most affected individuals would be persons living with AIDS, and no one in that situation was invited to serve on the panel. With the epicenter of the pandemic less than a mile away (the Castro district) in the city most affected at that time, it would have been easy to find someone to represent that community or to speak to the experience of living with AIDS, especially since the organizers themselves lived in the Bay Area. Instead of giving voice to those affected, the panelists addressed the crowd on their behalf. Given that two listed panelists (Scheper-Hughes and Kleinman) have focused their careers on the "suffering" of others, sensitivity to issues of representation of suffering is not an unreasonable expectation.

Third, no person on the panel was seriously involved in the major AIDS research organization AARG or deeply engaged with the pandemic on either a personal or professional level. The leading AIDS investigators in anthropology in those early years, I think it is fair to say, focused on the AIDS crisis in many ways and at some risk to their careers. Many dropped everything else to respond to the crisis. In my own case, I first learned about the existence of the "gay cancer" in early 1983 while cross-country skiing in Norway with a friend who asked me about it. I was oblivious at the time. When I returned home that summer, I became involved in multiple ways, with multiple organizations.[4] I began research in 1984 and began giving papers on AIDS topics in 1985. By the time of the AAA session on the social imaginary, I had given papers reporting on my work at conferences of the American Anthropological Association, the Society for Applied Anthropology, the Society for Cross-Cultural Research, and the Southwestern Anthropological Association, among others, in addition to participating in specialized conferences on HIV/AIDS. I had worked on an AIDS bibliography project (Bolton and Kempler 1992; Bolton and Orozco 1991, 1994) and had edited several journal issues (Bolton 1989; Bolton and Singer 1992a, 1992b). I incorporated AIDS into my medical anthropology course and began to teach human sexuality courses in order to promote knowledge that might save students' lives. I had also coauthored a book on Flemish gay male culture and AIDS (Vincke, Mak, and Bolton 1991).

Although I look back and take satisfaction in having done what I could during the early years of the AIDS crisis, I recite this not to pat myself on the back but rather to provide an example of an anthropologist who is committed to the cause. Other anthropologists, especially gay men in the first several years and later others, were doing as much or even more. AIDS was not a passing fad. It was not a bandwagon to enhance our careers or professional visibility; it was work on the ground, often with minimal resources, a matter of life and death, our own and those of our friends and communities. We were not pontificating about largely irrelevant grand theoretical schemes but were down in the trenches doing the necessary work of ordinary science in an extraordinary time on a topic neither fashionable nor likely to advance one's career. I have the greatest admiration for those who were in the trenches early and for whom there was nothing imaginary about what they faced. To name a few who deserve credit for being pioneers: Douglas Feldman, Norris Lang, Michael Clatts, Janet McGrath, Brooke Schoepf, Gilbert Herdt, Robert Carlson, Shirley Lindenbaum, Patricia Whelahan, Martha Ward, Moses Pound, Carl Kendall, Paul Farmer, Bryan Page, Stephen Eyre, Ron Stall, Joseph Carrier, Stephanie Kane, Susan McCombie, Raul Magaña, Douglas Goldsmith, Michael Gorman, Claire Sterk, Patricia Marshall, Ruth Wilson, Merrill Singer, Michele Shedlin (with apologies to others not mentioned by name). Indeed, a full six years before the panel, Ron Stall published in *Medical Anthropology Quarterly* an appeal to anthropologists to respond to AIDS. By the time of the "AIDS and the Social Imaginary" session, perhaps one hundred or more anthropologists were deeply involved in AIDS research in Africa, the United States, and Europe, among women, drug addicts, sex workers, and ethnic and sexual minorities. Although gay men may have been first to organize in response to AIDS and the first "risk group" studied, by 1992 they constituted a minority of anthropological researchers on AIDS, and overwhelmingly research was being carried out among populations other than gay men (Feldman 1986, 1989; Fernando 1993; Kane and Mason 1992).[5]

By the time of this session, anthropologists seriously engaged with the pandemic had participated in numerous major AIDS-focused conferences.[6] None of the panelists who spoke had participated in any of these AIDS conferences involving anthropologists; not one was an active member of AARG, the major organization of anthropologists involved in AIDS research; and for none of these panelists was AIDS a primary research concern either before or after the debacle.[7]

The session organizers were known to entertain or espouse views on the epidemic that most AIDS researchers considered both wrong and dangerous, in keeping with Scheper-Hughes's self-identification as an "AIDS heretic" (Bolton, n.d.; Scheper-Hughes 2021a, 2021b). Although I do not recall being aware of this at the time, evidence suggests that Rabinow was sympathetic toward the views of Peter Duesberg, a true AIDS heretic and a colleague at Berkeley.[8] Duesberg, it should be noted, claimed that HIV did not cause AIDS, blaming the syndrome instead on lifestyle factors (notably drug usage in gay communities that destroyed the immune system). Scheper-Hughes (2021a, 2021b) stated in an obituary for Rabinow: "Paul Rabinow had begun his study of the HIV/AIDS epidemic following Peter Duesberg, then a still highly respected UC Berkeley Professor of Molecular Biology, who in 1991 released a report entitled 'Everything You Know about AIDS Is Wrong.' Duesberg described HIV as a harmless fellow traveler along for the ride. Paul Rabinow was initially intrigued by Duesberg's conclusions." Translated into responses to COVID-19, this is the equivalent of denying the role of the coronavirus in the pandemic that has killed more than one million Americans. Duesberg was the primary figure in the AIDS denialism movement and used his prominence to bypass standard rules for publishing his unfounded views.[9]

Scheper-Hughes (1993a, 1993b, 1993c, 1994, 2020) also defended the quarantine policies implemented in Cuba to control the spread of HIV. This is not the place to rehash the arguments about the Cuban approach to AIDS (for Murray's position, see 1993a), but the context of the counter-reaction is significant. Similar policies were being advocated in the United States by prominent politicians such as Senator Jesse Helms, who urged rounding up infected individuals and placing them in quarantine. The targeted community fought against this threat. (There was a joke making the rounds in the gay community at the time that quarantine might not be too bad if they gave us an island in Hawai'i—a thinly veiled reference to the leprosy colony that had existed on the island of Molokai.) During the early years of the Cuban Revolution, the Castro regime had a terrible history of repression toward sexual "deviants"; re-education work camps were set up and gays were rounded up and sent to these forced labor camps to be turned into "real" men.[10] Quarantine for a disease that is spread behaviorally rather than airborne is an extreme measure that presumably would be instated for the duration of a person's life or until a cure could be found (no cure exists at the time of this writing, thirty years later). Quarantine was opposed by both national and international health agencies as inappropriate, misguided, and unnecessary. Scheper-Hughes's defense of quarantine measures came not from intensive fieldwork but rather from two brief trips to Cuba, where she was allowed to visit a sanitorium and interview a health authority. Conceivably, ideology overrode science in this matter. Such jet-set or tourist ethnography manifested itself during her talk when she discussed her visit to an AIDS ward in Brazil that reeked of feces, with patients uncared for as she interviewed the staff (Scheper-Hughes, Araujo, and Paredes 1992).

Perhaps the most significant factor that energized the negative response was the blatant exercise of power and influence by a small group of elite anthropologists for whom normal rules did not apply. Paraphrasing Leona Helmsley, "only little people have to pay taxes"; in the case of the "Social Imaginary" panel, the organizers of the panel demonstrated a total disregard for rules, specifically the AAA's rules about giving multiple papers at the annual meeting, and the procedures for approving and scheduling sessions and labeling papers or discussions accurately as such. This was particularly appalling given that some paper proposals dealing with AIDS had to be rejected for lack of space in the program.

The panel as constituted was a clear case of elitism, opportunism, and condescension. Now that AIDS research opportunities had expanded considerably, funding was becoming available and it was no longer as stigmatizing to do research on AIDS, the elite would swoop in, having ignored the pandemic for a decade, to appropriate the narrative whose way had been paved by serious anthropologists. The Johnny-come-latelies would legitimize the study of AIDS, though many others were already engaged in research and action on AIDS and it needed no legitimation. The panelists would represent the voices of people they claimed, falsely, were not being heard—women, heterosexuals, et cetera—they would blame the victims, in this instance, gay men. They acknowledged their intention to lend their "good names" and "celebrity" status to call attention to AIDS, which was viewed by many as arrogant, presumptuous, and reprehensible.[11] They also proclaimed: "we are all people living with AIDS" (a phrase lifted from an article with that title by Herbert Daniel, 1991), but they were living on the periphery, living with it in the imaginary worlds they inhabited. I have no doubt that some of the panelists knew people who had died from AIDS: students, colleagues, family members, or friends. Rabinow himself mourned the loss of his friend Foucault, who had died eight years earlier. Explaining Foucault to American academics had been, after all, one of Rabinow's missions in life and claims to fame. When it came to being the voice to be heard on AIDS, it was the panelists' voices, to the exclusion of people who were truly living with AIDS in their personal and professional lives.

It also was explicit that at least Scheper-Hughes dismissed most work done by anthropologists on AIDS as worthless, repetitive, and unimaginative. This disdain for the work of dozens of anthropologists, without going into details, was insulting and baseless. I do not claim that the work of anthropologists doing research on AIDS was above criticism; I myself have been critical of some of the research work being done, but it is indefensible as a blanket statement. Anthropologists were engaged in understanding AIDS and behavior on the ground, in difficult ethnographic fieldwork in shooting galleries, in favelas, among sex workers, in gay bathhouses, and in other poorly understood venues where transmission of HIV was allegedly taking place and were engaged in the search for ways to reduce transmission, among many other topics being studied, including healthcare access, stigma, and discrimination.

The opportunism was palpable: when it was unfashionable to be involved with AIDS, the panelists had remained quiet; when there was no funding for AIDS research, they stood back. But things had changed: now there was some funding that their good names would allow them to access; consultancies would be up for grabs.[12] Scheper-Hughes reported in 1992 that she served as a consultant to the Ford Foundation in Brazil on AIDS and reproductive health (Rabinow and Scheper-Hughes, letter to the panelists, October 16, 1992). To burnish one's AIDS credentials by placing a prominent session at the AAA on one's curriculum vitae would provide credibility. It is worth quoting this letter:

> We are writing to explain the thinking behind the organization of our panel "AIDS and the Social Imaginary," as well as its current status. We wanted our panel to contribute to underlining consciousness of AIDS at the meetings. We knew there would be other panels, quite possibly more specialized ones. We felt, and still feel, more presence, more discussion, more diversity is better than less. We felt, and still feel, that as critical cultural anthropologists of various stripes we could make a distinctive contribution both by highlighting some general issues but also by focusing attention on the importance of AIDS for everyone. We hoped that this gesture would be taken as it was intended—as one of solidarity aimed at enhancing the overall attention to the issue.
>
> We feel we are qualified to raise issues (and anthropological consciousness about AIDS). We have long-standing critical positions on methodology and politics in the social sciences which would lead us

to question and to critique some current work on AIDS. We put considerable thought into the composition of our panel which is a rather tightly organized 90-minute discussion among seven anthropologists. We would be happy to invite Ralph Bolton to open the discussion period, although we are concerned that there be enough time remaining for audience participation. We look forward to seeing you at the meetings.

What Did the Panelists Have to Say?

Absent a recording of the session, I must rely on what others close in time to the event reported on the content of the papers the five panelists presented and the atmosphere in which they were presented. To my knowledge, none of these papers were ever published. Scheper-Hughes (2021b) recalls the content of the presentations as follows:

> The room was a jumble, hot, loud and threatening. People were pushing each other to get inside the room. It felt like the beginning of an insurrection. I wanted to call the hotel security. But the speakers began. Jean Comaroff discussed the racism associating the origins of HIV with Black Africa (similar to today's Asian origin of Covid-19). Mick Taussig read a paper with extensive quotes from the book *Closer to the Knives*, an AIDS memoir by David Wojnarowicz supplemented with four slides of artwork which may have been painted or sketched by Taussig, but their relevance to the paper was questioned. I spoke about AIDS and Brazilian women, transvestites, prostitutes and street kids who had been infected with AIDS and left without any government health support, which I contrasted to the medical success of the Cuban AIDS sanatorium albeit at the cost of authoritarianism and individual freedom. Paul Rabinow spoke about AIDS, ethics, activism and politics in AIDS research. He compared the work of Peter Duesberg (the AIDS denier) and Robert Gallo, an American biomedical researcher who was once known for his discovery of HIV as the agent responsible for AIDS. Gallo and his collaborators published a series of papers in Science demonstrating that a retrovirus that they alone had isolated, called HTLV-III, was the cause of AIDS beating the French discovery. Both Rosaldo and Bolton were acutely aware of the situation and both stayed in the audience in an attempt to show their support for the protestors. When Bolton was

called up to speak as the invited discussant he introduced a second uninvited discussant, Steven O. Murray (who died in California in 2019 from an aggressive diffuse large B-cell lymphoma) repeated Bolton's "anti-elitist" and "anti-colonialist" accusation to the panelists and demanded that all AAA panels must include sexual diversity.

Scheper-Hughes's account is marred by a series of inaccuracies. It suggests that I spoke before Steve did. I spoke first only to introduce Steve; my own critique came after his. Elsewhere in her recollections of the session, Scheper-Hughes (2021b) alleges that a "protestor was swinging a chain that had been wrapped around her body toward Paul and me." Something that dramatic would certainly be remembered. No one to whom I have spoken about the sessions remembers any such occurrence. Inaccuracies aside, Scheper-Hughes's summation of the content and of the papers can stand as a description. Will Roscoe (n.d.), in a document he circulated but never published, wrote a scathing critique of each paper based on such points as the following: unoriginal appropriation of the work of others (Taussig on David Wojnarowicz); sensationalist gestures and assigning blame for AIDS conditions in Brazil on North American gay men and insensitivity in the field context (Scheper-Hughes); the use of an "arrival story" to assert claims of ethnographic authority (Comaroff and others), even when the material presented is derived from the work of a research assistant; apparent unfamiliarity of some presenters with relevant work (e.g., that of Paula Treichler, in the case of Comaroff); foci unrelated to the supposed subject of the session (Rosaldo discussed LGBTQ issues at Stanford); claiming authority to speak based on knowing someone who died of AIDS (Rabinow on Michel Foucault).

Contextualizing "AIDS and the Social Imaginary"

Understanding the intensity of the response to this panel necessitates placing it in the context of its time for both the AIDS pandemic and sexual minorities. The circumstances prevailing at that time may not be evident to younger generations, but the relevance to the present of what transpired then should be clear, especially given intensifying efforts to overturn the human rights gains achieved by LGBTQ communities in recent years as they come under assault by the Supreme Court and right-wing politicians at all levels of government—local, state, and national—in the United States and in other, fascist-leaning countries as well.

The AIDS Context

The year 1992 was several years before effective medications to prolong the lives of persons living with AIDS became available; AIDS was for most a death sentence. Stephen was among those labeled as long-term survivors; though spared death, long-term survivors suffered to varying degrees the maladies associated with an HIV infection. People living with AIDS also endured the stigma attached to the disease, and the blame was placed on these members of the gay community for bringing this disaster upon themselves and society. Moreover, various aspects of HIV/AIDS were criminalized.

Early in the epidemic, (unrealistic) promises were made that a vaccine or a cure or both would be forthcoming within a short time, but neither materialized. Nor did calls for quarantining people with AIDS. AIDS activism had exploded with the creative resistance to official neglect reflected in the media-savvy activities of ACT UP at this time. While gay institutions such as bathhouses were under attack by politicians and public health officials, gay men had responded to AIDS with one of the rapidest instances in history of behavioral transformation in response to a disease with the invention of safer sex. At the same time, while the Reagan administration ignored the crisis occurring predominantly in the first years in gay communities such as in San Francisco and New York, gay men, lesbians, and their allies mounted a massive response to the pandemic, creating nonprofit advocacy and activist organizations devoted to AIDS issues, caring for the sick and dying, and trying desperately to mobilize society as a whole to respond to the crisis. Enormous marches took place, and the AIDS Quilt, a memorial to those who had died from AIDS, went on display in 1987 at the National Mall in Washington DC (National AIDS Memorial n.d.). In 1992 AIDS was the number 1 cause of death for men between the ages of 25–44 in the United States, and 2,332 AIDS deaths were registered in San Francisco alone that year, according to the CDC.

The Gay Rights Context

The context of the social situation for sexual minorities is no less important than the AIDS context. Although there were antecedents in the United States and elsewhere, the impetus for the emergence of a major civil rights movement organizing to demand equal rights for sexual minorities sprang from the 1969 riots at the Stonewall Inn in Greenwich Village, New York. That event provided the spark that ignited what can be considered one of the top three civil rights movements in the history of the United States.[13] Responding to the repression exercised by police, brave individuals fought back, and riots raged for three days; gay rights organizations were formed, and the struggle was engaged in many arenas and on many issues, with considerable success. It is important to note, however, that sexual relations between members of the same sex were still illegal in twenty-two states in 1992. This was three years before the U.S. Supreme Court, in *Obergefell v. Hodges*, decriminalized same-sex behavior; it was before marriage equality was on the near horizon, although the issue was already being raised; it was around the time when gays and lesbians did not have the right to serve in the military, and the compromise worked out at the time allowed LGBTQ individuals to serve as long as they remained in the closet: "Don't Ask, Don't Tell." Discrimination against LGBTQ individuals was legal. Only days before the meeting, Colorado voters passed Amendment 2, which prohibited the state and municipalities from enacting antidiscrimination policies, an amendment eventually declared unconstitutional by the U.S. Supreme Court in 1996 (*Romer v. Evans*).

AIDS struck just as sexual minorities were beginning to get a taste of sexual freedom, and the 1970s had been an exuberant time. Members of sexual minorities flocked to places like San Francisco, forming ghettos where they could live as they pleased, though not entirely free of discrimination, homophobia, and violence. In San Francisco in 1978, Harvey Milk, a gay rights leader elected to the city council, was assassinated along with the mayor in an antigay hate crime. These events were part of the mindset of the anthropologists who reacted to what was perceived by protestors as the disguised homophobia of this panel, blaming gays for

AIDS and entertaining AIDS policies that would be harmful to them and their communities.

Anthropological Context

The discipline of anthropology was one of the slowest to respond to the movement for LGBTQ rights. Numerous prominent gay, lesbian, and bisexual anthropologists were professionally active in the 1960s and 1970s, but they were almost entirely closeted (Kutsche 1993; Read 1997). Younger anthropologists began to agitate for actions in defense of the LGBTQ minority. The first symposium on gay issues at an annual meeting took place in Mexico City in 1974, with Margaret Mead as a discussant. The activists were largely young scholars who were discriminated against in the job market, especially if they had studied gay and lesbian cultures. As Murray put it, in describing the problem in his own life, "With a partly 'lavender resumé,' I could not even get a job interview, let alone a tenure-track job" (2019; see Murray 1985 for a broader discussion). In 1978 a small group of activists founded the Anthropological Research Group on Homosexuality, better known as ARGOH. Some of these pioneers also became AIDS advocates, activists, or researchers early in the pandemic (e.g., Joe Carrier, Kenneth Payne, Stephen Murray, and Clark Taylor).

In 1987 the ARGOH membership approved a name change to become the Society of Lesbian and Gay Anthropologists. The name change reflected a greater openness and a move from an emphasis on who is studied to who is studying; in other words, it became an identity-based organization. In 2010 the name changed again to be even more inclusive, becoming the Association of Queer Anthropologists, a timid but also brave move from the testing of the waters in the previous incarnations to an in-your-face approach to the promotion of the interests of sexual minorities within the profession and beyond.[14]

What began as a small group of individuals gathering almost clandestinely at the AAA annual meetings became by the mid-1980s a vibrant organization with more than one hundred members. Initially, ARGOH/SOLGA had no official status within the AAA. Discussions were held on becoming an AAA unit (Rapaport 1988), but official status was not achieved until the late 1990s because of concern over the exposure of closeted individuals. One consequence of the emerging AIDS pandemic was a greater willingness to "come out" to confront the crisis and an enhanced sense of community ready to take on the tasks of fighting for recognition and equality. In 1993 over a million individuals converged on Washington in one of the largest civil rights marches in history. The planning for this had taken two years, and a contingent of LGBTQ anthropologists participated.

In the Aftermath of the Event

There was a flurry of post-session activity in terms of correspondence and publications dealing with the session, especially in the newsletters of the AAA (*Anthropology News*), the Society of Lesbian and Gay Anthropologists (*SOLGAN*), and the AIDS and Anthropology Research Group (*AIDS and Anthropology Bulletin*) in 1993 and 1994. Some panelists and their students wrote in defense of the session in May 1993 (Lancaster 1993; Rabinow 1993; Scheper-Hughes 1993d). But the preponderance of publications came from scholars critical of the session, and this discussion continued across multiple journals and over many months: in February (Amory 1993a, 1993b, 1993c, n.d.; "Big Names" 1993, Braiterman 1993; Murray 1993b; Roscoe 1993b), in April (Feldman 1993a), in May (Roscoe 1993a), and in September (Reynolds 1993; Robins 1993).

The controversy did not end in 1993 but continued in October 1994 after Scheper-Hughes (1993a) published her views on AIDS in Cuba in the *Anthropology News*. The *Anthropology News* editors refused to publish some letters critical of Scheper-Hughes's stance but instead gave her a platform to disseminate her comments on this topic, seen again as elite privilege; this was further exacerbated when, also in October, she published an article in *The Lancet* (1993b), more or less duplicating the *Anthropology News* publication. Correspondence with *The Lancet* editors indicated that they knew she had published something in the *Anthropology News* on the subject, but they had been assured that *The Lancet* article would be substantially different, thus not violating the normal rule of not accepting for publication something already in print. They expressed dismay on discovering the similarities, including the replication of entire paragraphs almost verbatim. Criticism by others continued in December, both in *Anthropology News* and *AIDS and Anthropology Bulletin* (De Gordon 1993; De Gordon et al. 1993;

Feldman 1993b; Sullivan 1993) and in *The Lancet* (De Gordon et al. 1993; Murray 1993a)—and again in *Anthropology News* in January (McCombie 1994; Murray 1994a), in SOLGAN in February (Kennedy and Lang 1994), in March (Singer 1994), and in AIDS *and Anthropology Bulletin* in April ("AARG Members Respond" 1994). Scheper-Hughes (1994a) revisited the topic yet again on television in October 1993 and then in October 1994 in an article in *Social Science and Medicine*.[15] Murray (1994b) wrote an unpublished response to Scheper-Hughes (1994a); while it is impossible to be sure now, it seems likely this was submitted to the same journal she had published in but was rejected.

Space limitations and legal impediments prevent me from discussing most of the post-session correspondence to which I have had access, including letters to and from Stephen. Even more recent communications between some principal opponents of the session cannot be quoted or cited. Some individuals, even this long after the event, still fear becoming embroiled in a controversy or wish to protect their legacy in other areas of their professional work or still experience pain when thinking about this event.

There is a certain surreal character to everything surrounding the "AIDS and the Social Imaginary" session, but perhaps the most surreal was an incident the following year, at the 1993 annual meeting of the AAA in Washington DC. Scheper-Hughes encountered Merrill Singer in the hotel lobby and told him she had heard a rumor that I was threatening to kill her. Singer acknowledges being an acquaintance if not a close friend (in his words) of Scheper-Hughes. He knew me also because we had worked together on publications. His reaction was that this rumor seemed unlikely. He decided to defuse the situation by arranging a meeting between Scheper-Hughes and me in his presence and with the participation of several AARG and SOLGA members. As I recall the encounter, Scheper-Hughes continued to insist that she had heard I was threatening to kill her, although I expressed my strong rejection of this absurd and serious allegation. I never leveled any kind of threat against her or anyone else. She was unable to provide the (perhaps imaginary) "source" from whom she had heard the rumor.

Reflecting on how she could have possibly imagined this, I recalled seeing her earlier at the 1993 AAA meeting at the business meeting of SOLGA. She attended not as a member but to be present when her student Roger Lancaster received the Ruth Benedict Prize for his book *Life Is Hard*. I was the cochair in charge of running the meeting. SOLGA business meetings were notorious for not proceeding efficiently, often running overtime, with members going off on tangents. As I started the meeting, attired in my black leather motorcycle jacket with a cock ring dangling from the left epaulet, I took a leather whip out of my briefcase and put it on the table in front of me, saying that we would run a disciplined meeting. Everyone in the room knew this was theater and a joke, except perhaps Scheper-Hughes, who may actually have thought this was aimed at her. The meeting proceeded normally with no threats of any kind.

Revisionist History

Following the event and even recently, some panelists have made false claims about what happened during the event that must not stand. It is unfortunate that we have not been able to locate a recording of the event, a videotape or audiotape of the session, or even photographs, aside from those published in the *Bay Area Reporter* and the *Chronicle of Higher Education*.

It has been claimed that the event was disrupted, although it was not; no one prevented the panelists from delivering their papers. Despite a few shouts at panelists, there was no inappropriate behavior from attendees in the large audience that included many people upset about the session. Two exceptions were reported by Amory (1993a). One involved a woman at the back of the auditorium who shouted *at me* during my remarks: "Sit down!" The other was some hissing and booing when Rabinow "opened his final comment with the remark, 'When my friend Michel Foucault died of AIDS,' a deeply offensive and condescending remark after the manner of 'Some of my best friends are Jews.'"[16] It is true that some individuals distributed handouts to the people entering the auditorium on their own, an activity not sponsored by either SOLGA or AARG. One handout was a pink card that read:

BY INVITATION ONLY

An exclusive panel on aids and the Social Imaginary

INVITED PANELISTS	INVITED LISTENERS
high profile, straight, self-proclaimed	wanna-be theory queens
low risk, tenured professors with	people living with HIV/AIDS
minimal previous involvement in	people of color, queers of all colors
AIDS activism or research,	people whose involvement with
"concerned people"	AIDS goes beyond the imaginary

Is this ANTHROPOLOGICAL BUSINESS as usual or AIDS PROFITEERING?

(invite yourself to imagine a AAA panel of queers analyzing straights, people of color analyzing whites, people living with HIV analyzing people without HIV)

It's 1992—is AIDS now safe for "everyone"?

I do not know who produced and distributed these handouts. Amory attributes them to "Jared Braiterman, and company." Braiterman was a graduate student at Stanford, and he indicates that the action was inspired (though not undertaken) by ACT UP, of which he was a member. Likewise, posters were scattered around with an image of Scheper-Hughes in a circle with a slash through it. None of this prevented the session from proceeding normally. What transpired during the brief discussion period following the paper presentations might be construed as "disruption," if by that term one means refusal to allow the panel to go unchallenged. Some audience members expressed their displeasure over the session, some of them passionately; they exercised their free speech rights in a peaceful fashion during the overtime following the panelists' papers.

It has also been asserted that the opponents of the session tried to have it canceled to prevent the panelists from speaking, which also is completely false. Correspondence before the event among leaders of SOLGA and AARG stressed the importance of hearing what the panelists had to say, which was emphasized to members of these organizations. Dickemann, in his role as outgoing senior co-chair of SOLGA, wrote the following chronology at the request of Sue-Ellen Jacobs, Carole Vance, and Esther Newton, who were preparing a document for submission to the AAA Board:

> At SOLGA's noon informal discussion on Friday, I reviewed the history of our efforts, and shared my impressions, as did others. After a

lengthy discussion, we urged members to attend and judge for themselves. Neither SOLGA nor AARG ever made any attempt to have the session cancelled, or in any way censor the meetings. Nor did we plan any "disturbance" or "action" or contact ACT-UP or any other outside organization. Drs. Bolton, Feldman and I were all agreed that we must first hear what the panel had to say before rendering any final judgment, even though the composition of the panel, and the Brazil paper of Dr. Scheper-Hughes were deeply disturbing. Indeed, we agreed that in spite of a great deal of suspicion and outrage, it was crucial that both organizations respond in a professional and rational fashion, and this we have done. (handwritten communication, n.d.)

Despite emotions running high, there were no plans to interfere with the panelists' right to speak, even though the organizers had violated the AAA rules on the limitation of participation in meetings to one paper presentation, which should have vitiated their right to hold this session and speak.

Some have falsely claimed that the organizers left plenty of time for comments from the audience. Their papers and comments lasted until the end of the time allotted for the session which may have been by design to short-circuit discussion. The attendees were not in a mood to leave, however, and a few were able to comment until it was absolutely necessary to vacate the room so the next session scheduled there could begin.

Another false claim has been that no rules were broken in scheduling this panel, since the participants would be holding a discussion, not giving papers, as asserted by the AAA president, Annette Weiner (1993). They actually delivered papers that they had tried to get scheduled by the program committee. Martha Ward, program chair for the San Francisco meeting, recalled that the organizers had submitted the session as a paper session. She refused to make an exception and exempt the session from the rules against multiple participation, specifically that no member was allowed to present two papers. Martha, an AIDS researcher herself, notes that the proposed session was rejected by the program committee (personal communication). The session organizers did an end-run at that point, going to the president of AAA to have their session scheduled during the lunch time slot when units of the AAA generally hold their business meetings. By labeling it a discussion panel, the organizers managed to get their papers on the program, overriding the rules. If the organizers had not been elite members of the profession, this maneuver probably would not have succeeded.

Scheper-Hughes (2021b) asserts that Murray and I both "demanded that all AAA panels must include sexual diversity." This is patently false and absurd; our position was that inclusiveness and representation should be honored in accordance with the specific topic of the panel. In the case of "AIDS and the Social Imaginary," it would make sense to have gay and AIDS representation because this was the most heavily affected community in the United States in those years. There was no demand for gay representation on all topics.

In defending the panel in a Rabinow obituary, Scheper-Hughes (2021b) included my name as being part of the "celebrity" panel. I was not a member of the panel. The blatant attempt to blunt my criticisms of the panel as elitist by claiming that I was a member and insinuating that I was also one of the elite fails to pass muster.[17] In her recent discussion of the event, Scheper-Hughes (2021b) claims that she and Rabinow had been naive in expecting their effort to demonstrate solidarity. That such distinguished, critical analysts would fall victim to naivete with respect to their professional activities strains credibility; the evidence suggests that psychological and social factors other than simply naivete were involved in this debacle.

It is difficult to determine whether the session affected the concerns raised by the protestors. The "hegemonic discourse" by the "Big Names" referred to by an anonymous writer of a letter to the *Anthropology Newsletter* continues (1993; the name was withheld by the editors of *Anthropology Newsletter* at the author's request to preclude retaliation). Within the AAA at the organizational level, however, it is worth underscoring certain developments. AAA named a committee to explore how to deal with LGBTQ and AIDS issues, resulting in the creation of two special commissions to replace the existing task forces. The Commission on AIDS Research and Education and the Commission on Lesbian and Gay Issues were created within a year of the "AIDS and the Social Imaginary" session (Givens 1994). Over the next several years, these commissions addressed problems raised in response to the session by the protestors. The executive director of AAA, John Cornman (1993b) wrote: "The AAA Executive Committee, meeting January 22 and 23, 1993, authorized creation of a

Department of Academic Relations and a Commission on Minority Issues in Anthropology. The Committee also adopted the 1993 operating budget and authorized creation of two planning groups: (1) to explore how the AAA might effectively address issues of discrimination against lesbians and gays in anthropology, and (2) to explore how the AAA might better focus its activities related to AIDS."

This action came less than two months after the session (Cornman 1993a). In October 1994 the executive board approved a resolution not to meet in locations where antigay legislation existed (such as sodomy laws, which were still on the books in places like Georgia, making criminals of AAA members who attended and engaged in sexual activity even with their own partners). This resolution was approved on December 1 at the business meeting and sent in spring 1995 for a vote by the full AAA membership. The message of the activist response seems to have gotten through.

Conclusion

The importance of this event is not due to the organizers' aim to call attention to AIDS or to the panelists' having said anything about AIDS of any value; indeed, we learned nothing new about AIDS from their papers. The real significance of the session was that it galvanized the LGBTQ and HIV/AIDS communities of anthropologists and their supporters. The event laid out in stark terms the grievances of a stigmatized minority, accustomed to either neglect or discrimination even within the AAA, that was unwilling to remain oppressed any longer. If the discipline had been slow to take on the AIDS pandemic, it had been even slower in responding to demands for equality, respect, and recognition by its LGBTQ members.

The panel also laid bare the power dynamics within the profession and its major organization. Privileges were accorded to prominent members employed at a handful of elite universities that produce most professional anthropologists. It was a moment of speaking truth to power when those most affected by AIDS (either in their personal lives or in their research commitment) would no longer sit back and allow the bystanders to take charge of the discourse or take on the label of victims. As the SOLGA T-shirt boldly asserted: "These natives can speak for themselves."

If this was a "turf war" as Roger Lancaster (1993) proclaimed in his defense of his mentor Scheper-Hughes and the panel, the turf was not AIDS. The struggle was over the misuse and abuse of power and privilege by a cadre of well-known scholars; it was a revolt against the professional establishment operating in its own self-interest. This could be considered as a point in a line of struggles against power and privilege, a forerunner to such movements as #MeToo and Black Lives Matter. It was a moment when LGBTQ anthropologists would not be silenced, would not sit back and allow others to speak for us. Evidence is easily found that the revolt succeeded, at least to some degree. "AIDS and the Social Imaginary" marked an important inflection point for the gay anthropological community. The 1990s would be a decade of an explosion of publications on LGBTQ topics and continued pressure on issues involving gay rights. While the AAA had plans to end the AIDS and Anthropology Task Force in 1991–92, after this panel the AAA committed itself to more intensive involvement in the issues raised by creating the commissions mentioned, even providing financial support for those commissions' work.

I would like to close by underscoring the importance of Stephen Murray's role in this event, in which he was initially a reluctant participant. I have always thought of Steve as an unpretentious, no-nonsense type of person. He played a minor role in one sense and spoke only briefly at the session. In the months after the event, however, he engaged in ongoing exchanges about the issues it raised. What stands out above all is the symbolic role thrust upon him. The image we retain is of him standing at the lectern in front of an enormous audience, a fourfold-stigmatized individual—as a gay man, as a scholar whose major contributions were on topics of sexuality and homosexuality, as someone who had never been appointed to a position as professor in any university, let alone an elite one, and as a person with AIDS. He was someone from the city where we were meeting, who was witness to the suffering and devastation of others caused by AIDS in his community and the effects on his own body and psyche. Getting Steve to take on this role is one of the accomplishments of which I am most pleased. Anthropologists play a good game of claiming to allow the people studied, the "natives," to have their voices heard. Too often, however, the anthropologist's voice drowns out the voices of the "other" (a topic on which Steve felt strongly; see Murray and Hong

1994). I have no doubt that most of the people in the audience that day were moved by Steve's words, by his mere presence, and his courage.

Perhaps this event has now faded from memory for many who attended it and is of little significance for those who came later and probably never even heard of it, but it is worth calling attention to because the battles being fought then are just as relevant today. The victories we achieved can be reversed and must be defended, as is evident every day on the national and international political scene, where our victories, our demands to be heard could turn out to have been pyrrhic, reversible. Stephen Murray was an early voice for the LGBTQ community within the anthropological profession and a scholar devoted to increasing knowledge about issues of sexual diversity globally. This volume honors him for his devotion and his contributions to the cause. I close by giving the last word to Steve, recording here a portion of what he said when he spoke in the session:

> This panel, that includes no one who has done anything about AIDS or been involved in the difficulties those of us who have tried to obtain funding for studying the horrors our own communities have been dealing with, mixes critics of past colonialisms with Stalinish fellow travelers of authoritarian regimes to colonize our sufferings. Professor Scheper-Hughes said at the beginning that we don't know who the panel organizers are. But we do. At an earlier AAA "star" panel I remember Paul Rabinow telling the audience that the panel had been tested and were all negative, so that it was safe to move closer. By that reasoning, some of you packed in here are in danger. And, at last year's meeting, Professor Scheper-Hughes took what was supposed to be a slot for a discussant to deliver a defense of the Cuban concentration camps for HIV+ people. We know that these organizers resisted requests to include gay or HIV+ panelists, even as substitutes. We just saw them read papers to fill every minute of the scheduled session after claiming that they wanted a discussion. We know them too well!
>
> Being rendered invisible here—looked through or looked beyond—I understand better what my Taiwanese friends feel about privileged outsiders coming in and profiting from their oppression, speaking in the language of the oppressor, and seizing their suffering as a means to advance their already-inflated reputations. With Keelung Hong I have

criticized two of the no-show panelists [Arthur Kleinman and Emily Martin] for complicity with domination by a minority ethnic oligarcy on Taiwan, and, more recently the gerontocracy oppressing China.

Until I saw the program, I would not have believed that San Francisco, an epicenter of the AIDS holocaust and one where 90% of the dead and dying are gay men, could be invaded by such a panel. San Francisco is my own place of refuge, my place of exile from academia in general and Berkeley anthropology in particular. Though my list of publications is 14 pages long and I have been involved in research on gay men and AIDS from the beginning of my career and of the epidemic, my application for a position at Berkeley in which I outlined the AIDS research I wanted to do was not considered seriously enough even to invite me to cross the bay and talk. My experience of being stigmatized for research on now-fashionable topics of sexuality is far from unique. I think of such pioneers as David Sonenschein, Clark Taylor, and Joseph Carrier, who never held university positions; of my friend and collaborator in critical analysis of AIDS discourse, Kenneth Payne, who died of AIDS; of the current and continuing struggles of people like Will Roscoe and others doing major work and not getting serious consideration for university positions.

Rather than deal point by point with what has been said, I would like to join the ranks of those people who have told anthropologists to "stay home, we don't want you making careers out of speaking about our sufferings. Stay in your ivory towers stroking each other's inflated egos. Get out of the way and let the natives speak for themselves."

Notes

1. Interested readers can consult the original materials, including the correspondence he received, in the Stephen O. Murray and Keelung Hong Special Collection at Michigan State University.
2. Scheper-Hughes describes papers by Comaroff, Taussig, Rosaldo, Rabinow, and herself. Will Roscoe, in a scathingly critical commentary on the talks (n.d., 1993b), mentions only the presentations by the same five participants. Finally, these same speakers are listed in the reports in the *Chronicle of Higher Education* (Coughlin 1992) and the *Bay Area Reporter* (Conkin 1992).
3. Extra police protection seems to have occurred previously on the Berkeley campus for a session organized by Scheper-Hughes. Her obituaries for Rabinow (2021a,

2021b) refer to Rabinow and herself as "AIDS Heretics: Comrades in Arms." (Web page of the Department of Anthropology, University of California, Berkeley. Accessed 11/8/2022. Dated: April 12, 2021. https://anthropology.berkeley.edu/sites/default/files/nancy-paul_rabinow_est_mort-editeddocx.pdf).

4. My involvement began with volunteering at the newly established AIDS Project Los Angeles, the leading AIDS NGO in Southern California. I cleaned the bathrooms in the small office complex of the organization and stuffed envelopes for mailings desperately seeking donations. I immediately volunteered as a subject in a large-scale AIDS research program, the Los Angeles Men's Study, donating blood and even semen specimens for multiple research projects. This project continues to this day and twice a year I submit to physical probing, psychological testing, behavioral questionnaires, and so forth. I underwent training in safer sex at the Institute of Advanced Study of Human Sexuality in San Francisco, where the anthropologist Clark Taylor taught, and participated in gay men's support groups in Los Angeles. I was active in AIDS awareness activities on campus at Pomona College, including on political decisions about placing condom dispensing machines in dorm bathrooms, and getting the college's program for charitable donations by faculty and staff to make the Foothill AIDS Project eligible to receive such contributions. I taught one of the first college courses devoted exclusively to AIDS; as part of the course, students were required to volunteer hours to one of several AIDS-related organizations in the region.

5. To cite only a sample, Brooke Schoepf (1998, 1993) on women in Africa; Michael Clatts (1993), Claire Sterk (1989, 1990), and Luis Kemnitzer and Moher Downing (1994) on drug users; Michele Shedlin (1990) on sex workers; Janet McGrath (1993) on women in Uganda. For a comprehensive list of what was already published by anthropologists prior to the "AIDS and the Social Imaginary" session, consult the bibliography published by Bolton and Orozco (1991, 1994) or consult the edited volumes and journal issues on the anthropology of AIDS published prior to or around the time of the session: Feldman (1990), Feldman and Johnson (1986), Herdt and Lindenbaum (1992), Bolton and Singer (1992a, 1992b).

6. E.g., the Wenner-Gren Symposium "AIDS Research: Issues for Anthropological Theory, Methods and Practice" held at Estes Park, Colorado, June 25–July 1, 1990 (Herdt and Lindenbaum 1992; Silverman 2002); the Conference on AIDS and Anthropology sponsored by the University of Miami and the Centers for Disease Control in Atlanta in 1991; a Conference on Theoretical Issues in AIDS Research held in Minneapolis in 1987; and a Conference on Representing AIDS: Confronting the AIDS Pandemic held at the University of Pennsylvania in 1991.

7. For the record, it should be noted that no-show Kleinman was second author on an early article written with Paul Farmer published in a non-anthropological journal, *Daedalus* (Farmer and Kleinman 1989), and several years later, Kleinman

did work on AIDS policies in China, coediting a book on the subject (Kaufman, Kleinman, and Saiche 2006). No-show Emily Martin became involved in AIDS as an "AIDS buddy," as a member of ACT UP, and as a researcher who focused on ideas about the human immune system (Martin, 1995).
8. During the fall semester of 1992 leading up to the meeting in December, Rabinow and Scheper-Hughes (1992) taught the first course on AIDS at Berkeley. Duesberg is listed on the syllabus for the course as a speaker for week 9 and the assigned readings that week were mostly his writings.
9. See the Wikipedia entry on AIDS denialism for a thorough discussion of the issues and the sources.
10. This is well documented, quite dramatically, in the works of Reynaldo Arenas (1994; see also Murray 1995a), a gay Cuban novelist; in Allen Young's analysis (1982), in the film "Fresas y Chocolate"; and elsewhere.
11. One organizer, Rabinow, ironically a disciple of and leading authority on Foucault, failed to apply a Foucauldian analysis of power to the panel itself or the institution of the AAA and the panelists' own positions in the dominant anthropology programs in the country. As one observer noted: "Foucault would have had a field day with it if he were still around because this is precisely the kind of abuse of power (in writing the history of science) that he raged against in all of his work" (Michael Clatts, personal communication, April 30, 2021).
12. Scheper-Hughes's (2019) curriculum vitae indicates that she was engaged in eighteen consultancies on multiple topics between 1996 and 2019—reported as a sample, not a complete list—none involving HIV/AIDS.
13. The movement for racial equality, and the suffrage and women's movement for gender equality, being the other two.
14. Some of the earliest pioneers lost their lives to AIDS before the 1992 session (e.g., Kenneth W. Payne, in 1988, for whom an annual prize is given by the Association of Queer Anthropologists).
15. Although listed on Scheper-Hughes's CV for 1994, the relevant episode of *60 Minutes* was apparently broadcast on October 3, 1993 (https://thetvdb.com/series/60-minutes/allseasons/official).
16. Foucault never acknowledged having AIDS, and his death was not officially attributed to AIDS by his partner until two years after he died.
17. I may have had some name recognition because of my Andean work and my work on AIDS, but I was never part of the professional power elite in any real sense. It is true that I taught at an outstanding undergraduate institution (with full scholarship support for any blind-admissions-accepted student), but it was not an institution that prepared professional anthropologists. One person noted, "if I didn't know Bolton was at Pomona, I wouldn't even know that they had an anthropology program" (the three-person department served the general edu-

cation needs of undergraduates). In comparison to the panelists, few anthropologists would have known of or read my work, and I had no disciples. Does it make me a member of the "elite" that I was the one who yielded my time to Steve to respond?

References

"AARG Members Respond to Commentary on AIDS in Cuba." 1994. *AIDS & Anthropology Bulletin* 5 (4): 1–2.
American Anthropological Association. 1992. Program, 91st Annual Meeting, San Francisco.
Amory, Deb. 1993a. "The 1992 AAA Panel from Hell: AIDS and the Social Imaginary: An Introduction." *Society of Lesbian and Gay Anthropologists Newsletter* 15 (1): 20–23.
———. 1993b. "On SOLGA: The Future and Queer Theory: An Introduction (with comments by Stephen Murray, William Leap, Esther Newton, Will Roscoe, Elizabeth Kennedy, Sue-Ellen Jacobs)." *Society of Lesbian and Gay Anthropologists Newsletter* 15 (2): 26–35.
———. 1993c. "SOLGA Annual Business Meeting Minutes: Friday, November 19, 1993." *Society of Lesbian and Gay Anthropologists Newsletter* 16 (1): 3–11.
———. n.d. "AQA History." Accessed March 14, 2023. https://queeranthro.org/business/aqa-history/.
Anwar, Yasmin. 2021. "World-Renowned Anthropologist Paul Rabinow Dies at 76." *Berkeley News*. Accessed November 8, 2022. https://news.berkeley.edu/2021/04/23/world-renowned-anthropologist-paul-rabinow-dies-at-76/.
Arenas, Reinaldo. 1994. *Before Night Falls: A Memoir*. London: Penguin.
"The Big Names and the Nameless." 1993. *Anthropology Newsletter* 34 (2): 3.
Bolton, Ralph, ed. 1989. *The AIDS Pandemic: A Global Emergency*. New York: Gordon and Breach.
———. n.d. "Ideology, Denial and the Self-Construction of an 'AIDS Heretic.'" Unpublished manuscript.
Bolton, Ralph, and Erika Kempler, eds. 1992. *The Anthropology of AIDS: Syllabi and Other Teaching Materials*. Washington DC: American Anthropological Association, AIDS and Anthropology Task Force.
Bolton, Ralph, and Gail Orozco. 1991. "AIDS Literature for Anthropologists: A Working Bibliography." *Journal of Sex Research* 28 (2): 307–46.
———. 1994. *The AIDS Bibliography: Studies in Anthropology and Related Fields*. Arlington VA: American Anthropological Association.
Bolton, Ralph, and Merrill Singer. 1992a. "Rethinking AIDS Prevention: Cultural Approaches." Special issue, *Medical Anthropology* 14 (2–4): 139–363.

———, eds. 1992b. *Rethinking AIDS Prevention: Cultural Approaches.* Philadelphia: Gordon and Breach.

Braiterman, Jared "Lee." 1993. "The 1992 AAA Panel from Hell: AIDS and the Social Imaginary: Some Thoughts about the AAA AIDS Panel Protest and the Uses of SOLGA." *Society of Lesbian and Gay Anthropologists Newsletter* 15 (1): 30–32.

Clatts, Michael. 1993. "Poverty, Drug Use and AIDS: Converging Issues in the Life Stories of Women in Harlem." In *Wings of Gauze: Women of Color and the Experience of Health and Illness* edited by Barbara Bair and Susan E. Cayleff, 312–39. Detroit: Wayne State University Press.

Conkin, Dennis. 1992. "Anthropologists Talk about AIDS, Enrage Colleagues." *Bay Area Reporter,* December 10: 5.

Cornman, John M. 1993a. "AAA Executive Committee Business." *Anthropology Newsletter* 34 (8): 4.

———. 1993b. "New Department, Commission Formed." *Anthropology Newsletter* 34 (3): 1, 28.

Coughlin, Ellen K. 1992. "Tempers Flare over AIDS Session at Anthropologists' Annual Meeting." *Chronicle of Higher Education,* December 16: A8.

Daniel, H. 1991. "We are All People Living with AIDS: Myths and Realities of AIDS in Brazil." *International Journal of Health Services* 21 (3): 539–51.

De Gordon, Antonio Maria. 1993. "AIDS in Cuba: Rights of the Uninfected." *Anthropology News* 34 (9): 2.

De Gordon, Antonio Maria, Shawn K. Centers, and L. P. Diovaldes. 1993. "Cuban AIDS Policy." *The Lancet* 342:1426.

Farmer, Paul. 1992. *AIDS and Accusation: Haiti and the Geography of Blame.* Berkeley: University of California Press.

Farmer, Paul, and Arthur Kleinman. 1989. "AIDS as Human Suffering." *Daedalus* 118 (2): 135–62.

Feldman, Douglas A. 1986. "Anthropology, AIDS, and Africa." *Medical Anthropology Quarterly.* 17 (2): 38–40.

———. 1989. "Developing AIDS Policy in a Low Prevalence Country: The Case of Bangladesh." *Practicing Anthropology* 11 (4): 2–12.

———. 1990. *Culture and AIDS.* Westport CT: Praeger.

———. 1993a. "Commentary: AIDS and the Social Imaginary." *AIDS & Anthropology Bulletin* 4 (4): 5–6.

———. 1993b. "Sacrificing Basic Civil Liberties." *Anthropology News* 34 (9): 2.

Feldman, Douglas A., and Thomas M. Johnson, eds. 1986. *The Social Dimensions of AIDS: Methods and Theory.* Westport CT: Praeger.

Fernando, Daniel. 1993. "AIDS and Injecting Drug Users." *Anthropology News* 34 (8): 2, 8.

Givens, David B. 1994. "Newton, Leap New Co-chairs of Commission on Lesbian and Gay Issues." *Anthropology News* 35 (5): 3.

Herdt, Gilbert and Shirley Lindenbaum, eds. 1992. *The Time of AIDS: Social Analysis, Theory, and Method*. Newbury Park CA: Sage.

Kane, Stephanie and Theresa Mason. 1992. "'IV Drug Users' and 'Sex Partners': The Limits of Epidemiological Categories and the Ethnography of Risk." In *The Time of AIDS: Social Analysis, Theory, and Method*, edited by Gilbert Herdt and Shirley Lindenbaum, 199–222. Newbury Park CA: Sage.

Kaufman, Joan, Arthur Kleinman, and Anthony Saich, eds. 2006. *AIDS and Social Policy in China*. Cambridge MA: Harvard University Press.

Kemnitzer, Luis S. and Moher Downing. 1994. "Needle Exchange: East vs. West." *Anthropology News* 3 (3): 4.

Kennedy, Liz, and Norris Lang. 1994. "Co-chairs Correspondence RE: Scheper-Hughes and the A.N." *Society of Lesbian and Gay Anthropologists Newsletter* 16 (1): 13–14. (Based on a draft prepared by Frank Proschan.)

Kutsche, Paul. 1993. "One View of Our History from 1984 to 1987." *Society of Lesbian and Gay Anthropologists Newsletter* 15 (3): 24–27.

Lancaster, Roger N. 1992. *Life Is Hard: Machismo, Danger, and the Intimacy of Power in Nicaragua*. Berkeley: University of California Press.

Lancaster, Roger. 1993. "Academic Turf War." *Anthropology News* 34 (5): 3, 21.

Martin, Emily. 1995. *Flexible Bodies*. Boston: Beacon.

McCombie, Susan. 1994. "AIDS in Cuba." *Anthropology News* 35 (1): 2.

McGrath, Janet W., Charles B. Rwabukwali, Debra A. Schumann, Jonnie Pearson-Marks, Sylvia Nakayiwa, Barbara Namande, Lucy Nakyobe, and Rebecca Mukasa. 1993. "Anthropology and AIDS: The Cultural Context of Sexual Risk Behaviour among Urban Baganda Women in Kampala, Uganda." *Social Science & Medicine* 36 (4): 429–39.

Murray, Stephen O. 1985. "The History of Anthropology's Lavender Fringe." *Anthropological Research Group on Homosexuality Newsletter* 6 (1): 8–10.

———. 1993a. "Cuban AIDS Policy." *The Lancet* 342 (December 4): 1426.

———. 1993b. "The 1992 AAA Panel from Hell: AIDS and the Social Imaginary: Colonizing AIDS Discourse." *Society of Lesbian and Gay Anthropologists Newsletter* 15 (1): 23–25.

———. 1994a. "Questions of Fairness." *Anthropology News* 35 (1): 2, 37.

———. 1994b. "Uncritical 'Critical' Medical Anthropology: Demonizing Gay Men." Unpublished manuscript.

———. 1995. "Heteronormative Cuban Sexual Policies and Resistance to Them." *GLQ: A Journal of Lesbian and Gay Studies* 2 (4): 473–77.

———. 2019. "Esther Newton's Memoir." Tangent Group, May 29, 2019. https://www.tangentgroup.org/58875-2/.

Murray, Stephen O., and Keelung Hong. 1994. *Taiwanese Culture, Taiwanese Society: A Critical Review of Social Science Research Done on Taiwan*. Lanham MD: University Press of America.

National AIDS Memorial. n.d. "The History of the Quilt." Accessed February 13, 2023. https://www.aidsmemorial.org/quilt-history.

O'Neill, John. 1990. "AIDS as a Globalizing Panic." *Theory, Culture & Society* 7 (2-3): 329–42.

Rabinow, Paul. 1993. "A More Fruitful Dialogue." *Anthropology News* 34 (5): 3.

Rabinow, Paul, and Nancy Scheper-Hughes. 1992. "Syllabus for Anthropology 119: AIDS: The Disease and Its Double." University of California, Berkeley, Department of Anthropology.

Rapaport, Roy. 1988. "Becoming a Section of AAA." *Society of Lesbian and Gay Anthropologists Newsletter* 11 (1): 3–4.

Read, Kenneth. 1997. "Founding of Anthropological Research Group on Homosexuality." With additional commentary by Larry Gross. *Society of Lesbian and Gay Anthropologists Newsletter* 19 (2): 1, 7–9.

Reynolds, Peter C. 1993. "Meeting the Needs of Members." *Anthropology News* 34 (6): 2.

Robins, Cynthia S. 1993. "Accountability and Responsibility." *Anthropology News* 34 (6): 2.

Rosaldo, Renato. 1994. "Whose Cultural Studies?" *American Anthropologist* 96 (3): 524–29.

Roscoe, Will. 1993a. "The 1992 AAA Panel from Hell: AIDS and the Social Imaginary: Correspondence to David B. Givens, Editor, *Anthropology Newsletter*, from Will Roscoe, dated December 21, 1992." *Society of Lesbian and Gay Anthropologists*.

———. 1993b. "AAA & HIV." *Anthropology News* 34 (5): 3.

———. n.d. "Observations on the Imaginary of Heterosexual Anthropologists." Unpublished manuscript.

Scheper-Hughes, Nancy. 1993a. "AIDS, Public Health and Human Rights in Cuba." *Anthropology Newsletter* 34 (7): 46, 48.

———. 1993b. "AIDS, Public Health and Human Rights in Cuba." *The Lancet* 342:965–67.

———. 1993c. "AIDS in Cuba: Fidel Castro's Health Plan." CBS *60 Minutes*, October 3, 1993.

———. 1993d. "AIDS Panel." *Anthropology News* 34 (5): 3.

———. 1994. "An Essay: AIDS and the Social Body." *Social Science & Medicine* 39 (7): 991–1003.

———. 2019. Curriculum Vitae. Accessed March 13, 2023. https://anthropology.berkeley.edu/file/503.

———. 2020. "Cuba HIV/AIDS: Epidemics and Containment." *Culture &Humanities*, Berkeley Blog, June 22. https://blogs.berkeley.edu/2020/06/22/cuba-hiv-aids-epidemic-epidemics-and-containment/.

———. 2021a. "Paul Rabinow (1944–2021): A Memoir." *Anthropology Today* 37 (3): 23–25.

———. 2021b. "*Paul Rabinow est mort*: A Memoir." Web page of the Department of Anthropology, University of California, Berkeley. Accessed November 8, 2022. https://anthropology.berkeley.edu/sites/default/files/nancy-paul_rabinow _est_mort-editeddocx.pdf.

Scheper-Hughes, Nancy, Mae Araujo, and Viva Paredes. 1992. "AIDS in Brazil—the 'Democratization of the Epidemic.'" Notes for a talk at Brazilian Action and Solidarity Exchange, San Francisco, November 22, 1992.

Schoepf, Brooke. 1988. "Women, AIDS, and Economic Crisis in Central Africa." *Canadian Journal of African Studies / Revue canadienne des études africaines* 22 (3): 625–44.

———. 1993. "AIDS Action-Research with Women in Kinshasa, Zaire." *Social Science & Medicine* 37 (11): 1401–13.

Shedlin, M. G. 1990. "An Ethnographic Approach to Understanding HIV High-Risk Behaviors: Prostitution and Drug Abuse." *NIDA Research Monograph Series* 93:134–49.

Silverman, Sydel. 2002. *The Beast on the Table: Conferencing with Anthropologists*. Walnut Creek CA: AltaMira.

Singer, Merrill. 1994. "Pointing Fingers at Needle Exchange." *Anthropology News* 35 (3): 4.

Stall, Ron. 1986. "AIDS: A Challenge to Anthropologists." *Medical Anthropology Quarterly* 17 (2): 36–37.

Sterk, Claire. 1989. "Prostitution, Drug Use, and AIDS." In *In the Field: Readings on the Field Research Experience*, edited by Carolyn D. Smith and William Kornblum, 91–99. New York: Praeger.

———. 1990. "AIDS Research Findings: Drug Use and AIDS in Street Prostitutes." In *The Effectiveness of Drug Abuse Treatment: Dutch and American Perspectives*, edited by Jerome J. Platt, Charles D. Kaplan, and Patricia J. McKim, 295–301. Malabar FL: Krieger.

Sullivan, Greg. 1993. "Coordination of Preventive Methods." *Anthropology News* 34 (9): 25.

Vincke, John, Ruud Mak, and Ralph Bolton, eds. 1991. *Mannen met Mannen: Welzijn, Relaties & Seksualiteit*. Ghent, Belgium: CGSO Forum.

Weiner, Annette. 1993. "Letter to Stephen O. Murray." *AIDS & Anthropology Bulletin* 4 (4): 1–2.

Young, Allen. 1981. *Gays under the Cuban Revolution*. San Francisco: Grey Fox.

Acknowledgments

In preparing this account, I have consulted numerous individuals who were present at the "AIDS and the Social Imaginary" session. I am grateful to the following scholars who responded to my requests for information: John O'Neil, Emily Martin, Arthur Kleinman, Martha Ward, and Robert Oppenheim; to Regna Darnell and Wendy Leeds-Hurwitz for spurring me on and for their editorial suggestions and corrections; and especially to Michael Clatts, Gilbert Herdt, Will Roscoe, and J. "Lee" Braiterman for in-person and email discussions that enhanced my personal understanding of the event. I also thank Jane Klain at the Paley Center for Media, who sorted out the date on which the *60 Minutes* episode mentioned was shown. I alone am responsible for any errors.

PART 3 Homosexualities

6 Stephen O. Murray's Legacy in the Comparative Study of Homosexualities

Barry D Adam

Stephen O. Murray's work, from his area surveys of same-sex behavior to his magnum opus, *Homosexualities* (2000), is grounded in a comparative, structural tradition of identifying major patterns from an encyclopedic array of data. A major theme of Murray's work was to make sense of a large but fragmentary set of observations on same-sex sexual bonding. Now that more than two decades have passed since the publication of *Homosexualities*, it is perhaps time to consider Murray's legacy in the systematic analysis of sexualities and the questions it raises for current scholarship in the field.

The Antecedents

Murray's work follows in the footsteps of great systematizing work like Claude Lévi-Strauss's (1969) *Elementary Structures of Kinship* which strives to map the immense variability and creativity of human societies in organizing themselves as kin. Perhaps the earliest landmark work to take on a global survey of same-sex relationships was Ferdinand Karsch-Haack's *Das gleichgeschlechtliche leben der Naturvölker*, published in 1911 in Munich during the first wave of modern gay cultural self-awareness and scholarship that emerged in Germany at the turn of the twentieth century. That tome of 668 pages sought to cumulate into a single compendium the extant body of far-flung references regarding same-sex sexuality. It came about during an era when scholars were trying to organize a vast array of textual traces, veiled comments, traveler reports, and ethnography into a coherent set of ideas about human sexuality, and it required the decoding of discourses of various, often antagonistic, observers embedded in colonial institutions, such as missionaries, administrators, prosecutors, and adventurers. As Paul Schrader (2020, 131–32) argues, Karsch-Haack relied mostly "on the writings of German travellers, missionaries, anthropologists and colonial civil servants who studied (or believed to do so) the sexual mores of African societies in the German colonies," which imbued the volume with "a set of discourses, administrative plans and racial stereotypes typical to the German colonial context." The book also tended to rely on the prevailing "belief that sexual orientation was fixed, biologically based, and transcultural, declaring that homoeroticism does not differ from culture to culture, but that only its 'characteristic form' might vary" (Tobin 2015, 137). Karsch-Haack did, however, establish definitively that homosexual relations were present—even widespread—among societies around the world, at a time when European church and state institutions and their attendant professions long denied their very existence or pushed them into the oblivion of perversion, crime, sickness, or sin. The amassing of a large cross-cultural evidentiary base also set the groundwork for the long-term reconceptualization of sexualities as social phenomena rooted in Indigenous cultural contexts, thereby gradually undermining the essentialist precepts circulating in the European societies that organized this early work.

The Revival of LGBTQ Studies

German sexual science perished with the destruction of the Weimar Republic at the hands of the Nazis. Indeed, the Institute for Sex Research in Berlin was a prime target by Nazi militants; the infamous book burnings recorded in news reels of the time in fact depicted the attack on the institute in 1933 (Isherwood, 1976, 129; Steakley 1975, 105). The worldwide ascendence of authoritarianism in states around the world in the mid-twentieth century largely erased these early initiatives, whether through fascism, Stalinism, or McCarthyism. The re-establishment of gender and sexual conservatism through state and church enforcement meant that scholarly examination of the social construction of gender and sexuality became too risky to pursue and largely fell into abeyance. Indeed, early postwar "scholarly debate, along with public discussion, largely addressed the issue of which tools of repression would prove most effective: psychiatry, law enforcement, or religious indoctrination" (Adam 2002, 15).

It is only with the emergence of feminism and gay liberation in the 1970s that it became possible again for a new generation of scholars to take up questions of subordination and equality in gender and sexuality. With these movements, both inside and outside the academy, "gay and lesbian studies, then, emerged as an effort to decolonize science in that it sought to break the pathology paradigm and wrest the stories of homosexual experience from the monopoly of the social-control professions" (Adam 2002, 15–16). As part of this new work on gender and sexuality, the early German scholarship began to be rediscovered. In 1975 Arno Press reissued the Karsch-Haack volume. LGBTQ studies caucuses formed in sociology and anthropology as well in the 1970s, and it is with this reopening and reinvigoration of the field that cross-cultural studies of sexualities developed a new momentum.

In this intellectual climate, Stephen O. Murray embarked on a series of publications, often with coauthors and coeditors like Will Roscoe, to recover and collect the evidence on homosexualities around the world. Between 1995 and 2002, he published volumes on *Latin American Male Homosexualities* (Murray 1995), *Islamic Homosexualities* (Murray and Roscoe 1997), *Boy-Wives and Female Husbands: Studies in African Homosexualities* (Murray and Roscoe 1998), *Pacific Homosexualities* (Murray 2002b), and his overview volume, *Homosexualities* (Murray 2000), plus an essay on "The Comparative Sociology of Homosexualities" (Murray 2002a). Murray was not alone in this quest for a global vision. Vern Bullough (1976) had offered something of a grand tour of "sexual variance in society and history," and David Greenberg (1988) devoted part 1 of his *Construction of Homosexuality* to examples of "kinship-structured" homosexual relations in addition to historical references in the West, before focusing on the question of the development of modern forms. Also contemporaneous with Murray's work were David Halperin's essays on literary and historical discourses on sodomy that led him to formulate a set of "transhistorical continuities" in the depiction of male same-sex relations that coalesced around four tropes: "(1) effeminacy, (2) paederasty or 'active' sodomy, (3) friendship or male love, and (4) passivity or inversion" (Halperin 2002, 109). Similarly, Martha Vicinus (1992) discerned a limited set of nineteenth-century social scripts in the depictions of gender and sexual variant women, namely the passing woman, the mannish woman, the libertine, and the romantic friend.

Murray's work still offers the most sustained, comprehensive, and foundational collection of anthropological observations available today. In this work, Murray (2000, 2002a) proposes a typology (the origins of which he credits to conversations he and I had in graduate school; Murray and Roscoe 1998; Murray 2000, 2) consisting of three broad patterns of homosexualities: "gender-stratified" relationships where gender-crossing or gender-mixed individuals typically enter into relationships with cisgender people; "age-stratified" relationships where younger men or adolescents enter into acolyte-mentor relationships with older men (Adam 1985); and "egalitarian" relationships where relationships between peers are predominant and status differences are optional rather than expected. Certainly, there are many variations within these themes: whether same-sex relations are valued or reviled within a society, they tend to be shaped by the kin rules that prescribe celebrated or forbidden relationships, including norms of gift exchange among the participating families. Just why different societies arrive at these patterns of same-sex relations is not easily discerned, but Murray (2000, 426, 436–37) comes to a few tentative conclusions concerning linkages between inheritance systems and patterns of homosexualities insofar as "societies with gender-stratified male homosexuality involving occupational specialties were four times more likely than the world average to have matrilineal inheritance" and "age-stratified male homosexuality was more common among urban and class-based societies than were the other two types . . . [and] were the most patrilineal in inheritance."

The Legacy

It is perhaps paradoxical that this landmark work of comparative structural analysis came at a time when grand, systematizing visions were already under attack by a wave of poststructuralist and deconstructionist critics. That critique was turning scholarly analysis toward a certain particularism that insisted on the uniqueness and incommensurability of each cultural form. Murray (2000, 8) was already feeling the sting of that critique when he remarked in the opening pages of *Homosexualities* that "in the current intellectual climate of postmodernist nihilism, stressing diversity within categories is less important than stressing that there are patternings, many of them recognized by those living within a society. . . . Individuals are more than 'carriers' of a modeled culture, but their acts are not random."

In the ensuing two decades, this collection and display of varying reports of gender and sexual nonconformity have generated a great many fundamental questions about how and why sexualities take the forms they do within their sociocultural contexts. Perhaps most remarkable has been the change in scholarship since Murray (2000, 424) lamented that "there is very little for ethnologists to work with except the record compiled by early European travellers and ethnographers operating under the protection of colonial regimes." The more supportive scholarly climate for gender and sexuality studies in the academy in the early 2000s has invigorated a new wealth of ethnographies that move beyond the colonial legacy. Especially encouraging has been the new work by scholars originating in the cultures once under European observation, many in diaspora or in collaboration with scholars in the Global North, but some working in their home environments.

Murray (2002a, 85) further lamented that "given the paucity of funding for research on the meanings of same-sex sex . . . , I cannot foresee the accumulation of the body of data necessary for serious comparative work of homosexual inwardness." The rise of HIV studies, with the resources provided by health granting agencies, now routinely identify and survey sizeable populations of "men who have sex with men" (MSM) in countries with no previous record of their existence in the anthropological literature. While funding has appeared, the MSM category has often been intentionally deployed to sidestep cultural contexts in order to shoehorn MSM into epidemiological profiles of potentially virus-transmitting genital connection (Young and Meyer 2005). The cultural work of translating epidemiology back into HIV prevention policy has often, then, been left to local public health authorities or community-based organizations, without the social science research that could help make sense of diverse local contexts (Adam 2011). There are some instances, however, where HIV research has also allowed for the development of sexuality studies by, or at least with, local collaborators, and supporting qualitative ethnography has been possible here and there (Parker, Aggleton, and Perez-Brumer 2016; see for example Alio et al. 2002 in Senegal; Boyce 2007 in India; and Wright 2000 in Bolivia). In a further twist in the story of sexual formation, HIV prevention work with MSM has even stimulated the adoption of the acronym as an identity and community in some places where these networks had previously been largely invisible and underground (Boellstorff 2011).

All of this new work raises questions concerning how sexual subjectivities and categories might be reconceptualized. While sexualities in the Global North/West have come to be posited in relation to liberal democratic states in terms of rights-bearing autonomous individuals (Adam 2016), knowledge systems grounded in Indigenous and Southern cultures may offer new avenues of thinking about sexualities (Seely 2020).

The early 2000s have also been a period of two major contradictory trends in the formation of homosexualities around the world. On the one hand, the rise of the internet has facilitated connections among homoerotically inclined people and given voice to many of them, unfiltered by media, church, or state institutions. It has brought many in contact with LGBTQ communities of the Global North, sparking debates about potentially neocolonial relationships between Indigenous and LGBTQ forms of sexuality and gender. On the other hand, new waves of repression have been directed against local homosexualities, whether LGBTQ identified or not, in the global culture wars that have pitted traditionalist, patriarchal, and authoritarian states against liberal democratic nations of the Global North and Latin America. Several of the ethnographic portraits of homosexualities in Murray's volumes seem almost idyllic in light of renewed regimes of criminalization and state persecution in places like Nigeria, Cameroon, Senegal, Tanzania, and Uganda in Africa; in Russia (particularly Chechnya); and in Iran, Afghanistan, and the terrorist Islamic State of Iraq and the Levant from 2014 to 2017, all of which have produced new streams of freedom-seeking LGBTQ refugees (Adam 2020a, 2020b).

Conclusions

The recurrence of these three patterns of homosexualities—gender-stratified, age-stratified, and egalitarian—among very different societies around the world, as documented in Murray's work, provides an occasion to reflect on the organization of sexualities even in the Global North of today. The increasing legalization of same-sex marriage (thirty-five countries as of 2024), primarily in Western Europe and the Americas, speaks to a parallel homogamy of heterosexual and homosexual relationships. As ideals of companionate marriage have been increasingly valued over a century and gender discipline has been increasingly challenged, marriage has become more conceivable for same-sex partners in tandem with the evolving meaning of marital relations for heterosexual partners. Increasing valuation of individual autonomy and the right to control one's own body have been absorbed as principles into democratic and human rights frameworks, helping to convert same-sex relationships from being unthinkable to being legally regulated. Queer theorists may very well be right that it is precisely the queer relationships that are least challenging to the heterosexual order that have been assimilated to it, leaving behind a great many other forms of sexual and emotional connection as irredeemably queer. From an anthropological perspective, at least as developed through Murray's work, this is far from surprising, as it is largely how same-sex relationships have always found a place among diverse kinship orders. Societies typically have a hierarchy of great and little traditions (to borrow Robert Redfield's terminology), some socially dominant—even hegemonic—and others submerged, niche, or stigmatized. As relatively egalitarian relationships have become elevated as socially desirable and valued in liberal democratic societies, there are nevertheless large sectors of the population, both heterosexual and not, who respond to and pursue differences defined by age, gender, and other statuses.

Turning to these little traditions, then, it is striking how gender may change, be deconstructed, or be reconceived but still nevertheless continue to be productive of relationships in new ways. It is out of the longstanding folk notion that assigned all gender and sexual nonconformity to a single category of the "deviant" or "perverse" that counter-assertions of gay masculinities arose through the 1970s to the 1990s (Humphreys 1972; Levine 1998). Murray's work, too, takes pains to affirm the viability of gay masculinities, both in terms of the gender-conforming partner in gender-stratified homosexualities and in terms of the modern gay male asserting himself at a time in Western societies when gender-similar men sought affirmation and recognition of their egalitarian-type relationships. Masculinity provided a vocabulary of empowerment and a demand for respect among a people long stigmatized as unmanly and weak, and as such, its affirmation was an understandable moment in the development of gay communities. Perhaps it is not surprising as well that female masculinity was not far behind (Halberstam 1998). And yet it may be that this trend to break away from femininity and effeminacy through the 1990s pressed gender nonconforming people to consolidate alternative identities in trans, queer, and nonbinary gender expressions through the early 2000s (Valentine 2007). Queering gender has given new visibility to attractions and bonding among nonbinary and gender-transgressing people: trans women migrating away from gay identities, trans men migrating into gay men's spaces (Scheim, Adam, and Marshall 2019), and nonbinary/queer people with their own homogamous and endogamous sexualities, without necessarily seeking cisgender partners—all of this at a time of unprecedented celebration of drag in popular culture (Feldman and Hakim 2020). Indeed, the critique of taxonomy in sexology and the deconstruction of its modernist and racial origins have ironically given rise *not* to the destruction of sexual categories but rather to a revived and unprecedented flourishing of them in ways that rival [Magnus] Hirschfeld a century ago. Kadji Amin (2023, 97) dubs this "combinatorial queerness," where the aim "is not to locate and fix an individual within a hierarchical pyramid or tree, but rather to put the key axes—gender, sexual, romantic, and relational orientation—into motion in order to capacitate a nearly infinite range of combinations, and thereby, forms of personhood."

Age-differentiated relationships occupy more marginal spaces in Western societies. They have come under considerable suspicion as violators of egalitarian norms of free consent and personal autonomy. The specter of pedophilia has stimulated moral panics, especially in the United States (Lancaster 2011), stiffer criminal penalties, widespread accusations by the Christian right of "grooming" directed at schools and LGBTQ communities, and a large research literature on child abuse that demonstrates negative physical and mental health outcomes among those affected (Monnat and Chandler 2015). LGBTQ people are certainly among those affected by childhood abuse, whether through bullying or sexual abuse. All the same, age-differentiated relationships among people above the age of consent remain not only possible but flourishing, at least among gay and bisexual men (Adam 2000). The migration of the dating world onto the internet and mobile apps has allowed the creation of a wide range of networks defined by sexual taste, and daddy-boy scenes have grown in this environment. These networks build on long-standing interests: it is worth recalling how kin terms like *tío* and *papi*, for example, have long been popular ways of describing boyfriends in Spanish. And despite the dominance of the child abuse framework, for the few researchers who have dared to ask, there are many narratives, at least among men, of youthful sexualized mentorship relationships that are recalled as supportive, valuable, and fundamental to their later well-being (Adam et al. 2019; Arreola et al. 2013).

Pulling on another thread in Murray's work, it remains an open question how sexualities articulate with divisions of labor. While the imbrication of gender with the division of labor has received a great deal of scrutiny, sexuality offers another intersection. In small societies with simple divisions of labor based primarily on gender, there seems to be an association between sexuality and the first steps toward greater complexity. On the one hand, there are eunuchs in early state formations and celibates in religious organizations who are intended to occupy gender locations that abstain from the reproductive and inheritance implications of heterosexual gender. On the other hand, there are the incipient priest/counselor/physician professions, often dubbed "shamans," that appear to innovate gender and sexual expression along with new roles in the division of labor. Even in advanced industrial societies, while LGBTQ people are "everywhere" in the division of labor, LGBTQ people have often been the first to integrate gender-identified occupations, but there remains some unevenness in their distribution among occupations despite their (often higher) educational attainment (Waite and Denier 2015). This leaves us with unresolved questions as to whether evolving complexity in the division of labor helps generate gender and sexual change and, conversely, whether gender and sexual innovators are also innovators in the division of labor.

The early mapping of sexual forms tended to start with the presumption that homosexuality is a primary force encoded and manifested in variable ways in different societies around the world. The view that homosexualities can at least be conceived as a sufficiently coherent entity that it can be studied cross-culturally is at least as legitimate as the cross-cultural study of "kinship," "family," or "power" that similarly start with the notion that these are sufficiently coherent concepts to capture similar human practices in diverse societies. That this commonality demonstrates something universal, natural, or biological about humans as a species is a further conceptual leap. The essentialist presumptions of early twentieth-century

German sexual science remain alive today, ranging from folk wisdom among many LGBTQ people who experience their sexuality as in-born, to biologists and geneticists who continue to search for gay genes and prenatal hormones or derive biological determination from studies of index finger length, birth order, and hypothalamus size (Kabátek, Perales, and Ablaza 2022; Diamond 2021). Still, increasingly sophisticated genetic analysis has yielded little that is definitive, rather returning to the realization that while genetics may provide a field of possibility and limitation, genes are not simply determinative. The variable manifestation of genes cannot take the status of first causes and genotypes cannot be disentangled from phenotypes.

The recurrence of structured patterns raises questions as well at the opposite end of the conceptual continuum, concerning how certain social divisions—not only gender—seem repeatedly to constitute fault lines that generate erotic tension and desire for different kinds of people. Many of the fundamental distinctions made in societies, such as age, social class, kinship, social status, and ethno-racial difference, can produce attraction and desire in a wide variety of circumstances. These taste groupings can consolidate into sexual "fields" (Green 2014) and cultures with varying degrees of public recognition. In societies of the Global North/West, they are often the stuff of classical and contemporary romances in literature, the theater, and cinema and continue to animate the human imagination. All of this leaves us with questions of how social organization and social structure may itself generate, or perhaps catalyze, sexualities.

Stephen O. Murray's work, then, set a benchmark in the comparative study of homosexualities. His exhaustive and meticulous scholarship brought to light forms of sexuality that had long suffered from an invisibility often reinforced by conservative forces that have been quick to turn to state repression to erase these long-standing human phenomena. His work remains highly relevant today as these repressive forces continue to censor homosexualities from the public record, from Florida to Russia and in many other places, in the name of either neocolonial or anticolonial initiatives. His work further challenges ethnographic scholars to document the cultural rootedness, as well as cross-cultural legibility, of homosexualities that are today flourishing in local contexts connected at the same time in far-flung internet networks, also often overshadowed by state homophobia (Bosia 2014). His work also poses fundamental questions concerning how cultures code, shape, and channel sexual expression, and how cultural discourses shape sexual subjectivity and even generate desire without entirely containing it.

References

Adam, Barry D. 1985. "Age, Structure and Sexuality." *Journal of Homosexuality* 11 (3–4): 19–33. doi:10.1300/j082v11n03_02.

———. 2000. "Age Preferences among Gay and Bisexual Men." *GLQ: A Journal of Lesbian and Gay Studies* 6 (3): 413–34. doi:10.1215/10642684-6-3-413.

———. 2002. "From Liberation to Transgression and Beyond." In *Handbook of Lesbian and Gay Studies*, edited by Diane Richardson and Steven Seidman, 15–26. London: Sage.

———. 2011. "Epistemic Fault Lines in Biomedical and Social Approaches to HIV Prevention." *Journal of the International AIDS Society* 14 (Supplement 2): S2. doi:10.1186/1758-2652-14-S2-S2.

———. 2016. "Neoliberalism, Masculinity, and HIV Risk." *Sexuality Research and Social Policy* 13:321–29. doi:10.1007/s13178-016-0232-2.

———. 2020a. "Global Anti-LGBT Politics." *Oxford Research Encyclopedia of Politics*. doi:10.1093/acrefore/9780190228637.013.1213.

———. 2020b. "Political Economy, Sexuality, and Intimacy." In *The Oxford Handbook of Global LGBT and Sexual Diversity Politics*, edited by Michael Bosia, Sandra M. McEvoy and Momin Rahman, 31–42. New York: Oxford University Press.

Adam, Barry D, Trevor Hart, Jack Mohr, Todd Coleman, and Julia Vernon. 2019. "Resilience Pathways, Childhood Escape Routes, and Mentors Reported by Gay and Bisexual Men Affected by Syndemic Conditions." *Sexualities* 22 (4): 622–42. doi:10.1177/1363460718758663.

Alio, Amina, Abdou Khoudia, Mamadou Thiam, Drusilla Talawa, Gradi Bamfonga, Abdoulaye Al Ansar, Cheikh Ndour, and Omar Ndoye. 2022. "They Call Us Goor-Jigeen: A Qualitative Exploration of the Experiences of Senegalese Muslim Men Who Have Sex with Men Living with HIV." *Culture, Health & Sexuality* 24 (9): 1289–1301. doi:10.1080/13691058.2022.2080273.

Amin, Kadji. 2023. "Taxonomically Queer?" *GLQ: A Journal of Lesbian and Gay Studies* 29 (1): 91–107. doi:10.1215/10642684-10144435.

Arreola, Sonya, George Ayala, Rafael Díaz, and Alex Kral. 2013. "Structure, Agency, and Sexual Development of Latino Gay Men." *Journal of Sex Research* 50 (3–4): 392–400. doi:10.1080/00224499.2011.648028.

Boellstorff, Tom. 2011. "But Do Not Identify as Gay: A Proleptic Genealogy of the MSM Category." *Cultural Anthropology* 26 (2): 287–312. doi:10.1111/j.1548-1360.2011.01100.x.

Bosia, Michael. 2014. "Strange Fruit: Homophobia, the State, and the Politics of LGBT Rights and Capabilities." *Journal of Human Rights* 13 (3): 256–73. doi:10.1080/14754835.2014.919217.

Boyce, Paul. 2007. "'Conceiving Kothis': Men Who Have Sex with Men in India and the Cultural Subject of HIV Prevention." *Medical Anthropology* 26 (2): 175–203. doi:10.1080/01459740701285582.

Bullough, Vern. 1976. *Sexual Variance in Society and History*. New York: Wiley.

Diamond, Lisa. 2021. "The New Genetic Evidence on Same-Gender Sexuality." *Journal of Sex Research* 58 (7): 818–37. doi:10.1080/00224499.2021.1879721.

Feldman, Zeena, and Jamie Hakim. 2020. "From *Paris Is Burning* to #dragrace." *Celebrity Studies* 11 (4): 386–401. doi:10.1080/19392397.2020.1765080.

Green, Adam, ed. 2014. *Sexual Fields*. Chicago: University of Chicago Press.

Greenberg, David. 1988. *The Construction of Homosexuality*. Chicago: University of Chicago Press.

Halberstam, Jack. 1998. *Female Masculinity*. Durham NC: Duke University Press.

Halperin, David. 2002. *How to Do the History of Homosexuality*. Chicago: University of Chicago Press.

Humphreys, Laud. 1972. "New Styles of Homosexual Manliness." In *The Homosexual Dialectic*, edited by Joseph McCaffrey. Englewood Cliffs NJ: Prentice-Hall.

Isherwood, Christopher. 1976. *Christopher and His Kind, 1929–1939*. New York: Farrar, Straus & Giroux.

Kabátek, Jan, Francisco Perales, and Christine Ablaza. 2022. "Evidence of Fraternal Birth Order Effect on Male and Female Same-Sex Marriage in the Dutch Population." *Journal of Sex Research* 59 (6): 697–703. doi:10.1080/00224499.2021.2002798.

Karsch-Haack, Ferdinand. 1911. *Das gleichgeschlechtliche Leben der Naturvölker*. Munich: Reinhardt.

Lancaster, Roger. 2011. *Sex Panic and the Punitive State*. Berkeley: University of California Press.

Levine, Martin. 1998. *Gay Macho*. New York: New York University Press.

Lévi-Strauss, Claude. 1969. *The Elementary Structures of Kinship*. Boston: Beacon.

Monnat, Shannon, and Raeven Chandler. 2015. "Long-Term Physical Health Consequences of Adverse Childhood Experiences." *Sociological Quarterly* 56 (4): 723–52 doi:10.1111/tsq.12107.

Murray, Stephen O. 1995. *Latin American Male Homosexualities*. Albuquerque: University of New Mexico Press.

———. 2000. *Homosexualities*. Chicago: University of Chicago Press.

———. 2002a. "The Comparative Sociology of Homosexualities." In *Handbook of Lesbian and Gay Studies*, edited by Diane Richardson and Steven Seidman, 83–96. London: Sage.

———. 2002b. *Pacific Homosexualities* Lincoln: Writers Club Press / iUniverse.

Murray, Stephen O., and Will Roscoe. 1997. *Islamic Homosexualities*. New York University Press.

———. 1998. *Boy-Wives and Female Husbands: Studies in African Homosexualities*. New York: St. Martin's.

Parker, Richard, Peter Aggleton, and Amaya Perez-Brumer. 2016. "The Trouble with 'Categories.'" *Global Public Health* 11 (7–8): 819–23. doi:10.1080/17441692.2016.1185138.

Scheim, Ayden, Barry D Adam, and Zack Marshall. 2019. "Gay, Bisexual, and Queer Trans Men Navigating Sexual Fields." *Sexualities* 22 (4): 566–86. doi:10.1177/1363460717716426.

Schrader, Paul. 2020. "Fears and Fantasies: German Sexual Science and Its Research on African Sexualities, 1890–1930." *Sexualities* 23 (1–2): 127–45. doi:10.1177/1363460718785109.

Seely, Stephen. 2020. "Queer Theory from the South." *Sexualities* 23 (7): 1228–47. doi:10.1177/1363460719893618.

Steakley, James. 1975. *The Homosexual Emancipation Movement in Germany*. New York: Arno.

Tobin, Robert Deam. 2015. *Peripheral Desires*. Philadelphia: University of Pennsylvania Press.

Valentine, David. 2007. *Imagining Transgender*. Durham NC: Duke University Press.

Vicinus, Martha. 1992. "They Wonder to Which Sex I Belong." *Feminist Studies* 18 (3): 467–97.

Waite, Sean, and Nicole Denier. 2015. "Gay Pay for Straight Work." *Gender & Society* 29 (4): 561–88. doi:10.1177/0891243215584761.

Wright, Timothy. 2000. "Gay Organizations, NGOs, and the Globalization of Sexual Identity: The Case of Bolivia." *Journal of Latin American Anthropology* 5 (2): 89–111.

Young, Rebecca, and Ilan Meyer. 2005. "The Trouble with 'MSM' and 'WSW.'" *American Journal of Public Health* 95 (7): 1144–49. doi:10.2.105/AJPH.2004.046714.

7 Stephen O. Murray's Contributions to Homosexuality Studies in Latin America

Milton Machuca-Gálvez

> "Culture," like "homosexuality" is an abstraction.
> —Stephen O. Murray, *Homosexualities*, 8

When I crossed the doors of Lambda Rising Bookstore near Dupont Circle, Washington DC in December of 1991, I learned to my surprise that I was in one of the pioneer lesbian, gay, bisexual, transgender, and queer bookstores in the nation. I had recently arrived from Panama and found it exhilarating and overwhelming to see so many more LGBTQ books than I had ever seen in a single place.[1] I came across *Male Homosexuality in Central and South America*, edited by Stephen O. Murray (1987), in browsing through the stacks; the price of $10 was costly for me, but I splurged and purchased it. I was born and raised in the so-called Mesoamerica area (specifically in El Salvador),[2] and, as I had started to come to terms with my own sexuality as a gay man earlier that year, the book offered me a timely window to explore male homosexuality from a scholarly perspective. Out of habit and to protect myself, I carefully placed a postcard to hide the title from prying eyes and covered it with a transparent self-adhesive plastic book cover. At that time, I did not know that I was opening the door to Stephen O. Murray's intellectual presence in my personal and professional life, which was amplified when I met him in person in 2008 and during subsequent visits I had with him and his husband, Keelung, in San Francisco and Philadelphia.

This chapter focuses on Barry D Adam's threefold typology of the social organization of male homosexuality (Adam 1979, 1985) as adopted, developed, and expanded upon by Murray; more specifically, I trace the history of the typology from its initial adoption by Murray in *Social Theory, Homosexual Realities* (1984) through its successive versions and eventual full articulation in *Homosexualities* (Murray 2000). Analyzing the key texts and works involved in the development of the typology, the chapter provides a sequential account of its adoption, development, and evolution with particular emphasis on Latin America in general and Mesoamerica in particular, examining Murray's theoretical contributions to Latin American male homosexuality studies.

During his lifetime, Stephen embedded himself in an intellectual project to examine male homosexual behavior in almost every geographic and cultural corner of the late twentieth- and early twenty-first-century worlds, as addressed by other chapters in this volume. My own research centers on Latin America, but I remain ever cognizant of Stephen's contributions to the broader global context in which these issues exist and persist and examine how they potentially intersect with other societal, cultural, and political factors beyond this specific region.

After carefully reviewing Murray's works on male homosexual behavior in Latin America, I realized that he was aware that he had greater familiarity with specific places, such as Mexico City and Guatemala City, compared to other urban areas or subregions. He recognized the value of the insights and research of other social scientists to better comprehend both the commonalities and differences among various locales and to fill the gaps in his own experience and expertise. I foreground his writings on Mesoamerica to retain this local perspective; the subregion holds particular significance as the place where Murray spent time collecting his data, and as a scholar, and he wanted his work to be accessible at the local level.

Essays about major urban centers may characterize social science writing in ways that seem to apply to the entire city but actually represent only a small area within it. Issues related to complex urban life, therefore, are distinct from those pertaining when countries or regions are viewed as homogeneous entities. Some social scientists mislead unintentionally when they refer to a province, country, or region when what they are actually addressing is a smaller geographic point. That Murray did not escape this pitfall reflects a disciplinary practice more than an individual's shortcoming.

The Basic Underlying Sexual Ideology

An earlier book by Murray, *Social Theory, Homosexual Realities* (1984), which he referred to as "*a preliminary reconnaissance*" (personal communication), surveys the theoretical scaffolding that informed his subsequent work on male homosexuality as a social science construct; Murray introduced Adam's threefold typology to explore the social organization of male homosexualities as manifested in different cultures. His central argument is a critique of the theoretical grand traditions in sociology: functionalism, symbolic interactionism, Essex deconstructivism,[3] and neo-Marxism; he argues that they are insufficient to address the social-historical challenges of the second half of the twentieth century and critiques the disconnection among the social theory perspectives current at the time he was addressing male homosexual realities. His focus shifts to the development and expansion of gay culture in North America after the advent of gay liberation post-Stonewall riots in the 1960s and the growing segregation of gay men and lesbians into communities separate from mainstream society.

In the chapter titled "Homosexual Categorization in Cross-Cultural Perspective," Murray (1984, 45) broadened his argument to encompass a worldwide point of view, noting that "while homosexual behavior probably occurs everywhere, the defining of persons by their sexual behavior does not seem to be a universal of categorization, i.e., sexual identity is not a domain of meaning for all peoples." Guiding us through the perilous course between an allegorical labeling Scylla and an allegorical non-labeling Charybdis, Murray (1984, 45) proposed to resolve this dilemma: "There is diversity, intra-culturally as well as cross-culturally, but there is not unlimited variation in social organization and categorization of sexuality. Despite pervasive intra-cultural variability which is highlighted by [the] anthropological tradition of seeking exotic variance, *relatively few of the imaginable mappings of cognitive space are recurrently used* by diverse cultures" (emphasis in original).

While human sexuality is extremely plastic and can manifest in a variety of ways, Murray argued that the ways in which society organizes sexuality are relatively limited, and are applicable to all forms of human sexuality. Murray (1984, 46–53) transformed Adams's typology into three organizing principles or categories of male homosexual-structuring relations in human societies, namely: *age-defined*, in which homosexual activity between older males and younger males is regarded as masculinizing, and in some cultures, as essential for the development of masculinity; *gender to gay*, where "the sexually receptive partner is expected to assume the feminine gender role, i.e., to act and dress in ways appropriate to women in that society"; and *age to gender*—although not explicitly defined by Murray, he pointed out that "an earlier transformation from age to gender occurred" in the seventeenth and eighteenth centuries when "the excoriations were of homosexual behavior rather than homosexual beings."

Murray summarized a comprehensive list of ethnographic, anthropological, and sociohistorical works to illustrate each category. He continued to use this typology in later writings, refining it into a fourfold typology that he referred to as *"the basic underlying sexual ideology"* for the social organization of homosexuality in different societies around the world (Murray 1995, 2000, emphasis added), but he ultimately returned to a threefold model (2000).

In the *gender-to-gay* type, Murray (1984, 48–49) typified the cultures of the Northern Mediterranean and Latin American area cultures as settings where the social organization of male homosexuality conforms to this category, resulting in a model entailing that "the '*active*' male in homosexual copulation is an unmarked male, not regarded by anyone, and least of all by himself, as male homosexual, whereas the '*passive*' partner is expected to conform to the female role." Social scientists working in the area refer to this as the "Mediterranean model" and point out that it encompasses a series of dichotomies underlying different characteristics of the model, namely: active/passive, penile/anal, honor/stigma-shame (e.g., Holcombe 2012, 201; Howe 2013, 17–18, 177–78; Lancaster 1992, 270).

Murray's scholarly production from the mid-1980s to the early 2000s included several edited and coauthored volumes that employed Adam's typology as the theoretical framework, covering a range of regions and countries, including Latin America (1995), the United States (1996a) Oceania (1992a), the Islamic world (with Roscoe, 1997), Africa (with Roscoe, 1998), and the Pacific Rim (2002). Each volume contained detailed case studies which focused on ethnographic, anthropological, and sociohistorical research.

The Gender-Defined Organization of Homosexuality in the Mediterranean Model

The edited volume *Male Homosexuality in Central and South America* (1987) appeared three years after *Social Theory, Homosexual Realities*. Murray's (1987, 1) introduction noted a subtle shift from the typology espoused in his previous work and affirmed that "the former Iberian colonies in the New World provide the prototype of the *gender-defined organization of homosexuality*" (emphasis added).

Murray's entry on Latin America for the *Encyclopedia of Homosexuality* (1990) elaborated that the former Iberian colonies in the New World exemplify gender-defined homosexuality, in which masculine insertors are not considered homosexuals, though feminine insertees are. He recognized that this typology is oversimplified because real-life behavior and identity are more complex and often chaotic; for example, a man's behavioral repertoire may diverge from a strict dichotomy over time or with different partners. The idea of an undifferentiated phallic supremacy among *hombres* (men) is simplistic because the sexually omnivorous *hombre* (man) is more of a fantasy of the *maricón* (faggot) than an empirical observation. The projection of this fantasy is flattering to the other, speaking to his insecurities about his masculinity in ways unlikely to contradict flattering *maricón* claims about the masculinity of the *hombre*. The typological system explaining these phenomena is simple, but the cultural and social contexts in which these norms are constructed and how they shape our understanding of gender and sexuality must be kept in mind (Murray 1990, 678). Murray (1992b, 29) reiterated: "In what has been written about male homosexuality in the world's cultures, *three basic social organizations recur. In so far as changes over history are visible, the types occur in the order (1) age-stratified, (2) gender-stratified, (3) gay*" (emphasis added). He acknowledged that the historical progression from age to gender to gay could lead one to believe it to be a necessary and evolutionary order if the typology were interpreted as a rigid sequence of stages; however, he contended that such an "evolution" is neither sequential nor inevitable (29).

Latin American Male Homosexualities (1995) is an edited volume consisting of twenty-two case studies, ten of which were authored by Murray, two in collaboration with another scholar, and ten by other scholars. It is divided into four sections: general context, Spanish-speaking societies, Brazil, and Indigenous. This work is reminiscent of *Male Homosexuality in Central and South America* (1987) but on a larger scale. Murray (1995, 5) introduced a subtle theoretical change to Adam's original threefold classification, revisiting Adam (1979, 1985) to formulate a new fourfold typology for the social structuring of homosexuality as "(1) age-structured, (2) gender-defined, (3) profession-defined, and (4) egalitarian/'gay' relations."

A profession-defined category previously appeared in "'Homosexual Occupations' in Mesoamerica?" (Murray 1991), published first as a journal article and later included in *Latin American Male Homosexualities* (1995). In it he critiqued the research of Frederick Whitam and Robin Mathy (1986) proposing homosexual occupational roles and argued that occupational choice is genetically determined by sexual desire rather than a product of choice. He conducted a study to explore a potential correlation between sexual orientation and occupation in Guatemala (a characteristic method reflecting his training in sociology), and found no necessary (let alone genetic!) connections between sexual orientation and occupation; the study revealed that certain occupational niches had a disproportionate percentage of gay men, which he attributed to insider trading of information about job vacancies and even secrecy about them; discrimination against persons viewed as homosexual and/or gender deviant; and the fact that certain occupations do not secure the kind of job that everyone wants. The study further suggested that specific concentration in service sectors probably also stems from more meritocratic evaluation of candidates than in other occupational sectors.

According to Murray (1995, 5) every society has a dominant discourse regarding male homosexuality, which is structured based on one of these ideal types; although relationships based on age, gender, profession, and comradeship may exist simultaneously, one of these will predominate, "both among those who are native to the society and in explanation to aliens who ask about same-sex relations." The profession-defined category did not last long as part of Murray's typology, even in *Latin American Male Homosexualities*; he confessed that he was not completely convinced and proposed that it would be preferable to include "profession-defined" homosexuality as part of "gender-defined" homosexuality because professions often entail associated gender roles (Murray 1995, 5).

Finally, Murray (2000, 5) provided a comprehensive analysis of male homosexuality across chronology and geography in *Homosexualities*, in which he revisited and abandoned the quadruple typology, returning to the original threefold model, concluding, "I shall argue that *most instances of 'profession-defined' homosexuality are kinds of 'gender-stratified' homosexuality*, especially those in which the bodies of males are penetrated by spirits of both sexes and by the appendages of male bodies" (emphasis added). With this theoretical framework in place, Murray divided his book into three parts, each corresponding to the threefold typology as the main classificatory criteria, and provided an abundance of localized case studies of male homosexual behavior in each category for different historical periods and cultures.

He eschewed a chronological sequential approach, providing independent examples of his typology for each occurrence. This heuristic device allowed him to compare and contrast examples to establish theoretical connections and recurring patterns in each successive part of the book, enabling *Homosexualities* to present a comprehensive survey of various types of homosexuality across different cultures and time periods. Part 1 focuses on age-structured homosexualities and includes examples of pederasty, effeminized boy entertainers, and feminized boy actors in different societies, including Australia and Melanesia, medieval Egypt, Sudan, Japan, ancient Korea, and Seville. Part 2 covers gender-stratified organization of homosexuality, including butch/femme relationships in North America, male receptacles for phallic discharges, and purportedly sacralized male homosexual roles illustrated by case studies from ancient Athens, Polynesia, northeastern Siberia, Afro-Brazil, and North America. Part 3 explores egalitarian homosexualities, including heroic male couples in ancient Greek literature, modern egalitarian homosexualities, and the correlation between organizations of homosexuality and other social structures such as Islamic societies, China, and "modern" Global North societies. The book concludes by raising the question of who is desiring whom and whether it matters; he argues that understanding the diversity of homosexualities across cultures and time periods is a necessary baseline to challenge the heteronormative assumptions underlying many contemporary debates about sexuality.

Murray's rigorous and meticulous research produced significant strides toward understanding the gender-defined organization of male homosexuality and became an essential reference point for further investigation and exploration in Latin America, particularly Mesoamerica.

Murray in Mesoamerica

Murray's research on male homosexuality in Latin America started almost serendipitously. As a graduate student, he was initially interested in ethnosemantics; his first research on male homosexuality focused on Anglo Canadians. He spent most of the late 1970s in Mesoamerica but had no specific "homosexual" research agenda and neither funding nor official authorization to conduct research (academic IRB clearances not being as common then). Murray acknowledged that his "research and life are not distinctly compartmentalized," and he found himself in a situation where his interest in alternative social, cultural, and sexual organizations motivated him to pursue graduate work in sociology, anthropology, and linguistics; this was a way for him to understand his own sexuality alongside the various social organizations of male homosexuality, including those in *mestizo/criollo* Mesoamerica (Murray 1996b, 236). Once he became a social scientist, he was always a social scientist, an analytical approach that informed his research.

Murray used participant observation to obtain fresh insights into male homosexual culture in Guatemala and quickly realized that the situation was different from what he had experienced in the 1970s United States. Guatemala, as well as all former Iberian colonies in the New World, exemplified gender-defined organization of male homosexuality, its most salient characteristic being that ideal cultural norms distinguish masculine insertors (*activos*), who are not considered homosexuals, from feminine insertees (*pasivos*), who are.

He was baffled to find himself in a social milieu where there existed male "homosexuality without a gay world" (Adam 1993), and he was left to wonder what this meant. What was missing? Male homosexual behavior in Parque Central in historic downtown Guatemala City provided ample confirmation; Murray collected and documented extensive examples to satisfy his curiosity and prove the point: Guatemalan society "has never had the accoutrements of a modern gay world, that is, *commercial enterprises, voluntary organizations,* or *a social movement composed of self-identified homosexual people*" were acutely missing (Adam 1993, 172, emphasis added). The "modern gay world," in this context, was equivalent to the Global North.

Obstacles to an Autonomous Gay Culture in Latin America

Murray wondered why a vibrant gay culture had not developed in Mesoamerica and decided that the main reason might be the influence of the family structure in the region, which could have altered attitudes toward same-sex relationships. The contemporary Mesoamerican family has more functions than does the contemporary family in the Global North (Murray 1987, 119): families in Guatemala fulfill many practical roles and provide many physical, psychological, social, and economic securities; all over the region, individuals live with their family of origin until they marry. What happens then to those homosexually oriented males? Unwritten Don't Ask, Don't Tell rules impose a premium on male homosexuals with negative consequences if they are not followed; Latin American male homosexuals in same-sex relationships risk being expelled from their homes and losing their family's economic and emotional support if their homosexuality is revealed and therefore tend to cultivate stronger family relationships than others who do not face such risks. They may exercise less freedom of movement than their heterosexual brothers because they fear that their absence from home may raise suspicion about their sexual orientation (Murray 1992a, 32; 1995, 36).

Families thus represent a safety network for adult children regardless of their sexual orientation. Aside from sociocultural factors, this pattern is reinforced by scarcity of economic resources to maintain a place of one's own and the general lack of available housing. Murray (1995, 38–40) observed, however, that this pattern generally crosses social class. He disputes "the popular psychoanalytic obsession with mothers, projected onto the etiology of homosexuality," adding that it "is useless in explaining [male] homosexuality in Latin America, because the veneration of martyr (Madonna/saintly) mothers is ubiquitous, while homosexuality is not."

He believed that these factors prevented the emergence of a gay culture in Latin America. It is surprising that he did not consider the significant impact of Christianity in controlling male homosexual conduct in the region, since the rejection of male homosexuality has strong Christian roots, whether in Roman Catholicism or evangelicalism.

After analyzing factors that hinder the development of a gay culture in Latin America, Murray identified lack of consciousness as another significant obstacle. Male homosexual behavior existed in Latin and Mesoamerica (Guatemala, in particular) during the last quarter of the twentieth century, according to Murray and other social scientists, but it was not easy to navigate. The threat of homophobia, AIDS, social unrest, and civil war posed a risk not just to homosexuals but to everyone in the area, making survival a day-to-day struggle. This challenging predicament made the idea of establishing gay institutions similar to those in the Global North simply unimaginable.

Murray (1995, 43) discussed the elements that facilitated the emergence of gay liberation movements and institutions in the 1960s and 1970s in the United States, remaining mindful that "Anglo America need not be assumed to constitute the only possible route to the rejection of pariah status" in light of the emergence of a similar movement elsewhere. The absence of a strong gay liberation movement in Mesoamerica due to a lack of gay consciousness does not indicate a lack of desire but rather is the outcome of several factors that disadvantage male homosexuals, including the absence of positive literature and role models, media misrepresentation of homosexuality, widespread homophobia, censorship, police oppression, and the fear of guilt by association (44–45). Murray identified "obstacles overcome by gay liberation movements in Anglo America, so there is evidence that such obstacles are surmountable" (44); things were unlikely to get better any time soon because "continued residence with families scattered throughout cities [was] a considerable obstacle to the formation of gay consciousness, culture and community as these have developed in Anglo North America." He concluded with a clairvoyant forecast: "Only time will tell if there are other routes to similar—or other—developments" (45).

Let us not forget that the United States has a long and often turbulent history with a strong geopolitical and strategic interest in the Mesoamerican and Latin American region. Murray developed his ideas about this area over a span of fifteen to twenty years, beginning in the 1980s, when U.S. interventionism was actively taking place. Throughout the era of the Reagan administration, the region was the stage for one of the final episodes of the Cold War, causing social unrest throughout the region on a scale never before seen. AIDS became a real threat to male homosexuals in the area at the same time. The direction and effects of the AIDS pandemic on the development of male homosexuality in Latin America was difficult to forecast from within its course, although the pandemic did spur the formation of new organizations dedicated to fighting the disease among men who have sex with other men and simultaneously became the catalyzing agent that helped to move male homosexuality into public view.

Murray in Perspective

The number of ethnographically oriented studies on male homosexuality in Latin America has increased dramatically since the publication of *Male Homosexuality in Central and South America* in 1987. Murray's work remains a point of reference for those who came after him because his description provides a valuable snapshot of the state of affairs of male homosexuality in Mesoamerica at that point. Over the past thirty-five years, there have been numerous changes, both positive and negative, in the perception of male homosexuality worldwide. As Murray predicted, new developments have contributed to greater visibility of male homosexuals in Latin America. The young Guatemalan informants he interviewed in the 1970s might be in their senior years now (assuming they survived the HIV/AIDS pandemic), and subsequent generations have followed. Attitudes toward male homosexuality have improved in some areas, in terms of increased legal protections and greater representation in media, but social pressures such as family expectations and honor continue to have a strong influence. For example, many cultures still stigmatize being openly gay, and family members may be reluctant to accept a gay son or brother. Much work remains to be done to promote acceptance and understanding of male homosexual individuals and the gay community despite progress in many areas.

The Global Divide on Homosexuality (Kohut 2014) found that age and religion play important roles in the acceptance or rejection of homosexuality in different countries. Homosexuality tends to be more accepted in countries where religion is no longer a dominant cultural force, and younger generations are generally more tolerant of different sexual orientations than their older counterparts. Out of seven Latin American countries surveyed, El Salvador was the most conservative about gay issues, with 62 percent of Salvadorans surveyed agreeing with the statement "homosexuality should not be accepted by society" (3); a closer look reveals Salvadorans under age thirty (as well as Russians and Venezuelans in the same age cohort) to be more tolerant of homosexuality than those fifty and older (Pousther and Kent 2020).

The violence and instability caused by armed conflicts in the region from the mid-1970s to the mid-1990s led a significant number of citizens, including male homosexuals, to migrate to the United States or other countries. Many male homosexuals who were doubly jeopardized by their sexual orientation fled the area and were exposed while abroad to a different approach to living their sexuality; they became active agents of cultural change upon returning by promoting greater acceptance of male homosexual individuals and issues. New organizations focused on the variety of non-heterosexual orientations have emerged in the region since the early 2000s, and these have been working to promote same-sex marriage, gay adoption, sexual education, safe sex, and other LGBTQIA+ issues; as a result, the LGBTQIA+ acronym has become more visible and generally accepted.

Gay pride parades are now ubiquitous in every capital of the Mesoamerican area. At the first gay pride parade in Mexico City in 1978, some thirty homosexuals who identified themselves as members of the Frente de Liberación Homosexual de México (Secretaría de Cultura, Gobierno de México 2019) were camouflaged during the "march for the anniversary of the Cuban Revolution." Emerging gay organizations in neighboring countries followed suit in organizing their version of gay pride in each respective capital city a decade or two later: San Salvador, El Salvador, in 1997 (Maire 2020); Tegucigalpa, Honduras, in 2000 (Varela-Huerta and Abrego 2020), and San Pedro Sula, Honduras, in 2009 (Orellana 2022; U.S. Department of State 2011); Guatemala in 2000 (Immigration and Refugee Board of Canada 2003); Costa Rica in 2003 (Jiménez Bolaños 2017), and Managua, Nicaragua, in 2009 (Kampwirth 2020).

Globalization and the internet have become powerful agents of cultural transformation, particularly in Latin America, where younger generations are increasingly adopting norms from beyond their borders. Male homosexuals, in particular, are harnessing these forces of change to assert their agency, making their voices more visible in positive and empowering ways. External influences are gradually fostering change, but societal stigma remains a persistent challenge. The term *gay* rapidly diffused in urban Latin America in the 1980s and nowadays has become integrated into everyday language in Latin American countries (e.g., Medina, Toro-Alfonso, and Baños 2008). In short, there is a movement toward diversity in the ways of organizing gay sexual orientation in particular and LGBTQIA+ life and identity in general.

Murray emphasized that his typology was developed after Adam's and should not be considered a rigid sequence of evolutionary stages. On the contrary, examples of the typology could coexist in a society, although one would dominate over the others. This translates in reality to a move toward gender equality in the gay community, with gender stratification giving way to egalitarianism, which fulfills Murray's earlier predictions and theories about its organization.

Since the early 2000s, Central American gay literature has flourished and expanded by leaps and bounds. A few concealed examples existed already during Murray's time in the region, demonstrating that literature by and about gay individuals in Central America is not a new phenomenon. The novelty lies in the way the theme is treated today; in a more positive light, literature acknowledges the stigma associated with being gay, and presents alternatives for living as such. This literature is available to any local reader, revealing the magnitude of the change that has occurred.

Gay literature in Mesoamerica is not uniform in production and varies from country to country. In El Salvador, one of the countries with the most abundant production, five novels with male homosexual characters as the protagonist have been published to date (Barrera 2013; Leiva Masín 2002; Orellana Suárez 2009, 2011; Soriano 2005), showing a growing trend of acceptance and awareness of the male homosexual community in El Salvador that seems to apply across the region. This trend demands a social science perspective to shed light on the main themes and treatment of the topic. Those who knew Stephen well have joked that he would most likely be preparing a critical book review of these novels. A renowned scholar of male homosexual literature, he would have been fascinated by this development and the progress made in promoting greater acceptance of male homosexual individuals in Mesoamerican culture.

Three decades after the publication of *Male Homosexuality in Central and South America*, significant progress points toward increasing acceptance, awareness, and recognition of the human rights of sexual minorities, although discrimination, harassment, and violence against LGBTQIA+ individuals remain prevalent based on various factors such as social class, ethnicity, age, gender, political ideology, and personal circumstances, especially among vulnerable populations. Those living in urban areas or from middle to high-income backgrounds, for instance, may experience less overt discrimination and have better access to resources and support networks than those from more marginalized groups.

The situation is not uniform across the region, and in some countries sexual orientation and gender identity can be matters of life or death. For instance, the alarming rates of violence against transgender individuals, particularly trans women, in Honduras highlight the extreme vulnerability of LGBTQ+ groups. While male homosexuals also face significant discrimination, including marginalization and criminalization, the broader LGBTQ+ community—especially those who challenge rigid gender norms—bears the brunt of this violence. These developments underscore the pervasive social stigmatization and the urgent need for more inclusive protections across the region. At the same time, we must search for the voices that have been silenced. Martin Nesvig (2001, 3), in his essay "The Complicated Terrain of Latin American Homosexuality," says that "the topic of male homosexuality offers a powerful lens through which social scientists can approach and problematize the dilemmas of reconstructing both the recent and remote social past."

Legal protections for LGBTQIA+ individuals in the region are still limited: same-sex marriage is not recognized and hate crimes against people who do not identify with heterosexuality and/or the gender binary are not considered a specific legal category, which results in perpetrators often escaping accountability for their actions, though LGBTQIA+ advocacy groups and support networks are working to promote awareness and advocate for legal protections and human rights.

There have been some positive developments despite these challenges. There has been a growing trend of acceptance and awareness of LGBTQIA+ issues, and the number of published works representing this group positively has increased. While there is still a long way to go, the increasing visibility and acceptance of LGBTQIA+ individuals in Central America is a step in the right direction, and the ongoing efforts of activists and allies are crucial to continue promoting progress and fighting against discrimination and inequality.

Conclusion

Since Murray's seminal publication of *Male Homosexuality in Central and South America* in 1987, ethnographic perspectives on male homosexuality in Latin America have burgeoned. Murray persistently revisited and refined his ideas, notably in his reflections as a gay anthropologist in Guatemala (1996b) and in his extensive examinations in *Latin American Male Homosexualities* (1995) and *Homosexualities* (2000). Yet despite his continuous efforts spanning three decades, external critiques or evaluations focusing on cultural continuity, shifting attitudes, and legal transformations in the region concerning his work remain scarce.

While it is conceivable that Stephen Murray might appreciate the strides taken in the study of Mesoamerican homosexuality, his own rigorous approach to scholarship and history of revising his work suggest he would probably encourage ongoing research efforts, emphasizing the need for building upon existing knowledge and perhaps seeking to expand the scope and depth of current scholarship. The Mesoamerican sociocultural terrain has evolved profoundly since Murray's first visit to the area, especially concerning views on homosexuality. Now, the region celebrates a vibrant gay culture, birthed from years of advocacy, activism, communal solidarity, and cultural change. The rise of this culture underscores the LGBTQIA+ community's tenacity and highlights a fertile ground for delving into the intricate realities of present-day queer life in Mesoamerica. Notably, terms like *nonbinary* or LGBTQIA+ are innovations of the late twentieth and early twenty-first century, postdating much of Murray's initial research.

Murray's scholarly contributions in this domain remain instrumental for both academia and the broader community. The synthesis of his pioneering insights with current research on the male homosexual experiences in Mesoamerica depicts a vibrant and evolving academic landscape. To truly appreciate Murray's evolving perspectives, one must grasp the nuances of his disciplinary stance. This chapter has elucidated Murray's fundamental ideas on homosexuality in Latin America, emphasizing his ethnographic endeavors in Mesoamerica and their significance for today's social scientists.

Postscript

In his 2012 annual report to friends and colleagues, Stephen announced that I was the first research fellow in residence at El Instituto Obregón, news that was both humbling and flattering for me and reminded me of the significance of Stephen's name in relation to El Instituto. The sound of El Instituto Obregón carries a twofold significance for a native speaker of Spanish: *institutos* have a long tradition as think tanks in Latin America, as places where intellectuals assiduously devote themselves to intellectual activity; the last name *Obregón* evokes the memory of Álvaro Obregón, a Sonoran-born general in the Mexican Revolution who became the forty-sixth president of Mexico and was assassinated in 1928. In the popular image of the revolution, Obregón was known as "the organizer, the peacemaker, the unifier" (Hall 1981, 3). During my residency at El Instituto, I asked Stephen why he had chosen Obregón. He simply replied, with his characteristic feline smile, "por el presidente," a brief response that both conveyed his characteristic wit and humor and encapsulated the significance of the name. Stephen's choice of name was a deliberate nod to the intellectual and historical legacy of the Mesoamerican region, not merely a coincidence. Stephen was a scholar and intellectual attuned to the significance of names and symbols, and his naming of El Instituto Obregón reflected his deep understanding and appreciation of the cultural and historical context of the region.

Notes

1. How the acronym LGBTQ (lesbian, gay, bisexual, transgender, and queer) morphed into LGBTQIA+ (lesbian, gay, bisexual, transgender, queer/questioning, intersex, and asexual/agender) is beyond the scope of this paper.
2. The term "Mesoamerica," coined by German-Mexican ethnologist Paul Kirchhoff (1900-1972), refers to a region characterized by archaeological, cultural, and

historical similarities among various pre-Columbian cultures in the region. This area encompasses southern Mexico, Guatemala, Belize, El Salvador, western Honduras, and the Pacific lowlands of Nicaragua and northwestern Costa Rica (Kirchhoff 1968).

3. The original reads "Sussex deconstructivists." In my personal copy, he corrected it and wrote a capital E on top of "Su." I forgot to ask him for clarification.

References

Adam, Barry D. 1979. "Reply." *Sociologists' Gay Caucus Newsletter* 18:8.

———. 1985. "Age, Structure, and Sexuality." *Journal of Homosexuality* 11 (3-4): 19–33.

———. 1993. "In Nicaragua: Homosexuality without a Gay World." *Journal of Homosexuality* 24 (3–4): 171–81. doi:10.1300/J082v24n03_13.

Barrera, Luis Carlos. 2013. *Entre él y yo*. Madrid: Ediciones Eride.

Hall, Linda B. 1981. *Alvaro Obregón: Power and Revolution in Mexico, 1911–1920*. College Station: Texas A&M University Press.

Holcombe, W. Daniel. 2012. "Desarrollando una óptica queer: coloquio con David William Foster." *Studies in Latin American Popular Culture* 30:194–214. doi:10.1353/sla.2012.0007.

Howe, Cymene. 2013. *Intimate Activism: The Struggle for Sexual Rights in Postrevolutionary Nicaragua*. Durham NC: Duke University Press.

Immigration and Refugee Board of Canada. 2003. "Guatemala: Update to GTM33228.E of 3 December 1999; Treatment of Gays, Lesbians, and Bisexuals in Guatemala City; Police Attitude towards Same-Sex Domestic Violence and State Protection Available to Its Victims (1999–2003)." UN Refugee Agency. https://www.refworld.org/docid/403dd1f64.html.

Jiménez Bolaños, José Manuel. 2017. "De lo privado a lo público: la celebración del orgullo LGBTI en Costa Rica, 2003–2016." *Diálogos: Revista de Historia* 18 (1). https://doi.org/10.15517/dre.v18i1.25719.

Kampwirth, Karen. 2022. *LGBTQ Politics in Nicaragua: Revolution, Dictatorship, and Social Movements*. Tucson: University of Arizona Press.

Kirchhoff, Paul. 1968. "Mesoamerica: Its Geographic Limits, Ethnic Composition and Cultural Characteristics." In *Heritage of Conquest*, edited by Sol Tax, 17–30. New York: Cooper Square.

Kohut, Andrew. 2014. *The Global Divide on Homosexuality: Greater Acceptance in Secular and More Affluent Countries*. Washington DC: Pew Research Trust. https://www.pewresearch.org/global/2013/06/04/the-global-divide-on-homosexuality/.

Lancaster, Roger N. 1992. *Life Is Hard: Machismo, Danger, and the Intimacy of Power in Nicaragua*. Berkeley: University of California Press.

Leiva Masín, Julio. 2002. *Más allá del horizonte*. San Salvador: Arco Iris.

Maire, Thierry. 2020. "La marcha del orgullo en El Salvador: (Re)Construcción de la memoria, del mito fundador a la realidad histórica." *Revista Controversia* 215:159–99. https://revistacontroversia.com/index.php/controversia/article/view/1212/978.

Medina, Edgardo Javier, José Toro-Alfonso, and Omar Baños. 2008. "No más en el tintero. Hombres gay: Nuestras vidas y el VIH en Centro América y el Caribe." Los Angeles: AIDS Project Los Angeles-International Programs and Coalition of Gay Organizations in Central America. https://healtheducationresources.unesco.org/sites/default/files/resources/santiago_tintero.pdf.

Murray, Stephen O. 1984. *Social Theory, Homosexual Realities*. New York: Gay Academic Union.

———. 1987. *Male Homosexuality in Central and South America*. New York: Gay Academic Union.

———. 1990. "Latin America." In *The Encyclopedia of Homosexuality*, edited by Wayne R. Dynes, vol. 1, 678–81. New York: Garland.

———. 1991. "Homosexual Occupations in Mesoamerica?" *Journal of Homosexuality* 21 (4): 57–64.

———. 1992a. *Oceanic Homosexualities*. New York: Garland.

———. 1992b. "The 'Underdevelopment' of Modern/Gay Homosexuality in Urban Mesoamerica." In *Modern Homosexualities*, edited by Ken Plummer, 29–38. London: Routledge.

———. 1995. *Latin American Male Homosexualities*. Albuquerque: University of New Mexico Press.

———. 1996a. *American Gay*. Chicago: University of Chicago Press.

———. 1996b. "Male Homosexuality in Guatemala." In *Out in the Field*, edited by William Leap and Ellen Lewin, 236–60. Urbana: University of Illinois Press.

———. 2000. *Homosexualities*. Chicago: University of Chicago Press.

———. 2002. *Pacific Homosexualities*. Lincoln: iUniverse.

Murray, Stephen O., and Will Roscoe. 1997. *Islamic Homosexualities*. New York: New York University Press.

———, eds. 1998. *Boy-Wives and Female Husbands: Studies in African Homosexualities*. New York: St. Martin's.

Nesvig, Martin Austin. 2001. "The Complicated Terrain of Latin American Homosexuality." *Hispanic American Historical Review* 81 (3–4): 689–729.

Orellana, Dunia. 2022. "Juventud LGBTQ+ hondureña renueva la marcha del orgullo: Unas mil personas participaron en el evento en San Pedro Sula." *Los Angeles Blade*, August 2. https://www.losangelesblade.com/2022/08/02/juventud-lgbtq-hondurena-renueva-la-marcha-del-orgullo/.

Orellana Suárez, Mauricio. 2009. *Ciudad de alado*. San Salvador: Uruk Editores.

———. 2011. *Heterocity*. San José, Costa Rica: Ediciones Lanzallamas.

Poushter, Jacob, and Nicholas Kent. 2020. "The Global Divide on Homosexuality Persists." Pew Research Center. https://www.pewresearch.org/global/2020/06/25/global-divide-on-homosexuality-persists/.

Secretaría de Cultura, Gobierno de México. 2019. "Breve historia de la primera marcha LGBT+ de México." *Blog de Cultura.* https://www.gob.mx/cultura/articulos/breve-historia-de-la-primera-marcha-lgbttti-de-mexico.

Soriano, Carlos Alberto. 2005. *Ángeles caídos.* San Salvador, El Salvador: Editorial Lis.

U.S. Department of State. 2011. "2010 Country Reports on Human Rights Practices—Honduras." https://www.refworld.org/docid/4da56dc0c.html.

Varela-Huerta, Amarela, and Leisy J. Abrego. 2021. "Somos más que testimonios, somos historiadoras encarnadas de la política interseccional e internacionalista: Entrevista con Suyapa Portillo Villeda." *Revista Andamios* 18 (45): 273–305. https://doi.org/10.29092/uacm.v18i45.819.

Whitam, Frederick J., and Robin Mathy. 1986. *Male Homosexuality in Four Societies.* New York: Praeger.

8 Stephen O. Murray and the Development of Queer African Studies

Marc Epprecht

The second-ever panel devoted to queer topics at the African Studies Association took place in San Francisco in November 1996—the first ever had happened the year before (Amory 1997).[1] I had traveled there from Zimbabwe to present an early analysis of evidence I had been uncovering in the colonial archives on the history of male-male sexual relations in what was then known as Southern Rhodesia. Extremely naive about the field of global queer studies, I had not read any of Stephen Murray's work, let alone that of Will Roscoe. I understood very well, however, the need to counter the dangerous political homophobia then emerging under the umbrella of African nationalism and hitched to a highly conservative interpretation of Christianity (Islamic leaders in the region would follow soon after). My hope was to do so not by speeches and denunciations but by the careful assembly of historical evidence. My belief at that time was that the evidence exposed the fundamental untruths of the main homophobic claims being floated, namely, that homosexuality was a "white man's disease" or "un-African" (Dunton and Palmberg 1996; Phillips 1997, 2004). By Steve's own account (Murray 2018), he "pleaded" with me after the conference presentation to contribute to a book that he and Will were putting together that aimed to do that very thing.

I was indeed skeptical of two more white boys joining the fray, especially as they were not Africanists. I was convinced, however, by some of the other company I would be keeping between the covers of the proposed book, Deborah Amory (1997) in particular. There was also the seeming urgency of getting a counternarrative to the political homophobia out into public discourse since virtually no African scholars at that time were engaging the project. I was proud, with reservations I discuss later, when the finished product finally came out as *Boy-Wives and Female Husbands* (Murray and Roscoe 1998, henceforth BWFH). This was not the first collection devoted to same-sex issues on the continent, but it was a pioneer for bringing a long historical lens, a wide-ranging geographical scope, and an abundance of anthropological and other source texts that showed a path forward for future research. It certainly launched me on my path. Has there been a single one of my publications on this topic that does not cite the book?[2]

BWFH was not well-distributed or reviewed in Africa and was never translated from English into any of the other international languages used on the continent. The trickle-down effect of its arguments was thus slow and often indirect. Nonetheless, it is safe to say that it helped to lay to ground for the development of a vibrant and diverse field of study now sometimes called "queer African studies." In this chapter, I reflect on ways that Murray's intellectual stamp is, and is not, visible in the field. I want to emphasize that I do so primarily because of my personal relationship with Stephen over a period that saw the field get launched and mature (1996–2019), and not from a desire by me to claim leadership in the field. Let me begin with the positive.

BWFH established fairly definitively what many of us beginning to work on the topic intuited: documents existed from around the continent that attested to a diversity of same-sex relationships among Africans from before contact with Europeans, Arabs, Persians, or any other supposedly culturally contaminating people. Vocabularies existed to name exceptions to the heteronorms otherwise on powerful display to various sojourners, missionaries, and anthropologists over the centuries. These changed over time in relation to many factors, not least of all the proselytization of explicitly homophobic Christian doctrine and a modernizing colonial ethic that sought to organize people into strict gender and sexual binaries, among other categories of convenience for governance and capitalist production. Africans today who feel erotically attracted to people of the same sex manage to live their lives through various strategies, but the political, religious, and other cultural stigma against them impose a heavy mental and other health toll.

The book intermingled historical texts with original research, including an interview (life story) conducted by Murray himself. The bibliography is more than thirty pages long. This was followed up by Murray's (2000) monograph, *Homosexualities* (with its fifty-plus pages of sources), weaving evidence from Africa south of the Sahara together thematically with histories of some of its colonizers, including the *mamluks* of Egypt, the Omanis and Persian traders along the Swahili coast, and of course the various Europeans who carved up the continent among themselves in the nineteenth century. *Homosexualities* received virtually no attention in Africa or among Africanists including, interestingly, at a forum devoted to critical reflections on BWFH with Murray himself in conversation (Epprecht et al. 2018).[3]

The immediate impact of BWFH in African studies came via three of its contributors. Speaking for myself, the bibliography alone was an invaluable tool for me to use in tracking down the often euphemistic and passing references to nonnormative sexuality hidden deeply in obscure texts that Murray had somehow found and that I needed to contextualize my findings in Zimbabwe. My first monograph on the topic (Epprecht 2004) thus stands directly on Murray's (and Roscoe's) shoulders. Perhaps to a lesser extent, the same applies to the second monograph to grow out of a key chapter in the book based on grinding doctoral research (Gaudio 2009).[4]

The third original contributor to run with the ball did so not with a monograph but by organizing a network to incubate new scholars, particularly Africans. Among other outcomes, therefore, I see BWFH leading in an almost direct line through Deborah Amory to the creation of the International Resources Network–Africa based at CLAGS (the Center for Lesbian and Gay Studies at City University of New York). IRN-Africa was an attempt to bridge the gaps between conventional academic research, activism, journalism, and artistic advocacy. Two further conferences aiming to mentor a new generation of African scholar-activists followed in Saly, Senegal (2005—the first time the topic was broached in a conference setting outside of South Africa) and Syracuse, New York (2009). Although IRN-Africa proved not to be sustainable, authors from those conferences went on to be published (Amory et al. 2022; Dankwa 2021; Ekine and Abbas 2013; Epprecht and Gueboguo 2009; Hackman 2018; Matebeni 2014; Matebeni, Munro, and Reddy 2018; Nyeck 2020, 2021; Nyeck and Epprecht 2013; Tamale 2011; "Zanele Muholi" n.d.; and others).[5] Most of the seventy-plus contributors on African topics to the *Global Encyclopedia of Lesbian, Gay, Bisexual, Transgender, and Queer (LGBTQ) History* (Chiang

2019) acknowledge their indebtedness to BWFH through reference to these second-generation works rather than BWFH itself.[6] Small wonder that Xavier Livermon (2019, 93) describes the book as "seminal." Despite its heavy reliance on colonial-language ethnographies of dubious integrity, it "paved an important path to engaging African-language vocabulary around queerness." Indeed, the new knowledge and cultural production across disciplines, the arts, popular and electronic media, and in every region of the continent is now so prodigious, it is difficult to stay abreast.

The shortcomings Livermon alludes to were discussed at the 2018 Canadian Association of African Studies roundtable (Epprecht et al. 2018) and acknowledged in the second edition of BWFH (Murray and Roscoe 2021). They are implicit as well in Rao's (2020, 19) critique of the book's "pinkwash" effect, meaning the occlusion of Indigenous sources of homophobia, and Dankwa's (2021, 24) description of Murray as an "ethnocartographer," drawing upon Kate Weston's (1993) history of the field. I understand ethnocartography to mean a facile mapping of ethnic groups or tribes based on highly select, colonial-era reifications of borders with the (good) intention of shoring up the construct of "homosexual" in the West as a rights-deserving category of person. Weston (1993, 341) put it this way: "an old-fashioned empiricist project allied to a hard-won understanding of the sexual politics that continue to target lesbian and gay male relationships in Anglo-European societies." Mapping nonnormative gender and sexuality in the Global South constitutes, in effect, a forward defense of sexual rights in the Global North. Notwithstanding the progressive politics at one level, ethnocartography in this view plays into a harmful essentialization and hierarchization of identities, perhaps in line with various critiques of "queer imperialism" or "The Gay International" (Massad 2002). The appendixes of BWFH listing "tribes" and their "social structures" did, and does, make me nervous about that, knowing how fluid and politicized ethnicity and language were in the colonial era. My own interpretation is that a fair reading of Murray (2000), among his other works, as well as his partnership with Roscoe, dispels the thought that he was seeking to conjure a single, transhistorical identity (or teleology toward it). Quite the contrary.[7]

Over the years I had intermittent communication with Steve, from whom I drew a lot of moral support. I learned something worrisome, however, when I invited him to write a review for a special issue of the *Canadian Journal of African Studies* on sexualities in Africa. It remains a regret of mine that I was not able as his editor to get him to tone down his attack on William Spurlin (2006; Murray 2009). To be fair, he may have interpreted my own earlier critique of Spurlin (Epprecht 2008) as an invitation to be combative. It nonetheless made me uncomfortable. Happily, this tone has not been emulated in queer African studies, as far as I can tell, which is mostly respectful to other members of the community of scholars, notwithstanding sometimes sharp divergence of opinion.

As noted, such criticism of Murray scarcely rippled in Africa itself until very recently (the new edition may change that, being now available as an open-source book). Dankwa (2021) deserves the last word on this debate for now, in my view, and not only because she was an original member of IRN and is the author of the very first monograph devoted to understanding the lives of African women with erotic relationships with women. She also takes the time to acknowledge Murray's theoretical and methodological work, including as articulated in his monograph (Murray 2000). Among other things, she challenges his relentless focus on sex and sexuality as reflecting a masculinist impulse that obscured more complex dynamics and the significance of everyday intimacies (erotic or not) under the umbrella of female friendship. This was, of course, something of little interest to Murray's colonial-era sources, who may have assumed Africans, and African women in particular, were not capable of such "higher" emotions. I would argue that the inclusion in BWFH of K. L. Kendall's chapter "When a Woman Loves a Woman in Lesotho" indicates an anticipation of and openness to Dankwa's critique.

Murray's pioneering role in establishing the historicity of same-sex relationships in Africa has now mostly receded into the background of assumed knowledge in queer African studies. I am uncertain, however, that all of his theoretical and methodological arguments have been evenly taken up. Briefly, taking Murray as a model implies the following: Read everything. If you cite something, make sure you understand and represent it correctly. Do not fetishize Foucault and other titans of the Western queer canon. Be skeptical of queer theory or any "postmodern" incantations that do not rest on a solid base of empirical evidence, understanding that the latter may be deeply flawed and patchy. Seek out diversity and complexity but do consider how they shed light on recurrent patterns that underscore the commonality of humanity.

To my mind, the most promising articulations of queer African studies today build upon these insights by, for example, foregrounding the work of African intellectuals who may be more attentive to nuance to African cultures and the role of racism in shaping sexual cultures than Foucault ever was. As well, they stress (with local evidence) that Africa's position in the global political economy is an empirical fact that should not be overlooked if we are going to understand sexual cultures (and gender relations and friendship networks, among many other topics). As Otu (2022) underlines in his pioneering study of *sasso* (male-bodied people who sometimes have erotic relationships with male-bodied people in Ghana), the brutality of Western-coached neoliberal structural adjustment policies upon the African poor is often rendered invisible by sanctimonious human rights and cultural identity discourses coming out of the West, ostensibly in the spirit of solidarity. This needs to be, and is being, corrected by much of the emerging body of African scholarship on sexuality, gender, and friendship, with or without reference to Murray's breakthrough scholarship.

Notes

1. Many thanks to Will Roscoe, Wendy Leeds-Hurwitz, and Regna Darnell, for inviting me to participate in the panel that has led to this book, and to my excellent colleagues Serena Owusu Dankwa, Rudolf Gaudio, and Deborah Amory for offering much welcome feedback on an early draft of this chapter upon very short notice.
2. For the record, I clock Gevisser and Cameron (1994) as the first (mostly) scholarly book on the topic, and it provided an important frame for our discussion in San Francisco. To the point about African scholars' initial reticence or inability to take on the research, Msibi (2018), Awondo (2019), and Dankwa (2021) appear to be the first peer-reviewed monographs by Africans on the topic, a two-decade lag now being addressed with some gusto.
3. Murray and Roscoe (1997) is also generally not cited by scholars of queer Africa, possibly on account of having little content from the region south of the Sahara,

possibly for its very harsh reception by Arab scholars like Massad (2002, 170–71). Ndzovu (2019) does cite Murray from *Islamic Homosexualities* as a passing support, but draws more directly upon BWFH alumni Amory, Gaudio, and myself. The genealogy of knowledge is certainly challenging to establish, and an adequate response requires multiple strategies. I note with interest, for example, that the relatively rich archive from the Portuguese colony of Angola that Murray discussed seems to have stimulated the emergence of a lively scholarship on the other Lusophone side of the continent, Mozambique (Araújo 2023; Miguel 2023), which today has a much more favorable research environment than Angola.

4. I want also to acknowledge Kendall (1995) and Nthunya (1996), the latter midwifed by Kendall. Their previous literary work led to Kendall's inclusion in BWFH as one of the commissioned chapters.

5. Cary Alan Johnson, who followed the activist path from IRN-Africa, also played a leadership role in various publications of a report and social media nature, notably Johnson (2007) and Thoreson and Cook (2011). Counting "grandchildren" of the original alumni, I could start with my own graduate and postgraduate students who have extended the work in francophone and Lusophone contexts. See Paszat (2022a, 2022b), Mbaye and Epprecht (2022), and Miguel (2023).

6. Murray (2019) appears in this massive undertaking along with several other IRN alumni and their students (Kwateng-Yeboah 2019 on Fanon, for example). Steve's brief contribution there was aimed, in part, and most discreetly, at correcting a misstep of mine in my reading of the ethnography (I had attributed self-censorship to Evans-Pritchard for the gap in time between his fieldwork and his most-cited article on the topic, which Steve demonstrated with meticulous attention to detail was not in fact the case).

7. See Roscoe (1998) for a challenge to ethnocartographic colonialism from Turtle Island.

References

Amory, Deborah P. 1997. "Homosexuality' in Africa: Issues and Debates." *Issue* 25 (1): 5–10.

Amory, Deborah P., Sean G. Massey, Jennifer Miller, and Allison P. Brown. 2022. *Introduction to LGBTQ+ Studies: A Cross-disciplinary Approach*. Albany: SUNY Press. Available as a free download at https://milnepublishing.geneseo.edu/introlgbtqstudies/front-matter/introduction/.

Araújo, Caio Simões de. 2023. "Sex, Lives and Videotape: The Transhistoricity of an Itinerant Visual Archive." *African Studies* 81 (3–4): 354–75. https://doi.org/10.1080/00020184.2023.2174076.

Awondo, Patrick. 2019. *Le sexe et ses doubles. (Homo)sexualités en postcolonie.* Lyon, France: ENS Éditions.

Chiang, Howard, ed. 2019. *Global Encyclopedia of Lesbian, Gay, Bisexual, Transgender, and Queer (LGBTQ) History.* New York: Charles Scribner's Sons.

Dankwa, Serena Owusua. 2021. *Knowing Women: Same-Sex Intimacy, Gender, and Identity in Postcolonial Ghana.* Cambridge, UK: Cambridge University Press.

Dunton, Chris and Mai Palmberg. 1996. *Human Rights and Homosexuality in Southern Africa.* Uppsala: Nordiska Afrikainstitutet.

Ekine, Sokari, and Hakima Abbas. 2013. *Queer African Reader.* Nairobi: Fahamu/Pambazuka Press.

Epprecht, Marc. 2004. *Hungochani: The History of a Dissident Sexuality in Southern Africa.* Montreal: McGill-Queen's University Press.

———. 2008. *Heterosexual Africa? The History of an Idea from the Age of Exploration to the Age of AIDS.* Athens: Ohio University Press.

Epprecht, Marc, and Charles Gueboguo, eds. 2009. "Special Issue: New Perspectives on Sexualities in Africa." *Canadian Journal of African Studies / Revue canadienne des études africaines* 43 (1).

Epprecht, Marc, Stephen O. Murray, Kuukuwa Andam, Francisco Miguel, Aminata Cécile Mbaye, and Rudolf P. Gaudio. 2018. "*Boy Wives, Female Husbands* Twenty Years On: Reflections on Scholarly Activism and the Struggle for Sexual Orientation and Gender Identity/Expression Rights in Africa." *Canadian Journal of African Studies / Revue canadienne des études africaines* 52 (3): 349–64.

Gaudio, Rudolf P. 2009. *Allah Made Us: Sexual Outlaws in an Islamic African City.* Hoboken NJ: Wiley-Blackwell.

Gevisser, Mark, and Edwin Cameron, eds. 1994. *Defiant Desire: Gay and Lesbian Lives in South Africa.* Johannesburg: Ravan Press.

Hackman, Melissa. 2018. *Desire Work: Ex-Gay and Pentecostal Masculinity in Democratic South Africa.* Durham NC: Duke University Press.

Johnson, Cary Alan. 2007. *Off the Map: How HIV/AIDS Programming Is Failing Same-Sex Practicing People in Africa.* New York: International Gay and Lesbian Human Rights Commission.

Kendall, K. Limakatso, ed. 1995. *Basali! Stories by and about Women in Lesotho.* Pietermaritzburg, South Africa: University of Natal Press.

Kwateng-Yeboah, James. 2019. "Frantz Fanon (1925–1961)." In *Global Encyclopedia of Lesbian, Gay, Bisexual, Transgender, and Queer (LGBTQ) History*, edited by Howard Chiang, 512–13. New York: Charles Scribner's Sons.

Livermon, Xavier. 2019. "Archives in Africa." In *Global Encyclopedia of Lesbian, Gay, Bisexual, Transgender, and Queer (LGBTQ) History*, edited by Howard Chiang, 91–95. New York: Charles Scribner's Sons.

Massad, Joseph. 2002. "Re-Orienting Desire: The Gay International and the Arab World." *Public Culture* 14 (2): 361–85.

Matebeni, Zethu, ed. 2014. *Reclaiming Afrikan: Queer Perspectives on Sexual and Gender Identities*. Cape Town: Modjaji.

Matebeni, Zethu, Surya Munro, and Vasu Reddy, eds. 2018. *Queer in Africa: LGBTQI Identities, Citizenship and Activism*. New York: Routledge.

Mbaye, Aminata Cécile, and Marc Epprecht. 2022. "New Studies of Sexual Orientation, Gender Identities and Expression in Africa South of the Sahara: Complicating the Narrative." *Canadian Journal of African Studies / Revue canadienne des études africaines* 57 (2): 479–88. https://doi.org/10.1080/00083968.2022.2142253.

Miguel, Francisco. 2023. "Mozambican 'Tolerance' toward Homosexuality: Luso-tropicalist Myth and Homonationalism." *Sexualities* 27 (8). https://doi.org/10.1177/13634607231160054.

Msibi, Thabo. 2018. *Hidden Sexualities of South African Teachers: Black Male Educators and Same-Sex Desire*. London: Routledge.

Murray, Stephen O. 2000. *Homosexualities*. Chicago: University of Chicago Press.

———. 2009. "Southern African Homosexualities and Denials." *Canadian Journal of African Studies/Revue canadienne des études africaines* 43 (1): 68–78.

———. 2019. "E. E. Evans-Pritchard (1902–1973)." In *Global Encyclopedia of Lesbian, Gay, Bisexual, Transgender, and Queer (LGBTQ) History*, edited by Howard Chiang, 64. New York: Charles Scribner's Sons.

Murray, Stephen O., and Will Roscoe, eds. 1997. *Islamic Homosexualities: Culture, History and Literature*. New York: New York University Press.

———. 1998. *Boy-Wives and Female Husbands: Studies in African Homosexualities*. New York: St. Martin's.

Ndzovu, Hassan J. 2019. "Islam in Africa, South of the Sahara." In *Global Encyclopedia of Lesbian, Gay, Bisexual, Transgender, and Queer (LGBTQ) History*, edited by Howard Chiang, 851–56. New York: Charles Scribner's Sons.

Nthunya, Mpho 'M'atsepho. 1996. *Singing Away the Hunger*. Edited by L. Limakatso Kendall. Pietermaritzburg, South Africa: University of Natal Press.

Nyeck, Sybille N., ed. 2020. *Routledge Handbook of Queer African Studies*. New York: Routledge.

———. 2021. *African(a) Queer Presence*. Cham, Switzerland: Palgrave Macmillan.

Nyeck, S. N., and Marc Epprecht. 2013 *Sexual Diversity in Africa: Politics, Theory, and Citizenship*. McGill-Queen's University Press.

Otu, Kwame Edwin. 2022. *Amphibious Subjects: Sasso and the Contested Politics of Queer Self-Making in Neoliberal Ghana*. Oakland: University of California Press.

Paszat, Emma. 2022a. "Criminalization and Rhetorical Nondiscrimination: Sex Work and Sexual Diversity Politics in Rwanda." *Journal of Human Rights* 21 (5): 542–57. doi:10.1080/14754835.2021.2013174.

———. 2022b. "Organizing Under Pressure: Authoritarianism, Respectability Politics, and LGBT Advocacy in Rwanda." *Social Movement Studies* 23 (2). doi:10.10 80/14742837.2022.2072287.

Phillips, Oliver. 1997. "Zimbabwean Law and the Production of a White Man's Disease." *Social and Legal Studies* 6 (4): 471–92.

———. 2004. "The Invisible Presence of Homosexuality: Implications for HIV/AIDS and Rights in Southern Africa." In *HIV and AIDS in Africa: Beyond Epistemology* edited by Ezekiel Kalipeni, Susan Craddock, Joseph Oppong, and Jayati Ghosh, 155–66. Oxford, UK: Blackwell.

Rao, Rahul. 2020. *Out of Time: The Queer Politics of Postcoloniality*. Oxford, UK: Oxford University Press.

Roscoe, Will. 1998. *Changing Ones: Third and Fourth Genders in Native North America*. New York: St. Martin's.

Spurlin, William J. 2006. *Imperialism within the Margins: Queer Representation and the Politics of Culture in Southern Africa*. New York: Houndmills.

Tamale, Sylvia, ed. 2011. *African Sexualities: A Reader*. Nairobi: Fahamu/Pambazuka Press.

Thoreson, Ryan, and Sam Cook, eds. 2011. *Nowhere to Turn: Blackmail and Extortion of LGBT People in Sub-Saharan Africa*. San Francisco: International Gay and Lesbian Human Rights Commission.

Weston, Kate. 1993. "Lesbian/Gay Studies in the House of Anthropology." *Annual Review of Anthropology* 22:339–67.

"Zanele Muholi." n.d. *Yancey Richardson*. Accessed February 7, 2023. http://www.yanceyrichardson.com/artists/zanele-muholi.

PART 4　Stephen O. Murray Gets the Last Word

9   John Gumperz in Context

1977 AND 1992 INTERVIEWS

Stephen O. Murray

Having been intrigued by sociolinguistics in a 1973–74 seminar with Keith H. Basso at the University of Arizona, and having worked through a lot of material in a year-long reading course with William J. Samarin at the University of Toronto in 1974–75, I undertook research for a PhD dissertation on social networks among linguistic anthropologists, in particular those then identified with the ethnography of speaking/communication and ethnoscience.

I attended the 1977 Georgetown University Round Table and Professor Samarin asked both Charles Ferguson and John Gumperz if they would be willing to sit down and be interviewed about their careers and networks by this sociology graduate student who was familiar with a lot of sociolinguistics work. Both agreed. I interviewed Ferguson at an office in the Center of Applied Linguistics, and Gumperz in an empty Georgetown University classroom. Both were very gracious and neither displayed any impatience with my questions.

I felt that John understood what I was looking for or at, more so than Dell Hymes, who had written extensively on history of American linguistics. Or perhaps Dell was just shyer than John. Keyboarding and rereading the 1977 interview just after John's death in Santa Barbara at the age of ninety-one, I wish that I had asked about the connections forged in India with Ferguson and Bill Bright, but my focus was on connections at Berkeley that led to the 1964 special issue of the *American Anthropologist*.[1] As is apparent in my questioning, I was also interested in how academics learned about the jobs they got, a larger study of which was published in 1981,[2] my most-cited sociology article, by the way, coauthored with my dissertation chair, Dennis Magill, and Joseph H. Rankin, who was in my

Arizona cohort and who now teaches at Wayne State University in Detroit. And I also asked John about finding interesting work, a question from my dissertation questionnaire and formal interviews that led to my 1982 paper.[3]

The ethnography of communication became the main example of a theory group (a concept pioneered with regard to American sociology theories by Nicholas Mullins in his 1973 book) producing a rhetoric of continuity, with Chomskian generative-transformationalist grammarians providing a better example than "the new ethnography" (ethnoscience) of a rhetoric of making revolutionary advances.[4] (In Mullins's terms, Gumperz was both an "intellectual leader" and an "organizational leader" of several "theory groups," as was Ferguson.)

Along with myriad other case studies, I wrote about all three of the roughly contemporary perspectives in my dissertation "Social Science Networks" in 1979, which was published in 1983 as *Group Formation in Social Science*, somewhat revised in *Theory Groups and the Study of Language in North America* and *American Sociolinguistics*.[5]

I had received a National Institute of Mental Health postdoctoral fellowship to work with John in the Language Behavior Research Laboratory at the University of California, Berkeley, during 1980–82. Though I had been endeavoring to "go native" and was more participant than observer while there, I did write about the third generation of Gumperz students at Berkeley in *American Sociolinguistics* and for a book chapter.[6]

A decade later, in 1992, we sat down again, this time in his office at the lab to talk again about his career trajectory, past and then-present networks. I'm not sure why the second interview has more about the Chomskian revolution and Labovian sociolinguistics than the first one.

A few months before his death, there was an all-morning double session of the American Anthropological Association annual meeting in an overflowing ballroom of the San Francisco Hilton called "Gumperz at 90." Between the two halves of the interesting and sometimes even entertaining program, I had the opportunity to greet John and his wife, Jenny [Cook-Gumperz]. Though in a wheelchair, he did not seem especially frail and corrected various pronunciations of names and places. I think and hope that he basked in the affection of the assemblage. He encouraged and refined a lot of research from a great many people across a wide range of topics.

His elders and most of his contemporaries mentioned or discussed in these interviews are dead, and I have long been aware that my sociology of networks from the late 1970s has turned into history. My dissertation and various publications of it were presented as histories, and so are these "raw data."

I have identified some references to particular publications. In addition to again acknowledging his encouragement of my sociological work on the history of linguistics and sociolinguistics, I want again to acknowledge my debt to William Samarin for his investment of time and patience in my sociolinguistic education and for introducing me to John Gumperz and Charles Ferguson, and for asking them and Dell Hymes to agree to be interviewed for my dissertation research.

Stephen O. Murray
SAN FRANCISCO, CALIFORNIA | *April 8, 2013*

First Interview

MARCH 18, 1977, GEORGETOWN

Stephen Murray: You were born in Germany [Hattingen, January 9, 1922] and were a native speaker of German?

John Gumperz: That's right.

SM: When did you learn English?

JG: I started learning English in high school [in Germany], but I didn't really learn English until I came to the United States in 1939—I was 17.

SM: What did your parents do?

JG: They had a small factory in Germany and they came over here because they had relatives here and they—started a business here.

SM: Skipping a bit [over starting out to be a chemist], your thesis was from Michigan in 1954 on Swabian dialects in Washtenaw County, Michigan—in Germanics?

JG: That's right, in Germanic linguistics.

SM: A dialectological study—

JG: Well, actually, it started out as a dialectological study, but actually it was a study in the German tradition of dialectology that was very much concerned with sort of the social forces as they affect language change and language mixture. One of the problems that intrigued me was the question of how—what would now be called creolization or dialect mixture [occurred]. The issue that emerged as I was working there was that there was no relationship between the dialect that people learned—the third generation speakers learned—when they were in the United States and the original dialects as they could be predicted from place of origin of the people [place from which they emigrated]. I went through the church records and found out where the people came from and I found that if I'd taken just the native dialect, I'd have predicted a completely different distribution of dialect features than what I actually found. What I actually found was that dialect mixture occurred and that the determining factor—indeed, the *over*determining factor—was church membership [in Michigan]. There were three main congregations, which roughly corresponded to the settlement patterns—three sort of village settlement patterns, which also corresponded to social groups. Each church had its own community hall and social group. People did all their socializing and it wasn't exactly geography. Some people lived in one area and went to another church. There was also factionalism, history, and tradition.

SM: But it was very much social grouping in America?

JG: That's right. What happened was that three distinct dialects formed, two of which I had quite a bit of information on. And certain forms generalized in one area and the other areas, so I see it as a sort of beginning of my sociolinguistic interest.

SM: What influences did you feel at that time?

JG: As I said, German dialectology. It was mainly the work of Germans like [Adolf] Bach, Hugo Moser, and [Theodor] Frings. And in the U.S. the person I learned some of this from was a man named Otto Springer, who is teaching Germanic linguistics at Pennsylvania. And, of course, I'd been to the Linguistics Institute—and to some extent Hans Kurath, and Herbert Penzl was my PhD supervisor.

SM: Who else was on your committee?

JG: Hans Kurath, Herbert Penzl, Albert Marckwardt—I think that's it.

SM: How did this lead into your work in India?

JG: What happened was that in doing this work—in trying to do this work—I became aware of the other interesting work that was going on in dialectology. I had gone to the [1953] LI [Linguistics Institute] at Indiana [University]. I found that I became aware of the work that Trager and [Henry Lee] Smith

Smith were doing,[7] which provided some theoretical basis for the kind of work I was doing. The earliest work I was doing was only strictly dialectological. Trager-Smith [provided] the notion of overall pattern and common core. I took courses from Hockett and from Trager and Smith, so I, as a result of taking those courses when I—a year before I finished my degree, I was appointed first as a predoctoral fellow, then as an instructor at Cornell, in the Division of Modern Language, and the first year I worked on the English for foreigners project, directed by Martin Joos and George Trager and Haxie Smith—working with William Welmers. And the second year I taught Hindi in the Division of Modern Languages. Basically, I became interested in what are the conditioning factors for language distribution, and I thought that a caste society would be an interesting society to study because of the so-called hard, harsh social boundaries. I'd also taken anthropology courses all along. At Michigan I had a course from Leslie White in anthropology, and I'd also audited some courses from Ted Newcomb, and I'd read the work of the Michigan sociologists [Hans Gerth, with whom Gumperz had a class while in the army]. Then when I came to Cornell, there was an advanced course, which was called an integrated course in social science, where ... we had regular lab work in social survey techniques, various kinds of historical techniques—I got a really good introduction to social science methodology which I took as a postdoc.

SM: So you got into Indian work primarily for theoretical reasons?

JG: That's right.

SM: When was your first fieldwork in India?

JG: In 1954, right after I got my degree. I got my degree, then I got my postdoctoral [fellowship] to go to India for two years. I taught Hindi in the way most linguists did in those days: acting as a linguist with an informant. I had to learn Hindi also when I got to India. I learned to speak it.

SM: Backtracking, did you have any contact with [Kenneth] Pike and [Eugene] Nida at Michigan?

JG: Oh, yeah, I'm sorry. Pike was one of my teachers, of course.

SM: And Nida?

JG: Pike was probably the first person I learned linguistics from. I didn't have any contact with Nida. Nida wasn't there.

SM: How did you find out about the Cornell position?

JG: Because I took this course at the LI at Indiana in 1953 and they were selecting people to work on various projects, and there were some jobs opening up at the Foreign Service Institute. Since there were no linguistics departments in those days, some people were selected for a job in the Foreign Service Institute, but then there was a cut in funds and they couldn't fill all these jobs, but then there were jobs [that] became available instead—these predoctoral fellowships working on this other ancillary project at Cornell. Then, after I'd been at Cornell, after the project was finished, I was appointed as an instructor there.

SM: How—when did you go to Berkeley?

JG: In 1956.

SM: How did you find out about that position?

JG: By that time Berkeley was interested in setting up a Hindi program. There was one person teaching Hindi in the United States, and that was at Penn, and I—there were two or three others—Oscar Aguilar and I who taught it, and there was a position opening and I got it.

SM: Did you apply for it or did [Murray] Emeneau recruit you?

JG: Actually, Richard Park and Emeneau recruited me, yes.

SM: Do you recall if you had anyone write references for you for Berkeley?

JG: I don't know whether people *wrote* references. I didn't formally request any references, but the people who knew me at the time who'd worked with me were the Cornell people and Henry Hoenigswald, and Charles Ferguson, with whom I taught in India—so I'm assuming that they were asked, but I didn't elicit any.

SM: So you went to Berkeley, and taught Hindi. Were you affiliated with—was there a linguistics department?

JG: In those days there was a linguistics department, but it had only one F.T.E. [full-time employee], everyone else was sort of informally connected. People met in the linguistics group. I think the year I came the linguistics department was formally established, but most people were still on part-time appointments. At first, I was full-time in Near Eastern languages. After three or four years, I got a part-time appointment in linguistics and part-time in Near Eastern languages.

SM: Not in anthropology until after Hymes left [in 1965]?

JG: Well—not until Hymes left, that's right.

SM: What kind of interaction did you have with the people in linguistics at Berkeley?

JG: It was a fairly close and friendly group, both with the Emeneaus and with Mary Haas. They were very welcoming toward younger people—students and [junior faculty]. It was sort of a mixed group of advanced graduate students who were sort of friends and—There were often parties at the Emeneaus' and Mary Haas's and we sort of [became] part of the same group, including people like Karl Teeter at Harvard, and Wick Miller, who is at Utah, Sid Lamb, Bill Shipley at Santa Cruz, and many others. We were all part of that group. I was the only sociolinguist among them.

SM: Do you feel that any of those people had an intellectual influence on you?

JG: Intellectual influence—contact was mainly with Sidney Lamb, who at the time was a really very important linguist—that was through Hockett. He really built on Hockett.

SM: I gather from talking to Dell Hymes that Lamb was rather anathema to Haas and Emeneau—

JG: that's right. Yeah.

SM: Did that, um, stigmatize you—associating with him?

JG: Well, there were factional problems that I think we shouldn't go into. But it wasn't just Lamb. It ended up being Lamb, Hymes, and myself.

SM: Okay. I understand you were the prime organizer of the Saturday group.

JG: That's right. We sort of had a luncheon group with Hymes, later on with Susan Ervin-Tripp, Dan Slobin, David Schroeder in philosophy, who's now at Illinois, John Searle, occasionally, and Wallace Chafe when he came to Berkeley. We all met on and off. We were all young people interested in various problems of cognition, sociolinguistics, social theory, philosophy.

SM: This was around 1960?

JG: Yeah, starting around '60.

SM: How did you meet Ervin-Tripp?

JG: She came to Berkeley in 1958, and I met her because she'd read my first paper in the *American Anthropologist* on dialect in an Indian village.[8]

SM: You had common interests?

JG: That's right, common interests. She, being a woman, was appointed for one year at Berkeley and then was let go by the psychology department for the overtly stated reason that they didn't like to employ women. So she had to get a job. She got a grant to do her child language work and the speech department took her in to teach English to Japanese and Korean second language teaching. It was forced on her.

SM: This Saturday group—

JG: Erving Goffman was part of that group occasionally, and we had very close relationships with the Stanford people—Kimball Romney, Charles Frake, Duane Metzger, and Roy D'Andrade, so the ethnography of communication when it was born was sort of a Berkeley-Stanford thing, not just a Berkeley thing.

SM: **Right, but certainly California based.**

JG: Originally, it was California based. That's right, yeah. In the initial stages of the field, Frake formed a bridge between ethnographers of communication and ethnographic semanticists. He was the only one of the Stanford ethnoscience people who actively participated in the original Southwestern Anthropology [Southwestern Anthropological Association] meeting symposium, and his paper on "how to get a drink" is still seen as one of the classics in the field.[9] In his later work, Frake is the first to take a cognitive—perhaps slightly Chomskian—view of the field in contrast to Hymes's basically functionalist, Durkheimian or Parsonian view.

SM: **These Saturday meetings, were they formal: papers—**

JG: Oh, no, no, no. We just had luncheons and talked, we talked very freely. Actually, we had meeting[s] in other persons' houses. Oh, and two other regular participants were Julian Boyd, who was an English linguist, and Josephine Miles, a poet and interested in studies of style. Boyd is a major theorist in the generative grammar tradition: Boyd and Thorne.[10]

SM: **Was generative grammar one of the things that was being discussed?**

JG: Oh yeah, oh yeah. I remember having long talks with Roman Jakobson, who was there for a time. We were fortunate, because we had the Stanford Center [for Advanced Study in the Behavioral Sciences], and Jakobson came and Morris Halle came out one year, and we talked. We had long discussions about the problems of rule-ordering, and all that sort of thing.

SM: **And at some point you coalesced into something more formal.**

JG: Well, it started with a symposium we did in the Southwest Anthropological Association. I don't know what it was called. The participants then were Goffman, Frake, Hymes, and myself. And I remember Nancy Tanner, who is now at UC Santa Cruz and who's published several papers on language usage.

SM: Ervin-Tripp—

JG: Ervin-Tripp? No, I don't think she was; I don't know whether she participated in that symposium or not.

SM: **And this became the basis for the AAA—**

JG: That's right, and then we had the AAA meeting. What happened is that through Roman Jakobson I was put in touch with some people in Norway who were interested in having someone who was interested in sociolinguistics, and I got a Fulbright to go to Norway and I came in contact with Fredrik Barth and Jan-Petter Blom, who were the major influences on me in anthropological theory, both, and who actually taught me Bateson,[11] which—I hadn't really read Bateson until then, and then I did my fieldwork with Blom in Norway and the influence there was ethnomusicology. He is an ethnomusicologist and a folklorist and a social anthropologist. So I think I really became a social anthropologist through working and talking with him. I also learned a great deal of anthropology before, because I'd spent two years in India as the only linguist working in a team of anthropologists, and, well, especially John Hitchcock, who's a professor of anthropology at Wisconsin now and my very close friend. We talked a great deal about problems of social structure and so on. And we were immersed in fieldwork. Part of that project, we actually had to produce fieldnotes and we did a lot of ethnography in common. In fact, I really learned. I'd had a one-year course in social survey methods. We had several sociologists there, and an economist, and a psychologist. Leigh Triandis was in the field with us, as part of the [John] Whiting project in socialization theory, so we really had contact with most of the major currents in social science. Then, later on in Norway, I was really lucky to meet Fredrik Barth. I tried to make contact with people who were interested in social philosophy—Arne Naess and people like that—and they couldn't [or] weren't really interested, and the sociologists I couldn't really talk to, but Fredrik read some of my papers and was interested. So I began, again through personal contact and collaboration with Fred and J.-P. Blom, I really again got to find out what good ethnographic fieldwork is.

SM: **They were going in the direction you were going?**

JG: Yeah.

SM: **Which was increasingly more anthropological?**

JG: Well not entirely, it was also linguistic. It was taking both anthropological and linguistic theories.

SM: **I meant that from linguistic training, moving in anthropological directions without ceasing to be a linguist. Will you accept that formulation?**

JG: Yeah.

SM: **Given that you're now a professor of anthropology—**

JG: Well, what happened was partly a matter of factionalism or alternative interests within the linguistics department. There was a split between empiricists and theorists, and although I wasn't a generative grammarian—there weren't any generative grammarians there—I was in the linguistics departments and there was some difficulty with theorists, either in the social area or in the linguistic area. I was seen as merely repeating what [Edward] Sapir had done. Lamb was seen as empty theorizing. So it wasn't comfortable. Dell Hymes was seen as not doing any fieldwork. I don't want to attribute it to any particular individual. I think it's a very common failing that people have of recognizing when others strike out in new directions, failing to see what's original about the new work.

SM: **Generational tension?**

JG: Yeah. I remember when Paul Friedrich reviewed the Ferguson and Gumperz *Linguistic Diversity in South Asia* book[12] and pointed out my drawing a parallel looking at phonemic systems in sort of reference group models for imitation, rather than the real thing that was an important thing. I remember that people at lunch pointed out to me, "Well, look, Sapir did all that."

SM: **So you moved to anthropology?**

JG: Well, no. I stayed in linguistics a year. Then it became administratively too difficult and I got to be wholly in anthropology. It was sort of a compromise. The linguistics department brought in some generative grammarians, they brought in Wallace Chafe, thinking he would be an anti-theorist, which he is far from. And they brought in Bill Wong, who was at first interested in generative grammar, and then, successively, they brought in more people, and I would go out into the anthropology department. Then we built up our own group of linguistic anthropology in the anthropology department.

SM: **It was still a group across departmental boundaries.**

JG: There's always been that group and we've always stayed, and we have, even though we don't see each other that much, we still have an intellectual relationship. Not with sociology at all since Erving Goffman left [in 1969]. I kept getting the last of his students for two or three years, but we've had no relationships with sociology. But we've certainly had a close relationship with anthropology with [ties to some of those in] linguistics and psychology maintained and philosophy.

SM: In sociology, there was never any relationship with symbolic interactionists?

JG: Vaguely. Most of the ethnomethodologists were Goffman students and the Goffman students had the same problem with Goffman, however, that we had with *our* ancestors. I remember when Harvey Sacks had his thesis finished and Goffman sat on it for a couple of years. He just didn't understand it, and some of us who had read it had to write him letters, and finally the committee had to be reconstituted so he could get his degree.[13]

SM: Were you on it?

JG: No, I was not, but I was one of the people who had to write letters, suggesting that the committee—and Blumer played an important role in seeing that he got his degree. I was on [Emanuel] Schegloff's committee, yes.[14]

SM: Even though Blumer played—

JG: —an important role—

SM: There was no—

JG: —no intellectual contact, no. [Theodore R.] Sarbin used to come and say, "Yeah we ought to talk some time," but no, no real contact.

SM: That seems to be a national pattern. Let's see, what year did you join the SSRC committee [Social Science Research Council Committee on Sociolinguistics]?

JG: I was in the original group.

SM: At the 1964 LI [Linguistics Institute]?

JG: Yeah, I was one of the org—yeah, but then, I think I was too far out. SSRC doesn't like people who are too far out in theory, so they picked a lot of older, senior people in the beginning. I've always been critical of the committee because they've skirted around theoretical issues. I was brought in, finally, after two years, after repeated attempts by Hymes and Ferguson, I think.

JG: They've had a succession: [Nathan] Keyfitz, Everett Hughes is really one of the fathers of sociolinguistics, but John Useem, I don't know, wasn't that interested. And Stan Lieberson: I think has done some very good work, but it's in a very special field. They were there for a while. Joshua Fishman has never really been interested in learning any linguistics. [something inaudible]

SM: Like Lambert, openly hostile to linguistics.

JG: That's right. He doesn't have to. They're social psychologists, they're using language for social measurement, which is fine.

SM: So, on the committee, you tended to be a dissenting voice?

JG: Well, I was usually a dissenting voice. I think we were the first to insist that the committee sponsor some empirical work. Then, we had this cross-cultural study of communicative competence with Slobin, Ervin-Tripp, and myself, which was the first comparative project [sponsored by the SSRC Committee on Sociolinguistics]. We started that. The rest of the activities of the committee were inviting conferences, running conferences where people who had names but weren't necessarily interested in each other talked at each other in conference. And I was a dissenting voice in the work on language planning, which I felt was completely asociological and atheoretical sociologically. I insisted on making conferences between people who really shared some interest, had a basis for talking, that that was confused with saying you want to invite you friends. It's not what I meant.

SM: I can see that that would be touchy.

JG: That's right, but the model that I had in mind was the kind of thing we had in the beginning of ethnomethodology, when Harold Garfinkel used to call. We would spend our own money and go down to UCLA and spend here days talking with Garfinkel, Aaron Cicourel, Bill Labov, Manny Schegloff, Harvey Sacks, and myself—people that are unlikely to be [conceived as being] together, who aren't usually grouped together. We just went down there and talked, I preferred that sort of thing, where people would come because they were interested in some of the same things, and we weren't necessarily friends. That was the first place I met Manny Schegloff, for example. I had met others. I knew Roy Turner, because he was the same building, but I never talked with him when he was at Berkeley. Now he's a very good friend.

SM: Does that say something about Berkeley or—

JG: It says something about Berkeley. It's hard to get across in Berkeley, yeah.

SM: Who do your trust to assess your work? Say, circa 1970. Who would have read what you were writing?

JG: 1966–70? Now? Now my work is quite different, straight phenomenological, ethnomethodological. I don't do any more traditional sociolinguistics anymore. I changed radically since I started working on my code-switching articles.

SM: Well—could you specify your reference group both then and now?

JG: My reference group then, in the early days, would have been someone like Hymes. Ethel Albert, certainly. Ethel Albert I would trust even now in linguistics. [pause]

SM: Was she part of the Saturday meetings in the early sixties?

JG: Occasionally, yes. Not as much as she should have been [pause]. Paul Friedrich, certainly, Robbins Burling, always. No sociologists that I can think of.

Now, among anthropologists, here are a group of people: Maurice Bloch in London, certainly. And, in the early days, Edmund Leach and Fredrik Barth, too. I don't think they're that interested now anymore. But in this kind of work I would say who I trust, anthropologists who read my work: Edmund Leach, Ned Hall, Fergie [Ferguson], I would still trust to read my work, Gillian Sankoff, Bill Labov always, Aaron Cicourel, Harold Garfinkel. Anyone with some kind of phenomenological bent. Aram Yengoyan and Pete Becker, certainly—Pete Becker is Alton S. Becker, who published a book on style with Kenneth Pike about eight or nine years ago and who I think is one of the major rising stars in anthropological linguistics and sociolinguistics.[15] He's the chairman of the linguistics department at Michigan. He's done some quite fascinating work on the things—whose work isn't mentioned here with these people—

SM: He was a student of Pike's?

JG: He was a student of Pike's. Fred Erickson at Harvard, who has done nonverbal communication in the phenomenology/ethnomethodology mold. I know most of them, but not as personal friends.

SM: People whose comments you'd pay some attention to?

JG: Yeah—creating a field is partly a matter of creating social networks of communicating individuals—and the other thing that I haven't mentioned is that I feel I've always kept out of paradigms, now even more consciously. Whenever someone starts categorizing me either as an ethnography of communication man, or—I got out of the linguistic variability business early in the game and became an ethnography of communication man and I've been out of that bag for the last four or five years. I'm more interested in interaction—I now don't want to be associated with ethnomethodology. As soon as—once you start crystallizing a paradigm, things get distorted by the paradigm elaborators, and I think that's a bad thing.

SM: You resist being called any particular label?

JG: That's right. And at the moment, I've moved. I think you have to realize that there is a whole new trend that's sociological that wasn't mentioned here [the 1977 Georgetown University Round Table]. There was a man who was here named Charles Li who's published several books on subject and topic and is just starting a journal, which is going to be expressly sociological on language. I think Ferguson was right that the trend in linguistics is to more sociological work and there is a whole movement in linguistics, which started partly at Berkeley toward a Heideggerian linguistics, which is in the social theory, so linguistics is getting much more interested. It's interesting for someone like me. I was asked in 1962 to go to MIT for a year, and I spent a summer there. That's when I went to Norway instead, because I felt I had little to learn at MIT at the time. I was in Cambridge the day before yesterday, and at a party I talked to a number of the MIT people, like Haj Ross, and people like that, and they're now very much interested in social issues. Ross is working on sound symbolism.

And at Berkeley now, some of the closest associates I have are people like Charles Fillmore, apart from the people in our group [the Language Behavior Research Laboratory, located in a converted residence, since demolished, on the eastern edge of the Berkeley campus] who are both linguists and know linguistics and all of whom [know] social theory. We have a lot of people—two of whom were trained as linguists—Brent Berlin and myself—and Eugene Hammel, who is mainly a mathematical anthropologist not—and Paul Kay and Bill Geoghegan were trained as anthropologists, but we all know linguistics, we all know social theory, but we don't distinguish between sociological and anthropological theory. We're interested in theory as such. I think progress has to do with social theory and social issues rather than getting immersed in either a paradigm or a discipline.

SM: **You think there's a current within anthropology as well?**

JG: It's always occurred [possibly "current"]. There's never been a unified way of defining anthropology, not more than there is a unified way of defining sociology. Of course, I think another major influence on me has been my wife—I think I've learned more social theory from my wife than I have from anyone else. And I think she is an important social theorist, even though she's not generally recognized. But I think she will be recognized as an important social theorist.

SM: **Would she accept the label "ethnomethodologist," or is she as resistant to labeling as you are?**

JG: I think she is, too, to some extent. Certainly, she's the only person—I think she's written what is generally considered *the* ethnomethodological statement of socialization theory. I don't know if you've read her article on the child as practical reasoner. She's writing a book now that will show— What I'm doing now is done basically jointly with her. We work on different kinds of data, but from the same perspective. She's not— She started out as a Bernstein student, but I mean that's been long since given up, outgrown.[16] On theoretical grounds, you can't talk phenomenology and do rather bad survey sociology.

SM: **What do you think of the work of Mary Douglas?**

JG: It's uninterpretable. I can't understand it. It's nice sentiment, nice Catholic sentiment, let's put it that way.

SM: **In the early days at Berkeley, you were not only in but organizing a network. Do you feel that now?**

JG: We are organizing networks of students, and we have a very close tie with the people at Texas, some of them Hymes's former students and partly our students: Ben Blount, Joel Sherzer, Brian Stross, Mary Sanches.

SM: **Do you still have ties to people at Stanford?**

JG: Less so, though we have new ties with Stanford, Ferguson, and even Herb Clark, Elizabeth Traugott—but less with anthropology, except Chuck Frake. He's the only one left. We have ties to San Diego, but we also have ties with other students of ours. For instance, there's starting in England now, Stephen Levinson and Penny Brown are teaching in Cambridge. In London, Maurice Bloch and Dave Parkin are starting a sort of new tradition of ethnography of communication. I've fairly strong ties at Harvard with Frederick Erickson and Courtney Cazden, who are doing the kind of ethnography of communication of classroom interaction that we're doing. At the moment, I'm involved in classroom interaction studies also. And we have other ties at Rockefeller now—beginning to form ties at Rockefeller with Michael Cole and William Hall, and their project on cross-cultural learning. They have a new newsletter on cross-cultural studies and expressly include sociolinguistics. You might find out also what are some of the new journals with sociolinguistic emphasis. There are three or four being formed. One is by Charles Li.[17] Another [*Discourse Processes*] is being sponsored by Roy O. Freedle at ETC, who has written a book on language with Hall.[18] And there is another one—in Alberta by [Tony] Vanek and Darnell [*Papers in Linguistics*]. A third independent tradition seems to be arising in Hawai'i among students of George Grace and Michael Forman. You might want to look at Ron Scollon's *Conversations with a Two-Year-Old* [*Conversations with a One Year Old*], published by the University of Hawai'i Press, and at Ann M. Peters's work on child language. [pause]

SM: **So, in contrast to Hymes and Ferguson [whom I had already interviewed], you are optimistic that sociolinguistic interests won't be wiped out—in anthropology or linguistics.**

JG: Sociolinguistics as a paradigm may be wiped out, but the ideas will survive. I have no regrets for sociolinguistics. I think discipline[s] ought to die if they—

SM: Not speaking about a particular paradigm, they seem pessimistic in a more general sense about the health of study—

JG: No, I don't think so at all. I think it's rising. I mean, it's no longer possible to capture it by a small group of people. There are so many different kinds of sociolinguistics. The sociolinguistic interest within linguistics might be the new typology—the sort of thing Gillian Sankoff talked about [at the Georgetown University Round Table]. She's not the only one doing this. There's a whole group of linguists doing this socially relevant work, including Charles Li, Bill Foley, Talmy Givon at UCLA. Ed Keenan to some extent, perhaps less, but certainly Elinor Keenan, Penny Brown in Cambridge, a number of people are doing this kind of work. I'm sure that people in Chicago and other places I don't know about are, too, and that is very, very relevant kind of work.

Then there's the whole group of people who are working conversational cooperation: Adam Kendon, Fred Erickson, Paul Byers, Ray McDermott—at least two of them, Erickson and McDermott—know linguistics quite well. Then there is the whole group of Frake students—Jean Jackson at MIT, Michael Agar, Mary Sanches—and people like Roy D'Andrade who are working on speech events as a cognitive anthropological point of view. These are getting to be different kinds of fields. Besides, there are the ethnomethodologists, who are spreading and some of whom are learning some linguistics. [end of tape] That doesn't even exhaust the inventory. I didn't even mention the work on variability, the work on creoles and pidgins [Derek] Bickerton and [Beryl L.] Bailey and people like that are doing. Besides that, there are all these applications now—to classroom interaction studies.

SM: Cazden and Mehan?

JG: Cazden and [Hugh] Mehan, yeah. You see, we're all part of the same informal group now. We have a grant now at Rockefeller than includes Cazden and Erickson and Mehan and the Fillmores [Charles and Lily Wong], my wife and myself, Roger Shuy is there, and the Rockefeller University people [McDermott was there at the time]. We have a grant that allows us to travel and visit each other's places and keep coordinated informally to work on classroom interaction, problems of cross-cultural communication.

SM: How do you find interesting work?

JG: Several things that I found very interesting. Something that's completely outside [my normal purview]: I saw two articles on reading and literacy that I found absolutely fascinating. One is the one done by [David R.] Olson who is at New Bailey Ontario. It's a fascinating article at a conference in epistemics in 1974 on reading and literacy that sort of makes sense of [Marshall] McLuhan. It's a major important article that he's making. And then an article that came out of a conference that Olson and Robbie Case from Ontario and Jack Goody and a number of other people were in Israel in the summer. And this is the article [on] anthropology of literacy by Goody.[19] I knew of his work on literacy, and he invited me to come to Cambridge and talk, and his wife actually attended a seminar that I taught at Cambridge: Esther Goody, his wife. And I knew this, and I just happened to talk to him and found out about—that he hadn't worked on this stuff for a while and showed me this article. The Olson article I got through a student. That's another new area that has relevance to sociolinguistics and builds on things, but it's not a small group any longer. I think maybe that's what Hymes and Ferguson were trying to say.

SM: They miss the ties of the small group?

JG: That's right.

SM: But *you* think it's alive and well and diversifying?

JG: Yes. It's multifarious. We're no longer in an age—well, we can form small groups oriented around particular interests, yes, but fields have gotten too big.

SM: So you don't need anymore to search out people—

JG: We don't need any more [SSRC] sociolinguistics committee, I'll tell you that much. We need issue-focused groups.

Second Interview

FEBRUARY 14, 1992, BERKELEY

SM: Back at Michigan, Herbert Penzl chaired your committee, with Albert Marckwardt and Kurath on it.

JG: That's right.

SM: Did you have contact with [Charles C.] Fries and Pike?

JG: Yes. I took courses from both of them. One of my first courses was with Fries, and I took a number of courses from Pike, but he was always away for part of the year. That's why he wasn't on my committee.

SM: Was Kurath active?

JG: He was primarily working on the dialect atlas of the U.S. in the European tradition. That's why I got interested. I was interested in dialects and so on and took some courses from him, and he was on my committee. I'm not quite sure that he was on my committee. He was also a friend of Penzl's, because they were both Austrians. Kurath did a study of the Austrian dialect of the first immigrants who came to the United States.

SM: Did they introduce you to the Cornell people?

JG: No, I met the Cornell people when as part of my program at the summer school Linguistic Institute. The first one I went to in [19]49 or '50 at Indiana University—they had been at Michigan, but I was a chemistry student and had never attended, but went to some lectures. I transferred over to the German department and worked with Penzl and took courses in linguistics. Then I got a traveling scholarship to go to the Linguistic Institute at Indiana. There I met Henry Lee Smith and George Trager, who were part of an international project preparing modular basic model texts for teaching English grammar, for teaching English to foreign students, which was then translated into their languages. I went to Cornell to work on this basic English grammar. I worked with William Welmers, an Africanist, but who had a job supervising the actual writings of these materials. I was in Cornell for two years: one working primarily on this grammar. That was done in 1953, and then I got an instructorship there in linguistics. I finished my thesis during that year. After collecting my fieldwork data, I went on to Cornell without finishing my dissertation.

SM: Was it a center for linguistics?

JG: In those days, for what was called descriptive linguistics, Cornell was one of the major centers. One of the most important influences in determining the course of American linguistics was where these foreign language texts that were prepared during the war for American soldiers going abroad. Cornell was one of the main centers. In fact, the chair of the department, Milton Cowan, was also director of that project during the war years, and he brought a number of people who had worked on it—most of them were linguists who had worked on American Indian languages and other things—to Cornell. So it was probably the largest linguistics department in the country. It was called the Division of Modern Languages, but it was explicitly linguistics rather than literature. There was another division of literature.

SM: Were you a neo-Bloomfieldian then?

JG: Yeah, that was the only game in town. I worked with and was influenced by Charles Hockett who was THE neo-Bloomfieldian, and I also talked quite a bit to others: Welmers was also a structuralist, descriptive linguistics; Gordon Fairbanks, a Slavicist, but also a descriptivist.

SM: **So you were doing distributional analysis, not the kind of metalinguistics that Trager was also trying to develop during the 1950s?**

JG: No. I was doing work on intonation, but mostly writing grammatical drills and exercises, things of that sort.

SM: **Was there a crisis, a Kuhnian-style crisis, in neo-Bloomfieldian linguistics in the early fifties?**

JG: The crisis didn't really emerge until the late fifties when Chomsky first appeared on the scene. There was always a crisis between the Bloomfieldians and the Sapirians, Bloomfield insisting on a more rigid formalism than Sapir. Sapir was an ethnographer and very much intuitive. Bloomfield was more of a formalist, trained in historical linguistics, which meant rigorous attention to linguistic form. Although ideologically Bloomfield and Sapir didn't differ that much, Sapir was more intuitive and more interested in language and culture.

SM: **Do you have any sense that Hockett and the others at Cornell then had any disaffection, felt that they couldn't explain intonation—**

JG: No. Trager and Smith were part of the project. We actually worked on intonation. We wrote these dialogs, then spoke about and transcribed them with intonation and everything, so we knew that intonation and all that stuff was important. In other words, I learned how to do that while I was there.

SM: **But they thought that they had a handle on it?**

JG: Yeah. Hockett was also a moving force in the famous *First Five Minutes* analysis,[20] which was inspired by Gregory Bateson. People were very eclectic in those days. There wasn't this rigid division in those days that there is now.

SM: **But they didn't feel that they were wandering in the wilderness, waiting for enlightenment?**

JG: No, no, no, no, no. There wasn't a sense of crisis at all, nor was there a rigid sense of paradigm. I know from talking to Pike that he always felt on the outs, but I think that had more to do with his religion than anything else.

SM: **Because he was a missionary, or because he brought it into linguistics?**

JG: Because he brought it into linguistics. He was a fundamentalist. In those days that was still far out.

SM: **You were present at the creation, being at MIT before the 1962 International Congress of Linguists.**

JG: They really did have a mission and a sense of "we" and "they." The "we" were those who had received their training at MIT and "they" was everybody else. In a way, there were a group of marginals, people who had undergone post hoc conversions, structuralists who had now somehow professed the Chomskian faith.

SM: **How did they regard you?**

JG: I never professed that faith. The reason I went to MIT was that in my first years here Roman Jakobson was at the Center for Advanced Study [in the Behavioral Sciences] in Palo Alto and I spent a lot of time with him and he and they had kind of a program with postdoctoral grants that they could give to people that enabled them to bring in others, presumably to be converted to the faith. It was a proselytizing exercise. I didn't take to that very well, because I was beginning to think out my own ideas. I was very interested in issues of LINGUISTIC DIFFUSION in those days and in things like bilingualism and those kinds of social issues and I saw what they did and couldn't see much relevance in what they did. Their view was just "Don't talk to us. Learn what we do." In those days there weren't any textbooks, so I had to try to read various drafts that were being passed around. Morris Halle's *Sound Patterns of Russian*,[21] and those things. I frankly was never interested in formalization of grammatical processes, grammatical patterns, so I didn't pay that much attention to that. Actually, they brought me in the summer while they were preparing for this International Congress. I worked on my own paper for the congress and attended some lectures and talked to people. I didn't have any obligations.

SM: **So Jakobson had vouched for you.**

JG: Yeah, he had recommended me. There were other people. An English linguist, William Sledd, who was a really hardcore transformationalist in those days. There were others like me who were just around and who were supposed to soak in the spirit and the word and so on.

SM: **How did Jakobson himself feel about that?**

JG: No, no, no, no. He never felt that way. Basically he always had a sense that there were certain universal things about language—his notions about distinctive features, the little booklet with Jakobson and Halle, pointing out that there were universal features to grammar. From that programmatic, ideological perspective, he agreed with what these people were doing, get away from the text-based particularistic analyses of particular languages each in their own terms to a series of investigations of what all human languages share that doesn't really fall into the earlier drafts of culture-or language-boundedness that characterized nineteenth century linguistics. From that perspective they liked Roman Jakobson, but when it came to the Chomskian formalism, he never had too much, too close connection with Chomsky. Morris Halle was his student and close connection. They were both Slavicists and close connections.

SM: Jakobson let what Chomsky pass—

JG: That's right.

SM: —never criticized it, never endorsed it.

JG: That's right. Jakobson was retired from Harvard about that time and had an appointment at MIT so he used that as an economic base when he retired—something that I understand now that I've retired.

SM: So do you know anything about how Chomsky came to give one of the plenary addresses at the 1962 Congress? He seems a generation younger than the other plenary speakers.

JG: He had clearly raised a lot of questions. He was the first challenge to the shared understanding that united linguists and he was seen as one of the major forces like [Michael] Halliday and [Louis] Hjelmslev, or [Jerzy] Kuryłowicz. Chomsky was the one with the school and the disciples, all of whom were presenting papers [at the congress] on the theories. I remember at lunch talk about what so-and-so is saying, so that we can argue against it. In fact, there was a systematic effort. There was a small army of scholars that was deployed to scout out the enemy and do battle. Like Terry Langendoen's dissertation on [John R.] Firth.[22] People started digging out [Wilhelm von] Humboldt again.

SM: When I interviewed you in 1977 and again when you read a draft of part of my dissertation, you said that I paid too little attention to the Stanford end of the Berkeley-Stanford axis with Metzger, Romney, and D'Andrade as well as Frake.

JG: It was kind of a Berkeley-Stanford axis with Kay and Berlin and Hammel in those days.

SM: Early sixties. It seems to me that Metzger and Romney and D'Andrade were never very interested in language.

JG: D'Andrade was basically a social psychologist. Metzger was interested in ethnography and discovery procedures and formalizing ethnographic inquiry.

SM: Never language in actual use.

JG: No. Certainly Frake was, and then there were Frake's students. The extent that there was a school can be seen in the contrast between the Sanches and Blount volumes on language use versus the [Richard] Bauman and [Joel]

Sherzer one on ethnography of communication. On the one hand people consciously spoke of cognitive processes. There was a serious attempt to marry the cognitive with the ethnographic, especially in the articles by Sanches and by Blount on the use of genealogies in disputes. There's always a great deal of latitude in constructing genealogies. Blount showed how they are constructed in the context of local disputes, claims to land, and claims to power. All of this was put in the context of language use. In contrast to description of speech events in terms of Jakobsonian factors with very little attention paid to the actual details of the talk. I mean the emphasis was on—the claim was that the speech event is to all intents and purposes a major social system. There are actors interacting in relation to certain norms. The trace of language reveals what those norms are. What they say has certain values.

It's basically a Goffmanian analysis. If you substitute Goffman's notion of situation for ethnography of communication notion of event, you get a kind of Goffmanian analysis. The only [thing] that the ethnographers of communication didn't take, didn't really pick up from Goffman was Goffman's insistence that when you create an interactive situation that it is a kind of universe of its own, apart from the broader social entity of which it is a part. He used the Batesonian image of lenses filtering out, using the example of a poker game. It's a world of its own. You don't get that out of the early ethnography of communication stuff. You get the descriptions and analysis into component features and descriptions of the ethnographically determined beliefs about the event—what's transacted, how they're valued, and so on—

SM: Isn't that true of Frake as much as of Hymes?

JG: Well, no. Frake, for example in his Yakan house paper, looks at, says that within the context of, entering a Yakan house is a speech event and within that context, certain values are assigned to the house and so on. Frake goes beyond. He still has that ethnosemantic perspective, whereas the others didn't, but it's not explicit.

SM: Meanwhile, back at contrasting Bauman and Sherzer with Sanches and Blount. The Bauman and Sherzer book got a lot of attention, a lot of it VERY critical; the Sanches and Blount volumes hardly got any.

JG: Cambridge University Press has a good distribution system and Academic Press didn't.

SM: They certainly got Newmeyer's book out to the whole world![23]

JG: That was quite a different Academic Press.

SM: They didn't know how to market anthropological linguistics?

JG: Not very much marketing was done. Newmeyer's was all Chomskian. The Sanches and Blount books did not get out very well. In Europe they're read quite a bit. The Bauman and Sherzer book was not bad.

SM: It got out, but Leach attacked it, Maurice Bloch, Ruth Borker... I don't know that it got ANY good reviews.

JG: Reviews don't matter very much. It's been republished, it's been much, much more successful.

SM: Whatever happened to Ethel Albert? I always liked the paper that she wrote for both Gumperz and Hymes volumes, but nothing followed them.

JG: As far as I remember she was very ill. Even when she was in Berkeley, we had the same doctor, and I would see her sometimes there. She really hasn't done very much. Frederick Erickson was her student. He was partly Hall's student, partly her student. I met her when she was at Northwestern, but she never went to meetings. That's right, she didn't do very much at all.

SM: Some people fall by the wayside—even with jobs! What was the relationship between Chafe coming to Berkeley and Hymes leaving and you leaving the linguistics department for anthropology?

JG: This was during the free speech movement. Hymes was always in favor of the underdog and took a very antiwar, antiestablishment position. He felt that the department didn't appreciate that. He got offers from Columbia and Penn and decided to leave. There wasn't too much sympathy in the department for what he did, academically or politically, so he left.

SM: So it wasn't feeling threatened by Chafe.

JG: No, no, no, no. Chafe was more of an orthodox neo-Bloomfieldian linguist at the time, or was said to be. The senior people told me. I was in the same department for a couple of years. I went into the linguistics department when Hymes left, a zero FTE appointment, but I had a vote in the faculty. I think that Hymes left and then Chafe came in the year after that. I remember that the rationale that the senior people gave was, "We want someone who's bright but isn't hung up on theory." That was Chafe.

SM: I remember Mary Haas complaining that Hymes and his students just "don't get the language."

JG: That's right: that's what she said. But subsequently, in his old days, he has learned the Oregon languages. He may not be able to speak them but he has certainly learned to read them.

SM: Chafe and Hymes got along all right when they were in the same department?

JG: Yeah.

SM: And Gumperz and Chafe?

JG: Oh, yes. We weren't close friends but we get along. I've never engaged in great theoretical battles.

SM: You missed your chance at Cambridge in 1962! [JG laughs] Where did Labov come from? It seems that he was in all the early sociolinguistic collections while he was still a graduate student.

JG: He was a chemist, but he had a degree in philosophy from Harvard and was clearly already a very mature scholar by the second year of graduate school, when he began to emerge on the national scene. Some of the articles that he wrote were very, very basic.

SM: But his first influential publication in *Word* wasn't until 1963, the same year as the session that became Gumperz and Hymes 1964.[24]

JG: The article on Martha's Vineyard was already around before it came out in *Word*. He was also the protégé of Uriel Weinreich, who sent him around. He got to be known. We brought him here for a meeting. That's when I first met him. Then in 1964 at a summer session at the LI in Indiana, where the [SSRC] sociolinguistics committee was first formed, he was certainly part of the group at the recommendation of Weinreich. Basically, if Weinreich was invited, his primary interest was in semantics and he'd say that sociolinguistics wasn't his main interest anymore, but here's this man who's going to be a great sociolinguist.

SM: So, pretty much, if you invited Weinreich, you got Labov.

JG: Yeah.

SM: How did you first encounter Basil Bernstein?

JG: In 1961–62 I was in Norway. My then-wife Ellen McDonald was doing her dissertation and was working in the library in London for a while. I went a couple of times to visit her. Bernstein's first articles had come out and I'd seen them, so I looked him up and we became friends.

SM: Did you meet him before Hymes did?

JG: About the same time, I think, but independently.

SM: But neither of you could teach him anything?

JG: I told Ernest Gellner that Bernstein had only had a few ideas in his life, and he said, "You're wrong: one idea!" He was a bright man. He had something to say and he was very clear about that, but he never bothered to relate to what it meant, to spell it out for social theory or for linguistic theory or for sociolinguistic theory. He was not interested in linguistics at all—like other sociologists. He doesn't know linguistics at all, let alone code-switching and speech communities.

SM: He seems to feel that he was some kind of Marxist who got a bad rap.

JG: That's right. He *did*, in the United States. He did write about class in a totally British way, where class is a relationship to the means of production with nothing to do with these Warner scales that Americans used.

SM: [Anthony] Giddens has gotten a long ways without appreciably more sophisticated ideas of—

JG: Class?

SM: Of anything.

JG: He had one or two good ideas, and a word: structuration. He knows Bourdieu and understands ethnomethodology, but if you're looking for real theory or detailed substance, you won't find it.

SM: How did Bourdieu become so pervasive here? Deborah Tannen, Susan Gal, and Kit Woolard all told me that they never heard of him while they were here, but just a short time after they left, when I came, it was like we were living and breathing cultural capital.

JG: I remember when I first read the *Practice* book and I thought that was great.[25] I felt that practice analysis is the social equivalent to what I'm doing. I certainly didn't have the courage to follow it up. I put it aside, thinking "this is absolutely great; I'll have to do something with that some time." But I didn't. But then people began to pick it up.

SM: You must have told someone about it, because there was at most a one-year gap between when Deborah left and when I arrived.

JG: I don't know. I wasn't interested in grand theory, and I still haven't thought it all out. I remember talking to Ron Scollon and he was all interested in Foucault, the archaeology of knowledge and all that stuff. I was trying to make sense of that, and I was trying to make sense of Antonio Gramsci. Then Kit wrote a paper, and I thought it was really good, but that she was wrong in a number of places and I tried to think about it. About seven years ago I started teaching a course in sociolinguistic theory.

SM: How did you know about Bourdieu's *Practice* book?

JG: It was a Cambridge book. I may have just picked it up. Very few people had heard about Bourdieu then. I was interested in reading history and I just picked it up, I think, without knowing that Bourdieu had thought about structure and language and so on, which has come out in his recent writing. The point is that the last few times that I've taught this course is not to start with [Alfred] Schutz and Garfinkel, like I used to. I didn't teach any Goffman. But now I realize what Goffman has contributed. He's the first one who's given us a language really to study interaction, a set of concepts: situation, encounter, focused interaction, and things of that sort, and involvement in particular, which have been really basic to conversational analysis, even though conversational analysts never mention these notions.

I realized that was one basis and the ethnomethodological Garfinkel and Cicourel differential processes. To figure out what was my theory, what would it be like. What are these processes. I realized that to do what I'm doing I don't need any assumptions about structure at all. All I have to know is look at practice, so what I started thinking, I started working with Goffman, Garfinkel, and Schutz and trying to relate it to broader things, language as a form of action in a Weberian sense, but that's very abstract. Practice has brought that down to everyday, creative situations. Then I also needed something else: to get over the notion in my early work on speech communities and networks. I needed to integrate that. Then I realized that things like group, culture, social system—they're all middle theory concepts and I needed something else, and I read Bourdieu again and got the economic metaphor rather than the social metaphor. You've got the notion of field and capital. Jenny was the first who read Bourdieu and [Jean-Claude] Passeron in education. She wrote something about that. FROM HER! When we look back at it, it was from her. That's right.

SM: Was Bourdieu the ladder from what you in 1977 called Heideggerian sociolinguistics back to society?

JG: Bourdieu is a bit Heideggerian, Sartrean, himself. The Heideggerian notion is the constructionist notion that by the way we act we constitute society to put it very simply. You go to Foucault's notion of discourse. You have a set of raw metaphors about which to construct a theory of how this works: situated practice to inference and discourse to broader social fields. There's a recent book, called *The Foucault Effect: Studies in Governmentality*,[26] which is quite good. Two of his articles, which have not been published before, are included.

In one of them he says what he means by "discourse." Governmentality for Foucault is what Bourdieu calls symbolic domination. Foucault talks about discourse in a very broad sense. It's very nice. As far as Foucault is concerned, discourse is what you can convincingly say, what topics can you convincingly talk about, what do you need to allude to indirectly, and so on.

SM: Here in Berkeley in the early eighties, how come we didn't know that Henri Tajfel existed?

JG: All I know of Tajfel is via his students. [Howard] Giles and company. As far as I could see he was an unreconstructed social psychologist. I don't see him as having much of relevance to say about the kinds of things in which I was interested. I admit I haven't read him.

SM: It seems that in the sixties there was a much more extensive collaboration between psychology and linguistic anthropology with Dan Slobin and Susan Ervin-Tripp than there was by the early eighties.

JG: Slobin has always been interested in grammar. He got interested in comparative acquisition and so on. Now he's getting more interested in semantics and spatial perception. But Tajfel as far as I could see via Giles is just reference group theory and that sort of thing. A lot has to do with what you are brought into contact with by the social relationships you participate in. Somehow. I know the work that Giles did. Giles sort of bridges Tajfel and Wally Lambert. That stuff turned me off, because it doesn't say anything. George Miller once told me he'd given up on Wally Lambert long, long ago.

SM: He had one good idea, too.

JG: That's right. The Tajfel tradition seems to me to have a social out there and a language out there. We've been wanting to stop that kind of view ever since the ethnography of communication.

SM: Perhaps I'll have to make the case!

JG: [laughs] If you can make the case and make me want to read and see what I missed, I'll be glad, delighted to read it.

SM: The burden's on me!

JG: That's right.

SM: One last thing, why didn't you respond to Singh and Lele?[27]

JG: Well, they're Indians. Their language: I don't think that they meant it that intemperately. But [pause] how can you respond? It just isn't true. They just haven't ever read what I've written. Why should I?

SM: Well, that was [B. F.] Skinner's response to Chomsky. There are people who infer that the criticism must be right when there is no response. Like silence is consent.

JG: I didn't consent! To the extent they had anything to propose it was "Gumperz should have read Paul Grice." That's ridiculous. I've said in a number of places that what I'm talking about are processes of implicature. They don't understand the difference between social phenomena and linguistic phenomena. I don't take the criticism seriously. Most people who have read it don't. Kit Woolard once sent me something she read by them for *Language in Society*. She said that she toned them down about 75 percent but didn't succeed in toning them down very much.

SM: Isn't it unpleasant in that they are native speakers from your region?

JG: Yes—well, I'm a native speaker of German, but I would not presume to talk about German culture. I think they are as much native speakers of my region as I am a native speaker of German. I'm no expert on Germany. I was sixteen when I left. Maybe they were a little bit older.

SM: Perhaps I have a more combative temperament, as several people have suggested.

JG: Have I attacked anyone in writing?

SM: Oh, sure! Practically everyone in the introduction to *Discourse Strategies*.[28]

JG: Not really attack them.

SM: Dismiss them.

JG: No. All I said is that they're not interested in what I'm interested in. No. I have my standard way of talking about Labov: it's a great thing if you're interested in comparing different macro-systems, but he doesn't deal with interaction. I don't have a problem with that.

SM: I guess no one else has ever really attacked you.

JG: Labov never attacked me. Some Labovians have attacked me. *Language in Society* is not such an exciting journal that I read every line.

SM: Now, now.

JG: Dell and I are very good friends now.

SM: There was a general feeling when I was here in the early eighties that our work couldn't be published in *Language in Society*.

JG: Yeah, well, you had some problems with Dell for not saying he was the greatest, didn't you.

SM: I had some problems with Dell over what I said about [Allen D.] Grimshaw, but he accepted the paper I submitted to *Language in Society*. And Keith Chick's and Sarah Michaels's articles, and one that he accepted from Niyi [Akinnaso] but that Niyi didn't get revisions back to him.[29]

JG: I felt at the time that he was getting away from it. Since that time, he has gotten back by going into performance studies and he's begun to see really. I don't think that he was ideologically a functionalist. He's seen that performance is a form of practice, so we're much closer now than we were.

SM: But Dell "broke through" to performance by 1975, before the time I'm talking about.[30] He seems to feel that your students didn't appreciate his work.

JG: Well, they did. [Tape recorder turned off.]

Notes

1. John J. Gumperz and Dell H. Hymes, eds., "The Ethnography of Communication," *American Anthropologist* 66, no. 6, part 2 (1964).
2. Stephen O. Murray, Joseph H. Rankin, and Dennis W. Magill, "Strong Ties and Academic Jobs," *Sociology of Work and Occupations* 8, no. 1 (1981): 119–36.
3. Stephen O. Murray and Robert C. Poolman, "Strong Ties and Scientific Information," *Social Networks* 4, no. 3 (1981): 225–32.
4. Nicholas Mullins, *Theories and Theory Groups in American Sociology* (New York: Harper and Row, 1973).
5. Stephen O. Murray, "Social Science Networks" (unpublished PhD diss., University of Toronto, 1979); Stephen O. Murray, *Group Formation in Social Science* (Edmonton, AB: Linguistic Research, 1983); Stephen O. Murray, *Theory Groups and the Study of Language in North America: A Social History* (Amsterdam: John Benjamins, 1994); Stephen O. Murray, *American Sociolinguistics: Theorists and Theory Groups* (Amsterdam: John Benjamins, 1998).
6. Stephen O. Murray, "Interactional Sociolinguistics at Berkeley," in *The Social History of Language and Social Interaction Research: People, Places, Ideas*, ed. Wendy Leeds-Hurwitz, 97–126 (Cresskill NJ: Hampton Press, 2010).
7. George L. Trager and Henry Lee Smith Jr., *An Outline of English Structure* (Norman OK: Battenberg Press, 1951).
8. John J. Gumperz, "Dialect Differences and Social Stratification in a North Indian Village," *American Anthropologist* 60 (1958): 668–81.

9. Charles Frake, "How to Ask for a Drink in Subanun," *American Anthropologist* 66, no. 6, part 2 (1964): 127–32.
10. Julian Boyd and J. P. Thorne, "The Semantics of Modal Verbs," *Journal of Linguistics* 5 (1969): 57–74.
11. Specifically, Gregory Bateson, *Naven* (Cambridge: Cambridge University Press, 1936).
12. Paul W. Friedrich, Review of *Linguistic Diversity in South Asia* by Charles A. Ferguson and John J. Gumperz, *Language* 37, no. 1 (1961): 163–68.
13. Harvey Sacks, "The Search for Help: No One to Turn To" (PhD diss., University of California, Berkeley, 1966).
14. Emanuel A. Schegloff, "The First Five Seconds: The Order of Conversational Opening" (PhD diss., University of California, Berkeley, 1967).
15. Richard Emerson Young, Alton L. Becker, and Kenneth Lee Pike, *Rhetoric: Discovery and Change* (New York: Harcourt, Brace & World 1970).
16. Jenny Cook-Gumperz, "The Child as Practical Reasoner," in *Sociocultural Dimensions of Language Use*, ed. Mary Sanches and Ben Blount, 137–62 (New York: Academic Press, 1975); probably Jenny Cook-Gumperz, *The Social Construction of Literacy* (Cambridge: Cambridge University Press, 1986); Basil Bernstein, *Social Control and Socialization: A Study of Class Differences in the Language of Maternal Control* (London: Routledge and Kegan Paul, 1973).
17. Li earned a PhD at Berkeley in 1971.
18. William S. Hall and Roy O. Freedle, *Culture and Language: The Black American Experience* (New York: Wiley, 1975).
19. Jack Goody and Ian Watt, "The Consequences of Literacy," *Comparative Studies in Society and History* 5, no. 3 (1963): 304–45.
20. Robert E. Pittenger, Charles F. Hockett, and John J. Danehy, *The First Five Minutes: A Sample of Microscopic Interview Analysis* (New York: Paul Martineau, 1960).
21. Morris Halle, *Sound Patterns of Russian: A Linguistic and Acoustical Investigation* (The Hague: Mouton, 1959).
22. Terry Langendoen, "Modern British Linguistics" (PhD diss., MIT, 1961).
23. Frederick Newmeyer, *Linguistic Theory in America: The First Quarter Century of Transformational Generative Grammar* (New York: Academic, 1980).
24. William Labov, "The Social Motivation of a Sound Change," *Word* 19, no. 3 (1963): 273–309; John J. Gumperz and Dell H. Hymes, eds., "The Ethnography of Communication," *American Anthropologist* 66, no. 6, part 2 (1964).
25. Pierre Bourdieu, *Outline of a Theory of Practice* (Cambridge: Cambridge University Press, 1977; originally published in French in 1972).
26. Graham Burchell, Colin Gordon, and Peter Miller, *The Foucault Effect: Studies in Governmentality* (Chicago: University of Chicago Press, 1991).

27. Rajendra Singh, Jayant Lele, and Gita Martohardjono, "Communication in a Multilingual Society: Some Missed Opportunities," *Language in Society* 17, no. 1 (1988): 43–59.
28. John J. Gumperz, *Discourse Strategies* (Cambridge: Cambridge University Press, 1971).
29. Stephen O. Murray, "Toward a Model of Members' Methods of Recognizing Interruptions," *Language in Society* 14, no. 1 (1985): 31–40; Keith Chick, "The Interactional Accomplishment of Discrimination in South Africa," *Language in Society* 14, no. 3 (1985): 299–326; Sarah Michaels, "'Sharing Time': Children's Narrative Styles and Differential Access to Literacy," *Language in Society* 10, no. 3 (1981): 423–42.
30. Dell H. Hymes, "Breakthrough into Performance," in *Folklore: Performance and Communication*, ed. Dan Ben-Amos and Kenneth Goldstein, 11–74 (The Hague: Mouton, 1975).

Selected Publications by John Gumperz

Blom, Jan-Petter, and John J. Gumperz. 1972. "Social Meaning in Linguistic Structure: Code-Switching in Norway." In *Directions in Sociolinguistics*, edited by John Gumperz and Dell Hymes, 707–34. New York: Holt, Rinehart & Winston.

Cook-Gumperz, Jenny, and John J. Gumperz. 1996. "Treacherous Words: Gender and Power in Academic Assessment." *Folia Linguistica* 30 (3-4): 167–88.

———. 2011. "Frames and Contexts: Another Look at the Macro-Micro Link." *Pragmatics* 21 (2): 285–88.

Gumperz, John J. 1955. "The Swabian Dialects of Washtenaw County, Michigan." PhD dissertation, University of Michigan.

———. 1958a. "Dialect Differences and Social Stratification in a North Indian Village." *American Anthropologist* 60 (4): 668–81. (Reprinted in Gumperz 1971, 25–47.)

———. 1958b. "Phonological Differences in Three Hindi Dialects." *Language* 34 (2): 212–24

———. 1962. "Types of Linguistic Communities." *Anthropological Linguistics* 4 (1): 28–40. (Reprinted in Gumperz 1971, 97–113.)

———. 1964. "Linguistic and Social Interaction in Two Communities." *American Anthropologist* 66 (6), part 2: 137–54. (Reprinted in Gumperz 1971, 151–76.)

———. 1966. "On the Ethnology of Linguistic Change." In *Sociolinguistics*, edited by William Bright, 27–49. The Hague: Mouton.

———. 1968. "The Speech Community." *International Encyclopedia of Social Science* 9:381–86. (Reprinted in Gumperz 1971, 114–28.)

———. 1969. "Communication in Multi-lingual Societies." In *Cognitive Anthropology*, edited by Stephen Tyler, 435–48. Long Grove IL: Waveland. (Reprinted in Gumperz 1971, 230–50.)

———. 1971. *Language in Social Groups*. Stanford: Stanford University Press.

———. 1972. "The Communicative Competence of Bilinguals." *Language in Society* 1 (1): 143–54.

———. 1974. "Linguistic Anthropology in Society." *American Anthropologist* 76 (4): 785–98.

———. 1976. "The Sociolinguistic Significance of Conversational Code-Switching." *Language Behavior Research Laboratory Working Paper* 46.

———. 1979. "The Retrieval of Socio-cultural Knowledge in Conversation." *Poetics Today* 1 (1–2): 273–86.

———. 1980. "The Sociolinguistic Basis of Speech Act Theory." In *Speech Acts Theory: Ten Years Later*, edited by Julian Boyd and Alessandro Ferrara, 101–21. Milan: Versus.

———. 1982a. *Discourse Strategies*. New York: Cambridge University Press.

———, ed. 1982b. *Language and Social Identity*. New York: Cambridge University Press.

———. 1983. "Interethnic Discourse." *Society* 20 (4): 64–69

———. 1992. "Contextualization and Understanding." In *Rethinking Context: Language as an Interactive Phenomenon*, edited by Alessandro Duranti and Charles Goodwin, 229–52. New York: Cambridge University Press.

———. 1997. *Discussing Communication Analysis*, edited by Susan Eerdmans, Carlo Prevignano, and Paul J. Thibault. Lausanne: Beta Press. (This seventy-five-page booklet includes a discussion between Gumperz and Aldo Di Luzio, commentary on that by Carlo Prevignano, a short piece on "Contextualizing 'contextualization cues'" by Stephen C. Levinson, and a short piece by Gumperz on "current contributions to interactional sociolinguistics.")

Gumperz, John J., and Margaret Field. 1995. "Children's Discourse and Inferential Practices in Cooperative Learning." *Discourse Practices* 19 (1): 133–47.

Gumperz, John J., and Eleanor Herasimchuk. 1972. "Conversational Analysis of Social Meaning: A Study of Classroom Interaction." In *Sociolinguistics: Current Trends and Prospects*, edited by Roger Shuy, 99–134. Washington DC: Georgetown University Press. (Reprinted in *Sociocultural Dimensions of Language Use*, edited by Mary Sanches and Ben Blount, 81–115. New York: Academic Press.)

Gumperz, John J., and Eduardo Hernández-Chavez. 1971. "Bilingualism, Bidialectalism and Classroom Interaction." (Reprinted in Gumperz 1971, 311–39.)

Gumperz, John J., and Dell H. Hymes, eds. 1964. *American Anthropologist* 66 (6), part 2: "The Ethnography of Communication."

———. 1972. *Directions in Sociolinguistics*. New York: Holt, Rinehart & Winston.

Gumperz, John J., Hannah Kaltman, and Mary Catherine O'Connor. 1984. "Cohesion in Spoken and Written Discourse: Ethnic Styles and Transition to Literacy." In *Coherence in Spoken and Written Discourse*, edited by Deborah Tannen, 3–20. Norwood NJ: Ablex.

Gumperz, John J. and Stephen C. Levinson. 1991. "Rethinking Linguistic Relativity." *Current Anthropology* 32 (5): 613–23.

———. 1996. *Rethinking Linguistic Relativity*. Cambridge: Cambridge University Press.

Gumperz, John J., and C. M. Naim. 1960. "Formal and Informal Standards in Hindi Regional Language Area." *International Journal of American Linguistics* 26 (3): 92–118. (Reprinted in Gumperz 1971, 48–76.)

Gumperz, John J., and Celia Roberts. 1978. *Developing Awareness Skills for Inter-ethnic Communication*. Singapore: Seameo Regional Language Center.

Gumperz, John J., and Robert Wilson. 1971. "Convergence and Creolization." In *Pidginization and Creolization of Languages*, edited by Dell Hymes, 151–67. Cambridge: Cambridge University Press. (Reprinted in Gumperz 1971, 251–73.)

10 Doing History of Anthropology

Stephen O. Murray

Those who followed the explorations of the historical connections in the preceding chapters [of Murray 2013] are unlikely to expect a conclusion that proclaims the Truth that anthropology or human sciences more generally should be pursuing or has discovered. Instead, I want to draw on my experience of questioning "just-so" stories about intellectual connections in the past to offer some suggestions about how not to do history of a field. I have given some thought of late to my own intellectual genealogy and, if that is not a sufficiently narcissistic topic to contemplate, to the history of the history of anthropology.

My PhD dissertation, titled "Social Science Networks," compared what have been called "schools." Robert Redfield (1953, 728) once said that an academic discipline is at once a group of people in persisting social relations and a method of investigation, further noting that "the two kinds of relations, social and methodological, are mutually influential, but neither determines the other." It seems to me that I began with a focus on the social and have drifted, not with conscious intent as to the outcome, to focus increasingly on shared practices, on methods rather than methodologies, and on shared assumptions about what should be studied and how. Trying to make sense of where the history of anthropology in general and my work in particular came from, it seems to me that I can identify two streams of what I would call emic history of anthropology. I want to discuss these streams both as social groupings and methods of investigation.

The first serious work on the history of anthropology aiming to understand the past in its own terms rather than to promote the author's position or positions in the present and aspiring to contextualize ideas from the past as something other than building blocks of current models was done by students trained in Frederick Teggart's Department of Social Institutions at Berkeley. Teggart taught a course on the history of the idea of progress in the 1930s that focused on making sense of the concept of "progress" in the intellectual contexts of different times in Western history. Robert Nisbet, one of his students and my first graduate school mentor in social theory, eventually crystallized that into a book, *History of the Idea of Progress*, which was only published in 1980; it should be but has not been of interest to historians of anthropology. Two of Teggart's other students examined the interrelations of social theory and the accounts by explorers, travelers and missionaries of the beliefs, institutions, and physical characteristics of the peoples encountered and subjugated by Europeans between the fifteenth and nineteenth centuries more directly. Katherine Oakes completed a dissertation in 1944 on the shifting representations of Africans. Under her married name, Katherine George, she published a synopsis in *Isis* in 1958. Margaret T. Hodgen, a student of Teggart who became his colleague, published what remains the standard and so-far definitive book *Early Anthropology in the Sixteenth and Seventeenth Centuries* in 1964. Drawing on similar insights much earlier, she published a history of the idea of "survivals" in 1936 and an exemplification of how to examine cultural innovation and diffusion across time and space in 1952, in an anthropological monograph series, and followed *Change and History* and *Early Anthropology in the Sixteenth and Seventeenth Centuries* with an attempt to tell anthropologists how to do history, *Anthropology, History, and Cultural Change* (Hodgen 1974).

A Teggartian tradition with a catastrophist rather than gradualist view of cultural change also includes repeated criticisms of the use of the comparative method and of unilinear cultural evolution (while recommending comparisons). Kenneth Bock, in addition to Nisbet, has continued this tradition of criticizing sociobiology. Both as a student of Teggart and Hodgen (i.e., Robert Nisbet) and as the author of a history of the Berkeley Department of Social Institutions based heavily on the views of Hodgen, Bock, and Nisbet, I can readily claim a legitimate genealogical connection to this academic tradition of intellectual history of social science.

Although I certainly share some of its assumptions, in particular catastrophism in its Kuhnian form as "scientific revolutions" (punctuating Brownian motion of professors' theoretical and methodological approaches) I don't think that my work much resembles that of Teggart's students. I am interested in the institutions and less formal social networks of twentieth-century American social science(s), whereas they examined the texts and memes (what they called "unit-ideas") of pre-academic science, generally over the course of centuries, and rarely into the twentieth century. In common with Arthur Lovejoy, Teggartians focused on unit-ideas like progress or community rather than on individual thinkers or schools of thought. I greatly admire Robert Nisbet's (1966) *Sociological Tradition* but am unlikely to emulate his approach; making the tradition plural would not resolve the differences in approach. I agree that there are anthropological traditions but associate them with prototype individuals rather than with unit-ideas. Or perhaps I simply failed to learn how to do what Teggart and Hodgen and (sometimes) Nesbit did, despite the place I could claim in their intellectual genealogy.

Although my own genealogy remains incomplete, I emphasize the first lesson for historical inference from this self-analysis: don't jump to any conclusions that because B studied with A, B is doing what A did, even if B calls himself or herself an A-ian. I admire the Teggartian tradition, and wouldn't reject the label "Teggartian," but it fails to predict or explain much of the work I do.

The year 1962 was a watershed for the traditions with which I identify. Thomas Kuhn published the first edition of *The Structure of Scientific Revolutions*, a book that significantly increased interest in social history of science, challenged the conception that progress in science is smooth and incremental, and turned at least some attention to social processes in accepting or rejecting old and new ideas and methods. The Social Science Research Council (SSRC) sponsored a conference on the History of Anthropology that legitimated the emerging historicist approach with which I identify my own work in the same year. I see this as a Pennsylvania tradition in good part because the conference's prime mover was A. Irving Hallowell, whose "The History of Anthropology as an Anthropological Problem" appeared in 1965 in the first issue of the *Journal of the History of the Behavioral Sciences*; this journal was a major outlet for my work and that of others trying to make sense out of past work in both psychology and the social sciences.[1]

The first volume of that journal contained George Stocking's (1965) "On the Limits of Presentism and Historicism in the Historiography of the Behavioral Sciences." I thought the paper was given at the 1962 conference, but the version in Stocking's 1968 book *Race, Culture, and Evolution* doesn't indicate provenance, so the connection of publication may have left me with the illusion that the two papers were presented at the same meeting. Looking again at Hallowell's "The History of Anthropology as an Anthropological Problem," I found that it drew only on the SSRC presentation and was more directly based on a paper presented at the 1962 American Anthropological Association meetings. Stocking, and also Dell Hymes, whose work to construct a tradition of American linguistic anthropology heavily influenced my work, were both at Berkeley then which made the connection a logical inference. Both soon took up positions at the University of Pennsylvania where Stocking had taken courses from Hallowell earlier. Regna Darnell, who as the external examiner of my dissertation defended it from the ad hoc committee that included none of the three professors with whom I had worked on the dissertation research (all three were on sabbatical), was a student at Penn not only of Hymes and Stocking but of Hallowell and as an undergraduate was a student of Frederica de Laguna, who was a student of Franz Boas.

A second lesson for doing history drawn from my too-facile identification with the Pennsylvania tradition is to keep track of the dates, of who was where and when, especially when reminiscences are flowing. My experience interviewing our elders has taught me that chronology is *not* remembered well, and what seems in retrospect to fit together has often been put together in recollection. Actual historical connections are rarely so tidy. My memory of the unity of a Pennsylvania tradition probably owed more to knowing that Darnell was a student of Hallowell and Stocking and Hymes at Pennsylvania during the 1960s and that she has identified the 1962 SSRC meeting as the starting point of a professional history of anthropology than to having given explicit thought to where those three were in 1962. Hymes was not yet at Pennsylvania and was unlikely to have been influenced by Hallowell. Hymes and Stocking were at Berkeley together only after Teggart's death in 1946 and the departure of both Hodgen and Nisbet. Hodgen's papers in the Bancroft Library document that she and Stocking were in correspondence about how to do history of anthropology.

Hallowell's article cites Hodgen, Teggart, Bock, and Oakes-George, and I suspect that he played some part in the publication of Hodgen's book by the University of Pennsylvania Press. He was the editor of the Viking Fund Publications in Anthropology series in which her *Change and History* was published in 1952, documenting that there were Berkeley connections to this Pennsylvania tradition as well as by teacher-student ties like those between Hallowell and Stocking and both to Darnell.

The methodological moral "seek and ye shall find" is often true but I prefer to look for connections beyond those based on propinquity. Geography is not the only basis for social ties and intellectual influence, especially in the development of sciences, including social. It is dangerous to assume that because C and D were in the same institution, for example in the same department at the same time necessitated any real interchange of ideas.[2] Professor E across the continent may have provided a more important source of ideas and support to C or D than they were to each other and they may or may not have had links to the same person located elsewhere or to each other.

Breaking out of that tangle of social connections, let me turn now to what I see as essential in the tradition within which I work to finally say something about the content of the "Pennsylvania tradition" in the history of anthropology. Hallowell approached historical research the same way he approached fieldwork, with respect for difference and an aspiration to understand alien assumptions, beliefs, institutions, and so on; "the past is a different country" is the formula for this approach. Anthropologists are supposed to suspend a commitment to their own culture's ways in order to try to understand those of another contemporary culture and, accordingly Hallowell (and Hodgen) explored why earlier anthropologists thought what they did, and how what they thought made sense by their own cultural logic rather than by searching for precursors or attacking the follies of the past. He did not scorn ideas that differed from his own or condemn past writers for failing to understand cultures the way he did. He tried to make sense of chronologically alien worldviews of anthropologists in the same way that he tried to make sense of Ojibway cultural assumptions and cosmology (Hallowell 2010).

My third point for doing history of anthropology (or of any other discourse) is not to assume that the same word means the same thing in older texts; in his 1965 paper, Hallowell uses *nature* as an example. I have had to deal with quite different senses of *phonology, etymology, revolution,* and *personality* than are common in current discourse. I think these historically variable meanings of "the same word" are the equivalent to false cognates across languages in which the familiar word only *looks* the same across time and may have been used quite differently in the old text that one is reading.

Hallowell and Hodgen raised the question of the reliability of reports, with both recalling the spectacular example of the *monopoli*, headless men with faces on their chests that John Mandeville supposedly saw in his travels, although these travels never took place. Mandeville appropriated the label *monopoli* from Pliny, which is comparable to what Carlos Castaneda did when he constructed the teachings of "Don Juan" out of the books in the UCLA library. Many editions and translations ensued before Mandeville's non-travels and non-observations were established, and the Library of Congress continued to classify Castaneda novels in the part of the E99 cataloging for work about the Yaqui tribe. Reports of observation are easy to fake, and it is impossible to know how many more accounts that are plausible on the surface pass as observations rather than hearsay or outright invention. My second lesson to know who was where when applies. This means that even "modern, professional" observers need to preserve fieldnotes and letters from the field and to realize that they are as or more important sources to interpret what anthropologists did, and the basis for what they have written (see Sanjek 1990); these need to be subjected to the same scrutiny as other sources of evidence in my interviews.

For understanding Edward Sapir's Southern Paiute work, for example, it is important to know that the data were elicited from a single person, Tony Tillohash, far from any Paiute world; Sapir encountered him at the Carlisle School in Pennsylvania and brought him to Philadelphia where almost all the material on Paiute language and culture was located in 1910 (see Fowler and Fowler 1986). When attempting to establish who "discovered" phonemic analysis, it is important to know not only that Sapir wrote what he published in 1930–31 (Sapir 1930) but that it was written before 1917. In a 1916 letter to Alfred Kroeber, Sapir had already communicated what would be the prime example in his 1933 paper on the psychological reality of the phoneme. This chronology virtually to eliminates the possibility that Sapir's "discovery" of phonemic analysis was sparked by either [Ferdinand de] Saussure or gestalt psychology (Murray 1981). Sapir's classic publication reveals that he relied on Tillohash's feelings and even on his analyses of the forms of his own language. The great remove from the speech community is important to demonstrate the lack of connection between Sapir's linguistic methods and the ethnography of speaking or other sociolinguistic traditions (a topic considered at length in Murray 2013, 172–93); he largely avoided both ethnography and naturally occurring speech. When he did spend some time in a functioning native speech community among the Navajo, he was perplexed by individual differences and fled from participant observation, preferring the controlled elicitation sometimes called "white room ethnography."[3]

Joseph Casagrande's *In the Company of Man* (1965) deserves some credit for moving toward a focus on the natives who form the basis of anthropologists' pronouncements about alien culture. My reservation is that the anthropologists again speak about (and for) the natives. It would be more interesting in my view for the natives to speak for themselves about how the ethnographers behaved, what sort of weird questions they asked, and about the quality of their representations that eventually were published. I wish someone in Chan Kom or Tepotzlán would write the history of American anthropologists' involvement there.[4] Alfonso Villa Rojas wrote a manuscript autobiography for Robert Redfield; he was not a native of Chan Kom so it is a suspect source to document how Redfield was perceived in "the village that chose progress" (Redfield 1950).

In the same vein, I wonder what Balinese and Javanese villagers recall about Clifford Geertz's fieldwork as well as their interpretations of cockfights. Close reading of his famous article on the Balinese cockfight (Geertz 1972) suffices to show lack of Balinese support for his interpretations, but the text of his 1966 monograph on the lack of a conception of personhood in Bali renders it impossible to know how much came from observation, how much from native testimony, and how much from his own preconceptions emanating from Gregory Bateson and Margaret Mead (1942), which, in a further distancing from firsthand experience, was facilitated by and to some degree based on the interpretations of Walter Spies and other Dutch romanticizers (see Vickers 1997). I wonder what the Balinese photographed as children for *Balinese Character* say as they examine

Bateson's photos to make sense of what was and wasn't published. These are necessarily interpretive endeavors; even if I had Geertz's fieldnotes, I would still have questions about how he framed whatever questions he asked. If Mark Hobart (1986) and Unna Wikan (1990) are correct in alleging that Geertz's account is totally wrong, a serious historian of anthropology must ask why he thought what he did when he fashioned his model of the Balinese. The extent to which the Balinese Geertz lived with wanted the Balinese as he portrayed or whether they cared about his representations that were irrelevant to their everyday experience must be distinguished from his emphasis on accentuating cultural differences; what he recorded must be distinguished from what he "knew" in advance from reading Bateson and Mead (1942).

Winkin (1988), Daubenmier (2008), and Migliore and colleagues (2009) provide exemplars of what I would like to see explored more often in field sites, to wit: eliciting memories from the "natives" and their views on how their culture was represented by the alien observer.

In accordance with his own agenda, Derek Freeman (1991, 1999), the rabid critic of Mead's first fieldwork report, set out to reconstruct where Mead was and what she was doing in Samoa in 1925.[5] He documented though did not seem to notice that she spent considerable time on problems other than the one he maintains was set for her by Boas, namely, to show that that adolescent turmoil didn't exist. Despite doing that research Freeman still attacked what I published in *Current Anthropology* (Murray 1990, 1991), asserting that she did what she thought was interesting throughout her life and was too inner-directed to be "set" a task unless she wanted to do it. To my mind, Freeman as a historian is so eager to undercut what Mead wrote about Samoan adolescence that he fails to see or willfully ignores her intensive work on other topics, although the evidence undercuts his own representation of her as Boas's puppet. Although pursuing the documentation for the wrong reasons, Freeman contributed to understanding what a "Boasian anthropologist" did in one field setting at one time. (This does not redeem his account of Boasian theory!) A sympathetic attempt to understand what Mead was doing would have enhanced understanding of his chronicle of what she did, but relating what she wrote to what she did seems to me more revealing than labeling her work "Boasian," as if that label constituted an explanation.

In recent years Jennifer Brown has done some of this with descendants of Hallowell's Ojibwe sources, as have Sally Cole (2009) with descendants of those with whom Ruth Landes worked and Judith Daubenmier (2008) with those with whom University of Chicago anthropologists worked on the "Fox Project" in rural Iowa in the years after World War II. Although I know less about archaeology and nothing about physical anthropology, I am relatively confident that to understand the contributions of past practitioners of those to me arcane subdisciplines also requires examining what they actually did, that is, their practices rather than their pronouncements about methodology (fascinatingly exemplified by Pykles 2009).

Describing practices that differ from current standards risks being interpreted as criticizing the past for not being the present, and for doing things differently then and there. Even marginal outsiders who hold non-anthropology degrees, like Hodgen, Stocking, and I do have presentist concerns and sometimes at least implicitly criticize those we write about; for example, Hodgen aimed to discredit the "age and area hypothesis."[6] At least consciously, in writing my dissertation, I thought I had license to criticize lines of work with still active proponents, such as conversation analysis, but not how Boas or [Albert] Gallatin or [Lewis H.] Morgan went about studying and writing about Native Peoples. In the decades since then I have vacillated between thinking it impossible not to judge theoretical and methodological approaches, whether past or present, and thinking I should attempt sympathetic understanding from within the past paradigms, in their own terms, even (or especially) what I regard as ludicrous. Kuhn wrote somewhere that the historian of science should try to understand what it felt like to believe in phlogiston.[7] Some historians of anthropology try to understand what it was like to conceive of Caribs or Iroquois as lost tribes of Israel; others of us grapple with concepts like kinship and structure, for example, *the* Kwagiutl culture inscribed by a half-Tlingit, half-white trader named George Hunt, and *the* Southern Paiute language that Edward Sapir and Tony Tillohash constructed from their sense of patterning of sound and sense.

We can no more recover the past than we can enter into the full native sense of cultures other than those in which we were raised. Again, searching across time is similar to reaching across space or across social/cultural distances within a place to so-called subcultures. These ultimately impossible goals are nonetheless ones we *should* reach for and try to approximate. I do not approve of jettisoning attempts at sympathetic understanding of other cultures or of other anthropologies. Berating those who came before us for not seeing things the way we see them is equivalent to berating other peoples for not doing things the way we do them, or patronizing them for their apparent similarities to "our way" the "right way" or the way we should be in some imagined future, or the way we were in some imagined golden past age.

Some work in emic anthropology has achieved wide circulation, along with such etic anthropology as Marvin Harris's popular books or Margaret Mead's (1928) quite etic *Coming of Age in Samoa*. In the history of anthropology, the emic writings are known only to other historians of anthropology, and to some extent to other anthropologists, rather than to the general public. The three most widely-disseminated books dealing with anthropology in the past or anthropology over time, in chronological order of publication, are H. R. Hays (1958), *From Ape to Angel*, which no one reads anymore; Marvin Harris's (1968) *The Rise of Anthropological Theory*, which perhaps some anthropologists read, though it is unlikely anyone else does; and Derek Freeman's (1983) *Margaret Mead and Samoa*.[8] All three books are resolutely presentist. Hays presents a longer version of a typical introductory textbook review of the progress of the field. The other two explore what went wrong, specifically, how did the bad guys, and in Freeman's case a fallen woman as well, go wrong. Marvin Harris and Derek Freeman both have what they consider proper and adequate understandings of humankind and have revealed this understanding of what they consider the proper program for the science of humankind. Puzzled that not all anthropologists march under their banner, angry and resentful that most anthropologists persist in what they see as error, both turned toward the past to explore the sources of the contemporary error. Harris was rather grudging in crediting forerunners of his own cultural materialism but his account generated some interest in developments that led up to and presumably culminated in his theory. Freeman thought that anthropology, particularly American cultural anthropology, was benighted and persisted in its folly.

The popular histories and textbook histories of all sciences are what Herbert Butterfield (1931) called "presentist," which is to say that in writing about the past their primary purpose is in making sense of the present, legitimating present preoccupations with some sort of tradition and development, and lauding those who made contributions that are either accepted in the present or are believed to have led to present understandings of whatever phenomena are of concern to the contemporary science. Popular accounts of all sciences are "presentist," what Thomas Kuhn called "textbook history," and could more properly be called textbook substitutes for history. These do not aim to make sense of scientists in their own world with their own assumptions, but to prefigure "what we know now." The past is usually represented as a glorious march or fitful but heroic advance to present understanding. Harris and Freeman have positive visions but they are more visions of what anthropology *should* be than of what it is; most of the present discipline, not just the past is, in their view, lost in error.[9] Ancestors were not groping toward the truth as it is now properly understood by Harris or by Freeman but building intellectual structures designed to keep human self-understanding in the dark. Franz Boas, cast as the king of darkness by both Harris and Freeman and earlier by Leslie White (1966), has had plenty of hagiographers. Earlier books, including Robert Lowie's (1937) *History of Ethnological Theory*, Margaret Mead's (1972) autobiography and her book on Ruth Benedict (1959), and Melville Herskovits's book on Boas (1953), portrayed him as a culture hero, dispelling the racist darkness of nineteenth-century unilinear evolutionism and building science on its wreckage. Boas's admirers were every bit as much presentist as his detractors.

Perhaps one or more of these authors really does have the truth. My own view of anthropology doubtless colors my view that etic history is spurious That it is bad history goes without saying, but I am not certain that anthropology or any science needs good history, or that bad history is harmful to it. If someone today has a completely adequate understanding of our species, it doesn't matter whether she or he distorts the history of anthropology either as a path to the present or a bog from which their revelation will rescue anthropology. Those of us who are less confident that we hold the final truth should be aware that what we do and think may seem as stupid or inexplicable from the perspective of the future as some of what our predecessors did and thought seem to us. Perhaps some of what we know will be forgotten, just as some of what our predecessors knew has been forgotten. What has been forgotten is not necessarily the error. Lines of inquiry are dropped, new paradigms ask new questions, as Kuhn observed, but they do not necessarily offer new answers to the old questions, and the old questions may arise again or keep nagging in the background.

I am not sure why anyone should attempt the ultimately impossible task of making sense across time or across space, but for those so inclined, I have made some suggestions about how to do history of anthropology better, that I think apply to the history of ideas as well as to the history of institutions.

Recapitulating the maxims, drawn if not deduced, from my experiences in trying to understand the history of social science:

1. Don't jump to any conclusions that because B studies with A that B is doing what A did—even if others, or even B, calls B an A-ian.
2. Keep track of the dates, of who was where when, especially when using material elicited from informants or from public recollections. When working with published texts, it is important to ascertain when the texts were written, not just when they were published. In making inferences based on chronology, it is often important to find out whether a work circulated before publication. It's great to *know* that B had a copy of A's work, but in the absence of citation or a dated inventory of B's library the historian often has to assess the probability that A sent her work to B before B wrote whatever work the historian is trying to place and make sense of.

It's nice to know what the persons you are trying to understand were doing, especially when they were "in the field." "Fieldwork" would be another good example of a term that means different things to different people and at different times, and to different disciplines, which brings us to:

3. Don't assume that the same word means the same thing in older texts as it means when you use the word. Indeed, don't assume that the same word means the same thing to people writing at the same time. Meanings are constantly shifting, and one person may use an older sense of a word after someone else has used it with a newer meaning.

4. A subsidiary fourth point is that geography isn't destiny. Action at a distance occurs in anthropology and other sciences, while inaction at proximity also recurs. The fathers of ethnoscience, Harold Conklin, Ward Goodenough, and Floyd Lounsbury all studied with George Peter Murdock at Yale after World War II, yet they developed emic componential analysis independently of each other—and with only vague and general encouragement from Murdock, whose assumptions that the same etic domains can be coded in all cultures are institutionalized in the Human Relations Area Files. Similarly, Edward Sapir seems to have had precious little interchange with his urban ethnographer colleagues in the University of Chicago Sociology and Anthropology Department, and was on better terms with the positivist, quantitativist William Ogburn and his students than with the urban ethnographers and symbolic interactionists. Don't assume important contact from proximity or exclude it on the basis of geographical distance.

5. My fifth and final maxim is to treat schools as possibly useful fictions, not as explanations. That Ruth Bunzel or Ruth Underhill or Gladys Reichard wrote down texts as the natives dictated them because she was a Boasian is a pseudo-explanation. They may have been Boasians because they understood the point of collecting native texts—as Radcliffe-Brown did not; Boas may even have been the one to suggest the activity to them, but whomever we have in mind as the paradigmatic Boasian woman, you can be sure that there were other influences on her, and that being a Boasian was not the beginning and ending of her self-understanding. There are some shared assumptions between

say, Benedict and Mead, and Kroeber and Sapir. They certainly knew each other, and all had been influenced by Franz Boas, but there are considerable differences in what each of them did, and substantial shifts of interest over the life course of each. Kroeber's views on kinship didn't change much between 1909 and his death in 1960, but his views on evolution changed markedly, just as Mead's views on the extent of biological constraints on cultural difference did. Sapir gave up hypothesizing historical linguistic connections, and all four of them gave up tabulating trait distributions, albeit at different times. and for different reasons.

When I looked closely at much that has been written about named traditions in American social science, in particular the Chicago school of sociology, functionalism, ethnoscience, Boasian anthropology, and so on, they didn't so much dissolve as shatter into smaller molecules. Not atoms, but smaller molecules—three simultaneous Chicago schools, four ethnoscience groupings plus a residue of fellow travelers not very connected to each other, and two sets of Boasians, with Papa Franz himself turning against the historical inferences of the first generation of his students, in particular Alfred Kroeber and Edward Sapir.

I now think of theory groups as loose amalgams of individuals pursuing often different objectives, held together more by a common labeling by outsiders than by allegiance to such a label from inside. As with Boasian anthropologists, those viewed as a school often deny that they are a school and emphasize intra-group differences, even though these may strike outsiders as narcissism over small differences among those with distinctive shared assumptions and practices.

Similarities are salient for some purposes, but theoretical traditions within anthropology or any other discipline are not homogeneous and are fuzzily bounded. Boas became anti-Boasian as some so-called Boasians defined it; even prototypes can get fuzzy. When trying to make sense of what one person did or what a number of people with some link (like having studied with Boas) did, one must first examine what they actually did; their practices may be sufficiently similar that a label condenses them and is heuristic. The danger for history, as for anthropology, is inordinate haste in applying etic labels, for example, this is a "shaman," that is a "structuralist."

I am Sapirian enough to think we need to understand how various influences come together in an individual culture carrier, whether the culture being carried is that of Samoans or of Oceanist social anthropologists. In this ego-centered talk I have linked my own assumptions to Sapirian, Teggartian, and a University of Pennsylvania tradition.[10] This implies that I think such labels make some sense and specifically that they make some sense in understanding what I do. I don't think my cravings to be viewed as legitimate are so keen that I need so many families, and what has been transmitted through the genealogy I have made visible in this chapter is open to question. I've at least hinted at both the personal and the intellectual connections between the Teggartian and Hallowellian traditions in the history of anthropology but I can't imagine anyone claiming they formed a group.

I think, alongside Hallowell, that trying to understand across time takes the same effort to suspend judgment and to make sense of others in their own frame of reference as understanding across space does. Depending on how far back one goes, the possibility of natives being around to reject one's interpretations disappears. I have preferred in my own work to risk the wrath of the living, which constitutes an interesting if not necessarily privileged insight on the past. When the natives are literate, as most anthropologists are (even if they tend to eschew reading what others wrote about their fieldwork sites), and combative, as many are, a dialog of interpretation can occur that does not have to be imagined. What people think they are doing or think that they did and what they think they meant provide interesting data; criticism by peers and by natives makes better sense of cultures, including historical professional cultures. I understand making sense of the ways of others as the raison d'être of social science, including of history and anthropology, and the history of anthropology.

Notes

1. Including George W. Stocking Jr., A. Irving Hallowell, Edwin G. Boring, and David Bakan.
2. During my last year in residence in Toronto, I had an office just down the hall at St. Michael's from Marshall McLuhan. I saw another University of Toronto

celebrity, novelist Robertson Davies, master of Massey College, several times a week but never saw, let alone talked to, McLuhan. (I also never saw Lewis Feuer, whom Robert Nisbet sent me to work with at Toronto: Feuer was on sabbatical when I arrived and then left the University of Toronto.)

3. That is, taking the native informant out of context for the convenience of the researcher, rather than observing a functioning culture; see Murray 1992, 680; and 2013, 279 and 312 for discussion.

4. See Kemper and Royce (1997) for discussion of this issue.

5. I was naive to think Freeman's modus operandi of cherry-picking quotations and ignoring explicit rejection of what he wanted to argue had changed for his second Mead/Samoa book. In a paper presented at the 2012 American Anthropological Association meetings (2013), Paul Shankman showed that Freeman's hoaxing claims were based on flagrant misrepresentation of what his prime informant, Fa'apua'a Fa'amū, had said: "An analysis of Mead's relationship with Fa'apua'a demonstrates that she was not an informant for Mead on adolescent sex, and an examination of the three interviews used by Freeman does not support his interpretation of them. In fact, responding to direct questioning during the interviews, Fa'apua'a stated that Mead did not ask her questions about her own sexual conduct or about adolescent sexual conduct. Nor did she provide Mead with information on this subject" (quote from the abstract; also see Shankman and Boyer 2009).

6. Having taken postgraduate courses in anthropology for four years at three universities, I "went native" to some extent, joined the American Anthropological Association, presented research, and served as a discussant at sessions of its annual meetings (on subjects other than the history of anthropology), and have published research that is not history of the fields in anthropological and linguistic anthropology journals.

Briefly, *historicism* means examining what previous scholars did in context, while *presentism* means looking to see how the early work led to the modern work.

7. Kuhn (1983), 674–78.

8. Some favor its techno-environmental determinism and use uncritically as a textbook.

9. More properly, since both are now dead, in the views propounded in their books.

10. Each of my successive anthropological linguistic mentors provide a link to Sapir: Keith Basso through Clyde Kluckhohn, William Samarin through Mary Haas and Murray Emeneau, John Gumperz through Kenneth Pike. I also consider myself a "Weberian" comparativist more than a little influenced by Alexis de Tocqueville. I was introduced to their ideas as an undergraduate student at James Madison College by Peter Lyman, Bruce Miller, and Richard Zinman (before

being a graduate student of Robert Nisbet and Irving Zeitlin, both of whom wrote books about Tocqueville).

References

Bateson, Gregory, and Margaret Mead. 1942. *Balinese Character: A Photographic Analysis*. New York: New York Academy of Sciences.

Butterfield, Herbert. 1931. *The Whig Interpretation of History*. London: George Bell and Sons.

Casagrande, Joseph B., ed. 1965. *In the Company of Man: Twenty Portraits by Anthropologists*. New York: Harper.

Cole, Sally. 2009. *Rainy River Lives: Stories Told by Maggie Wilson*. Lincoln: University of Nebraska Press.

Daubenmier, Judith. 2008. *The Meskwaki and Anthropologists*. Lincoln: University of Nebraska Press.

Fowler, Catherine S., and Don D. Fowler. 1986. "Edward Sapir, Tony Tillohash and Southern Paiute Studies." In *New Perspectives in Language, Culture, and Personality: Proceedings of the Edward Sapir Centenary Conference (Ottawa, 1–3 October 1984)*, edited by William Cowan, Michael Foster, and E. F. K. Koerner, 41–65. Amsterdam: John Benjamins.

Freeman, Derek. 1983. *Margaret Mead and Samoa*. Cambridge MA: Harvard University Press.

———. 1991. "'There's Tricks i' th' World': An Historical Analysis of the Samoan Researches of Margaret Mead." *Visual Anthropology Review* 7 (1): 103–28.

———. 1999. *The Fateful Hoaxing of Margaret Mead: A Historical Analysis of Her Samoan Research*. Boulder CO: Westview.

Geertz, Clifford. 1966. *Person, Time, and Conduct in Bali: An Essay in Cultural Analysis*. New Haven CT: Yale Southeast Asia Program.

———. 1972. "Deep Play: Notes on the Balinese Cockfight." *Daedalus* 101 (1): 1–37

George, Katherine. 1958. "The Civilized West Looks at Primitive Africa, 1400–1800: A Study in Ethnocentrism." *Isis* 49 (1): 62–72.

Hallowell, A. Irving. 1965. "The History of Anthropology as an Anthropological Problem." *Journal of the History of the Behavioral Sciences* 1 (1): 24–38.

———. 2010. *Contributions to Ojibwe Studies: Essays, 1934–1972*. Edited by Jennifer S. H. Brown and Susan Elaine Gray. Lincoln: University of Nebraska Press.

Harris, Marvin. 1968. *The Rise of Anthropological Theory*. New York: Crowell.

Hays, Hoffman Reynolds. 1958. *From Ape to Angel: An Informal History of Social Anthropology*. New York: Knopf.

Herskovits, Melville J. 1953. *Franz Boas: The Science of Man in the Making*. New York: Charles.

Hobart, Mark. 1986. "Thinker, Thespian, Soldier, Slave? Assumptions about Human Nature in the Study of Balinese Society." In *Context, Meaning, and Power in Southeast Asia*, edited by Mark Hobart and Robert Taylor, 131–56. Ithaca: Cornell Southeast Asia Program.

Hodgen, Margaret T. 1936. *The Doctrine of Survivals: A History of Scientific Method in the Study of Man*. London: Allenson.

———. 1952. *Change and History: A Study of the Dated Distributions of Technological Innovations in England*. New York: Wenner-Gren.

———. 1964. *Early Anthropology in the Sixteenth and Seventeenth Centuries*. Philadelphia: University of Pennsylvania Press.

———. 1974. *Anthropology, History, and Cultural Change*. Tucson: University of Arizona Press.

Kemper, Robert V., and Anya P. Royce. 1997. "Ethical Issues for Social Anthropologists: A North American Perspective on Long-Term Research in Mexico." *Human Organization* 56 (4): 479–83.

Kuhn, Thomas S. 1962. *The Structure of Scientific Revolutions*. Chicago: University of Chicago Press.

———. 1983. "Commensurability, Comparability, Communicability." In *Proceedings of the 1982 Biennial Meeting of the Philosophy of Science Association*, edited by Peter D. Asquith and Thomas Nickles, vol. 2, 669–88. East Lansing MI: Philosophy of Science Association.

Lowie, Robert. 1937. *The History of Ethnological Theory*. New York: Holt.

Mead, Margaret. 1928. *Coming of Age in Samoa*. New York: Morrow.

———. 1959. *An Anthropologist at Work*. Boston: Houghton-Mifflin.

———. 1972. *Blackberry Winter: My Earlier Years*. New York: Simon and Schuster.

Migliore, Sam, Margaret Dorazio-Migliore, and Vincenzo Ingrasci. 2009. "Living Memory: Milocca's Charlotte Gower Chapman." *Histories of Anthropology Annual* 5:110–51.

Murray, Stephen O. 1981. "Sapir's Gestalt." *Anthropological Linguistics* 23 (1): 8–12.

———. 1990. "Problematic Aspects of Freeman's Account of Boasian Culture." *Current Anthropology* 31 (4): 401–7.

———. 1991. "On Boasians and Margaret Mead." *Current Anthropology* 32 (4): 448–52.

———. 1992. Review of *Bodies, Pleasures, and Passions: Sexual Culture in Contemporary Brazil* by Richard G. Parker. *Journal of the History of Sexuality* 2 (4): 679–82.

———. 2013. *American Anthropology and Company: Historical Explorations*. Lincoln: University of Nebraska Press.

Nisbet, Robert A. 1966. *The Sociological Tradition*. New York: Basic.

———. 1980. *History of the Idea of Progress*. New York: Basic.

Pykles, Benjamin C. 2009. *"The Archaeology of the Mormons Themselves": The Restoration of Nauvoo and the Rise of Historical Archaeology in America.* Lincoln: University of Nebraska Press.

Redfield, Robert. 1950. *A Village That Chose Progress: Chan Kom Revisited.* Chicago: University of Chicago Press.

———. 1953. "Relations of Anthropology to the Social Sciences and to the Humanities." In *Anthropology Today: An Encyclopedia Inventory,* edited by Alfred A. Kroeber, 728–38. Chicago: University of Chicago Press.

Sanjek, Roger. 1990. *Fieldnotes: The Makings of Anthropology.* Ithaca NY: Cornell University Press.

Sapir, Edward. 1930. "Southern Paiute, a Shoshonean language." *Proceedings of the American Academy of Arts and Sciences* 65 (1): 1–296.

———. 1933. "La réalité psychologique des phonèmes." *Journal de psychologie normale et pathologique* 30:247–65.

Shankman, Paul. 2013. "The 'Fateful Hoaxing' of Margaret Mead: A Cautionary Tale." *Current Anthropology* 54 (1): 51–70.

Shankman, Paul, and Paul S. Boyer. 2009. *The Trashing of Margaret Mead: Anatomy of an Anthropological Controversy.* Madison: University of Wisconsin Press.

Stocking, George W., Jr. 1965. "On the Limits of 'Presentism' and 'Historicism' in the Historiography of the Behavioral Sciences." *Journal of the History of the Behavioral Sciences* 1 (3): 211–18.

———. 1968. *Race, Culture, and Evolution: Essays in the History of Anthropology.* New York: Free Press.

Vickers, Adrian. 1997. *Bali: A Paradise Created.* Singapore: Periplus.

White, Leslie A. 1966. *The Social Organization of Ethnological Theory.* Houston: Rice University.

Wikan, Unni. *Managing Turbulent Hearts: A Balinese Formula for Living.* Chicago: University of Chicago Press, 1990.

Winkin, Yves. 1988. "Goffman à Baltasound." *Politex* 3/4:66–70.

11   What Is a Conversation (in Anglo America)?

Stephen O. Murray

> What passed for conversation at Carlo's [Carl Van Vechten's]; in all the years I spent in that place I never heard nor took part in a conversation as I define the word; at Carlo's there were monologues, exchanges of bon mots, bitchery, some facts, but there was never the give-and-take of conversation.
> —Coleman Dowell, *A Star Bright Life*, 126

Sacks, Schegloff, and Jefferson (1974, 700) claimed that their model of turn-taking was "a basic form of organization: 'basic' in that it would be invariant to parties" in all cultures, that it "accommodated grossly apparent facts," and that the fourteen features which they listed could be observed "in any conversation" anywhere.[1] Schegloff (1987, 101) reiterated that conversation analysis (CA): "takes ordinary conversation to be the fundamental form of talk-in-interaction (in the sense that other, task-or context-specialized forms are transformations of it: Sacks et al. 1974, 730–31), and a/the primordial site of human sociality and social life."

Conversation analysts, because they take for granted that any instance of interaction will reveal the purportedly universal features of the turn-taking model, rarely bother to distinguish what native "members" of a society consider distinct communicative events.[2] Edelsky (1981, 5) noted that conversation analysts' conception of "conversation" is quite at variance with members' models: "The usual direction in scientific inquiry [fundamental to early ethnomethodological programs: see Garfinkel and Sacks 1970], that of taking the imprecise 'lay' notions and discovering boundaries of sub-notions within them, was reversed in the case of analyses of 'conversation.' Instead, researchers have tended to collapse more distinct speech community notions (e.g., classroom lessons, therapy sessions, coffee klatch conversations) into one category designated as 'conversation.'"

I argue, en route to a typology of speech situations used by "members" of the Anglo-American (Californian) "speech community" from which CA generalizations derive, that the speech setting from which microanalysis of interaction has been drawn inordinately differs significantly from what members recognize as "conversation."

Therapeutic Conversation?

Whereas the communicative setting of psychotherapist-patient interaction is one kind of naturally occurring interaction in North America, we may still wonder if we live in so therapeutically oriented a society (Rieff 1966) that therapy talk has become paradigmatic of naturally occurring interaction. The folk view is that one party (the patient) is not typical or representative; perceived deviance in interaction often occasions being placed in the patient role whether by persuasion ("You need professional help!") or coercion (involuntary psychiatric holds and commitments) and the other party (the therapist) has asymmetric control over the frequency, duration, and topics (Turner 1972) of the interaction, whether or not s/he controls the allocation of speaking turns. Goffman (1983, 11; also see 1981, 14n8) noted in his valediction that "even apart from *what* is said, turn-taking rules in informal talk differ somewhat from those in family therapy sessions." Yet, in many of the seminal works of microanalysis, the specific context of therapy is ignored because "conversation analysts" generalize from therapeutic settings with the implicit but unquestioned assumption that how interaction is done in therapeutic settings is the same as how interaction is done elsewhere.

In *The First Five Minutes*, Pittenger, Hockett, and Danehy (1960) describe differentia in prosodic cues in detail, while in *The Natural History of an Interview*, Bateson, Birdwhistell, Brosin, Hockett, and McQuown (McQuown 1971, 1983) further complicate generalization with their painstaking analysis of kinesic and paralinguistic detail in an assessment interview. This line of work "testifies to the richness of the phenomenon being studied. It also demonstrates the great difficulty in reducing this information to a parsimonious statement that would allow the knowledge gained to be disseminated broadly and confirmed by other researchers" (Labov and

Fanshel 1977, 20; also see Leeds-Hurwitz 1987). Similar charges have been leveled at the analyses of Harvey Sacks, although his work utilizing therapy talk is atypically concerned with content and motivation rather than mechanics (Sacks 1975).[3]

Many publications by other analysts based upon data consisting of therapy talk without any explanation of their choice of research site and without mentioning what might be atypical of conversation in what they simply refer to as dubious "conversations." Turner's recognition of something out of the ordinary in the speech situation was an exception (Turner 1972): he specifically distinguished "pre-therapy talk," in which the therapist answered questions if and when asked, from "therapy talk," during which the therapist did not answer even direct questions. The asymmetry marked the power of the therapist "answerable to no one" within therapy talk even if it did not produce it. "Patients" were answerable to the therapist and to each other but had no "answer right" (see Basso 1974) if they asked anything of the therapist [that is, they had no right to receive an answer]. The same caveat tends to apply more generally in medical "consultations" (see Tannen and Wallat 1986).

Conversation analysts inclined toward ethnomethodology usually assume that "members" use the "devices" inferred/identified by the analysts, ignoring interactants' intentions. On an ad hoc basis, they may depart from proclaiming mechanisms and impute motivation for a speech turn/speech act (e.g., Schegloff 1987, 109–11; Schegloff and Sacks 1973). They do not seek, even then, to find out if "members" share the interpretations of what they were doing or trying to do with the "devices" that the analyst has posited.

Labov and Fanshel (1977, 1) sought better grounding their analysis by examining the first five minutes of psychotherapy, mostly its paralinguistic features, "to grasp some of the general principles of conversation." They employed a technique in which they sought the therapist's interpretation of what went on in the conversation they taped but did not seek the interpretations of the patient.[4]

Robin Lakoff (1978) contended that the psychoanalytical interview is a system fundamentally deviating from the rules employed in ordinary conversation rather than being typical of naturally occurring conversation. The "principle of rationality" (i.e., the working assumption that participants are rational) that undergirds and facilitates most interaction, and conversation in particular, is suspended in psychoanalytical interviews, and in most other forms of therapy. Statements that would be "passed over" in ordinary conversation are seized upon by therapists and on occasion by patients and may even be elevated to the status of "keys"; she also contended that another fundamental assumption of ordinary conversation, the "principle of benefit," is also suspended. Both parties in (voluntary) therapeutic talk may expect instrumental benefits such as income for the therapist or improved functioning for the patient. Some patients assuredly seek "someone to talk to" in renting a therapist's ears. Therapists rarely regard therapy as social pleasantry; it is hard work that they believe deserves ample compensation. Disjunctive motivations, and even cross purposes, however, do not distinguish therapy talk from ordinary conversation. The "principle of benefit," therefore, proves problematic in distinguishing speech events.[5]

The extraordinary features of "therapeutic discourse" include an unusually high frequency of metacommunicative utterances: participants are more self-conscious about communicating (nonverbally as well as verbally) than in other speech settings. Patients must not follow rules of coherence ordinarily used to make sense when undergoing psychoanalysis and various primal therapies but must free associate, in various expressions, "get down" or "get in touch with" variously conceived basic processes or prior levels. While therapists may delude themselves about their power (be possessed by false consciousness), they are not releasing patients from constraints in ordering them to free associate but merely imposing new constraints. The patient doesn't decide that it is time to free associate because the analyst directs the patient to begin. "Non-directive therapists," albeit with greater subtlety (which provides more cover for self-delusion), also control conversation, by choosing what is therapeutic to reflect back. A patient who was seriously pondering the drug use of significant others, for instance, attempted to discuss the topic. The therapist "heard her saying" as an evasion of talking about the personal problem that the therapy was "supposed to be about" (even though this was a major difficulty in sustaining relationships). Newer "client-centered" therapies mask the concept of "resistance," but it has not perished.

Therapists exercise floor control in addition to topic control, although social psychologists in the [Robert F.] Bales tradition who confuse power with talking a lot or with monopolizing the floor may miss this fact. In American culture, as in many tribal cultures (see Albert 1972; Basso 1970; Breiness 1988; Samarin 1965), having the last word (making the decision after hearing various views) is more important than having more turns at talk. "Dominating" the conversation may be a means to gain power in a group of strangers in a social psychology laboratory or even in a naturally occurring grouping of strangers, such as a jury (Collins and Guetzkow 1964; Strodtbeck, James and Hawkins 1957), but in groups in which the greater power of one party is firmly established in everyone's mind, the mystery of having to guess what the powerful person wants or thinks can be enhanced by silence (see Hymes 1974, 110; Murray 1975; Tannen 1985, 1989).

"Therapy talk," in common with all dyadic interaction, violates the "turn order is not fixed" feature of the Sacks and colleagues (1974:700–701) model; length of interaction is fixed in advance, as is the number of parties. "Therapy talk" deviates markedly from three of their fourteen allegedly "grossly apparent" universal features.[6] The applicability of other features of the model, such as "One party talks at a time" and "Occurrences of more than one speaker at a time are common, but brief," should be empirical questions, but they have not yet been addressed in this favored locale for analysis.[7]

Anglo-American Speech Situations

Native speakers of American English distinguish several kinds of verbal interaction.[8] Conversation is certainly among them. The relative status of participants in distinguishing kinds of talk is more salient to members of the culture than the formal features of turn-taking. These dual approaches to modeling a typology of speech situations are not orthogonal, however, because control of the floor (not occupation or monopolization of the floor, but the ability to choose who will speak about what) is a prerogative of the higher status interactant in *all* types of interaction. Differences in relative status also define who should speak and who should listen in various kinds of speech situations.

Kinds of talk elicited from Anglo Californians as "kinds of conversations" include dialog/multilog, chat, conversation, discussion, gossip, and argument. Whatever status differences exist between interlocutors tend to be ignored or downplayed in "conversation," and there is no expectation that one party will control topic, length of speaking turns, or length of interaction within a conversation. Although many conversations are dominated by one party, this is neither a defining feature nor part of a prototypical instance of "conversation." The interaction as a whole (as well as segments within it) may be goal-directed, but goals are typically more diffuse and plural than those found in some other kinds of interaction.[9]

A second kind of talk in which one participant normatively controls the floor and prototypically is confined to a single topic is the *lecture* (see Goffman 1981, 162–96); other instances or labels include a sermon, an address, a speech, "a talk to [about topic T]", a briefing, a "formal presentation," a "guided tour," and a "calling on the carpet." The speaker of these kinds of talk does not necessarily have higher status than the listeners, especially in the case of a briefing, rather the speaker is listened to because s/he has special competence or information, without necessarily having higher social status, so that one person has inordinately long turns in contrast to everyday "conversation," and one person chooses the "next speaker." A briefing by a subordinate does not differ from a supervisor "calling on the carpet" employees and warning them they will be fired if they repeat some error, as only considering turn-taking patterns would predict. The voluntary character of attendance by those whose role is to listen (and occasionally to ask questions) is important in distinguishing among the kinds of interaction in which one person mostly monopolizes the floor. Actual control of topic and floor varies according to the status of the person(s) in the hearer role. Conveying information is the manifest goal of such talk, although additional subsidiary motivations frequently are involved.

Natives (if not analysts) also distinguish a kind of talk in which speakers alternate more frequently than in lectures. Although length of turns and frequency of topic changes in *interviews* may approximate those in everyday conversation, native speakers do not confuse interviews with conversation, no matter how artful the facade of informality. One informant put it this way in describing his perspective on job interviews: "Of course you have to play along, but you always have to remember that they [interviewers] are deciding your fate. How you evaluate them can only matter if they first decide they want you." More coercive categories of interviews include interrogation, inquiry, and examination. The interlocutor with higher status or some control over matters of importance to the other asks the questions and can interrupt and change topics seemingly at will (although usually constrained by certain probably unconscious cultural proscriptions on abruptness).

Although spoken exchanges are transcribed in court, doctors, lawyers, and other professionals conducting interviews often take notes, but a written record of the interaction was not regarded as a necessary feature of interviews by most Californians. Notes about "passing conversations" may be made in personal journals, memoranda, et cetera. Whereas minutes of some "*meetings*" are recorded, transcribing of interaction is not regarded as a defining characteristic of a "meeting" by native speakers. The manifest goal of interviews is commonly information, but displays of power or of solidarity are recurrent, and attempts are sometimes made to amuse the interlocutors.

Individuals may go to doctors, lawyers, or other consultants with some expectation of setting at least an initial topic (the problem presented), but this topic may be redefined totally by the professional consulted. Professionals are paid to winnow out what is clinically or legally significant and control floor and topic on the basis of this expertise. Clients expect the professional to focus on "real problems." Despite considerable deference to (expected) medical and legal expertise, patients want to be taken seriously and "treated like human beings." This last desideratum again constrains abruptness. Varying amounts of explanation for disregarding lay opinion are offered depending on the social status of the patient or client. The expectations of conversational equality proffered by West (1984) are not the same as those of interactants in the setting of medical consultation. The doctor is paid to find out what, if anything, is wrong, but some patients may be motivated in making a medical appointment (especially for psychotherapy) by a need for human sociation; they still generally expect the doctor to "take charge" of the interaction and defer to the special competence of the practitioner which legitimates bodily intrusion as well as interactional control.

Doctors, lawyers, and other professionals are perceived as having special competence. In functioning as gatekeepers (to courts, hospital, prescriptions, etc.), they resemble interviewers. "Medical interview" is a reasonable label for much interaction between medical practitioners and clients/patients. I do not think such interactions are generally viewed by participants as being *"service encounters"* (Merritt 1975).[10] Waiters, salespeople, and cashiers are also gatekeepers, but their special expertise rarely receives the same deference as that given to doctors and lawyers. Second-guessing the client in ways that doctors and lawyers routinely do may be perceived in service encounters as "attitude" or "rudeness" where those paying expect higher degrees of deference than they do from those socially defined as professionals who are also said to "serve" them. Some doctors may produce the prescriptions ordered by the client in the same way a waiter delivers an entrée, but such interaction deviates from general expectation. Salespeople may be paid a percentage of the sales price, but salespeople are not paid directly by the buyer for spending time with him or her, even though they may be paid a percentage of the sales price, much as doctors are when they write prescriptions and operate as signature machines. Ethical doctors do not receive commissions based on volume of prescriptions, nor do they often receive tips beyond charges for services rendered, as waiters do.

The norm in service encounters is that "the customer is always right," although those providing the service frequently think otherwise (at least west of New Jersey; cf. Tannen 1981, 1984) and they are generally expected to act under the fiction that the customer is right. Medical practitioners are trained to act under a nearly opposite assumption that serves to maintain the high rewards allocated for special medical competence. Patient conceptions are often undercut systematically which is tolerated more readily than are the airs of superior knowledge or taste sometimes perceived in service encounters.

Some informants suggested "negotiation" as a speech situation distinct in formality and instrumentality from "conversation." "Negotiation" is a term used by social scientists to describe aspects of all interaction (Strauss 1978), so that folk and technical usage can easily become confused. Despite the claims to generic status as the key to "the interaction order" (Goffman 1983), negotiation should probably be considered at the level of speech *event* within the typology of Anglo North American speech situations presented here.

Even more asymmetric than the interview is giving orders/commands/ *directives*, a usually brief segment of speech. A parent telling a child to halt or a commanding officer telling troops to advance are not instances of "conversation," whether or not there is a speaking turn of the "Yes, sir" or "Why, Mommy?" form. This kind of speech is possible because of the relative status of interactants and the intent of the higher status individual make this kind of speech possible; turn-taking is irrelevant to identifying instances. Although some orders may be motivated by a desire to demonstrate dominance, the prototypical goal of an order is to commence or to halt an action by an other or others.

Religious services are the setting for some speech events not found elsewhere in Anglo culture, such as chanting, praying aloud, and responsive readings.[11] One party, generally the person with higher status (within the sacred domain, not necessarily in secular status hierarchies), often has disproportionate control of the floor relative to other participants or some borrowed authority (as in a layperson designated by the minister to read a scriptural passage). The addressee is not visible but may be represented and felt by those involved to be "present in spirit."

Watching *performances* on stage or screen also requires notice. Dramaturgical sociology (building on Kenneth Burke's work) has given generic senses to "staged," "performance," and "scripted." Although psychotherapy has adapted "role playing," natives still distinguish the stage of life in which a speaker may re-enact a previous interaction from a stage for which they pay to watch impersonations, re-enactments, and even some improvisations. The person performing (like popular lecturers or emissaries being debriefed) does not necessarily possess higher status than audience members. A few performers have great wealth, but status may lag behind wealth, and especially far behind income (Weber [1922] 1978, 926–40).

An Instance of Native Concern about Distinguishing "Conversation"

These distinctions may become important in real interaction, as shown in the following example taken from testimony before the U.S. Joint Senate/House Committee that was investigating National Security Council activities during the summer of 1987. In reviewing the initial investigations by the attorney general of the United States, two senators defined all the inquiries to possibly culpable officials he had made as "interviews." The attorney general did not accept this definition of some key events. In EM1, he first uses "conversation" in a generic sense, in which "casual conversation" and "interview" are both kinds of "conversation." An "interview" has a purpose, in contrast to "casual conversation." Short duration seems to be a defining feature of the latter, but there is also the implication that one only interviews persons with lower status. GM2 accepts a distinction between casual conversation and interview, but Senator George Mitchell does not accept that the importance of the interlocutor precludes conducting an interview with a witness present and some record being kept. In GM3 and GM5 he rejects the predictability of the interchange as a reason not to conduct an interview. Attorney General Edwin Meese does not further discuss the propriety of interviewing high-ranking officials but continues to defend only having had "a conversation" (as a distinct, not generic classification of an occasion of interaction).

Senator George Mitchell 1: As to the interviewing that you conducted on Friday, Saturday, and Sunday/ your recollection has been supported / and you have relied extensively on notes taken of those meetings // As to the critical events of Monday and Tuesday / there is only your undocumented recollection / and it does raise a question which I would like to ask you // Is there a reason why / at each interview you had up to and including the meeting with Col. North/ there was always another member of your staff present who took notes /but that with respect to every interview thereafter you were alone and no notes were taken /or is that pure accident.

Attorney General Edwin Meese 1: It's not totally pure accident // It's pure accident in a general sense // but they were totally different types of conversations // In the meetings I had with / Secretary Schultz // the meeting with Mr. Sporkin / uh / the meeting with Mr. McFarlane / the meeting with / uh/ Mr. North // All these are what you might call / uh / interviews where we were seeking to elicit a great deal of information / and in which notes were important in order to record that information which we were hearing in each case for the first time // uh / The other conversations that took place were not for the purpose of eliciting great amounts of information // They were the casual conversations // conversations in which / uh / I was the only person present / for example/ with the President and Don Regan in which I don't usually take notes in those quick meetings.

GM2: Giving you every benefit of the doubt / uh / uh / I think it's difficult to understand that you did not regard Adm. Poindexter // one of the three people in the government who is alleged to have had information about it/ the president's national security adviser / as a person not sufficiently important enough to have an interview with / but rather a casual conversation.

EM2: Well / the reason that it / that there was no interview / is that what he said essentially confirmed what—

GM3: But you couldn't have known beforehand what he was going to say/ could you?

EM3: No / I was just trying to find out because / I had very little time before the national security planning group meeting/ and my meeting with the president and I thought it was important to confirm with Adm. Poindexter / the idea being that there would be ample time / uh / to go into a formal interview situation/ had that been necessary.

GM4: Well I'll leave it at that and say that it's / it's really very difficult to accept. I/d like to

EM4: I don't understand why it's difficult to accept

GM5: Well, Adm. Poindexter was a central figure and to say that you didn't interview him

EM5: but everything he told me was totally consistent

GM6: But you could / not / have / known / before you talked to him what he was going to say.

EM6: That's right.

GM7: That's the very purpose of having someone there to record the meeting.

EM7: Well / that's right / but had he said anything differently from that we would have had a more formal interview to get that information . . .

The chairman of the committee did not accept the interview/conversation distinction, but the attorney general reiterated the distinction in the following:

EM8: Mr. Chairman / as I think you'll remember / from my discussion with Senator Mitchell / most of the times in the interviews / notes were taken / in fact / those notes have been relied on here for the information about which I've testified / and there were only a few instances / that notes were not taken.

Senator Daniel Inouye: But these were / the / important / interviews // after you began to get suspicious / that something was WRONG.

EM9: The only interview I would say / I wouldn't even call them interviews / They were conversations / I would say the only / uh conversation even / in which probably notes would be valuable / and had I had the time / on the occasion /uh I would have uh jotted them down although / I must say I have a very good recollection of them / would be the discussion with Admiral Poindexter// Notes were taken in the ensuing interviews.

The senators were less interested in what the interchange was called than in the lack of any record of what someone suspected of wrongdoing told an investigator suspected by many as colluding in the destruction of evidence and limiting political embarrassment for the administration of which he was a part. In invoking the folk understanding of speech situations, Meese backed off from the appeal to common sense that one doesn't interview the powerful but continued to appeal to the common sense that interviews are not conducted on the fly, and that note-taking is not a part of conversation. Senators Mitchell and Inouye did not challenge this common sense about conversation but stressed the impropriety of the nation's highest law enforcement official having casual conversations rather than conducting formal inquiries when exploring possibly criminal acts.[12]

Conclusion

It is clear from elicitation of native Anglo-American categories of kinds of speech settings and from the contested use of the category "conversation" in the preceding example that "conversation" (1) is a native category and (2) is not a generic category for all verbal interactions. Other emic [local] categories such as "shaman" and "taboo" have been used as etic labels by anthropologists in ways that might startle Tungus and Polynesian readers. I do not think that "conversation" is like this.[13] "Conversation" is not only an inapt generalization but also an obfuscation used by interlocutors such as doctors and attorneys general to mask micro-level manifestations of power/domination that sustain inequality. Although "conversations" may be interesting to analyze, analysts should not collude with the dominant participants in interaction to confuse asymmetrical encounters with the native category "conversation."[14]

Notes

1. To some extent, this research was supported by National Institute of Mental Health research grant 08371-02, and it was influenced in various ways by Deborah Tannen, Wendy Leeds-Hurwitz, Keelung Hong, and John Gumperz. I am grateful to Pablo Tellez for assuring me that my critique applies to "conversación" as a generic category in Spanish, the second most commonly spoken language in California, and to four Californians born in four different decades who worked out the typology of speech events presented here while crossing Austria by train.
2. See Hymes (1974, 51–52) on the levels of speech act, event, situation, and on the plurifunctionality of speech. Exemplary analyses of genres in other (than Anglo North American) cultures include Gossen (1974) and Sherzer (1983).
3. Indeed, it includes a (partial) hierarchical taxonomy of genre (a level between speech act and speech event).
4. The work of John Gumperz and his associates (see Gumperz 1982a, 1982b; Murray 1985) on interethnic miscommunication includes playback for comments by interviewees as well as interviewers, workers as well as managers and does not perpetuate (collude with) the greater ability of those in place with power to define for analysts what was going on (see Singh, Lele, and Martohardjono,1988). The method is cogently defended by Tannen (1984, 32–40). The ethnography of communication tradition (see Hymes 1974) has always focused on native rather than analysts' models, following the example of Sapir, rather than of Bloomfield (see Murray 1991b).
5. Furthermore, I think that Lakoff (also see West 1984) projects her own egalitarian norms onto the expectations of interactants in all settings, particularly consultations with professionals.
6. Schegloff, in particular, further conflates analysts' models based on repeated listening with how the natives accomplish interaction in real time. This is the sort of "it must be this way" approach that Garfinkel criticized in the functionalist sociology of the 1950s. As Wieder (1992n37) reminds, "Just because recognized things are orderly is not a good reason to suppose that they can be formulated in terms of criterial attributes."
7. North American doctor-patient interaction became the pervasive site for conversation analysis during the 1980s, with the papers in Fisher and Todd (1983), Frankel (1984), Heller and Freeman (1987); along with Mishler (1984), West (1984), Tannen and Wallat (1986), Cicourel (1987), and numerous other works by these authors and by others. The critique of generalizing from psychotherapy to "conversation" applies almost wholesale to the asymmetries of doctor-patient interaction with the exception of free association being a part. The "answer right" of medical patients is only slightly greater than that of those treated for mental illnesses (see Erickson and Rittenberg 1987).

8. Goffman (1981, 48) cautioned that while "verbal exchanges may be the natural unit of plays, novels, audiotapes, and other forms of literary life wherein words can be transcribed much more effectively than actions can be described, natural conversation, however, is not subject to this recording bias—not subject to systematic transformation into words." Nonetheless expected kinds of speaking seem basic to the native conceptions of kinds of interaction. Still, more than speaking is important in "speech situations." Silence, as more than the absence of speech, is one aspect (see Basso 1970; Bauman 1983; Samarin 1965; Tannen 1985, 1989), along with what is glossed as "nonverbal communication," a label that suggests a residual category, and also recreates in a wider sphere the unifunctional view of language as communication.

9. It seems to me that Goffman (1981, 14n8) went too far in considering "conversation" to be critically "cut off from or carried on to the side of instrumental tasks, a period of idling felt to be an end in itself." After all, there is the marked category "idle conversation" which would be redundant if Goffman's description was apposite. However, he rightly stressed the lack of a fixed schedule and the rough equality of status of participants for the purposes (and duration) of a "conversation."

10. This label was not elicited but was quickly understood by informants as a kind of talk for which they did not have a label at the level of speech settings. At the level of speech acts there are servers taking or asking for orders. The served are being waited on, or ordering.

11. A "sermon" can be considered a kind of "lecture" in this typology.

12. Halkowski (1990) showed, from another part of the Iran-Contra hearing testimony of Lt. Col. Oliver North, a distinction between the attorney general conducting a "full-fledged investigation" and "the attorney general in his role as Mr. Meese," the president's friend. The conception of roles exactly parallels the conception of differing appropriate speech events.

13. It is more like "chief," a misrepresentation with damaging consequences (see Clemmer 1986).

14. It may even be important to examine what happens and what fails to happen in "informal conversation." Murray (1991a) contends that failure of conversational involvement constitutes part of the "glass ceiling" constraining the promotion of Asian Americans.

References

Albert, Ethel. 1964. "'Rhetoric,' 'Logic' and 'Poetics' in Burundi." *American Anthropologist* 44 (2): 35–54.

Basso, Keith H. 1970. "To Give Up on Words." *Southwestern Journal of Anthropology* 26:213–30.

———. 1974. "Basic Conversation Rules." Unpublished manuscript.
Bauman, Richard. 1983. *"Let Your Words Be Few": Symbolism of Speaking and Silence among Seventeenth Century Quakers.* Cambridge: Cambridge University Press.
Brenneis, Donald. 1988. "Language and Disputing." *Annual Review of Anthropology* 17:221–37.
Cicourel, Aaron V. 1987. "The Interpretation of Communicative Contexts: Examples from Medical Encounters." *Social Psychology Quarterly* 50 (2): 217–26.
Clemmer, Richard O. 1986. "Hopis, Western Shoshones, and Southern Utes: Three Different Responses to the Indian Reorganization Act of 1934." *American Indian Culture and Research Journal* 10 (2): 15–40.
Collins, Barry, and Harold Guetzkow. 1964. *A Social Psychology of Group Processes for Decision-Making.* New York: Wiley.
Edelsky, Carol. 1981. "Introduction." *Journal of the Linguistic Association of the Southwest* 4:5–8.
Erickson, Frederick, and William Rittenberg. 1987. "Topic Control and Person Control: A Thorny Problem for Foreign Physicians in Interaction with American Patients." *Discourse Processes* 10 (4): 401–15.
Fisher, Sue, and Alexandra Dundas Todd. 1983. *The Social Organization of Doctor-Patient Communication.* Washington DC: Center for Applied Linguistics.
Frankel, Richard M. 1984. "Special Issue: Physicians and Patients in Social Interaction: Medical Encounters as a Discourse Process." *Discourse Processes* 7 (2).
Garfinkel, Harold, and Harvey Sacks. 1970. On Formal Structures and Practical Action. In *Theoretical Sociology*, edited by John C. McKinney, and Edward A. Tiryakian, 338–66. New York: Appleton, Century & Crofts.
Goffman, Erving. 1981. *Forms of Talk.* Philadelphia: University of Pennsylvania Press.
———. 1983. "The Interaction Order." *American Sociological Review* 48 (1): 1–17
Gossen, Gary H. 1974. *Chamula in the World of the Sun.* Cambridge MA: Harvard University Press.
Gumperz, John J. 1982a. *Discourse Strategies.* Cambridge: Cambridge University Press.
———. 1982b. *Language and Social Identity.* Cambridge: Cambridge University Press.
Halkowski, Timothy. 1990. "'Role' as an Interactional Device." *Social Problems* 37 (4): 564–77.
Heller, Monica, and Sarah Freeman. 1987. "Special Issue: Discourse as Organizational Process." *Discourse Processes* 10 (4).
Hymes, Dell H. 1974. *Foundations in Sociolinguistics.* Philadelphia: University of Pennsylvania Press.
Labov, William, and David Fanshel. 1978. *Therapeutic Discourse.* New York: Academic Press.
Lakoff, Robin T. 1978. Review of *Language and Interpretation in Psychoanalysis. Language* 54:377–94.

Leeds-Hurwitz, Wendy. 1987. "The Social History of *The Natural History of an Interview.*" *Research on Language and Social Interaction* 20:1–51.

McQuown, Norman A., ed. 1971. *The Natural History of an Interview.* Chicago: Microfilm Collection of Manuscripts on Cultural Anthropology, University of Chicago, Joseph Regenstein Library, Department of Photoduplication.

———. 1983. *El microanálisis de entrevistas.* Mexico City: Universidad Nacional Autónoma de México.

Merritt, Marilyn. 1975. "On Questions Following Questions in Service Encounters." *Language in Society* 5 (3): 315–57.

Mishler, Elliot. 1984. *The Discourse of Medicine: Dialectics of Medical Interviews.* Norwood NJ: Ablex.

Murray, Stephen O. 1975. "Power and Solidarity in the Oval Office." Paper presented at the annual meeting of the American Sociological Association, San Francisco.

———. 1985. "Toward a Model of Members' Methods for Recognizing Interruptions." *Language in Society* 14 (1): 31–40.

———. 1991a. "Ethnic Differences in Interpretive Conventions and the Reproduction of Inequality in Everyday Life." *Symbolic Interaction* 14 (2): 187–204.

———. 1991b. "The First Quarter Century of the Linguistic Society of America." *Historiographia Linguistica* 18 (1): 1–47.

Pittenger, Robert, Charles Hockett, and John Danehy. 1960. *The First Five Minutes.* Ithaca NY: Martineau.

Rieff, Philip. 1966. *The Triumph of the Therapeutic: Uses of Faith after Freud.* New York: Harper and Row.

Sacks, Harvey. 1975. "Everyone Has to Lie." In *Sociocultural Dimensions of Language Use*, edited by Mary Sanches and Ben G. Blount, 57–80. New York: Academic Press.

Sacks, Harvey, Emanuel Schegloff, and Gail Jefferson. 1974. "A Simplest Systematics for the Organization of Turn-Taking." *Language* 50 (4), part 1: 696–735

Samarin, William J. 1965. "The Language of Silence." *Practical Anthropology* 12 (2): 115–19.

Schegloff, Emanuel A. 1987. "Analyzing Single Episodes of Interaction." *Social Psychology Quarterly* 50 (2): 101–14.

Schegloff, Emanuel A., and Harvey Sacks. 1973. "Opening Up Closings." *Semiotica* 8 (4): 289–327.

Sherzer, Joel. 1983. *Kuna Ways of Speaking.* Austin: University of Texas Press.

Singh, Rajdendra, Jayant Lele, and Gita Martohardjono. 1988. "Communication in a Multilingual Society: Some Missed Opportunities." *Language in Society* 17 (1): 43–59.

Strauss, Anselm L. 1978. *Negotiations: Varieties, Contexts, Processes, and Social Order.* San Francisco: Jossey-Bass.

Strodtbeck, Fred, Rita James, and Charles Hawkins. 1957. "Social Status in Jury Deliberations." *American Sociological Review* 22:713–19.
Tannen, Deborah. 1981. "New York Jewish Conversational Style." *International Journal of the Sociology of Language* 30:133–49.
———. 1984. *Conversational Style*. New York: Ablex.
———. 1985. "Silence: Anything But." In *Perspectives on Silence*, edited by Deborah Tannen and Muriel Saville-Troike, 93–111. Norwood NJ: Ablex.
———. 1989. "Silence as Conflict Management." In *Conflict Talk*, edited by Allen D. Grimshaw, 260–79. Cambridge: Cambridge University Press.
Tannen, Deborah, and Cynthia Wallat. 1986. "Medical Professionals and Parents: A Linguistic Analysis of Communication across Contexts." *Language in Society* 15 (3): 295–312.
Turner, Roy. 1972. "Some Formal Properties of Therapy Talk." In *Studies in Social Interaction*, edited by David Sudnow, 367–96. New York: Free Press.
Weber, Max. (1922) 1978. *Economy and Society*. Berkeley: University of California Press.
West, Candace. 1984. *Routine Complications*. Bloomington: Indiana University Press.
Wieder, D. Lawrence. 1992. "Notes on Goffman, Ethnomethodology, and Conversational Analysis Connection." Paper presented at the International Communication Association, Miami.

12 Introduction to *Male Sexual Subjectivities*

Stephen O. Murray

For a more than a third of a century, I have been writing about gay identity and community, and about various roles around the world and across millennia that have involved same-sex sex. One of my chief frustrations with the historical and ethnographic literatures is the paucity of detailed data on same-sex desires and what the desires (and behaviors) mean for individuals. I would very much have loved to compare systematic data about the subjectivities of those engaged in same-sex sex across space and time, but these data are nearly nonexistent, so my ethnology and comparative history of homosexual relations (culminating in *Homosexualities* [Murray 2000a]) had to rely heavily on what those not engaging in same-sex sex wrote about the doings of others, not on the carefully contextualized and fine-grained data about individual meanings and desires that I wish were available for comparison.

As I was concluding that long-running project of sorting out types of same-sex sexual relationships, I was also trying to encourage honest accounts of male-male sexual desire. In addition to the lengthy recollections of sexual encounters I elicited for "Self Size and Observable Sex" (Murray 1999b) and the young Kenyan man's sexual life history in *Boy-Wives and Female Husbands* (Murray 1998), I arranged the publication of a gay Pakistani Canadian's sexually graphic memoir, *Sex, Longing and Not Belonging* (Khan 1997, for which I wrote an afterword, Murray 1997). *Flipping*, a flamboyant roman à clef from a gay Filipino American (Ramos 1998, for which I wrote a cover blurb), and *My Black Book* (Adams 2004, for which I wrote a preface that was not used). I have also written about Latino (1995a,

1995b, 1996c), African American (1996d), and Asian-Pacific Islander homoerotic subjectivities (1996a, 1999a, 2000b), based on published fictional and autobiographical materials, and even ventured a bit about my own sexual socialization (1996b) in writing skeptically about Mesoamerican men's self-reports of homosexual behavior. Bill Simon was central in inspiring me to try to get at individual meanings of recurrent desires and patterns of sexual conduct in the complexity of the postmodernist present. "As never before, more than finding the origins of sexuality in the history of their culture, we must seek these origins in the varied histories of individuals," he convincingly wrote (Simon 1996, 117). But how, Bill? But how?

In this introduction, I will get into what is not (re)cognized about sexual behavior and sexual desire and thereby cannot reliably be reported to interviewers. I nevertheless wish there were more sexual life history documents available. In their absence, I have looked elsewhere for what is available. "Poems, plays, and fiction speak from the inside," as literary historian Bruce Smith (1991, 25) wrote. Literature written for native audiences provides a "noetic expression of a social and cultural milieu . . . [that] provide[s] readers with a codification of the world that is cognitively and aesthetically credible" apart from its aesthetic accomplishments, according to anthropologist Herbert Phillips (1987, 3–4). Although literary works "are refractions and distillations, rather than reflections or replicas," they provide an important "source of indigenous meanings, assumptions, and purposes," he added (27, 61). Or, as Prince Genji explained in the twenty-fifth book of *Genji Monogatari*,

> The fact is that works of fiction set down things that have happened in this world ever since the days of the gods. Writings like the *Chronicles of Japan* really give only one side of the picture, whereas these romances must be full of just the right sort of details. The authors certainly do not write about specific people, recording all the actual circumstances of their lives. Rather it is a matter of their being so moved by things, both good and bad, which they have heard and seen happening to men and women that they cannot keep it all to themselves but wants to commit it to writing and make it known to other people—even to those of later generations. This, I feel sure, is the origin of fiction. . . . In every case the things they write about will belong to this actual world of ours. (Morris 1964, 316)[1]

And not just things but attitudes, values, and desires: "The mode of discourse that gives us most intimate access to scripts of sexual desire is not moral, legal, or medical, but literary.... Moral, legal, and medical discourse are concerned with sexual acts; only poetic discourse can address homosexual desire" (Smith 1991, 16–17) is only a slight overstatement. Except in personal narratives, desire must be inferred from behavior, even though it takes little reflection to know there is a lot of sexual desire that does not produce manifest behavior and a lot of sexual behavior that has little to do with what one or more of the partners desire.

I am not assuming that the representations in the fictions I discuss are autobiographical, only that they are mimetic, that is, that they detail culturally and psychologically plausible (imaginable) relations and relationships. First-person narratives in first novels are widely presumed to be autobiographical, but for my purposes it is not particularly important whether these books provide *self*-representations or of representations of similarly situated males. Desire, even in the narrow sense of desire for corporeal contact (sexual congress), is more about what someone thinks than about her/his experience (sexual behavior).

Notes

1. I have altered the masculine singular pronouns to gender-unmarked plurals in this passage written by a woman in the eleventh century, a time in which women writers predominated (28). Morris's (1964) book from which this quotation is taken is itself a superb exemplar of using works of fiction to reconstruct aspects of a particular past social structure. Another is Friedrich (1966). For comparative history, Brown and Gilman (1960) was my first model of systematically examining data from literary texts. The pattern they found was increasing egalitarianism—specifically, less status-marking in forms of address.

References

Adams, Nicholas C. 2004. *My Black Book*. Lincoln: iUniverse.
Brown, Roger, and Albert Gilman. 1960. "The Pronouns of Power and Solidarity." In *Style in Language*, edited by Thomas Sebeok, 253–76. Cambridge: MIT Press.
Friedrich, Paul. 1966. "The Linguistic Reflex of Social Change from Tsarist to Soviet Russian Kinship." *Sociological Inquiry* 36 (2): 31–57.
Khan, Badruddin. 1997. *Sex, Longing, and Belonging: A Gay Muslim Life*. Bangkok: Bua Luang.

Morris, Ivan. 1964. *The World of the Shining Prince: Court Life in Ancient Japan.* New York: Knopf.

Murray, Stephen O. 1995a. "Ethnicity, Homosexuality, and Closetry in Recent Gay Mexican-American Fiction in English." In *Latin American Male Homosexualities,* 158–69. Albuquerque: University of New Mexico Press.

———. 1995b. "Machismo, Male Homosexuality, and Latino Culture." In *Latin American Male Homosexualities,* 49–69. Albuquerque: University of New Mexico Press.

———. 1996a. "Gay Asian/Pacific-Americans." In *American Gay,* 261–68. Chicago: University of Chicago Press.

———. 1996b. "Male Homosexuality in Guatemala: Possible Insights and Certain Confusions from Sleeping with the Natives." In *Out in the Field: Reflections of Lesbian and Gay Anthropologists,* edited by Ellen Lewin and William L. Leap, 236–60. Urbana: University of Illinois Press.

———. 1996c. "Mexican American Homosexuality." In *American Gay,* 258–60. Chicago: University of Chicago Press.

———. 1996d. "Some Gay African-American Self-Representations from the 1980s and 1990s." In *American Gay,* 246–57. Chicago: University of Chicago Press.

———. 1997. Afterword. In *Sex, Longing, and Belonging: A Gay Muslim Life,* by Badruddin Khan, 220–38. Bangkok: Bua Luang.

———. 1998. "'A Feeling within Me': Kamau, a Twenty-Five-Year-Old Kikuyu." In *Boy-Wives and Female Husbands: Studies in African Homosexualities,* edited by Stephen O. Murray and Will Roscoe, 41–65. New York: St. Martin's.

———. 1999a. "Increasingly Gay Self-Representations of Male-Male Sexual Experiences in Thailand." In *Lady Boys, Tom Boys, Rent Boys: Male and Female Homosexualities in Contemporary Thailand,* edited by Peter Jackson and Gerard Sullivan, 81–96. Binghamton NY: Harrington Park Press.

———. 1999b. "Self Size and Observable Sex." In *Public Sex/Gay Space,* edited by William L. Leap, 157–86. New York: Columbia University Press.

———. 2000a. *Homosexualities.* Chicago: University of Chicago Press.

———. 2000b. "Transformed Shamans in Borneo, the Philippines, and Mainland Southeast Asia." In *Homosexualities,* 328–35. Chicago: University of Chicago Press.

Phillips, Herbert. 1987. *Modern Thai Literature: With an Ethnographic Interpretation.* Honolulu: University of Hawai'i Press.

Ramos, Ricardo. 1998. *Flipping.* Bangkok: Bua Luang.

Simon, William. 1996. *Sexual Postmodernity.* London: Routledge.

Smith, Bruce. 1991. *Desire in Shakespeare's England: A Cultural Poetics.* Chicago: University of Chicago Press.

What Had Been

Stephen O. Murray

What had been dauntingly abstract /
Became vividly teal. /
Do we really need /
Anything more to celebrate?

Source Acknowledgments

Chapter 9 originally appeared as *John Gumperz in Context: 1977 and 1992 Interviews*, by Stephen O. Murray, published as a Kindle book, and is reprinted by permission of Keelung Hong.

Chapter 10 originally appeared in Stephen O. Murray, *American Anthropology and Company*, University of Nebraska Press, and is reprinted by permission of Keelung Hong.

Chapter 13 originally appeared in Stephen O. Murray, *Collected Stories*, published as a Kindle book, and is reprinted by permission of Keelung Hong.

Unpublished work by Stephen O. Murray appearing in chapters 1, 11, and 12 has been included here by permission of Keelung Hong.

Appendix

STEPHEN O. MURRAY'S
COMPLETE LIST OF PUBLICATIONS

Compiled by Wendy Leeds-Hurwitz

Books and Book Chapters

"The Invisibility of Scientific Scorn." In *The Don Juan Papers: Further Castaneda Controversies*, edited by Richard de Mille, 198–202. Santa Barbara: Ross-Erikson, 1980. Reprint, Belmont CA: Wadsworth, 1990. Reprint, Lincoln: iUniverse.com, 2001.

"Die Ethnoromantische versuchung." *Der Wissenschaftler und das Irrationale. Band 1: Beiträge aus Ethnologie und Anthropologie*, edited by Hans-Peter Duerr, 377–85. Frankfurt: Syndikat, 1981.

Group Formation in Social Science. Edmonton AB: Linguistic Research, 1983.
 Revised in *Theory Groups and the Study of Language in North America: A Social History*. Amsterdam: John Benjamins, 1994.
 Revised again in *American Sociolinguistics: Theorists and Theory Groups*. Amsterdam: John Benjamins, 1998.

Social Theory, Homosexual Realities. New York: Gay Academic Union, 1984.
 Revised in *American Gay*, 13–98. Chicago: University of Chicago Press, 1996.

"Edward Sapir in the 'Chicago School of Sociology.'" In *New Perspectives on Language, Culture and Personality: Proceedings of the Sapir Centenary Conference (Ottawa, 1–3 October 1984)*, edited by William Cowan, Michael Foster, and E. F. K. Koerner, 241–92. Amsterdam: John Benjamins, 1986.

Ed. *Male Homosexuality in Central and South America*. New York: Gay Academic Union, 1987.

"Dangers of Lexical Inference II: Some Aymara Terms." 165–67.
 Revised in *Latin American Male Homosexualities*, 282–84. Albuquerque: University of New Mexico Press, 1995.

"The Family as an Obstacle to the Growth of a Gay Subculture in Mesoamerica." 118–29.
 Revised as "Family, Social Insecurity, and the Underdevelopment of Gay Institutions in Latin America." In *Latin American Male Homosexualities*, 33–48. Albuquerque: University of New Mexico Press, 1995.

Revised in *Contemporary Cultures and Societies of Latin America: A Reader in the Social Anthropology of Middle and South America*, 3rd ed., edited by Dwight Heath, 284–93. Prospect Heights IL: Waveland, 2002.

"Introduction." 1–3.

"Postscript [Latino Conceptions of Male Homosexuality]." 192–99.

"Sentimental Effusions of Genital Contact in Upper Amazonia." 139–51.

    Reprinted in *Ethnographic Studies of Homosexuality*, vol. 2, edited by Wayne R. Dynes and Stephen Donaldson, 339–51. New York: Garland, 1992.

    Revised as "'Sentimental Effusions' of Genital Contact in Upper Amazonia." In *Latin American Male Homosexualities*, 264–73. Albuquerque: University of New Mexico Press, 1995.

"Third (and Fourth?) Sex Araucanian Shamans?" 159–64.

    Revised as part of the chapter "South American West Coast Indigenous Homosexualities." In *Latin American Male Homosexualities*, 279–92. Albuquerque: University of New Mexico Press, 1995.

With Manuel Arboleda G. "Stigma Transformation and Relexification: 'Gay' in Latin America." 130–38.

    Reprinted in *Coming Out: International Lesbian and Gay Writing*, edited by Stephan Likosky, 412–18. New York: Pantheon, 1992.

    Reprinted as "Stigma Transformation and Relexification: 'Gay' in Latin America." In *Ethnographic Studies of Homosexuality*, vol. 2, edited by Wayne R. Dynes and Stephen Donaldson, 330–38. New York: Garland, 1992.

    Revised in *Latin American Male Homosexualities*, 138–44. Albuquerque: University of New Mexico Press, 1995.

With Wayne R. Dynes. "Hispanic Homosexuals: A Spanish Lexicon." 170–82.

    Revised in *Latin American Male Homosexualities*, 180–92. Albuquerque: University of New Mexico Press, 1995.

"Haitian (In?)tolerance of Homosexuality." In *Homosexuality: Which Homosexuality? International Conference on Gay and Lesbian Studies*, edited by Dennis Altman, Carole Vance, Martha Vicinus, Jeffrey Weeks, et al., 101–8. Amsterdam: Free University Press, 1989.

    Reprinted as "A Note on Haitian Homosexuality." In *Male Homosexuality in Central and South America*, 92–100. New York: Gay Academic Union, 1987.

    Revised as part of "Haitian (In?)tolerance of Homosexuality and 'Scientific' Fantasies about 'Alien Corruption' of Black 'Innocents.'" In *Pieces for a History of Gay Studies*, 33–42. San Francisco: El Instituto Obregón, 2012.

In *The Encyclopedia of Homosexuality*, vols. 1–2. Edited by Wayne R. Dynes. New York: Garland, 1990.

"Ackerley, Joseph Randolph (1896–1967)." 9.

"Africa, Sub-Saharan." 22–24.

"Amazonia." 45–46.
"Andean Cultures." 52–54.
"Benedict, Ruth F." 126–27.
"Community." 258–60.
    Revised as part of "Ethnic and Temporal Differences in Coming Out and in Moving to San Francisco." In *American Gay*, 182–216. Chicago: University of Chicago Press, 1996.
"Couples." 272–77.
    Revised in *American Gay*, 167–81. Chicago: University of Chicago Press, 1996.
"Haiti." 516.
"Latin America." 678–81.
"Mamluks." 760–61.
"Nicolson, Harold." 901.
"Pacific Cultures." 937–40.
"Role." 1112–15.
    Revised as "'The Homosexual Role' and Lesbigay Roles." In *American Gay*, 143–66. Chicago: University of Chicago Press, 1996.
"Sociology." 1219–27.
With Clark L. Taylor. "México." 803–7.
In *International Dictionary of Anthropologists*. Edited by Christopher Winters. New York: Garland, 1991.
    "Dixon, Roland B. (Roland Burrage)." 149–50.
    "Ogburn, William F. (William Fielding)." 517–18.
    "Parsons, Elsie Clews." 529.
    "Shternberg, Leo [Lev]." 639–40.
    "Swanton, John Reed." 680.
    "Thomas, W. I. (William Isaac)." 691–93.
    Reprinted in *American Anthropology and Company: Historical Explorations*, 161–71. Lincoln: University of Nebraska Press, 2013.
"Components of Gay Community in San Francisco." In *Gay Culture in America: Essays from the Field*, edited by Gilbert Herdt, 107–46. Boston: Beacon, 1992.
    Revised as part of "Ethnic and Temporal Differences in Coming Out and in Moving to San Francisco." In *American Gay*, 182–216. Chicago: University of Chicago Press, 1996.
Oceanic Homosexualities. New York: Garland, 1992.
    "Age-Stratified Homosexuality." 3–23.
        Revised in *Pacific Homosexualities*, 23–58. Lincoln: iUniverse, 2002.
    "Austronesian Gender-Defined Homosexuality." 151–70.
        Revised as "Gender-Defined Homosexuality." In *Pacific Homosexualities*, 105–56. Lincoln: iUniverse, 2002.

"Czaplicka's Interpretation of Kamchadal Slavery and of Siberian Transformed Shamans as a Third Gender." 329–39.

"Early Reports of Cebuano, Tinguian, and Sambal 'Berdache.'" 185–92.

"Early Reports of Malagasy 'Berdaches.'" 249–56.

"Egalitarian Relationships: Introduction." 353–62.

"Female Homosexuality in Pacific Societies: Introduction." 397–405.

"Homosexual Categorization in Cross-Cultural Perspective." xiii–xl.

> Revised as "Homosexual Categorization in Cross-Cultural Perspective." In *Latin American Male Homosexualities*, 3–32. Albuquerque: University of New Mexico Press, 1995.
>
> Revised as "Introduction: Homosexual Categorization in Cross-Cultural Perspective." In *Pacific Homosexualities*, 1–22. Lincoln: iUniverse, 2002.

"The Hwarang of Ancient Korea." 103–9.

> Revised in *Homosexualities*, 65–69. Chicago: University of Chicago Press, 2000.

"Late 19th-Century Reports of Manangs in Northern Borneo." 285–92.

"Male Homosexuality in Japan before the Meiji Restoration." 111–50.

> Revised in *Pacific Homosexualities*, 59–104. Lincoln: iUniverse, 2002.

"Peter Jackson's Account of Emergent Gay Homosexuality in Contemporary Thailand." 387–96.

"Profession-Defined Homosexuality." 257–72.

> Revised as "Profession-Defined Homosexuality I: Transformed Shamans" and "Profession-Defined Homosexuality II: Entertainers." In *Pacific Homosexualities*, 157–252. Lincoln: iUniverse, 2002.
>
> Revised as "Transformed Shamans in Borneo, the Philippines, and Mainland Southeast Asia." In *Homosexualities*, 328–35. Chicago: University of Chicago Press, 2000.

"The Traditional Kodiak and Aleutian Islanders' Non-Sacralized, Trans-Generational, Trans-Role." 341–52.

"Vladimir Bogoraz's Account of Chukchi Transformed Shamans." 293–312.

"Vladimir Iokalson's Reports of Northeastern Siberian Transformed Shamans." 313–27.

"The 'Underdevelopment' of Modern/Gay Homosexuality in Mesoamerica." In *Modern Homosexualities: Fragments of Lesbian and Gay Experience*, edited by Ken Plummer, 29–38. London: Routledge, 1992.

In *The Encyclopedia of Language and Linguistics*. Edited by Ron E. Asher. London: Pergamon, 1994.

"Bloomfield, Leonard (1887–1949)." Vol. 1. 374–75.

"Hoijer, Harry (1904–76)." Vol. 3. 1588.

"Li, Fang-Kuei (1902–87)." Vol. 4. 2206.

"Swadesh, Morris (1909–67)." Vol. 8. 4421.

With Keelung Hong. *Taiwanese Culture, Taiwanese Society: A Critical Review of Social Science Research Done on Taiwan.* Lanham MD: University Press of America, 1994.
"Studies of Land Reform on Taiwan." 69–76.

Latin American Male Homosexualities. Albuquerque: University of New Mexico Press, 1995.
"Changes and Variations in Male Homosexuality in Latino and Indigenous Societies." xi–xvi.
"Ethnicity, Homosexuality, and Closetry in Recent Gay Mexican-American Fiction in English." 158–69.
"Homosexuality and AIDS in Latinos in the United States." 170–79.
"Machismo, Male Homosexuality, and Latino Culture." 49–69.
"Modern Male Homosexuality in México and Peru." 145–49.
Revised as "'Modern' Homosexual Behavior in Mexico and Peru." In *Homosexualities*, 408–12. Chicago: University of Chicago Press, 2000.

"Stigma Transformation and Relexification in the International Diffusion of *Gay*." In *Beyond the Lavender Lexicon: Authenticity, Imagination and Appropriation in Lesbian and Gay Languages*, edited by William L. Leap, 297–315. New York: Gordon and Breach, 1995.
Revised as "New Bottles: Stigma Transformation and Relexification of Gendered Homosexuality in the International Diffusion of *Gay* and *Lesbian*." In *Homosexualities*, 393–402. Chicago: University of Chicago Press, 2000.

American Gay. Chicago: University of Chicago Press, 1996.

Angkor Life: Pre-Cambodian Life 800 Years Ago in the Society That Created the Stupendous Monuments of Angkor Wat and Angkor Thom. Bangkok: Bua Luang, 1996.

"Male Homosexuality in Guatemala: Possible Insights and Certain Confusions from Sleeping with the Natives." In *Out in the Field: Reflections of Lesbian and Gay Anthropologists*, edited by Ellen Lewin and William L. Leap, 236–60. Urbana: University of Illinois Press, 1996.

"Afterword." In *Sex, Longing, and Belonging: A Gay Muslim Life* by Badruddin Khan, 220–38. Bangkok: Bua Luang, 1997.

"Homosexuality." In *Dictionary of Anthropology*, edited by Thomas Barfield, 241–43. London: Blackwell, 1997.

With Badruddin Khan. "Pakistan." In *Sociolegal Control of Homosexuality: A Multi-Nation Comparison*, edited by Donald J. West and Richard Green, 119–26. New York: Plenum, 1997.

With Will Roscoe, eds. *Islamic Homosexualities: Culture, History, and Literature.* New York: New York University Press, 1997.
"Corporealizing Medieval Persian and Turkish Tropes." 132–41.
"Gender-Defined Homosexual Roles in Sub-Saharan African Islamic Cultures." 222–29.

"Homosexuality Among Slave Elites in Ottoman Turkey." 174–86.
"Male Actresses in Islamic Parts of Indonesia and the Southern Philippines." 256–61.
"Male Homosexuality in Ottoman Albania." 187–96.
"Male Homosexuality, Inheritance Rules, and the Status of Women in Medieval Egypt: The Case of the Mamlûks." 161–73.
> Revised as "The Mamlûks of Medieval Egypt." In *Homosexualities*, 43–50. Chicago: University of Chicago Press, 2000.

"The Sohari *Khanith*." 244–55.
> Revised in *Homosexualities*, 275–79. Chicago: University of Chicago Press, 2000.

"Some Nineteenth-Century Reports of Islamic Homosexualities." 204–21.
"The Will Not to Know: Islamic Accommodations of Male Homosexuality." 14–54.
"Woman-Woman Love in Islamic Societies." 97–104.
With Eric G. Allyn. "Two Islamic AIDS Education Organizations." 297–301.
With Will Roscoe. "Conclusion." 302–19.
With Will Roscoe. "Introduction." 3–13.

With Will Roscoe, eds. *Boy-Wives and Female Husbands: Studies in African Homosexualities*. New York: St. Martin's, 1998.
"Appendix 2: Organizations of Homosexuality and Other Social Structures in Sub-Saharan Africa." 283–97.
"'A Feeling within Me': Kamau, a Twenty-Five-Year-Old Kikuyu." 41–65.
"Sexual Politics in Contemporary Southern Africa." 243–54.
With Joseph M. Carrier. "Woman-Woman Marriage in Africa." 255–66.
With Will Roscoe. "Africa and African Homosexualities: An Introduction." 1–18.
With Will Roscoe. "Appendix 1: African Groups with Same-Sex Patterns." 279–82.
With Will Roscoe. "Diversity and Identity: The Challenge of African Homosexualities." 267–78.
With Will Roscoe. "Overview [Central Africa]." 141–48.
With Will Roscoe. "Overview [Horn of Africa, Sudan, and East Africa]." 21–40.
With Will Roscoe. "Overview [Southern Africa]." 173–85.
With Will Roscoe. "Overview [West Africa]." 91–109.
With Will Roscoe. "Preface: 'All Very Confusing.'" xi–xxii.
Revised ed., Albany: State University of New York Press, 2021.

"The Development of Lesbigay Studies in the United States of America." In *Guide to Lesbian, Gay and Queer Studies*, edited by Raymond Donovan and Leong K. Chan, 47–60. Sydney: University of Sydney Centre for Lesbian and Gay Research, 1999.
> Revised as "An Overview of Lesbigay Studies in North America." In *Pieces for a History of Gay Studies*, 15–25. San Francisco: El Instituto Obregón, 2012.

"Dixon, Roland Burrage." In *American National Biography*, vol. 6, edited by John A. Garrety and Mark C. Carnes, 650–51. New York: Oxford University Press, 1999.

"How 'The Logical Structure of Linguistic Theory' Did Not Appear during the 1950s or 60s." In *The Emergence of the Modern Language Sciences: Studies on the Transition from Historical-Comparative to Structural Linguistics in Honour of E. F. Konrad Koerner*, vol. 1, edited by Sheila Embleton, John E. Joseph, and Hans-Josef Niederhe, 261–66. Amsterdam: John Benjamins, 1999.

"Increasingly Gay Self-Representations of Male-Male Sexual Experiences in Thailand." In *Lady Boys, Tom Boys, Rent Boys: Male and Female Homosexualities in Contemporary Thailand*, edited by Peter Jackson and Gerard Sullivan, 81–96. Binghamton NY: Harrington Park, 1999.

    Co-published simultaneously in *Journal of Gay and Lesbian Social Services* 9, no. 2–3 (1999): 81–96.

"The Non-Eclipse of Americanist Anthropology During the 1930s and 1940s." In *Theorizing the Americanist Tradition*, edited by Lisa Phillips Valentine and Regna Darnell, 52–74. Toronto: University of Toronto Press, 1999.

    Revised in *American Anthropology and Company: Historical Explorations*, 88–101. Lincoln: University of Nebraska Press, 2013.

"Self Size and Observable Sex." In *Public Sex/Gay Space*, edited by William L. Leap, 157–86. New York: Columbia University Press, 1999.

Homosexualities. Chicago: University of Chicago Press, 2000.

In *History of the Language Sciences/Geschichte der Sprachwissenschaften/Histoire des sciences du langage*, vol. 2, edited by Sylvain Auroux, E. F. K. Koerner, Hans-Josef Niederehe, and Kees Versteegh. Berlin: Walter de Gruyter, 2001.

    "Attempts at the Professionalization of American Linguistics: The Role of the Linguistic Society of America." 1932–35.

    "The Ethnolinguistic Tradition in 19th-Century America: From the Earliest Beginnings to Boas." 1909–23.

In *Who's Who in Gay and Lesbian History: From Antiquity to World War II.* Edited by Robert Aldrich and Garry Wotherspoon. London: Routledge, 2001.

    "Hafiz." 195–96.

    "Joey Stefano." 387–88.

    "Laud Humphreys." 200–201.

    "Margaret Mead." 304.

    "Roger Brown." 60–61.

    "Ruth Benedict." 48.

    "Wallace Thurman." 442–43.

With Regna Darnell. "Series Editors' Introduction." In *Invisible Genealogies: A History of Americanist Anthropology* by Regna Darnell, xiii–xv. Lincoln: University of Nebraska Press, 2001.

With Regna Darnell. "Series Editors' Introduction." In *The Shaping of American Ethnography: The Wilkes Exploring Expedition, 1838–1842* by Barry Alan Joyce, ix–xi. Lincoln: University of Nebraska Press, 2001.

"The Comparative Sociology of Homosexualities." In *The Handbook of Lesbian and Gay Studies*, edited by Diane Richardson and Steven Seidman, 83–96. London: Sage, 2002.

"Five Reasons I Don't Take 'Queer Theory' Seriously." In *Sexualities: Critical Concepts in Sociology*, vol. 4, *Sexualities and Their Futures*, edited by Ken Plummer, 245–48. London: Routledge, 2002.

> Revised as part of "Theoretical Nihilism Calling Itself a 'Theory.'" In *Pieces for a History of Gay Studies*, 97–101. San Francisco: El Instituto Obregón, 2012.

In *Celebrating a Century of the American Anthropological Association*. Edited by Regna Darnell and Frederick W. Gleach. Lincoln: University of Nebraska Press, 2002.
> "Edward H. Spicer." 229–32.
> "Francis L. K. Hsu." 245–48.
> "George M. Foster." 213–16.
> "Harry Hoijer." 165–68.
> "John R. Swanton." 61–64.
> "Ralph L. Beals." 133–36.
> "Robert Redfield." 105–8.

In *Before Stonewall: Activists for Gay and Lesbian Rights in Historical Context*. Edited by Vern L. Bullough. New York: Haworth, 2002.
> "Donald Webster Cory (1913–1936)." 333–43.
> With Jim Kepner. "Henry Gerber (1895–1972): Grandfather of the American Gay Movement." 24–34.

Pacific Homosexualities. Lincoln: iUniverse, 2002.

With Manuel Fernández-Alemany. *Heterogender Homosexuality in Honduras*. Lincoln: iUniverse, 2002.

With Regna Darnell. "Series Editors' Introduction." In *Ruth Landes: A Life in Anthropology* by Sally Cole. Lincoln: University of Nebraska Press, 2003, ix–xi.

In *Encyclopedia of Lesbian, Gay, Bisexual and Transgender History in America*, vols. 1–3. Edited by Marc Stein. New York: Scribner's Sons, 2004.
> "Benedict, Ruth." Vol. 1. 132–33.
> "Language." Vol. 2, 132–38.
> "Sociology." Vol. 3, 134–38.

In *Biographical Dictionary of Social and Cultural Anthropology*. Edited by Vered Amit. London: Routledge, 2004.
> With Frederic W. Gleach. "Edward H. Spicer." 479–80.
> With Frederic W. Gleach. "George M. Foster." 169–71.

With Regna Darnell. "Series Editors' Introduction." In *Irregular Connections: A History of Anthropology and Sexuality* by Andrew P. Lyons and Harriet D. Lyons, xiii–xiv. Lincoln: University of Nebraska Press, 2004.

With Regna Darnell. "Series Editors' Introduction." In *Leslie A. White: Evolution and Revolution in Anthropology* by William J. Peace, xi–xii. Lincoln: University of Nebraska Press, 2004.

With Regna Darnell. "Series Editors' Introduction." In *Melville J. Herskovits and the Racial Politics of Knowledge* by Jerry Gershenhorn, xi–xiii. Lincoln: University of Nebraska Press, 2004.

With Regna Darnell. "Series Editors' Introduction." In *Rolling in Ditches with Shamans: Jaime de Angulo and the Professionalization of American Anthropology* by Wendy Leeds-Hurwitz, ix–xi. Lincoln: University of Nebraska Press, 2004.

With Regna Darnell. "Series Editors' Introduction." In *Ephraim George Squier and the Development of American Anthropology* by Terry A. Barnhart, xv–xvi. Lincoln: University of Nebraska Press, 2005.

With Regna Darnell. "Series Editors' Introduction." In *Ruth Benedict: Beyond Relativity, Beyond Pattern* by Virginia Heyer Young, vii–viii. Lincoln: University of Nebraska Press, 2005.

With Keelung Hong. *Looking through Taiwan: American Anthropologists' Collusion with Ethnic Domination*. Lincoln: University of Nebraska Press, 2005.

With Regna Darnell. "Series Editors' Introduction." vii–ix.

"William Fielding Ogburn's Fostering of Sol Tax's Explorations of Small-Scale Mercantile Capitalism in Highland Guatemala." In *Histories of Anthropology Annual*, vol. 3, edited by Regna Darnell and Frederic W. Gleach, 38–50. Lincoln: University of Nebraska Press, 2007.

With Regna Darnell. "Series Editors' Introduction." In *Anthropology Goes to the Fair: The 1904 Louisiana Purchase Exposition* by Nancy J. Parezo and Don D. Fowler, xi–xiii. Lincoln: University of Nebraska Press, 2007.

In *The Oxford Encyclopedia of Women in World History*, vol. 3, edited by Bonnie G. Smith. Oxford, UK: Oxford University Press, 2008.

"Pederasty." 426–28.

"Sexuality: Homosexuality." 20–25.

With Regna Darnell. "Series Editors' Introduction." In *The 1904 Anthropology Days and Olympic Games: Sport, Race, and American Imperialism*, edited by Susan Brownell, xvii–xviii. Lincoln: University of Nebraska Press, 2008.

With Regna Darnell. "Series Editors' Introduction." to *Lev Shternberg: Anthropologist, Russian Socialist, Jewish Activist* by Sergei Kan, xi–xii. Lincoln: University of Nebraska Press, 2009.

With Regna Darnell. "Series Editors' Introduction." In *The Meskwaki and Anthropologists: Action Anthropology Reconsidered* by Judith M. Daubenmier, xi–xiii. Lincoln: University of Nebraska Press, 2008.

"Interactional Sociolinguistics at Berkeley." In *The Social History of Language and Social Interaction Research: People, Places, Ideas*, edited by Wendy Leeds-Hurwitz, 97–126. Cresskill NJ: Hampton Press, 2010.

"Mexico." In *The Politics of Sexuality in Latin America: A Reader on Lesbian, Gay, Bisexual, and Transgender Rights*, edited by Javier Corrales and Mario Pecheny, 60–65. Pittsburgh: University of Pittsburgh Press, 2010.

"'Scientific Revolutions' and Other Kinds of Regime Change." In *Chomskyan (R)evolutions*, edited by Douglas Kibbee, 75–101. Amsterdam: John Benjamins, 2010.

With Regna Darnell. "Series Editors' Introduction." In *Contributions to Ojibwe Studies: Essays, 1934–1972* by A. Irving Hallowell, edited and with introductions by Jennifer S. H. Brown and Susan Elaine Gray, ix–xi. Lincoln: University of Nebraska Press, 2010.

With Regna Darnell. "Series Editors' Introduction." In *Excavating Nauvoo: The Mormons and the Rise of Historical Archaeology in America* by Benjamin C. Pykles, xix–xxi. Lincoln: University of Nebraska Press, 2010.

"Introduction." In *Watercolors* by Gary Bukovnik, 10. San Francisco: Norfolk Press, 2011.
  Reprinted in English and translated into Chinese for the catalog of Bukovnik's show at the Shanghai HongQiao Contemporary Art Museum, December 18, 2015–January 9, 2016.

21st-Century Representations of Muslim Homosexualities. San Francisco: El Instituto Obregón, 2012.

Collected Stories. San Francisco: El Instituto Obregón, 2012.
  Reissued in 2019 as *Collected Stories and Poems*.

Pieces for a History of Gay Studies. San Francisco: El Instituto Obregón, 2012.

Reading 20th-Century Italian Fiction. San Francisco: El Instituto Obregón, 2012.

Reading Sicily (in English). San Francisco: El Instituto Obregón, 2012.

An Introduction to African Cinema. San Francisco: El Instituto Obregón, 2013.
  Revised and reissued in 2016 and 2017 under the same title.

American Anthropology and Company: Historical Explorations. Lincoln: University of Nebraska Press, 2013.
  With Regna Darnell. "Series Editors' Introduction." xi–xiii.

John Gumperz in Context: 1977 and 1992 Interviews. San Francisco: El Instituto Obregón, 2013.

With Regna Darnell. "Series Editors' Introduction." In *Cultural Negotiations: The Role of Women in the Founding of Americanist Archaeology* by David L. Browman, vii–ix. Lincoln: University of Nebraska Press, 2013.

With Regna Darnell. "Series Editors' Introduction." In *Homo Imperii: A History of Physical Anthropology in Russia* by Marina Mogilner, ix–xi. Lincoln: University of Nebraska, 2013.

With Regna Darnell. "Series Editors' Introduction." In *Racial Science in Hitler's New Europe, 1938–1945*, edited by Anton Weiss-Wendt and Rory Yeomans, ix–x. Lincoln: University of Nebraska Press, 2013.

"Appendix: 1997 and 2002 Interviews of the Author by Stephen Murray." In *Flipping* by Ricardo Ramos, 141–60. Floating Lotus, 2014.

With Regna Darnell. "Series Editors' Introduction." In *American Antiquities: Revisiting the Origins of American Archaeology* by Terry A. Barnhart, xi–xiii. Lincoln: University of Nebraska Press, 2015.

With Regna Darnell. "Series Editors' Introduction." In *Before Boas: The Genesis of Ethnography and Ethnology in the German Enlightenment* by Han F. Vermeulen, xxi–xxiii. Lincoln: University of Nebraska Press, 2015.

With Regna Darnell. "Series Editors' Introduction." In *Cora Du Bois: Anthropologist, Diplomat, Agent*, by Susan C. Seymour, xi–xii. Lincoln: University of Nebraska Press, 2015.

With Regna Darnell. "Series Editors' Introduction." In *An Asian Frontier: American Anthropology and Korea, 1882–1945* by Robert Oppenheim, xi–xii. Lincoln: University of Nebraska Press, 2016.

With Regna Darnell. "Series Editors' Introduction." In *Theodore E. White and the Development of Zooarchaeology in North America* by R. Lee Lyman, xv–xvi. Lincoln: University of Nebraska Press, 2016.

"Karl Popper's Enheartening of Derek Freeman's Attacks on Margaret Mead's *Coming of Age in Samoa*." In *Tracking Anthropology's Engagements*, edited by Regna Darnell and Frederic W. Gleach, 199–212. Lincoln: University of Nebraska Press, 2018.

With Regna Darnell. "Series Editors' Introduction." In *Declared Defective: Native Americans, Eugenics and the Myth of Nam Hollow* by Robert Jarvenpa, xi–xii. Lincoln: University of Nebraska Press, 2018.

With Regna Darnell. "Series Editors' Introduction." In *The Enigma of Max Gluckman: The Ethnographic Life of a 'Luckyman' in Africa*, by Robert J. Gordon, ix–xi. Lincoln: University of Nebraska Press, 2018.

With Regna Darnell. "Series Editors' Introduction." In *Glory, Trouble, and the Renaissance at the Robert S. Peabody Museum of Archaeology*, edited by Malinda Stafford Blustain and Ryan J. Wheeler, xi–xii. Lincoln: University of Nebraska Press, 2018.

With Regna Darnell. "Series Editors' Introduction." In *Race Experts: Sculpture, Anthropology, and the American Public in Malvina Hoffman's "Races of Mankind"* by Linda Kim, xv–xvii. Lincoln: University of Nebraska Press, 2018.

"Sidebar: E. E. Evans-Pritchard (1902–1973)." In *Global Encyclopedia of Lesbian, Gay, Bisexual, and Transgender and Queer (LGBTQ) History*, vol. 1, edited by Howard Chiang and Anjali R Arondekar, 64. New York: Charles Scribner's Sons, 2019.

With Regna Darnell. "Series Editors' Introduction." In *National Races: Transnational Power Struggles in the Sciences and Politics of Human Diversity, 1840–1945*, edited by Richard McMahon, ix–x. Lincoln: University of Nebraska Press, 2019.

With Regna Darnell. "Series Editors' Introduction." In *Franz Boas: The Emergence of the Anthropologist* by Rosemary Lévy Zumwalt, xi–xii. Lincoln: University of Nebraska Press, 2019.

With Regna Darnell and Robert Oppenheim. "Series Editors' Introduction." In *Maria Czaplicka: Gender, Shamanism, Race* by Grażyna Kubica, translated by Ben Koshalka, xi–xiii. Lincoln: University of Nebraska Press, 2020.

"The Genesis of *Boy-Wives and Female Husbands*." In *Boy-Wives and Female Husbands: Studies in African Homosexualities*, 2nd ed., edited by Stephen O. Murray and Will Roscoe, xix–xxiv. New York: St. Martin's, 2021.

"Appendix 2: Organization of Homosexuality and Other Social Structures in Sub-Saharan Africa." 281–95.

"'A Feeling within Me': Kamau, a Twenty-Five-Year-Old Kikuyu." 41–60.

"The Genesis of Boy-Wives and Female Husbands." xix–xxiv.

"Sexual Politics in Contemporary Southern Africa." 239–50.

With Joseph M. Carrier. "Woman-Woman Marriage in Africa." 253–64.

With Will Roscoe. "Africa and African Homosexualities: An Introduction." 1–16.

With Will Roscoe. "Appendix 1: African Groups with Same-Sex Patterns." 277–80.

With Will Roscoe. "Diversity and Identity: The Challenge of African Homosexualities." 265–75.

With Will Roscoe. "Overview [Central Africa]." 137–44.

With Will Roscoe. "Overview [Horn of Africa, Sudan, and East Africa]." 19–39.

With Will Roscoe. "Overview [Southern Africa]." 169–81.

With Will Roscoe. "Overview [West Africa]." 87–105.

With Will Roscoe. "Preface: 'All Very Confusing.'" xxv–xxxvi.

With Wendy Leeds-Hurwitz, Regna Darnell, Nathan Dawthorne, and Robert Oppenheim. "An Interview with Stephen O. Murray on Stephen O. Murray as Historian of Anthropology (and More)." In *Centering the Margins of Anthropology's History*, edited by Regna Darnell and Frederick W. Gleach, 243–68. Lincoln: University of Nebraska Press, 2021.

Articles, Book Reviews, and Other Writing

"Alternative Life Styles Part 2: Lord Krsna in America." *Phalanstery Review* 3, no. 11 (1972): 3–5.

Review of *The Church and the Homosexual* by John J. McNeill. *The Body Politic* 20 (October 1975): 44.

Review of *Comparative Studies in Science and Society*, edited by Sal Restivo and Christopher K. Vanderpool. *Contemporary Sociology* 5, no. 5 (1976): 690–69l.

Review of *Studies in the History of Linguistics: Traditions and Paradigms*, edited by Dell Hymes. *Contemporary Sociology* 5, no. 3 (1976): 371.

Review of *Village of Curers and Assassins: On the Production of Fala Kpelle Cosmological Categories* by Beryl Larry Bellman. *Contemporary Sociology* 5, no. 6 (1976): 749–50.

Review of *Another Kind of Love* by Richard Woods; *The Homosexual Question* by Marc Oraison; and *Am I Running with You, God?* by Malcolm Boyd. *The Body Politic* 37, October (1977): 20.

Review of *The National Interest: The Politics of Northern Development, 1968–75* by Edgar J. Dosman; *As Long as This Land Shall Last* by Rene Fumoleau; and *This Land Is Not for Sale: Canada's Original People and Their Land* by Hugh McCullum and Karmel McCullum. *Contemporary Sociology* 6, no. 2 (1977): 218–19.

"To the Editor: Prescriptive Misuse of Sociology of Science Indicators." *Contemporary Sociology* 6, no. 5 (1977): 524–25.

"No Fun [Letter to the Editor]." *The Advocate* 231 (December 28, 1977), 44.

"Sins of Omission [Letter to the Editor: Response to Morgado]." *The Body Politic* 32 (April 1977): 3.

"Notes from the Front Lines: California." *Sociologists' Gay Caucus Newsletter* 15 (1978): 9.

"Promoting Linguistic Diversity." *The Ecumenist* 16, no. 3 (1978): 38–40.

"Relationships." *Sociologists' Gay Caucus Newsletter* 14 (1978): 6–7.

Review of *Africville: The Life and Death of a Canadian Black Community* by Donald H. Clairmont and Dennis William Magill. *Contemporary Sociology* 7, no. 1 (1978): 34–35.

Review of *Tu, Vous, Usted: A Social-Psychological Study of Address Patterns* by Wallace E. Lambert and G. Richard Tucker. *Papers in Linguistics* 11, no. 1–2 (1978): 261–66.

"The Art of Gay Insulting." *Anthropological Linguistics* 21, no. 5 (1979): 211–23.

"An Aberration of Late Capitalism: Comment on Adam." *Sociologists' Gay Caucus Newsletter* 18: 7–8, 20 (1979): 4.

"The Institutional Elaboration of a Quasi-Ethnic Community." *International Review of Modern Sociology* 9, no. 2 (1979): 165–77.

Reprinted in *Homosexuality in International Perspective*, edited by Joseph Harry and Man Singh Das, 33–44. New Delhi: Vikas, 1980.

Revised as part of "Ethnic and Temporal Differences in Coming Out and in Moving to San Francisco." In *American Gay*, 182–216. Chicago: University of Chicago Press, 1996.

Reprinted in *Social Perspectives on Lesbian and Gay Studies: A Reader*, edited by Peter M. Nardi and Beth E. Schneider, 207–14. London: Routledge, 1998.

"Mistaking Fantasy for Ethnography." *Anthropological Research Group on Homosexuality Newsletter* 1, no. 3 (1979): 3.

Translated as "Ein Homoerotisches Phantásien—Ethnographisch Mißdeutet." In *Authentizität und Betrug in der Ethnologie*, edited by Hans-Peter Duerr, 58–62. Frankfurt: Suhrkamp, 1987.

Reprinted in *Male Homosexuality in Central and South America*, 155–58. New York: Gay Academic Union, 1987.

Reprinted in *Ethnographic Studies of Homosexuality*, vol. 2, edited by Wayne R. Dynes and Stephen Donaldson, 353–56. New York: Garland, 1992.

Reprinted in *Latin American Male Homosexualities*, 274–78. Albuquerque: University of New Mexico Press, 1995.

"Review: The Scientific Reception of Castaneda, *The Second Ring of Power* by Carlos Castaneda; *Castaneda's Journey: The Power and the Allegory* by Richard de Mille; *Seeing Casteneda: Reactions to the 'Don Juan' Writings by Carlos Castaneda* by Daniel C. Noel; *Reading Castaneda: A Prologue to the Social Sciences* by David Silverman." *Contemporary Sociology* 8, no. 2 (1979): 189–92.

"Screening Information: The Functions and Fetishism of Types." *Sociologists' Gay Caucus Newsletter* 17 (1979): 8–10.

Reprinted as "Appendix: Screening Information: The Functions and Fetishism of 'My Type.'" In *American Gay*, 178–81. Chicago: University of Chicago Press, 1996.

"The Uniqueness of San Francisco: Comment on Weinberg." *Sociologists' Gay Caucus Newsletter* 17 (1979): 5–7.

"Gatekeepers and the 'Chomskian Revolution.'" *Journal of the History of the Behavioral Sciences* 16 (1980): 73–88.

"Lexical and Institutional Elaboration: The 'Species Homosexual' in Guatemala." *Anthropological Linguistics* 22, no. 4 (1980): 177–85.

Reprinted in *Homosexuality and Homosexuals in the Arts*, edited by Wayne R. Dynes and Stephen Donaldson, 361–69. New York: Garland, 1992.

"Resistance to Sociology at Berkeley." *Journal of the History of Sociology* 2, no. 2 (1980): 61–84.

Revised in *American Anthropology and Company: Historical Explorations*, 246–63. Lincoln: University of Nebraska Press, 2013.

Review of *The Unmentionable Vice: Homosexuality in the Later Medieval Period* by Michael Goodich. *Sociologists' Gay Caucus Newsletter* 23 (1980): 3.

Reprinted as "Saints and Profits: Review of *The Unmentionable Vice: Homosexuality in the Later Medieval Period* by Michael Goodich." *Boston Gay Review* 9 (1981): 19.

With Lucille H. Covelli. "Accomplishing Topic Change." *Anthropological Linguistics* 22, no. 9 (1980): 382–89.

With Joseph H. Rankin. "Use Diffusion: An Extension and Critique." *Technological Forecasting and Social Change* 16, no. 4 (1980): 331–41.

"The Canadian 'Winter' of Edward Sapir." *Historiographia Linguistica* 8, no. 1 (1981): 63–68.

"What Is a Conversation? When Is an Interruption?" *Working Papers of the Language Behavior Research Laboratory*, no. 52 (1981).

"A Self-Defeating Quest for an Ideal Friend: J. R. Ackerley Revisited." *Advocate* 332 (December 10, 1981): 34–35, 41.

Review of *Language and Control* by Roger Fowler, Gunter Kress and Tony Trew; *Language as Ideology* by Gunther Kress and Robert Hodge. *American Journal of Sociology* 87, no. 3 (1981): 743–45.

Review of *Linguistic Theory in America: The First Quarter Century of Transformational Generative Grammar* by Frederick J. Newmeyer. *Historiographia Linguistica* 8, no. 1 (1981): 107–12.

Review of *Myth and Meaning* by Claude Lévi-Strauss; *The Origin of Table Manners* by Claude Lévi-Strauss; *Structural Anthropology*, vol. 2 by Claude Lévi-Strauss; and *Claude Lévi-Strauss: Social Psychotherapy and the Collective Unconscious* by Thomas Shalvey. *Contemporary Sociology* 10, no. 2 (1981): 222–23.

"Sapir's Gestalt." *Anthropological Linguistics* 23, no. 1 (1981): 8–12.

With Joseph H. Rankin, and Dennis W. Magill. "Informelle Rationalität und Wissenschaftlichen Gemeinschaften." *DerWissenschaftler und das Irrationale* 2 (1981): 219–25.

With Joseph H. Rankin, and Dennis W. Magill. "Strong Ties and Job Information." *Sociology of Work and Occupations* 8, no. 1 (1981): 119–36.

"The Dissolution of Classical Ethnoscience." *Journal of the History of the Behavioral Sciences* 18, no. 2 (1982): 163–75.

"A Latter-Day Yankee Prophet: Review of *Benjamin Lee Whorf: Lost Generation Theories of Mind, Language, and Religion* by Peter C. Rollins." *Historiographia Linguistica* 9, no. 1/2 (1982): 156–61.

"Panic in the Streets." *Sociologists' Gay Caucus Newsletter* 33 (1982): 5–6.

Review of *Adonis García: A Picaresque Novel* by Luis Zapata. *Advocate* 346 (July 8, 1982): 53.

Review of *Crime and Society in Early Modern Seville* by Mary Elizabeth Perry; and *Bluebeard* by Leonard Wolf. *Gay Books Bulletin* 8 (1982): 8–9.

Review of *Gayspeak: Gay Male/Lesbian Communication* by James W. Chesebro. *Advocate* 334 (January 7, 1982): 31.

Review of *Language as a Social Resource: Essays by Allen D. Grimshaw*, edited by Anwar S. Dil. *American Anthropologist* 84, no. 3 (1982): 743–45.

Review of *Profane Culture* by Paul Willis; *Sexual Meanings: The Cultural Construction of Gender and Sexuality* by Sherry B. Ortner and Harriet Whitehead; *Gayspeak:*

Gay Male/Lesbian Communication by James W. Chesebro; *The Celluloid Closet: Homosexuality in the Movies* by Vito Russo. *Sociologists' Gay Caucus Newsletter* 31 (1982): 5–7.

"The Reviewer Responds [Reply to Newmeyer]." *Historiographia Linguistica* 9, no. 1/2 (1982): 187.

"Role Distance 'South of the Slot.'" *Journal of the History of Sociology* 4, no. 2 (1982): 90–95.

With Keelung Hong. "Commentary: Eurocentrism in American Ethnic Studies." *Contemporary Sociology* 11, no. 2 (1982): 129.

With Robert C. Poolman. "Strong Ties and Scientific Information." *Social Networks* 4, no. 3 (1982): 225–32.

> Reprinted in *Social Networks: Critical Concepts*, edited by John Scott, 459–66. New York: Routledge, 2002.

With Joseph R. Rankin. "Extrapolation, Hart, and Ogburn." *Journal of the History of Sociology* 4, no. 2 (1982): 96–102.

"The Creation of Linguistic Structure." *American Anthropologist* 85, no. 2 (1983): 356–62.

> Revised as "The Manufacture of Linguistic Structure." In *American Anthropology and Company: Historical Explorations*, 22–30. Lincoln: University of Nebraska Press, 2013.

"Fuzzy Sets and Abominations." *Man* 18, no. 2 (1983): 396–99.

> Reprinted in *Ethnographic Studies of Homosexuality*, vol. 2, edited by Wayne R. Dynes and Stephen Donaldson, 326–29. New York: Garland, 1992.

Review of *Eclogues: Eight Stories* by Guy Davenport. *Advocate* 364 (March 31, 1983): 52.

"Ritual and Personal Insults in Stigmatized Subcultures: Gay, Black, Jew." *Maledicta* 7 (1983): 189–211.

> Reprinted in *The Best of Maledicta*, edited by Reinhold Aman, 118–40. Philadelphia: Running Press, 1987.

> Reprinted in *Opus Maledicta*, edited by Reinhold Aman, 213–35. New York: Marlowe, 1996.

"Sociology and the AIDS Panic III." *Sociologists' Gay Caucus Newsletter* 35 (1983): 4–6.

With Kent Gerard. "Renaissance Sodomite Subcultures?" *Onder Vrouwen, Onder Mannen* 1 (1983): 182–96.

With Kenneth W. Payne. "Historical Inferences from Ethnohistorical Data: Boasian Views." *Journal of the History of the Behavioral Sciences* 19, no. 4 (1983): 335–40.

> Reprinted in *American Anthropology and Company: Historical Explorations*, 15–21. Lincoln: University of Nebraska Press, 2013.

"Comment on Yuchtman-Yaar's 'Tension . . . in the Modern Kibbutz.'" *Contemporary Sociology* 13, no. 2 (1984): 130.

"Fauler Zauber in der Südsee." *Psychologie Heute* 3, no. 11 (1984): 68–72.

"Murray Comments on Ethnography Authenticity." *Anthropology Newsletter* 25, no. 9 (1984): 2.

"Notes on the History of Linguistic Anthropology." *Historiographia Linguistica* 11, no. 3 (1984): 449–60.

Review of *Margaret Mead and Samoa: The Making and Unmaking of an Anthropological Myth* by Derek Freeman. *Psychologie Heute* 3, no. 11 (1984): 68–72.

With Chen Bousee. Review of *The Lesbian Community* by Deborah Goleman Wolf. *Urban Life* 13, no. 1 (1984): 113–15.

With Robert C. Poolman Jr. "Socially Structuring Prototype Semantics." *Forum Linguisticum* 8, no. 1 (1984): 95–102.

"The History of Anthropology's Lavender Fringe." *Anthropological Research Group on Homosexuality Newsletter* 6, no. 1 (1985): 8–10.

"A Pre-Boasian Sapir?" *Historiographia Linguistica* 12, no. 1–2 (1985): 267–69.

"Remembering Michel Foucault." *Sociologists' Gay Caucus Newsletter* 43 (1985): 9–12. Revised in *Pieces for a History of Gay Studies*, 80–87. San Francisco: El Instituto Obregón, 2012.

Review of *A Woman's Quest for Science: Portrait of Anthropologist Elsie Clews Parsons* by Peter H. Hare. *Journal of the History of Sociology* 6, no. 1 (1985): 173–74.

"Toward a Model of Members' Methods of Recognizing Interruptions." *Language in Society* 14, no. 1 (1985): 31–40.

"Comment on Newmeyer." *Language* 62, no. 4 (1986): 966–67.

"More on the Sources and Fallacies of Social Constructionisms." *Sociologists' Gay Caucus Newsletter* 46 (1986): 6.

"The Postmaturity of Sociolinguistics: Edward Sapir and Personality Studies in the Chicago Department of Sociology." *Journal of the History of Sociology* 6, no. 2 (1986): 75–108.

Revised in *American Anthropology and Company: Historical Explorations*, 172–93. Lincoln: University of Nebraska Press, 2013.

Review of *AIDS in the Mind of America* by Dennis Altman. SIECUS *[Sex Information and Education Council of the U.S.] Report* 14, no. 3 (1986): 19.

Review of *Other Voices: The Style of a Male Homosexual Tavern* by Kenneth E. Read. *Urban Life* 15, no. 3–4 (1987): 479–82.

"STDs, 'Promiscuity' and Societal Differences in Acceptance of Homosexuality." *Sociologists' Gay Caucus Newsletter* 46 (1986): 5.

With Manuel Arboleda G. "The Dangers of Lexical Inference with Special Reference to Maori Homosexuality." *Journal of Homosexuality* 12, no. 1 (1986): 129–34.

With Wayne R. Dynes. "Edward Sapir's Coursework in Linguistics and Anthropology." *Historiographia Linguistica* 13, no. 1 (1986): 125–29.

"Genital Mutilation [Letter to the Editor, Response to Linke]." *Rites for Lesbian and Gay Liberation* 4, no. 4 (1987): 3.

"A Loaded Gun: Some Thoughts on American Concentration Camps and the AIDS Epidemic." *New York Native* (July 27, 1987), 15–17.

Obituary: Jesse O. Sawyer. *Anthropological Research Group on Homosexuality Newsletter* 9, no. 2 (1987): 6.

"Power and Solidarity in 'Interruption': A Critique of the Santa Barbara School Conception and its Application by Orcutt and Harvey (1985)." *Symbolic Interaction* 10, no. 1 (1987): 101–110.

Review of *Homosexuality in Greek Myth* by Bernard Sergent. *Anthropological Research Group on Homosexuality Newsletter* 9, no. 2 (1987): 14–15.

Review of *Spanish Language Use and Public Life in the USA*, edited by Lucía Elías-Olivares, Elizabeth A. Leone, René Cisneros, and John R. Gutiérrez. *Contemporary Sociology* 16, no. 5 (1987): 618–19.

"Snowing Canonical Texts." *American Anthropologist* 89, no. 2 (1987): 443–44.

With Kenneth W. Payne. "AIDS." *Anthropology Today* 3, no. 3 (1987): 1–2.

"Berkeley Sociology before Blumer." *Society for the Study of Symbolic Interaction Notes* 15, no. 2 (1988): 8.

"The Invisibility of the Taiwanese." *Taiwan Culture* 10 (1988): 3–8.

"The Reception of Anthropological Work in Sociology Journals, 1922–1951." *Journal of the History of the Behavioral Sciences* 24, no. 2 (1988): 135–51.

> Revised as "The Reception of Anthropological Work in American Sociology, 1921–1951." In *American Anthropology and Company: Historical Explorations*, 194–210. Lincoln: University of Nebraska Press, 2013.

Review of *Disease and Representation: Images of Illness from Madness to AIDS* by Sander L. Gilman. *Society of Lesbian and Gay Anthropologists Newsletter* 10, no. 3 (1988): 9–10.

Review of *Sexuality and Its Discontents: Meanings, Myths, and Modern Sexualities* by Jeffrey Weeks. *Journal of Homosexuality* 15, no. 3–4 (1988): 183–86.

Review of *Sodomy and the Perception of Evil: English Sea Rovers in the 17th Century Caribbean* by Barry Richard Burg. *Journal of Homosexuality* 16, no. 1–2 (1988): 484–85.

"The Sound of Simultaneous Speech, the Meaning of Interruption: A Rejoinder." *Journal of Pragmatics* 12, no. 1 (1988): 115–16.

"W. I. Thomas, Behaviorist Ethnologist." *Journal of the History of the Behavioral Science* 24, no. 4 (1988): 381–91.

> Reprinted in *American Anthropology and Company: Historical Explorations*, 161–71. Lincoln: University of Nebraska Press, 2013.

"Too Establishment? [Response to Helquist]." *The Advocate* 506 (August 30, 1988): 6.

With Lucille H. Covelli. "Women and Men Speaking at the Same Time." *Journal of Pragmatics* 12, no. 1 (1988): 103–11.

With Keelung Hong. "Taiwan, China, and the 'Objectivity' of Dictatorial Elites." *American Anthropologist* 90, no. 4 (1988): 976–78.

With Kenneth W. Payne. "Medical Policy without Scientific Evidence: The Promiscuity Paradigm and AIDS." *California Sociologist* 11, no. 1–2 (1988): 13–54.
- Reprinted in *Homosexuality and Medicine, Health, and Science*, edited by Wayne R. Dynes and Stephen Donaldson, 119–60. New York: Garland, 1992.
- Revised as "The Promiscuity Paradigm, AIDS, and Gay Complicity with the Remedicalization of Homosexuality." In *American Gay*, 99–125. Chicago: University of Chicago Press, 1996.

"AIDS, Gay Men and Their (Invisible) Sociology." *American Sociological Association Footnotes* 17, no. 3 (1989): 8.

"Homosexual Acts and Selves in Early Modern Europe." *Journal of Homosexuality* 16, no. 1–2 (1989): 457–77.
- Reprinted in *The Pursuit of Sodomy: Male Homosexuality in Renaissance and Enlightenment Europe*, edited by Kent Gerard and Gert Hekma, 457–78. New York: Haworth, 1989.

Obituaries: Kenneth W. Payne and Eric Michaels. *Society of Lesbian and Gay Anthropologists Newsletter* 11, no. 1 (1989): 5–6.
- Reprinted in *Anthropology Newsletter*, February 1989, 4.

"Recent Studies of American Linguistics: Review of *Science Encounters the Indian, 1820–1880*" by Robert E. Bieder; *Daniel Garrison Brinton* by Regna Darnell; *The Politics of Linguistics* by Frederick J. Newmeyer; and *Notes on the Development of the Linguistic Society of America, 1924–1950* by Martin Joos. *Historiographia Linguistica* 16, no. 1/2 (1989): 149–71.

Review of *AIDS: The Burden of History*, edited by Elizabeth Fee and Daniel M. Fox; and *AIDS: Cultural Analysis, Cultural Activism*, edited by Douglas Crimp. *Society of Lesbian and Gay Anthropologists Newsletter* 11, no. 1 (1989): 16–19.

Review of *Male Homosexuality in Thailand* by Peter A. Jackson. *Society of Lesbian and Gay Anthropologists Newsletter* 11, no. 3 (1989):15–18.
- Reprinted in *Sociologists' Lesbian and Gay Caucus Newsletter* 64 (1990): 7–10.
- Revised as "Peter Jackson's Account of Emergent Gay Homosexuality in Contemporary Thailand." In *Oceanic Homosexualities*, 387–96. New York: Garland, 1992.

"Robert Allan (Laud) Humphreys, 1930–1988." *Society of Lesbian and Gay Anthropologists Newsletter* 11, no. 2 (1989): 3–4.

"Sodomites in Pre-Inca Cultures on the West Coast of South America." *Society of Lesbian and Gay Anthropologists Newsletter* 11, no. 2 (1989): 14–19.
- Reprinted in *Committee on Lesbian and Gay History Newsletter* 3, no. 2 (1989): 26–29.
- Revised in *Latin American Male Homosexualities*, 279–82. Albuquerque: University of New Mexico Press, 1995.

"Urban Land Values, Public Safety, and Visible Gay Culture: A Reply to Scott Bravmann." *Sociologists' Lesbian and Gay Caucus Newsletter* 59 (1989): 7–8.

With Keelung Hong. "Complicity with Domination." *American Anthropologist* 91, no. 4 (1989): 1028–30.

With Marcel Mauss. "A 1934 Interview with Marcel Mauss." *American Ethnologist* 16, no. 1 (1989): 163–68.

With Kenneth W. Payne. "The Social Classification of AIDS in American Epidemiology." *Medical Anthropology* 10, no. 2–3 (1989): 115–28.

> Reprinted in *The AIDS Pandemic: A Global Emergency*, edited by Ralph Bolton, 23–36. Amsterdam: Gordon and Breach, 1989.
>
> Revised as part of "Haitian (In?)tolerance of Homosexuality and 'Scientific' Fantasies about 'Alien Corruption' of Black 'Innocents.'" In *Pieces for a History of Gay Studies*, 33–42. San Francisco: El Instituto Obregón, 2012.

"More on *The Construction of Homosexuality*." *Contemporary Sociology* 19, no. 1 (1990): 1–2.

"Problematic Aspects of Freeman's Account of Boasian Culture." *Current Anthropology* 31, no. 4 (1990): 401–7.

Review of *The Great Mirror of Male Love* by Ihara Saikaku. *Society of Lesbian and Gay Anthropologists Newsletter* 12, no. 3 (1990): 54–61.

Review of *More Man than You'll Ever Be! Gay Folklore and Acculturation in Middle America* by Joseph P. Goodwin. *Society of Lesbian and Gay Anthropologists Newsletter* 12, no. 2 (1990): 9–10.

> Reprinted in *Journal of American Folklore* 104, no. 413 (1991): 397–99.

"The Reviewer Responds [Reply to Hall]." *Historiographia Linguistica* 17, no. 1/2 (1990): 234–36.

With Keelung Hong. "American Anthropologists Looking through Taiwanese Culture." *Taiwan Tribune* 825 (1990): 2–3.

> Republished in *Dialectical Anthropology* 16, no. 3/4 (1991): 273–99.
>
> Republished in *Taiwanese Culture, Taiwanese Society: A Critical Review of Social Science Research Done on Taiwan*. Lanham MD: University Press of America, 1994.
>
> Revised as "American Anthropologists Looking through Taiwan to see 'Traditional' China, 1950–1990." In *American Anthropology and Company: Historical Explorations*, 122–56. Lincoln: University of Nebraska Press, 2013.
>
> Revised in Keelung Hong and Stephen O. Murray, *Looking through Taiwan: American Anthropologists' Collusion with Ethnic Domination*, 48–75. Lincoln: University of Nebraska Press, 2005.

"Blaming the Victim." *American Anthropologist* 93, no. 3 (1991): 700–701.

"Ethnic Differences in Interpretive Conventions and the Reproduction of Inequality in Everyday Life." *Symbolic Interaction* 14, no. 2 (1991): 187–204.

"The First Quarter Century of the Linguistic Society of America, 1924–1949." *Historiographia Linguistica* 18, no. 1 (1991): 1–48.

"'Homosexual Occupations' in Mesoamerica?" *Journal of Homosexuality* 21, no. 4 (1991): 57–66.
> Revised in *Latin American Male Homosexualities*, 71–79. Albuquerque: University of New Mexico Press, 1995.

"How Dark was the Eclipse of Bloomfield?" *Historiographia Linguistica* 18, no. 1 (1991): 251–53.

"Knowledge, Beliefs and Attitudes about AIDS in Los Angeles." *Society of Lesbian and Gay Anthropologists Newsletter* 13, no. 3 (1991): 54–55.

"Letter to the Editor: Response to Whitam." *Archives of Sexual Behavior* 20, no. 6 (1991): 587–88.

"On Boasians and Margaret Mead: Reply to Freeman." *Current Anthropology* 32, no. 4 (1991): 448–52.

"A Parting Shot." *Society of Lesbian and Gay Anthropologists Newsletter* 13, no. 3 (1991): 75.

Review of *Achilles: Paradigms of the War Hero from Homer to the Middle Ages* by Katherine Callen King. *Society of Lesbian and Gay Anthropologists Newsletter* 13, no. 2 (1991): 42.

Review of *AIDS: Individual, Cultural, and Policy Dimensions* by Peter Aggleton, Peter Davies, and Graham Hart. *Social Forces* 70, no. 1 (1991): 299–300.
> Revised as Review of *AIDS: Individual, Cultural and Policy Dimensions*, edited by Peter Aggleton, Peter Davies, and Graham Hart; and *Inventing AIDS* by Cindy Patton. *Society of Lesbian and Gay Anthropologists Newsletter* 13, no. 2 (1991): 41–42.

Review of *Edward Sapir: Linguist, Anthropologist, Humanist* by Regna Darnell. *Language in Society* 20, no. 2 (1991): 317–22.

Review of *The Greeks and Their Legacy* by Kenneth J. Dover. *Society of Lesbian and Gay Anthropologists Newsletter* 13, no. 1 (1991): 28.

Review of *Journal of the History of Sexuality*, edited by John C. Fout. *Society of Lesbian and Gay Anthropologists Newsletter* 13, no. 3 (1991): 66–67.

Review of *A Life for Language: A Biographical Memoir of Leonard Bloomfield* by Robert A. Hall Jr. *Language* 67, no. 3 (1991): 653–54.
> Revised in *Word* 43, no. 1 (1992): 138–45.

"The Rights of Research Assistants and the Rhetoric of Political Suppression: Morton Grodzins and the University of California Japanese-American Evacuation and Resettlement Study." *Journal of the History of the Behavioral Sciences* 27, no. 2 (1991): 130–56.
> Revised in *American Anthropology and Company: Historical Explorations*, 211–45. Lincoln: University of Nebraska Press, 2013.

"Sleeping with the Natives as a Source of Data." *Society of Lesbian and Gay Anthropologists Newsletter* 13, no. 3 (1991): 49–51.

"Social Constructionism and Ancient Greek Homosexualities: The State of the Art; A Review of *The Constraints of Desire: The Anthropology of Sex and Gender in Ancient Greece* by John J. Winkler; *One Hundred Years of Homosexuality and Other Essays on Greek Love* by David M. Halperin; and *Forms of Desire: Sexual Orientation and the Social Constructionist Controversy*, edited by Edward Stein." *Society of Lesbian and Gay Anthropologists Newsletter* 13, no. 1 (1991): 21–28.

Revised as "Explorations of Gender and Homosexualities in Ancient Greece: Social Constructionists ca. 1990 within the Empire of Gender." In *Pieces for a History of Gay Studies*, 88–96. San Francisco: El Instituto Obregón, 2012.

"SOLGA Publications: A Status Report and Results of a Reader Survey." *Society of Lesbian and Gay Anthropologists Newsletter* 13, no. 2 (1991): 28–30.

"Invidious Comparisons." *Society of Lesbian and Gay Anthropologists Newsletter* 14, no. 1 (1992): 19–20.

"Male Homosexual Elders: Notes on *Incidents* by Roland Barthes; *Bringing Out Roland Barthes* by David A. Miller; *Understanding the Male Hustler* by Sam Steward; and *Colin McPhee: Composer in Two Worlds* by Carol J. Oja." *Society of Lesbian and Gay Anthropologists Newsletter* 14, no. 3 (1992): 42–43.

"More Passions about *Passions of the Cut Sleeve*." *Society of Lesbian and Gay Anthropologists Newsletter* 14, no. 2 (1992): 23.

Review of *AIDS and Accusation: Haiti and the Geography of Blame* by Paul Farmer. *Society of Lesbian and Gay Anthropologists Newsletter* 14, no. 3 (1992): 40–42.

Review of *Bodies, Pleasures, and Passions: Sexual Culture in Contemporary Brazil* by Richard G. Parker. *Journal of the History of Sexuality* 2, no. 4 (1992): 679–82.

Review of *Dictionary of Latin American Racial and Ethnic Terminology* by Thomas M. Stephens. *Word* 43, no. 1 (1992): 105–7.

Reprinted in *Lingüística* 5 (1993): 231–32.

Review of *Homosexuality, Society, and the State in Mexico* by Ian G. Lumsden. *Society of Lesbian and Gay Anthropologists Newsletter* 14, no. 2 (1992): 30–31.

Review of *Language Maintenance in Melanesia: Sociolinguistics and Social Networks in New Caledonia* by Stephen Schooling. *Word* 43, no. 3 (1992): 462–65.

Review of *North American Contributions to the History of Linguistics* by Francis P. Dinneen, and E. F. Konrad Koerner. *Journal of Linguistic Anthropology* 2, no. 2 (1992): 233–34.

Review of *Practicing Linguistic Historiography*, edited by E. F. Konrad Koerner; and *First Person Singular II*, edited by E. F. Konrad Koerner. *Journal of the History of the Behavioral Sciences* 28, no. 1 (1992): 63–68.

Review of *You Just Don't Understand! Women and Men in Conversation* by Deborah Tannen. *Journal of Pragmatics* 18, no. 5 (1992): 507–14.

With Keelung Hong. "Pseudo-Objectivity." *Northern California Formosan Federation Newsletter* 4, no. 1 (1992): 70–75.

Reprinted in *Typhoon* 2, no. 4.

Revised as "A Case Study of Pseudo-Objectivity: The Hoover Institution Analysis of 1947 Resistance and Repression." In Keelung Hong and Stephen O. Murray, *Looking through Taiwan: American Anthropologists' Collusion with Ethnic Domination*, 27–38. Lincoln: University of Nebraska Press, 2005.

"Cuban AIDS policy." *Lancet* 342, no. 8884 (1993): 1426.

"Colonizing AIDS Discourse." *Society of Lesbian and Gay Anthropologists Newsletter* 15, no. 1 (1993): 23–25.

"The Editor's Response: Reply to Lewin." *Society of Lesbian and Gay Anthropologists Newsletter* 15, no. 2 (1993): 37–38.

"Network Determination of Linguistic Variables?" *American Speech* 68, no. 2 (1993): 161–77.

"Not Male vs. Female, but Activist vs. Quietist." *Society of Lesbian and Gay Anthropologists Newsletter* 15, no. 3 (1993): 6–7.

"Notes on Some Recently Published Collections: *Studies in Homosexuality*, edited by Wayne R. Dynes and Stephen Donaldson; *Ritualized Homosexuality in Melanesia* by Gilbert H. Herdt; *Coming Out* by Stephen Likosky; *The Golden Boy* by James Melson; *Hometowns: Gay Men Write about Where They Belong* by John Preston; *Only Entertainment* by Richard Dyer; *Inside/Out: Lesbian Theories, Gay Theories* by Diana Fuss; and *Anthropology and Autobiography: Participatory Experience and Embodied Knowledge* by Judith Okely and Helen Callaway." *Society of Lesbian and Gay Anthropologists Newsletter* 15, no. 3 (1993): 37–39.

"On SOLGA, the Future, and Queer Theory." *Society of Lesbian and Gay Anthropologists Newsletter* 15, no. 2 (1993): 33–34.

Review of *Games of Venus: An Anthology of Greek and Roman Erotic Verse from Sappho to Ovid*, edited by Peter Bing and Rip Cohen; *Homosexual Desire in Shakespeare's England: A Cultural Poetics* by Bruce R. Smith. *Society of Lesbian and Gay Anthropologists Newsletter* 15, no. 2 (1993): 43–44.

Review of *Life Is Hard: Machismo, Danger, and the Intimacy of Power in Nicaragua* by Roger N. Lancaster. *Society of Lesbian and Gay Anthropologists Newsletter* 15, no. 1 (1993): 32–35.

With Keelung Hong. Review of *A Thrice Told Tale: Feminism, Postmodernism and Ethnographic Responsibility* by Margery Wolf. *Typhoon* 3, no. 4 (1993): 4–6.

"Joel I. Brodsky, 1947–1994." *Sociologists' Lesbian and Gay Caucus Newsletter* 78 (1994): 3.

"A Memoir of the Founding of the Caucus." *Sociologists' Lesbian and Gay Caucus Newsletter* 79 (1994): 1–2.

Revised as "Memoirs of the Founding of Gay/Lesbian Organizations within the American Sociological Association and the American Anthropological Association: SGC and ARGOH." In *Pieces for a History of Gay Studies*, 70–73. San Francisco: El Instituto Obregón, 2012.

"On Subordinating Native American Cosmologies to the Empire of Gender." *Current Anthropology* 35, no. 1 (1994): 59–61.

Revised as "Appendix: A Note on a Purported 'Third Gender' Aboriginal Role." In *American Gay*, 161–66. Chicago: University of Chicago Press, 1996.

Revised as "Subordinating Native American Cosmologies to the Empire of Gender." In *Pieces for a History of Gay Studies*, 43–48. San Francisco: El Instituto Obregón, 2012.

"Questions of Fairness." *Anthropology Newsletter* 35, no. 2 (1994): 2, 37.

Review of *Children of Horizons: How Gay and Lesbian Teens are Leading a New Way Out of the Closet* by Gilbert Herdt and Andrew Boxer. *Sociologists' Lesbian and Gay Caucus Newsletter* 76 (1994): 8–9.

Review of *The Dove Coos: Gay Experiences by the Men of Thailand* by Eric Allyn. *Society of Lesbian and Gay Anthropologists Newsletter* 16, no. 1 (1994): 28–30.

Review of *Politeness in Language: Studies in Its History, Theory and Practice* by Richard J. Watts, Sachiko Ide, and Konrad Ehlich. *Word* 45, no. 2 (1994): 236–38.

Review of *The Time of AIDS: Social Analysis, Theory, and Method* by Gilbert Herdt and Shirley Lindenbaum; *AIDS: The Making of a Chronic Disease*, edited by Elizabeth Fee and Daniel M. Fox. *Contemporary Sociology* 23, no. 5 (1994): 751–53.

"Sex and the Economy of Speaking Turns." *Journal of Pragmatics* 21, no. 2 (1994): 215–24.

"A Thirteenth-Century Imperial Ethnography." *Anthropology Today* 10, no. 5 (1994): 15–18.

"Caucus Prehistory: A 1969 ASA Resolution." *Sociologists' Lesbian and Gay Caucus Newsletter* 82 (1995): 2.

"Discourse Creationism: Review of *The Invention of Heterosexuality* by Jonathan Ned Katz." *Journal of Sex Research* 32, no. 3 (1995): 263–65.

"Heteronormative Cuban Sexual Policies and Resistance to Them: Review of *Before Night Falls: A Memoir* by Reinaldo Arenas; and *Sexual Politics in Cuba: Machismo, Homosexuality, and AIDS* by Marvin Leiner." *GLQ: A Journal of Lesbian and Gay Studies* 2, no. 4 (1995): 473–77.

"Picano's 'Violet Quill Club.'" *Harvard Gay and Lesbian Review* 2, no. 3 (1995): 52.

Review of *Growing Up Before Stonewall: Life Stories of Some Gay Men* by Peter M. Nardi, David Sanders, and Judd Marmor. *Society of Lesbian and Gay Anthropologists Newsletter* 17, no. 1 (1995): 17.

Review of *The Psychology of Culture: A Course of Lectures* by Edward Sapir. *Historiographia Linguistica* 22, no. 3 (1995): 419–21.

"Some Southwest Asian and North African Terms for Homosexual Roles." *Archives of Sexual Behavior* 24, no. 6 (1995): 623–29.

"Historical Truths and Partisan Misrepresentations." *Anthropological Linguistics* 38, no. 2 (1996): 355–60.

Review of *Language, Culture, and Society: An Introduction to Linguistic Anthropology* by Zdenek Salzmann. *Word* 47, no. 1 (1996): 131–32.

Review of *Male Colors: The Construction of Homosexuality in Tokugawa Japan* by Gary P. Leupp. *Society of Lesbian and Gay Anthropologists Newsletter* 18, no. 1 (1996): 14–16.
Revised in *Contemporary Sociology* 26, no. 1 (1997): 73–74.

Review of *The Meanings of Macho: Being a Man in Mexico City* by Matthew C. Guttman. *Society of Lesbian and Gay Anthropologists Newsletter* 18, no. 2 (1996): 8–9.

Review of *Word's Out: Gay Men's English* by William L. Leap. *Anthropological Linguistics* 38, no. 4 (1996): 747–50.

"Free Speech and Thought Control [Response to Varnell]." *Out Now* 4, no. 2 (1996), 16.

"A 1978 Interview with Mary Haas." *Anthropological Linguistics* 39, no. 4 (1997): 695–722.

"An African-American's Representation of Internalized Homophobia during the Early 1930s: Chester Himes's *Cast the First Stone*." *Journal of Homosexuality* 34, no. 1 (1997): 31–46.

"Explaining Away Same-Sex Sexualities When They Obtrude on Anthropologists' Notice at All." *Anthropology Today* 13, no. 3 (1997): 2–5.
Revised as "The Anthropological Tradition of Explaining Away Same-Sex Sexuality When It Obtrudes on Anthropologists' Notice." *Kea* 14 (2001): 171–79.
Revised as "The Anthropological Tradition of Explaining Away Same-Sex Sexuality When It Obtrudes on Anthropologists' Notice." In *Pieces for a History of Gay Studies*, 26–32. San Francisco: El Instituto Obregón, 2012.

"Motive and Opportunity." *American Ethnologist* 24, no. 4 (1997): 934.

Review of *The Cree Language Is Our Identity: The La Ronge Lectures of Sarah Whitecalf*, edited by H. C. Wolfart and Freda Ahenakew; and *Multiple Identities: A Phenomenology of Multicultural Communication* by Pradeep Ajit Dhillon. *Word* 48, no. 1 (1997): 121–24.

Review of *Farm Boys: Lives of Gay Men from the Rural Midwest* by Will Fellows; and *Autopornography: A Memoir of Life in the Lust Lane* by Scott O'Hara. *Committee on Lesbian and Gay History Newsletter* 11, no. 2/3 (1997): 17–19.
Reprinted in *Internet History Sourcebooks Project*, 1998. https://sourcebooks.fordham.edu/pwh/clgh/clgh1997-11-2-3murray.asp.

Review of *Status and Power in Verbal Interaction: A Study of Discourse in a Close-Knit Social Network* by Julie Diamond. *Word* 48, no. 3 (1997): 450–53.

"Big-Name Gay Books Fizzled [Response to Schwartz]." *Out Now* 5, no. 4 (1997): 14.

"A SOD Day [Letter to the Editor]." *San Francisco Bay Times* 18, no. 18 (June 26, 1997): 34.

"New Gay Books: Review of *Gay and After* by Alan Sinfield." *Sexualities* 1, no. 4 (1998): 495–96.

Review of *Academic Outlaws: Queer Theory and Cultural Studies in the Academy* by William G. Tierney. *American Anthropologist* 100, no. 2 (1998): 565–66.

Review of *One of the Children: Gay Black Men in Harlem* by William G. Hawkeswood; and *Gay Macho: The Life and Death of the Homosexual Clone* by Martin Levine. *Journal of the Royal Anthropological Institute* 4, no. 3 (1998): 586–87.

"Subjectivities of Some Dark(-Haired) Objects of Desire: Reviews of *Young Man from the Provinces: A Gay Life before Stonewall* by Alan Helms; *Breaking the Surface* by Greg Louganis with Eric Marcus; *Wonder Bread and Ecstasy: The Life and Death of Joey Stefano* by Charles Isherwood; *Gary in Your Pocket* by Gary Fisher; *Honey, Honey, Miss Thang: Being Black, Gay, and on the Streets* by Leon E. Pettiway; *Last Night on Earth* by Bill T. Jones with Peggy Gillespie." *Journal of Homosexuality* 35, no. 1 (1998): 114–33.

"More on Gatekeepers and Chomsky's Writings of the 1950s." *Historiographia Linguistica* 26, no. 3 (1999): 343–53.

Review of *Machos, Maricones, and Gays: Cuba and Homosexuality* by Ian G. Lumsden. *Archives of Sexual Behavior* 28, no. 6 (1999): 575–77.

Review of *Mema's House: On Transvestites, Queens, and Machos* by Annick Prieur. *Journal of the Royal Anthropological Institute* 5, no. 2 (1999): 294–95.

Review of *Men as Women, Women as Men: Changing Gender in Native American Cultures* by Sabine Lang. *Journal of the Royal Anthropological Institute* 5, no. 4 (1999): 643–44.

Review of *Queerly Phrased: Language, Gender, and Sexuality*, edited by Anna Livia and Kira Hall. *Language in Society* 28, no. 2 (1999): 304–8.

"Roger Brown (1925–1997): A Memorial." *Journal of Homosexuality* 37, no. 1 (1999): 1–2.

"Tracing the Rise of the Gay Rights Movement: Review of *Out for Good: The Struggle to Build a Gay Rights Movement in America* by Dudley Clendinen and Adam Nagourney." *New York Times*, July 5, 1999, E13.

"Widely Plausible Deniability." *Sexualities* 2, no. 2 (1999): 252–55.

Review of *Beyond Carnival: Male Homosexuality in Twentieth-Century Brazil* by James N. Green; *Beneath the Equator: Cultures of Desire, Male Homosexuality, and Emerging Gay Communities in Brazil* by Richard Parker. *Journal of the Royal Anthropological Institute* 6, no. 4 (2000): 747–48.

With Regna Darnell. "Margaret Mead and Paradigm Shifts within Anthropology during the 1920s." *Journal of Youth and Adolescence* 29, no. 5 (2000): 557–73.

Revised as "Margaret Mead and the Professional Unpopularity of Popularizers." In *American Anthropology and Company: Historical Explorations*, 31–51. Lincoln: University of Nebraska Press, 2013.

"The Anthropological Tradition of Explaining Away Same-Sex Sexuality When It Obtrudes on Anthropologists' Notice." *Kea* 14 (2001): 171–78.

"Does Editing a Journal Increase One's Citations in It?" *Anthropology Newsletter* 42, no. 2 (2001): 16–17.

Revised as "Does Editing Core Anthropology Journals Increase Citations to the Editor?" In *American Anthropology and Company: Historical Explorations*, 264–72. Lincoln: University of Nebraska Press, 2013.

Review of *The Early Days of Sociolinguistics: Memories and Reflections*, edited by Christina Bratt Paulston and G. Richard Tucker. *Word* 52, no. 3 (2001): 459–62.

"Attempting to Manage Homosexuality before and after the Bolshevik Revolution: Review of *Homosexual Desire in Revolutionary Russia: The Regulation of Sexual and Gender Dissent* by Dan Healey." *Journal of Sex Research* 39, no. 3 (2002): 246–48.

"Gender-Mixing Roles, Gender-Crossing Roles, and the Sexuality of Transgendered Roles: Review Essay of *Beauty and Power: Transgendering and Cultural Transformation in the Southern Philippines* by Mark Johnson; *Travesti: Sex, Gender, and Culture among Brazilian Transgendered Prostitutes* by Don Kulick; *Neither Man nor Woman: The Hijras of India* by Serena Nanda; *Gender Diversity: Crosscultural Variations* by Serena Nanda; *Changing Ones: Third and Fourth Genders in Native North America* by Will Roscoe; *When Men Become Women: Manhood among the Gabra Nomads of East Africa* by John C. Wood; and *Women Become Men: Albanian Sworn Virgins* by Antonia Young." *Reviews in Anthropology* 31, no. 4 (2002): 291–308.

"Homosexuality in the Imagining of a Cuban Nation: Review of *Gay Cuban Nation* by Emilio Bejel." *Journal of Sex Research* 39, no. 3 (2002): 244–46.

Review of *Images of Ambiente: Homotextuality and Latino/a American Art, 1810–Today* by Rudy Bleys. *Committee on Lesbian and Gay History Newsletter* 16, no. 2 (2002): 8–9.

Review of *Masculine Domination* by Pierre Bourdieu. *Journal of the Royal Anthropological Institute* 8, no. 2 (2002): 389–90.

"Representations of Desires in Some Recent Gay Asian-American Writings." *Journal of Homosexuality* 45, no. 1 (2003): 111–42.

Review of *The Making of a Gay Asian Community: An Oral History of a Pre-AIDS Los Angeles* by Eric C. Wat. *Society of Lesbian and Gay Anthropologists Newsletter* 22, no. 2 (2003): 7.

"Striving to De-exoticize Japanese Marriage Avoiders: Review of *Beyond Common Sense: Sexuality and Gender in Contemporary Japan* by Wim Lunsing." *Journal of Sex Research* 40, no. 1 (2003): 111–12.

"Humphreys vs. Sagarin in the Sociological Study of Gay Movements." *International Journal of Sociology and Social Policy* 24, no. 3/4/5 (2004): 128–45.

Revised as "Humphreys vs. Sagarin in the Study of Gay Movements." In *Pieces for a History of Gay Studies*, 59–69. San Francisco: El Instituto Obregón, 2012.

"Panting for 'the Wild Man' and Tobias Schneebaum: A Review of *Keep the River on Your Right: A Modern Cannibal Tale* by David Shapiro and Laurie Shapiro." *Anthropology Today* 20, no. 4 (2004): 25–26.

"Pseudonyms and Maoists: A response to Pettigrew et al." *Anthropology Today* 20, no. 3 (2004): 25.

Review of *Colonial Affairs: Bowles, Burroughs, and Chester Write Tangier* by Greg Mullins. *Journal of Homosexuality* 47, no. 1 (2004): 170–78.

Review of *The Famous 41: Sexuality and Social Control in Mexico, 1901*, edited by Robert McKee Irwin, Edward J. McCaughan, and Michelle Rocío Nasser. *Committee on Lesbian and Gay History Newsletter* 18, no. 1 (2004): 18–19.

"American Anthropologists Discover Peasants." *Histories of Anthropology Annual* 1 (2005): 61–98.

Revised in *American Anthropology and Company: Historical Explorations*. Lincoln: University of Nebraska Press, 2013, 52–87.

Review of *Global Divas: Filipino Gay Men in the Diaspora* by Martin F. Manalansan. *Journal of the Royal Anthropological Institute* 10, no. 4 (2005): 952–53.

"The Use of 'Islamism.'" *Anthropology News* 46, no. 5 (2005): 3.

Review of *Before Homosexuality in the Arab-Islamic World, 1500–1800* by Khaled el-Rouayheb. *Committee on Lesbian and Gay History Newsletter* 20, no. 2 (2006): 11–12.

Reprinted as "An Antihistorical Examination of Some Arab Discourses: Khaled El-Rouayheb's *Before Homosexuality in the Arab-Islamic World, 1500–1800*." In *21st-Century Representations of Muslim Homosexualities*. San Francisco: El Instituto Obregón, 2012.

"Homosexuality in the Ottoman Empire." *Historical Reflections / Réflexions historiques* 31, no. 1 (2007): 101–16.

"The Pre-Freudian Georges Devereux, the Post-Freudian Alfred Kroeber, and Mohave Sexuality." *Histories of Anthropology Annual* 5 (2009): 12–27.

Revised in *American Anthropology and Company: Historical Explorations*, 102–13. Lincoln: University of Nebraska Press, 2013.

"Review: Southern African Homosexualities and Denials, *African Intimacies: Race, Homosexuality, and Globalization* by Neville Hoad; *Imperialism within the Margins: Queer Representations and the Politics of Culture in Southern Africa* by William J. Sperlin; and *Unspoken Facts: A History of African Homosexualities* by Gays and Lesbians of Zimbabwe." *Canadian Journal of African Studies / Revue canadienne des études africaines* 43, no. 1 (2009): 167–72.

Review of *Allah Made Us: Sexual Outlaws in an Islamic African City* by Rudolf Gaudio. *Language in Society* 39, no. 5 (2010): 696–99.

Reprinted as "An Antihistorical Examination of Some Arab Discourses: Khaled El-Rouayheb's *Before Homosexuality in the Arab-Islamic World, 1500–1800*." In *21st-Century Representations of Muslim Homosexualities*. San Francisco: El Instituto Obregón, 2012.

"Conceptions about and Representations of Male Homosexuality in the Popular Book and Movie, *The Yacoubian Building*." *Journal of Homosexuality* 60, no. 7 (2013): 1081–89.
   Reprinted in *21st-Century Representations of Muslim Homosexualities*. San Francisco: El Instituto Obregón, 2012.

"Dr. John Alan Lee: In Memoriam." *Journal of Homosexuality* 62, no. 1 (2015): 1–3.

Review of *Intimate Activism: The Struggle for Sexual Rights in Postrevolutionary Nicaragua* by Cymene Howe. *American Anthropologist* 117, no. 2 (2015): 429–30.

With Marc Epprecht, Kuukuwa Andam, Francisco Miguel, Aminata Cécile Mbaye, and Rudolf P. Gaudio. "*Boy-Wives, Female Husbands* Twenty Years On: Reflections on Scholarly Activism and the Struggle for Sexual Orientation and Gender Identity/Expression Rights in Africa." *Canadian Journal of African Studies / Revue canadienne des études africaines*, 52, no. 3 (2018): 349–64.

Contributors

BARRY D ADAM, Department of Sociology, University of Windsor, emeritus

RALPH BOLTON, Department of Anthropology, Pomona College, emeritus

REGNA DARNELL, Department of Anthropology, Western University, emerita

MARC EPPRECHT, Department of History, Queen's University

WENDY LEEDS-HURWITZ, Department of Communication, University of Wisconsin–Parkside, emerita

MILTON MACHUCA-GÁLVEZ, librarian for Spanish, Portuguese, Latin America, and Caribbean Studies, University of Kansas

PETER M. NARDI, Department of Sociology, Pitzer College, The Claremont Colleges, emeritus

ROBERT OPPENHEIM, Department of Asian Studies, University of Texas at Austin

Index

Abbas, Hakima, 189
academia, 71n4, 141, 181
Academic Press, 220–21
acknowledgments, 10, 62–65, 150, 277
activism, xi, 3, 24, 107, 128, 181, 189. *See also* AIDS
ACT UP, 130, 136, 143
Adams, Nicholas Charles, 11, 271
advocacy, 130, 180–81, 189
Africa, 128, 154, 158, 170, 188–89, 191, 280, 283; AIDS research in, 124; films from, 19; homosexualities in, 24; representations of, 234; women in, 143n5
African(s), 17, 189, 192, 234; American, 272; cinema, xi, 4, 19–20, 22, 30; colleagues, 14; homosexualities, xii, 78; nationalism, 187; scholar-activists, 189; societies, 154; studies, 12, 189; women, 191. See also *An Introduction to African Cinema* (Murray); *Boy-Wives and Female Husbands* (*BWFH*) (Murray and Roscoe); queer African studies; South Africa
African Studies Association, 16–17
Africanist, 24, 187, 189, 216
Agar, Michael, 214
age, 19, 35, 45–46, 130, 156, 158–60, 162, 170–73, 177–78, 180, 199, 215, 242, 281; and area hypothesis, 241; of consent, 160
Aguilar, Oscar, 204
AIDS, 7, 16, 23, 41–43, 58, 107, 176–77; activism, 107, 135; advocates, 132; bibliography project, 123; Cuban approach to, 125; denialism, 125, 144n9; heretics, 124, 142n3; and HIV, vii, xii, 23, 85, 116, 123–24, 130, 144; pandemic, 129, 132, 139, 143, 177; people with, 22, 119–20, 122, 126, 130, 135, 140; policies, 131, 143; quilt, 130; researchers, 23, 121, 124, 137
AIDS and Anthropology Research Group (AARG), 22, 118–24, 133–36
AIDS and the Social Imaginary (panel), 22, 107, 115–50
Ajirotuto, Cheryl, 6
Akinnaso, Niyi, 6, 227
Albert, Ethel, 210, 221, 257
Alio, Amina, 157
Alsford, Niki J. P., 102–3
American Anthropological Association (AAA), xi, 3, 6, 15–18, 22, 45, 54, 68, 87, 115, 118–19, 123, 127, 129, 132–41, 144n11, 200, 207, 236, 248; AIDS and Anthropology Task Force, 119, 140; Commission on AIDS Research and Education, 138; Commission on Lesbian and Gay Issues, 138; Commission on Minority Issues in Anthropology, 138; Department of Academic Relations, 138
American Anthropologist (journal), 65, 72n17, 89–91, 122, 199, 205
American Anthropology and Company (Murray), 4, 8, 53
American Gay (Murray), 4, 13, 44, 50, 56
Americanist tradition, 15, 71n5

American Sociolinguistics (journal), 4, 6, 200
American Sociological Association (ASA), xi, 15–16, 46, 119
Amin, Kadji, 160
Amory, Deborah "Deb," 107, 110n15, 133, 135–36, 187, 189, 192n1, 193n3
Angkor Life (Murray), 4, 18, 42, 50n6, 56
Anglo America, 176, 253–69
anthropological linguistics. *See* linguistics
Anthropological Research Group on Homosexuality (ARGOH), 14, 132. *See also* Association of Queer Anthropologists; Society of Lesbian and Gay Anthropologists (SOLGA)
anthropology, xi, 3, 5–6, 9–11, 13, 16–18, 20–23, 43, 49, 53–56, 59, 65, 72n17, 82, 89–90, 92, 94, 98, 119, 123, 131, 143, 174, 181, 203–4, 207–8, 212–13, 221, 247, 272; cultural, 242; history of, 24–25, 54, 70, 81–83, 87–113, 106, 116, 118, 233–51; linguistic, 3, 8, 58, 208, 225; of literacy, 215; medical, 118, 123; sociocultural, 54–55
Arab peoples, 59, 188, 193
archival research, 11, 13
archives, 49, 61–63, 64, 72n18, 73n28, 187, 193n3
areal studies, 4, 18–19, 87–113
ARGOH. *See* Anthropological Research Group on Homosexuality
Aristotle, 36
Asad, Talal, 90
Association of Queer Anthropologists, 118, 132, 144n14. *See also* Anthropological Research Group on Homosexuality; Society of Lesbian and Gay Anthropologists (SOLGA)
Augustine, 36

Austronesian languages, 93; and studies, 105
autobiography, 21, 239, 243, 272–73
autonomy, 38–41, 159–60, 175

Bailey, Beryl L. 214
Bach, Adolf, 202
Bales, Robert F., 267
Barnhart, Terry A., 84
Barth, Frederick, 6, 207, 211
Basso, Keith, 10, 54, 199, 248n10, 255, 257, 266n8
Bateson, Gregory, 6, 207, 217, 220, 228n11, 239–40, 254
Bauman, Richard, 220–21, 266n8
Bay Area, 6, 115–16, 122; and *Bay Area Reporter*, 135, 142n2
Becker, Alton S. "Pete," 6, 211
Beijing, 92
Beijinghua (dialect), 87, 93–94
Benedict, Ruth, 73n22, 243, 246
Berlin, Brent, 212, 219
Bernstein, Basil, 212, 222–23
Bernstein, Jay, 65
Bickerton, Derek, 214
biographies, 4, 45, 73n22, 84, 89, 107
Birdwhistell, Ray, 254
Bloch, Maurice, 211, 213, 221
Blom, Jan-Petter, 207
Bloomfield, Leonard, 67–68, 216–17, 221, 265
Blount, Ben, 213, 220–21
Blumer, Herbert, 64, 209
Blustain, Malinda Stafford, 84
Boas, Franz "Papa Franz," 72n18, 236, 240–41, 243, 245, 246
Boasian, 105, 240, 245–46
Bock, Kenneth, 234, 237
book reviews, 4, 14, 27, 55, 60, 180
Borker, Ruth, 6, 221

Bosco, Joseph, 96–97, 99, 101, 109n7
Bourdieu, Pierre, 6, 63, 223–25
Boyce, Paul, 157
Boyd, Julian, 206
Boy-Wives and Female Husbands (BWFH) (Murray and Roscoe), xii, 4, 12, 16, 155, 188, 271
Braiterman, Jared "Lee," 133, 136, 150
Bright, Bill, 199
Brosin, Henry, 254
Brown, Jennifer S. H., 241
Brown, Melissa J., 103, 110n10
Brown, Penelope "Penny," 213–14
Brown, Roger, 72n17, 273n1
Brownell, Susan, 83–84
Bullough, Vern, 155
Bulmer, Martin, 64
Bunzel, Ruth, 245
Burling, Robbins, 211
Bush, George W., 36
Butterfield, Herbert, 242
Byers, Paul, 214

Campbell, Douglas, 6
Camus, Albert, 45
Canada, 20, 66, 81, 118
Canadian, 15, 66, 81, 174; Anthropology Society, 81; Association of African Studies, 16, 190; *Journal of African Studies*, 28, 149, 191; Sociology and Anthropological Association, 15
Carlson, Robert, 123
Carrier, Joseph, 124, 132, 142
Casagrande, Joseph, 239
Case, Robbie, 215
case studies, 170–71, 173, 200
Castaneda, Carlos, 238
Cazden, Courtney, 213–14
Central America, 179, 181

Center for Advanced Studies in the Behavioral Sciences (Stanford Center), 206, 218
Center for Lesbian and Gay Studies, 16, 189
Chafe, Wallace, 205, 208, 221–22
Cheney, Dick, 36
Chick, Keith, 227, 229n29
China, 18, 22, 73n28, 87–88, 91–98, 101–6, 108, 141, 143n7, 173; People's Republic of, 22, 87–88, 102–3, 108–9
Chomsky, Noam, 71, 73, 200, 206, 217–19, 221, 226
Christian: doctrine, 188; right, 160
Christianity, 176, 187
The Chronicle of Higher Education (journal), 115, 135, 142n2
Churchill, Caryl, xii
Cicourel, Aaron, 210–11, 224, 265n7
citation, 65–66, 84, 244n2
citation analysis, 70, 73
citation patterns, 62
civil rights, 130–32
Clark, Herb, 213
classroom interaction, 213–14
Clatts, Michael, 120, 123, 143n5, 144n11, 150
Clinton, Bill, 35–36
Cole, Michael, 213
Cole, Sally, 84, 241
Collected Stories (Murray), 4, 19, 26, 277
colonialism, 87, 90, 93, 98, 141, 188, 193n7; and culture, xiii; archives, 187; civil servants, 154; era, 190–91; ethnocartographic, 193n7; in institutions, 153; and politics, 116; regimes of, 90, 157
Comaroff, Jean, 117, 128–29, 142n2
Committee on Sociolinguistics. *See* Social Science Research Council

community, 47, 119, 122, 125, 132, 138, 157–58, 176, 202, 235; gay, 11, 47, 66, 125, 130, 140–41, 177, 179–81, 271; research, 22, 98; of scholars, 92, 191; speech, 239, 254; studies, 90, 98, 102, 104
Conklin, Harold, 245n4
continuity: cultural, 23, 181; rhetoric of, 9, 200
contrarian, xi–xiii, 10, 59, 83
conversation analysis, 25–26, 241, 253, 265
Cook-Gumperz, Jenny, 200, 224, 228n16
Cornman, John, 138–39
Cornell University, 203–4, 216–17
Costa Rica, 50n10, 178, 183n2
Cowan, Milton, 216
Crane, Diana, 64–65
Creole language, and pidgins, 214
Critical Studies in the History of Anthropology, xii, 17, 22, 81–82, 97
cross-cultural, 123, 154, 162, 169; analysis, 11; communication, 214; social organization, xi; studies, 155, 161, 210, 213
Cuba, 144n10; AIDS in, 128, 133; concentration camps, 141; Revolution, 125, 178
cultural: assumptions, 237; authenticity, 97; capital, 6, 223; change, 23; continuity, 23, 181; differences, 94, 96, 240, 246; discourses, 163; distances, 70, 241; distinctiveness, 97, 99; evolution, 234; identity, 192; innovation, 234; materialism, 242; milieu, 272; practices, 87; production, 190; proscriptions, 259; regions, 12; rootedness, 162; stigma, 188; studies, 122, 303; transformation, 179; unity, 88; whole, 104. *See also* anthropology, cultural.
culture: and personality, 55; hero, 243

Dai, Bingham, 64
D'Andrade, Roy, 206, 214, 219
Dankwa, Serena Owusu, 189–92
Daubenmier, Judith M., 67, 240–41
Danehy, John, 254
De Gordon, Antonio Maria, 133
desire, 13, 162–63, 172, 176, 271–73
dialect, 91, 201–2, 205, 215–16
diaspora, 104, 106, 157
Dickemann, Jeffrey M., 60, 119, 136
disciples, 144, 219
disciplinary history, 3–4, 8–11, 17–18, 21, 25, 53
discrimination, xi, 120, 127, 131, 138–39, 172, 180–81
dissertations, 5, 8–10, 13–14, 24, 27n3, 56, 58, 60–61, 72n18, 73n23, 81–82, 199–201, 216, 219, 222, 233–34, 236, 241
Douglas, Mary, 213
Dowell, Coleman, 253
Duesberg, Peter, 124–25, 128, 144n8
Durkheim, Émile, 11, 55, 206

Edelsky, Carol, 253
egalitarian, 158, 172–73, 179, 265n5, 273n1; norms, 160; relationships, 156, 159
Eggan, Fred, 64
Egypt, 173, 189
Ekine, Sokari, 189
elders, 24–25, 61, 201, 236
Elementary Structures of Kinship (Lévi-Strauss), 23, 153
el-Rouayheb, Khaled, 69

El Salvador, 167, 178–79, 183n2
Emeneau, Murray, 54, 64, 204–5, 248n10
empirical: evidence, 192; observation, 171; questions, 257; studies, 72n15; work, 10, 66, 210
Epstein, Steven, 72n16
Erickson, Frederick, 6, 211, 213–14, 221, 265n7
Ervin-Tripp, Susan, 205–7, 210, 225
ethics, 60, 128
ethnographers, 72n17, 157, 206, 217, 239; of communication, 220; urban, 245n4
ethnographic: authority, 129; endeavors, 182; ethnographically oriented studies, 177; fieldwork, 127, 207; inquiry, 219; literatures, 271; perspectives, 23, 181; portraits, 158; practice, 104; present, 67; research, 10, 102, 170; reports, 19; scholars, 162; work, 24; writing, 110
ethnographies, 22, 47, 63, 65, 73n24, 153, 190, 193n6, 219; of communication, 9, 199–200, 206, 211, 213, 220, 225, 265n4; of Native American groups, 98; of South Korea, 108; qualitative, 157; of speaking, 10, 199, 239; regional, 3–4; salvage, 98; tourist, 125; village, 94; white-room, 66–67, 72, 239
ethnomethodology, 209, 210–11, 214, 223–24, 253, 255
ethnomusicology, 207
ethnoscience, 199–200, 206, 245n4, 246
Eubank, Earle Edward, 61
Europe, 124, 158, 221

Europeans, 100, 154, 157, 188–90, 215, 234
evolution, 106, 168, 171, 179, 243, 246; cultural, 234
Eyre, Stephen, 124

Fairbanks, Gordon, 216
Fanshel, David, 255
Faris, Robert, 64
Farmer, Paul, 121–22, 124, 143n7
Feldman, Douglas A., 123–24, 133, 136, 143n5
Feldman, Zeena, 160
Fell, Dafydd, 102–3, 110
fellowships, 24; postdoctoral, xii, 5–10, 18, 24, 54, 62, 71n6, 200, 203; predoctoral, 204
Fenton, William, 64
Ferguson, James, 110n12
Ferguson, Charles, 199–201, 204, 208–9, 211, 213, 215
Fernández-Alemany, Manuel, 7, 12–13, 59, 66, 69, 71n14
fiction works, xi, 4, 19, 26, 42, 46, 88, 94, 245, 272–73
fieldnotes, 61, 207, 238, 240
fieldwork, 19–20, 66, 93, 98, 125, 203, 207–8, 216, 237, 239–40, 244, 247
Fillmore, Charles, 212, 214
Fillmore, Lily Wong, 214
films, xiii, 4, 13, 19–21, 144n10
Firth, John R., 219
Fishman, Joshua, 209
The First Five Minutes (Pittenger, Hockett, and Danehy), 217, 254–55
Foley, Bill, 214
formalism, 217, 219
Forman, Michael, 213

Foucault, Michel, 6, 126, 129, 135, 144n11, 144n16, 191–92, 223–25, 229n26
Fowler, Catherine S., 238
Fowler, Don D., 238
Frake, Charles "Chuck," 206, 213–14, 219–20, 228n9
Freedle, Roy O., 213, 228n18
Freedman, Maurice, 106, 110n13
Freeman, Derek, 63, 73n21, 240, 242–43, 248n5
Freeman, Sarah, 265
Friedrich, Paul, 64, 208, 211, 228n12, 273n1
Fries, Charles C., 215
Frings, Theodor, 202
functionalism, 169, 246; view of, 206, 227, 265n6

Gal, Susan, 223
Galileo, 68
Gallatin, Albert, 241
Gallo, Robert, 128
Garfinkel, Harold, 210–11, 224, 253, 265n6
Gaudio, Rudolf, 189, 192n1, 193n3
gay, 42, 48, 89, 119, 153, 179; adoption, 178; and lesbian studies, xii, 155; consciousness, 176; culture, 169, 175–76, 181; genes, 162; identities, 11, 160, 271; issues, 132, 178; liberation, 155, 169, 176; masculinities, 159; men, xiii, 5, 123–24, 126, 129–30, 141–43, 160, 169, 172; pride parades, 178; representation, 138; rights, 116, 120, 130–31, 140; speech, 20; studies, 12, 20, 42, 47; world, 174–75. *See also* community
Geertz, Clifford, 239–40
Gellner, Ernest, 223

gender, 6, 154–62, 170–74, 188, 190; crossing 156; equality, 144n13, 179; identity, 180; identity, 161, 180; nonconforming, 160; relations, 192; stratified, 156, 159, 171, 173; stratification, 179; roles, 173; transgressing, 160
genealogy, 247; academic, 9; intellectual, 8, 233, 235; of anthropological practice, 98; of knowledge, 193
generative grammar, 73n27, 206, 208
Georgetown University Round Table, 15, 62, 199, 211, 214
Geoghegan, Bill, 212
Germany, 153, 201, 226
Gershenhorn, Jerry, 84
Gerth, Hans, 203
Giddens, Anthony, 223
Giles, Howie, 225
Gleach, Frederic W., 82
Givon, Talmy, 214
global, 105, 168; culture, 158; North, 157–58, 162, 173, 175–76, 190; political economy, 192; queer studies, 187; South, 190; survey, 153; synthesis, 23; vision, 155
globalization, 104, 179
"go native," 54, 62, 200, 248n6
Goffman, Erving, 6, 17, 206, 208–9, 220, 224, 254, 258, 260, 266n8, 266n9
Goldwater, Barry, 35–36
Goldsmith, Douglas, 124
Goodenough, Ward, 245
Goody, Esther, 215
Goody, Jack, 215
Gordon, Robert J., 84
Gorman, Michael, 124
Grace, George, 213
Gramsci, Antonio, 224

Greenberg, David, 155
Grice, Paul, 226
Group Formation in Social Science (Murray), 4, 8, 84, 200
Guatemala, 19–20, 23, 66, 172, 174–78, 181, 183n2; Guatemala City in, 168, 174
Gueboguo, Charles, 189
Gumperz, John, 4–6, 9–10, 24–25, 54, 62, 199–231, 248n10, 265n1

Haas, Mary, 54, 61, 64, 205, 221, 248n10
Hackman, Melissa, 189
Hakka, 87, 91, 93, 102
Hall, Edward T. "Ned", 211
Hall, Linda B., 182
Hall, William, 213
Halle, Morris, 206, 218–19
Hallowell, A. Irving, 235–38, 241, 247
Halperin, David, 155
Hammel, Eugene, 212, 219
Hanks, Judith, 46
Harrell, Stevan, 91–93, 96–97, 109
Harris, Marvin, 242–43
Harvard University, 109n5, 121, 205, 211, 213, 219, 222
Hauser, Philip, 64
Hawaiʻi, 43, 125, 213
Hays, Hoffman Reynolds, 242
Helms, Jesse, 125
Helmsley, Leona, 126
Herdt, Gilbert, 121–23, 143n5, 143n6, 150
Herskovits, Melville, 243
Herz, Peter Jeffrey, 97, 101
Heterogender Homosexuality in Honduras (Fernández-Alemany and Murray), 5, 12
Hindi language, 203–4
Hirschfeld, Magnus, 160
historical research, 24, 61, 68, 170, 237

historians, 37, 55, 58, 64, 67, 71n8, 240, 244; of anthropology, 234, 241–42; disciplinary, 65; insider/outsider, 57; literary, 272; of anthropology, 89, 234; of ideas and institutions, 55, 58; of linguistic anthropology, 3, 8; of science, 241; of social sciences, 89
historicism, 57, 235–36, 248n6. *See also* presentism
history: of ideas, 244; of linguistics, 54, 201; of science, 9, 144n11, 235. *See also* anthropology
Hitchcock, John, 207
HIV, 37, 44, 119, 125, 127–28, 136; and AIDS, xii, 23, 85, 116, 123–24, 130, 135, 139, 144n12, 177; positive (HIV+), 7, 16, 41, 48, 107, 141; prevention, 157–58; research, 157; studies, 157
Hjelmslev, Louis, 219
Hoad, Neville, 69
Hobart, Mark, 240
Hobbes, Thomas, 36
Hockett, Charles, 58, 203, 205, 216–17, 254
Hodgen, Margaret T., 234–38, 241
Hoenigswald, Henry, 204
Hokkien, 87, 90–94, 102
Holo, 87, 94
homophobia, 131, 163, 176, 187, 190
homosexual, 155, 157, 174–79, 190; behavior, 168–70, 272; beings, 170; professional, 18, 42; relations, 154–55, 271; relationships, 159.
homosexuality, xi–xii, 3–5, 11–15, 17–18, 20–21, 23–24, 27n3, 42, 55, 66, 72n16, 107, 119, 140, 153; age-stratified, 156; anthropologist of, 89; egalitarian, 173; gender-defined, 171–72; gender-stratified, 159. *See also* desire

INDEX | 317

Homosexualities (Murray), 5, 12, 17, 23, 44–45, 56, 153–56, 167–68, 181, 189, 271

Honduras, 178, 180, 183n2. See also *Heterogender Homosexuality in Honduras*

Hong, Keelung, xii–xiii, 6–7, 14, 18, 22, 43–44, 65, 67, 73n28, 83, 87–113, 140–41, 167, 265n1, 277

Hong Kong, 99, 103, 108

Hoover, Herbert, 35; Institution, 98, 100

Hsiao, Hsin-Huang Michael, 102–3

Hughes, Everett, 64, 209

human, 119, 143, 162, 242, 259; behavior, xi, 65; imagination, 23, 162; languages, 218; practices, 161; rights, 129, 153, 159, 180, 192; sciences, 56, 71n12, 233; self-understanding, 243; sexuality, xii–xiii, 123, 169; sociality, 253; societies, 170

Human Relations Area Files, 245

Humboldt, Wilhelm von, 219

Humphrey, Hubert, 35–36

Humphreys, Laud, 159

Hunt, George, 241

Hymes, Dell, 9, 199, 201, 204–10, 213, 215, 220–23, 236, 257, 265n2, 265n4

Iberian colonies, 171, 174

identity, xi, 132, 158, 171, 179; interdisciplinary, 82; political, 104; sexual, 169; Taiwanese, 22, 87, 100; transhistorical, 190. *See also* cultural; gay; gender

immigrants, 45, 216

inclusive, 122, 132, 13, 180

independent scholar, xi, 7, 14, 18

India, 59, 157, 199, 202–7, 226; languages of, 216

Indiana University, 202, 204, 216, 222

Indigenous, 158, 172, 190, 272; in cultural contexts, 154; studies, 104–5; Taiwanese, 98

inequality, 181, 264

Inouye, Daniel, 264

insiders, 9, 57–58, 71n6, 102

El Instituto Obregón, 7, 182

interactants, 255, 257, 259, 261, 265n5

interactional breakdowns, 6

interactions, 6, 54, 61, 82, 205, 211, 226, 253–54, 256–62, 265n6, 266; classroom, 213–14; control of, 259; doctor-patient, 265n7; in-context, 25; order, 11, 66, 260; studies of, 214, 224; talk-in, 253; verbal, 264

interdisciplinary, xi, 3, 5, 9–10, 81–82, 108n2

interethnic, 6, 265n4

interlocutors, 258–59, 262, 264

International Congress of Linguists, 217–18

International Resources Network-Africa "IRN-Africa," 189, 193n5

Internet, 158, 160, 163, 179

"Interruptions" and Other Messy Things in Language Use (Murray), 10, 20, 25, 66

interviews, 10, 20, 24–25, 38, 49, 61–63, 68, 70, 71n14, 90, 125, 177, 188, 199–231, 238, 248n5, 254–64, 265n4; Amazon, 17, 27; job, 132, 258

An Introduction to African Cinema (Murray), 4, 20

invisible college, 9, 55, 64–65

Islamic Homosexualities (Murray and Roscoe), 4, 12–13, 56, 155, 193n3

318 | INDEX

Jackson, Jean, 214
Jacobs, Sue-Ellen, 136
Jakobson, Roman, 206–7, 218–20
Japan, xi, 87, 93, 98, 108, 173, 206, 272
Japanese Culture Reflections (website), 21
Jarvenpa, Robert, 83
Jefferson, Gail, 253
Jefferson, Thomas, 93
Jews, 122, 135
John Gumperz in Context (Murray), 4, 10, 24, 199–231, 277
Johnson, Cary Alan, 193
Johnson, Corey W., 73n26
Johnson, Lyndon B., 34–36
Johnson, Thomas A., 143
Joos, Martin, 203
Joyce, Barry Alan, 84
Julian the Apostate, 35
Justice, Morality, and Constitutional Democracy, xii, 5, 36, 71n9

Kan, Sergei, 84
Kane, Stephanie, 124
Karsch-Haack, Ferdinand, 153–55
Kay, Paul, 212, 219
Keenan, Ed, 214
Keenan, Elinor, 214
Kendall, Carl, 124
Kendall, K. Limakatso, 191, 193n4
Kendall, Laurel, 109
Kendon, Adam, 214
Kennedy, Liz, 133
Keyfitz, Nathan, 209
kinship, 155, 159, 161–62, 241, 246
Kleinman, Arthur, 117, 122, 141, 143n7, 150
Kluckhohn, Clyde, 54, 248n10
Koerner, Konrad, 37, 49, 68, 72n16

Korea, 88, 105–6, 108n2, 109, 173, 206; North, 109n2; South, 88, 108n2, 109n2
Kroeber, Alfred, 59, 238, 246; collection, 64
Kroeber Anthropological Association, 15
Kroeber, Theodora, 64
Kubica, Grażyna, 82, 84
Kuhn, Thomas, 9, 217, 234–35, 241, 243–44, 248n7
Kuomintang "KMT," 22, 88, 91–94, 97–101
Kurath, Hans, 202, 215–16
Kurylowicz, Jerzy, 219

LaBarre, Weston, 64
Labov, Bill, 210–11, 200, 222, 226, 228n24, 255
Laguna, Frederica de, 236
Lakoff, Robin T., 255, 265n5
Lamb, Sidney, 205, 208
Lambert, Wallace T., 209, 225
Lancaster, Roger N., 133–34, 139, 160, 170
Landes, Ruth, 241
Lang, Norris, 123, 133
Langendoen, Terry, 219
languages, 54, 64, 81, 87–88, 90–94, 96–927, 102, 106, 179, 209–11, 213, 218–26, 239, 265n1, 266n8; African, 190; American Indian, 216; and culture, 81, 217; and social identity, 6; change, 202; child, 206; distribution, 203; everyday, 179; foreign, 216; international, 188; Near Eastern, 204; of the oppressor, 107, 141; Paiute, 238, 241; patterns, 6; use, 54, 220; teaching, 206

Language Behavior Research Laboratory. *See* University of California, Berkeley
Language in Society (journal), 226–27
Laslett, Barbara, 64
Latin American, 12, 23–24, 82, 158, 167–85
Latin American Male Homosexualities (Murray), 4, 12, 23, 155, 171–72, 181
lavender resumé, 7, 49, 132
lawyers, 36, 41, 259–60
Leach, Edmund, 211, 221
Lele, Jayant, 225, 229, 265n4
lesbians, 130–31, 138, 169
Lévi-Strauss, Claude, 23, 27, 153; tradition, 55
Levinson, Stephen, 213
LGBTQ, 16, 23, 26, 167, 178, 182n1, 189; anthropological community, 22; anthropologists, 132; caucus, xi; communities, 129, 141, 160; individuals, 131; issues, 138; people, 119, 160–62; publication, 115; refugees, 158; rights, 131; studies, 154–56; topics, 140
LGBTQ+, 180
LBGTQIA+, 178–81, 182n1
Li, Charles, 211, 213–14
Lieberson, Stan, 209
Lin, Sylvia Li-chun, 99–101
Lincoln, Abraham, 34
Lindenbaum, Shirley, 123–24, 143n5, 143n6
Linguistic Society of America, 60, 67
linguistics, xii, 3, 6, 9–10, 20–21, 23, 53–55, 67, 71n5, 81, 174, 199, 201–5, 207–14, 216–17, 219, 221, 223; American, 9; anthropological, 10, 66, 211, 221; Heideggerian, 212, 224; historical, 217; unanthropological, 8. *See also* sociolinguistics
Linguistics Institute "LI", 202, 204, 209, 222
literature, xiii, 19, 43, 74, 95, 110n12, 162, 176, 216, 272; anthropological, 157; area, 107; Central American, 179; ethnographic, 271; gay, 179; Greek, 173; homosexual, 180; research, 62, 160; social-scientific, 72n16
Livermon, Xavier, 190
Locke, John, 36
Looking Through Taiwan (Hong and Murray), 4, 18, 22, 83, 87–113
Lounsbury, Floyd, 245
Lovejoy, Arthur, 235
Lowie, Robert, 64, 243; collection, 64
Lyman, Peter, 248n10
Lyman, R. Lee, 83–84
Lyons, Andrew P., 83
Lyons, Harriet D., 83

Machiavelli, Nicollo, 36
Magaña, Raul, 124
Magill, Dennis W., 54, 199
Male Homosexuality in Central and South America (Murray), 4, 12, 23–24, 167–85
Male Sexual Subjectivities (Murray), 13, 26, 271–74
Malkiel, Yakov, 64
Maltz, Daniel, 6
Mandarin, 87, 90–94, 97, 102
Mandelbaum, David, 64
Mandeville, John, 238
Marckwardt, Albert, 202, 215
marriage: companionate, 159; equality, 131; forms, 97; same-sex, 158, 178, 180
Marshall, Patricia, 124
Marshall, Zack, 160

Martin, Emily, 109n4, 117, 141, 143, 150
Martin, Laura, 72n17
Marx, Karl, 36, 169, 223
Massachusetts Institute of Technology (MIT), 212, 214, 217–19
Matebeni, Zethu, 189
Mathy, Robin, 172
Mauss, Marcel, 61
McCarthy, Eugene, 36; and McCarthyism, 154
McCombie, Susan, 124, 133
McDermott, Ray, 213–14
McDonald, Ellen, 222
McGrath, Janet, 123, 143n5
McKinley, William, 34
McLuhan, Marshall, 215, 247–48
McMahon, Richard, 83–84
McQuown, Norman, 254
Mead, Margaret, 73n21, 132, 239–40, 242–43, 246, 248n5
Meese, Edwin, 262, 264, 266n12
men who have sex with men (MSM), 157–58
Merton, Robert K., 64
Mesoamerican, 24, 167–68, 172, 174–84
methods, 3, 21–22, 24–25, 53, 57, 60–62, 65–68, 70, 73n24, 83, 85, 143, 172, 191, 233, 235, 237, 241, 265n4; comparative, 234; linguistic, 239; qualitative/quantitative, 61, 68, 157; social survey, 207; topological, 106
methodology, 92, 104, 127, 203, 233, 241
Metzger, Duane, 206, 219
Mexico, 19–20, 66, 182, 183n2; City, 132, 168, 178
Michaels, Sarah, 227
Michigan State University, xii, 5, 11, 17, 27n1, 28n7, 36, 142n1
Migliore, Sam, 67, 240

migration, 91–92, 160; studies, 3
Miles, Josephine, 206
Miller, Bruce, 248n10
Miller, George, 225
Miller, Peter, 229n26
Miller, Wick, 205
Minnesota, xii, 5, 33–35
minorities: ethnic, 94, 124, 141; linguistic, 93; sexual, 23, 124, 129–32, 180; stigmatized, 139
misrepresentation, 18, 93, 176–77, 266n13, 248n5. *See also* representation
missionaries, 153–54, 188, 217, 234
Mitchell, George J., 262–64
Montini, Theresa, 65
Morgan, Lewis H., 241
Moser, Hugo, 202
Mullins, Nicholas C., 8–9, 200
Munro, Surya, 189
Murdock, George Peter, 245
music, xiii, 4, 46

Naess, Arne, 207
National Institute of Mental Health, 5, 62, 200, 265n1
nationalism, 87, 96, 101, 104–5, 109n7, 110n8, 187
Native peoples, 63, 67, 70, 71n7, 72n17, 90, 98, 120, 139–40, 142, 172, 239–40, 241, 245, 247, 253, 258, 261, 265n6; American, 98; Anglo-American, 264; and audience, 272; category of, 264; conceptions about, 266n8; dialect, 202; informant, 67, 248n3; models of, 265n4; speakers, 182, 201, 226, 257–59; speech community, 239; terms from, 90, 93, 96; testimony of, 239; texts from, 245; views, 19; voices, 107. *See also* "go native"

Nesvig, Martin, 180
Newcomb, Ted, 203
Newman, Stanley S., 64
Newmeyer, Frederick J., 220–21
Newton, Esther, 136
Nicaragua, 178, 183n2
Nida, Eugene, 203
Nietzsche, Friedrich, 100, 104
Nigeria, 6, 158
Nisbet, Robert, 10, 37, 234–36, 248n2, 249n10
Nixon, Richard, 36
nonbinary, 160, 181
nonverbal communication, 211, 256, 266n8
North American, 3–4, 15–16, 129, 169, 173, 254, 265n7; Anglo, 56, 176, 260, 265n2; anthropology, 65
North, Oliver, 266n12
Norway, 123, 207, 212, 222
Nyce, James, 64
Nyeck, Sybille N., 189

Oakes, Katherine (*nee* George), 234, 237
Obregón, Álvaro, 182. *See also* El Instituto Obregón
observers, 62, 144n11, 200, 238; alien, 63, 67, 240; antagonistic, 153; foreign, 93; military, 35
occupations, 172, 257; gender-identified, 161; specialties in, 156
Oceanic Homosexualities (Murray), 4, 12–13
Ogburn, William, 64, 245n4
oligarchy, 94, 141
Olson, David R., 214–15
O'Neil, John, 117–18, 150
O'Neill, John, 118
Ontario, 15, 214–15

oppression, 107, 139, 141, 176
Orozco, Gail, 123, 143n5
Otu, Kwame Edwin, 192
Outline of a Theory of Practice "Practice" (Bourdieu), 223–24
outsiders, 9, 57–58, 65, 107, 141, 241, 246. *See also* insiders

Pacific Homosexualities (Murray), 5, 12, 155
Page, Bryan, 124
Park, Richard, 204
Park, Robert E., 64
Parkin, Dave, 213
participant observation, 20, 65, 174, 239
Passeron, Jean-Claude, 224
Peace, William J., 84
Pennsylvania tradition, 9, 235–37, 247. *See also* University of Pennsylvania
Penzl, Herbert, 202, 215–16
People's Republic of China. *See* China
Persians, 188–89
Phillips, Herbert, 272
Phillips, Kevin, 36
Phillips, Oliver, 187
philosophy, 205, 207–8, 222
Pieces for a History of Gay Studies (Murray), 5, 11, 50n11
Pike, Kenneth L., 54, 64, 203, 211, 215, 217
Pittenger, Robert, 254
Plato, 36
plays, 26, 266n8, 272
Pliny, 238
poetry, 19, 26, 272
Poindexter, John, 263–64
Polynesians, 97, 173, 264
postmodern, 73n24, 156, 192, 272
Pound, Moses, 124
presentism, 57, 241–43, 248n6. *See also* historicism

psychology, 18, 21, 53, 55–56, 71n9, 205, 207–9, 219, 225, 235, 238, 273, 257; gestalt, 239; social, xii, 5, 36, 257

psychotherapy, 245, 254–55, 259, 261, 265. *See also* therapy

public health, 91; authorities, 157; officials, 130

Pykles, Benjamin C., 241

Quayle, Dan, 36

queer, 116, 135–36, 159–60, 182n1; African studies, viii, xi, 12, 24, 187–97; bookstores, 167; imperialism, 190; life, 181; studies, 23, 187; theorists, 159

question authority generation, 36–37

questionnaire, 14, 17–18, 60, 67–68, 81, 200

Qing, 87, 91–92

Rabinow, Paul, 115, 117–19, 124–29, 133, 135, 138, 141, 142n2, 142n3, 143n8, 144n11

racism, 122, 128, 192

Radcliffe-Brown, Alfred, 245

Rankin, Joseph H., 54, 199

Rao, Rahul, 190

raw data, 62, 201

Reading 20th-Century Italian Fiction (Murray), 4, 19

Reading Sicily (Murray), 4, 18–20

Reagan administration, 130, 177

Reddy, Vasu, 189

Redfield, Robert, 64, 72n10, 73n22, 159, 233, 239

reference group, 210; models, 208; theory, 225

Regan, Don, 262

regional ethnography, 3–4

Reichard, Gladys, 245

religion, 89–92, 95–96, 99, 177–78, 217; 95, 99, 154, 161, 188, 261

representations, 88, 95, 104, 107–9, 122, 137–38, 234, 239–40, 273. *See also* misrepresentation

repression, 98, 108, 125, 131, 154, 158, 162

Republican, 5, 34–36

resistance, 115, 118, 130, 256

revolutions, 46, 200, 238; rhetoric of, 9; scientific, 234–35

Romney, Kimball, 206, 219

Roosevelt, Franklin D., 34

Rosaldo, Renato, 117, 122, 128–29, 142n2

Ross, Haj, 212

Rubin, Gayle, 47

Rubinstein, Murray, 102–3

Russia, 109, 158, 162, 178, 218

Ruth Benedict Prize, 17, 134

Sacks, Harvey, 209–10, 253, 255, 257

Saharan, 189, 192n3

Samarin, William J., 54, 64, 199, 201, 248n10, 257, 266n8

same-sex: behavior, 23, 131, 153; issues, 188; marriage, 158, 178, 180; partners, 159; patterns, 12; relations, 155–56, 172; relationships, 153, 159, 175, 180, 188, 191; sex, 11, 157, 271; sexual bonding, 23, 153; sexual relations, 3, 12, 271; sexuality, 153

Samoa, 240, 242, 248n5

Sanches, Mary, 213–14, 220–21

San Diego, 13, 16, 34–35, 42, 213

San Francisco, xii, 5, 15–16, 20, 38–39, 50n8, 66, 115, 117, 130–31, 137, 141, 143, 167, 187, 192n2, 200–201; University of California-San Francisco, 65

Sankoff, Gillian, 211, 214

Sapir, Edward, 8–9, 15, 54–55, 58, 208, 217, 238–39, 241, 245–47, 248n10, 265n4; Centenary Conference, 15, 64; papers, 64

Sarbin, Theodore R., 209
Sartrean, 224
Saturday group, 205–6, 211
Saussure, Ferdinand de, 239
Schegloff, Emanuel "Manny," 209–10, 253, 255, 265n6
Scheper-Hughes, Nancy, 115, 117–20, 122, 124–29, 133–39, 141, 142n2, 142n3, 143n8, 144n12, 144n15
Schoepf, Brooke, 123, 143n5
Schroeder, David, 205
Schultz, George, 262
Schutz, Alfred, 224
Scollon, Ronald, 6, 213, 223
Searle, John, 205
semantics, 222, 225
Senegal, 157–58, 189
sexual, 46, 131, 139, 154–63, 174, 190, 192, 271–73; binaries, 188; conduct, 248n5, 272; conservatism, 154; deviants, 125; diversity, xi, 129, 137, 141; freedom, 131; ideology, 169–70; life history, 271–72; minorities, 124, 129–32, 180; orientation, 172, 175, 178–80
Seymour, Susan C., 84
Shedlin, Michelle G., 124, 143
Sherzer, Joel, 213, 220–21, 265n2
Shih, Shu-Mei, 102–3
Shils, Edward, 64
Shipley, Bill, 205
Shuy, Roger, 214
silence, 108, 140, 180, 226, 257, 266n8
Silverstein, Michael, 64
Simon, Bill, 272
Simon, Scott, 104–5
Singer, Merrill, 123–24, 133–34, 143n5
Singh, Rajendra, 225, 265n4
Skinner, B. F., 226
Slobin, Dan, 205, 210, 225

Smith, Bruce, 26, 272–73
Smith, Henry Lee "Haxie," 203, 216–17
social: circles, 65; class, 162, 175, 180; constructions, 153–54; groups, 202; networks, 199, 211, 235; structures, 162, 173, 190, 207, 273n1; theory, 37, 205, 212, 223, 234
socialization theory, 207, 212
Social Science Networks (Murray), 8, 200, 233
Social Science Research Council (SSRC), 235–36; Committee on Sociolinguistics of, 209–10, 215, 222
Social Theory, Homosexual Realities (Murray), 4, 11, 13, 168–69, 171
Society of Lesbian and Gay Anthropologists (SOLGA), xi, 107, 118–21, 132–36, 139; newsletter (SOLGAN), 14, 133. *See also* Anthropological Research Group on Homosexuality (ARGOH); Association of Queer Anthropologists
sociolinguistics, xi, 3–4, 9, 20, 24, 55, 64, 71n5, 199–201, 205, 207, 209–11, 213–15, 222, 224. *See also* linguistics
sociology, xi–xii, 5–6, 8–11, 15, 17, 20–24, 36–37, 49, 53–58, 64, 82, 155, 169, 172, 174, 199–200, 208, 212; Chicago school of, 246; dramaturgical, 261; functionalist, 265n6; of knowledge, 106; of networks, 201; of science, 64
Sonenschein, David, 142
Sontag, Susan, 46
speaking truth to power, 120, 139
speech, 26, 36, 93, 206, 261; act, 255, 265n1, 265n3, 266n10; community, 223–24, 254; events, 214, 220, 256, 260–61, 265n1, 265n3, 266n12; free, 136, 221; gay, 20; genre, 66; naturally

occurring, 239; situations, 254–60, 264, 266n8
Spies, Walter, 239
Springer, Otto, 202
Spurlin, William, 191
Stall, Ron, 124
Stanford University, 117, 129, 136, 206, 213, 219. *See also* Center for Advanced Study in the Behavioral Sciences
Stassen, Harold, 34
Steffen, Megan, 103–4, 108
Sterk, Claire, 124, 143n5
Stevenson, Adlai, 36
stigma, 126–27, 130, 139–40, 142, 159, 170, 177, 179–80, 188, 205
Strauss, Anselm L., 260
Strauss, Leo, 36
Stocking, George W., Jr., 9, 57, 236–37, 241, 247n1
Stross, Brian, 213
suicide, 45, 49
symbolic: domination, 169; interactionism, 103, 169, 208, 225, 245n4; role of, 23, 140
synthesis, 12, 23, 62, 181

Taft, Robert A., 34
Taiwan, 18, 20, 22, 67, 73n28, 87–113, 141. See also *Looking Through Taiwan* (Hong and Murray); *Taiwanese Culture, Taiwanese Society* (Murray and Hong)
Taiwanese, 15–16, 22, 87–113, 141
Taiwanese Culture, Taiwanese Society (Murray and Hong), 4, 18, 65
Tajfel, Henri, 225
Tamale, Sylvia, 189
Tannen, Deborah, 6, 223, 255, 257, 260, 265n1, 265n4, 265n7, 266n8

Tanner, Nancy, 206
Taussig, Michael, 117, 128–29, 142n2
Taylor, Clark, 71n10, 132, 142, 143n4
Teeter, Karl, 205
Teggart, Frederick, 234–37, 247
textbook histories, 242–43
theorists, 206, 208; armchair, 67; queer, 159; social, 212
theory groups, 8–9, 14, 21, 62, 89, 200, 246
Theory Groups and the Study of Language in North America (Murray), 4, 8, 49n2, 49n3, 65, 200
therapy, 254–57. *See also* psychotherapy
Thorne, James Peter, 206
Tibet, 96, 108; Tibetan, 109n5
Tillohash, Tony, 238–39, 241
Tocqueville, Alexis de, 36; 248n10
Toronto, 66, 81; Gay Academic Union in, 14. See also University of Toronto
Trager, George, 203, 216–17
transcribed, 25, 90, 217, 256n8, 259, 266n8
transcriptions, 61, 90–91, 93
transhistorical: continuities, 155; identity, 190
Traugott, Elizabeth, 213
Treichler, Paula A., 129
Tremlett, Paul-François, 100–101, 104, 107
Triandis, Leigh, 207
Truman, Harry S., 34
truth, 233, 243; proclaim, 70
Turner, Roy, 210, 254–55
Tusón, Amparo, 6
21st-Century Representations of Muslim Homosexualities (Murray), 5, 12–13

UCLA, 210, 214, 238
Underhill, Ruth, 245

United States, 5, 13, 18, 20, 66, 124–25, 129–31, 138, 160, 170, 174, 176, 178, 201–2, 204, 216, 223, 261
universal features, 218, 253, 257
University of Arizona, xii, 5, 10, 20, 199–200
University of California, Berkeley, xii, 5–6, 10, 15–16, 18, 24–25, 28n7, 38–39, 54, 59, 62, 64–65, 68, 116–17, 124, 142, 143n8, 199–200, 204–6, 210, 212–13, 215, 219, 221, 225, 234, 236–37; Language Behavior Research Laboratory at, 71n6, 200, 212
University of Cambridge, 69, 212–15, 222
University of Chicago, 56, 61, 64, 117, 121, 214, 241, 245
University of Pennsylvania, 28n7, 143n6, 202, 204, 221, 236–37, 247. *See also* Pennsylvania tradition
University of Toronto, xii, 5, 10, 20, 54, 199, 227n5, 247n2, 248
Useem, John, 209

Vance, Carole, 136
Vanek, Tony, 213
Vasantkumar, Chris, 106–7
Vechten, Carl Van, 253
Vicinus, Martha, 155
Vidal, Gore, 35
Vietnam, 35–36, 109, 116
Villa Rojas, Alfonso, 239

Wallace, Anthony F. C., 64
Ward, Martha, 124, 137, 150
Washington DC, 15–16, 130, 132, 134, 167
Weber, Max, 11, 36, 224, 248n10, 261
Weiner, Annette, 137
Weinreich, Uriel, 222
Weiss-Wendt, Anton, 83–84

Weller, Robert P., 89–92, 94
Welmers, William, 203, 216
West, Candace, 259, 265n5, 265n7
Weston, Kate, 190
Wheeler, Ryan J., 84
Whelahan, Patricia, 124
Whitam, Frederick J., 172
White, Leslie, 203, 243
Whiting, John, 207
Whorf, Benjamin Lee, 72
Wikan, Unni, 240
Wilkie, Wendell, 34
Wilson, Ruth, 124
Wilson, Woodrow, 34
Winkin, Yves, 67, 240
Winston, Ellen Black, 64
Winterhalder, Astrid, 97
Wirth, Louis, 64
Wojnarowicz, David, 128–29
Wolin, Sheldon, 36
Wolf, Arthur, 71n15, 95, 97
Wong, Bill, 208
Wong-Fillmore, Lily, 214
Woolard, Kit, 223, 226
Wright, Timothy, 157

Yengoyan, Aram, 211
Yeomans, Rory, 83–84
Young, Allen, 144n10
Young, Rebecca, 157
Young, Virginia Heyer, 84

Zeitlin, Irving, 249n10
Zheng, Chantal, 100
Zhou, Daguan, 59
Zimbabwe, 187, 189
Zinman, Richard, 248n10
Zumwalt, Rosemary Lévy, 84

In the Critical Studies in the History of Anthropology series

Invisible Genealogies: A History of Americanist Anthropology
Regna Darnell

The Shaping of American Ethnography: The Wilkes Exploring Expedition, 1838–1842
Barry Alan Joyce

Ruth Landes: A Life in Anthropology
Sally Cole

Melville J. Herskovits and the Racial Politics of Knowledge
Jerry Gershenhorn

Leslie A. White: Evolution and Revolution in Anthropology
William J. Peace

Rolling in Ditches with Shamans: Jaime de Angulo and the Professionalization of American Anthropology
Wendy Leeds-Hurwitz

Irregular Connections: A History of Anthropology and Sexuality
Andrew P. Lyons and Harriet D. Lyons

Ephraim George Squier and the Development of American Anthropology
Terry A. Barnhart

Ruth Benedict: Beyond Relativity, Beyond Pattern
Virginia Heyer Young

Looking through Taiwan: American Anthropologists' Collusion with Ethnic Domination
Keelung Hong and Stephen O. Murray

Visionary Observers: Anthropological Inquiry and Education
Jill B. R. Cherneff and Eve Hochwald
Foreword by Sydel Silverman

Anthropology Goes to the Fair: The 1904 Louisiana Purchase Exposition
Nancy J. Parezo and Don D. Fowler

The Meskwaki and Anthropologists: Action Anthropology Reconsidered
Judith M. Daubenmier

The 1904 Anthropology Days and Olympic Games: Sport, Race, and American Imperialism
Edited by Susan Brownell

Lev Shternberg: Anthropologist, Russian Socialist, Jewish Activist
Sergei Kan

Contributions to Ojibwe Studies: Essays, 1934–1972
A. Irving Hallowell
Edited and with introductions by Jennifer S. H. Brown and Susan Elaine Gray

Excavating Nauvoo: The Mormons and the Rise of Historical Archaeology in America
Benjamin C. Pykles
Foreword by Robert L. Schuyler

Cultural Negotiations: The Role of Women in the Founding of Americanist Archaeology
David L. Browman

*Homo Imperii: A History of
Physical Anthropology in Russia*
Marina Mogilner

*American Anthropology and
Company: Historical Explorations*
Stephen O. Murray

*Racial Science in Hitler's
New Europe, 1938–1945*
Edited by Anton Weiss-
Wendt and Rory Yeomans

*Cora Du Bois: Anthropologist,
Diplomat, Agent*
Susan C. Seymour

*Before Boas: The Genesis of
Ethnography and Ethnology in
the German Enlightenment*
Han F. Vermeulen

*American Antiquities: Revisiting the
Origins of American Archaeology*
Terry A. Barnhart

*An Asian Frontier: American
Anthropology and Korea, 1882–1945*
Robert Oppenheim

*Theodore E. White and the Development
of Zooarchaeology in North America*
R. Lee Lyman

*Declared Defective: Native Americans,
Eugenics, and the Myth of Nam Hollow*
Robert Jarvenpa

*Glory, Trouble, and Renaissance
at the Robert S. Peabody
Museum of Archaeology*
Edited and with an introduction
by Malinda Stafford Blustain
and Ryan J. Wheeler

*Race Experts: Sculpture, Anthropology,
and the American Public in Malvina
Hoffman's Races of Mankind*
Linda Kim

*The Enigma of Max Gluckman:
The Ethnographic Life of a
"Luckyman" in Africa*
Robert J. Gordon

*National Races: Transnational Power
Struggles in the Sciences and Politics
of Human Diversity, 1840–1945*
Edited by Richard McMahon

*Franz Boas: The Emergence
of the Anthropologist*
Rosemary Lévy Zumwalt

*Maria Czaplicka: Gender,
Shamanism, Race*
Grażyna Kubica

*Writing Anthropologists, Sounding
Primitives: The Poetry and
Scholarship of Edward Sapir,
Margaret Mead, and Ruth Benedict*
A. Elisabeth Reichel

*The History of Anthropology:
A Critical Window on the
Discipline in North America*
Regna Darnell

*History of Theory and
Method in Anthropology*
Regna Darnell

*Franz Boas: Shaping Anthropology
and Working for Social Justice*
Rosemary Lévy Zumwalt

A Maverick Boasian: The Life and Work of Alexander A. Goldenweiser
Sergei Kan

Hoarding New Guinea: Writing Colonial Ethnographic Collection Histories for Postcolonial Futures
Rainer F. Buschmann

Truth and Power in American Archaeology
Alice Beck Kehoe

Turning the Power: Indian Boarding Schools, Native American Anthropologists, and the Race to Preserve Indigenous Cultures
Nathan Sowry

James Cowles Prichard of the Red Lodge: A Life of Science during the Age of Improvement
Margaret M. Crump

Invisible Contrarian: Essays in Honor of Stephen O. Murray
Edited by Regna Darnell and Wendy Leeds-Hurwitz

To order or obtain more information on these or other University of Nebraska Press titles, visit nebraskapress.unl.edu.

www.ingramcontent.com/pod-product-compliance
Lightning Source LLC
LaVergne TN
LVHW051817060925
820435LV00002B/8